P9-ELX-116

Flunk. Start.

Flunk. Start.

Reclaiming My Decade Lost in Scientology

Sands Hall

COUNTERPOINT
BERKELEY, CALIFORNIA

FLUNK. START.

First hardcover edition: 2018

Library of Congress Cataloging-in-Publication Data
Names: Hall, Sands, author.
Title: Flunk, start : reclaiming my decade lost in scientology : a memoir / Sands Hall.
Description: Berkeley : Counterpoint Press, 2018.
Identifiers: LCCN 2017038728 | ISBN 9781619021785
Subjects: LCSH: Hall, Sands. | Ex-church members—United States—Biography. | Scientologists—United States—Biography. | Scientology.
Classification: LCC BP605.S2 H345 2018 | DDC 299/.936092 [B] — dc23
LC record available at https://lccn.loc.gov/2017038728

Jacket designed by Jarrod Taylor
Book designed by Wah-Ming Chang

COUNTERPOINT
2560 Ninth Street, Suite 318
Berkeley, CA 94710
www.counterpointpress.com

Printed in the United States of America
Distributed by Publishers Group West

10 9 8 7 6 5 4 3 2 1

This book is a memoir. The events, locales, and people described are as the author remembers them. In order to maintain anonymity and preserve privacy, she has changed the names and identifying characteristics of certain locales and individuals.

For Tom—

who lived so much of it with me

'Tis the temper of the hot and superstitious part of mankind in matters of religion ever to be fond of mysteries & for that reason to like best what they understand least.

ISAAC NEWTON, *A Historical Account of Two Notable Corruptions of Scripture*

. . . later he believed he had learned the truth of Paul's words where he said that God's Word was like a mirror in which a man might see not only the man he was, but the man he might be, and he came to understand that the proper business of life was trying to do something about the difference.

HARLAN, in *Unassigned Territory* by Kem Nunn

CONTENTS

FOREWORD

KNOWLEDGE REPORT

For a decade, I pretended that a decade of my life hadn't happened. Those "lost" years included the seven I was involved with the Church of Scientology and the three it took to be certain I wouldn't, again, return. Eventually, I began to peer and prod and then write about those years, and just as I'd completed a shaggy draft of this memoir, I found out that Jamie, the man who'd introduced me to the Church, had died. A memorial was planned for him in Los Angeles, a city I'd fled decades before and since visited just once—and then only because a book tour took me there. Because I'd been examining what had come of meeting and then marrying Jamie, it seemed imperative to attend his memorial, even though it meant putting myself back in the maw of what I'd found first scary, then intriguing and even engrossing, and then, during the awful time of leaving, terrifying.

I would also see people who'd once been incredibly dear to me but with whom, since leaving the Church, I'd lost contact. One of them, Paloma, who'd been not only a close friend but also one of my auditors (Scientology's form of counselor), even offered her guest room. Paloma's openheartedness and willingness to walk outside Scientology's boundaries moved and surprised me. Generally, those in the Church do not associate with those who have defected from it. But Paloma welcomed me, and, as we always had, we talked deeply, including about what we were currently writing. She pressed, and finally I offered up that I'd finished a draft of a memoir.

"About Scientology!" She looked shocked.

I told her it was also about my family, "which was, in a way, its own kind of cult," I said, laughing.

Clearly troubled, she asked me what I meant. After a bit more discussion, I suggested we not talk further about it. "When you get your next chunk of auditing," I said, "you'll have to answer all those security questions. I don't want to make trouble for you in any way."

Paloma shook her head. "I won't let the Church dictate who are and are not my friends."

I found this admirable, and, though surprising, even possible: Paloma has been married to a non-Scientologist for three decades; perhaps she and the Church—she and her own psyche—had figured things out. And for a few months after that remarkable and unexpectedly heartwarming time in Los Angeles, she and I stayed in touch. In one startling phone call she even implied that she might have accomplished all she needed to with and in the Church.

However, almost immediately after that confidence, if that's what it was, the phone calls and emails stopped. As Scientologists put it, we "fell out of comm." I was not surprised. I knew she was regretting our candid discussions.

A few months later, a mutual friend told me Paloma was very ill. This, too, I did not find surprising. Because Scientology—like Christian Science and other spiritual paths—believes that physical troubles are linked to emotional and psychological ones, I was fairly sure that Paloma was tracing her illness back to our talks. If she had entertained any doubts, and certainly by communicating such feelings to an ex-Scientologist, she was guilty of transgressions against the Church. By now she'd be seeing someone known as the Ethics Officer. Maybe getting auditing. In any case, spending lots of money "handling" that she'd talked to an apostate. She would not be in touch again.

So I was startled when, a few months later, I received a business-sized envelope with her name and address in the upper left-hand corner.

Standing in the morning sun next to my mailbox, which is at the end of my driveway in the rural area where I live, I opened it. Inside were three typed pages. Centered at the top of the first page were the words:

Knowledge Report

For even a seasoned member of the Church of Scientology, the phrase "Knowledge Report" can buckle the knees; to be the subject of one can curdle the blood.[1] Knowledge Reports are one of the increasingly totalitarian tactics L. Ron Hubbard employed as Scientology became bigger and more successful—and more controversial. In a 1982 policy letter, "Keeping Scientology Working," he writes that for an organization to run effectively, "the individual members themselves enforce the actions and mores of the group."[2] This can lead to rampant paranoia, as it's possible to imagine that every step you take in your job (especially in an organization established on Hubbard's principles), and indeed in your life, is being observed. Snitching is actively encouraged. As a Knowledge Report may lead to intense disciplinary measures, to receive one is literally hair-raising.

The walk out to my mailbox that morning had been to take a break from writing; I was almost done with a second draft of the memoir. By that time, I had processed enough of my emotions about the Church to be able to give a laugh at what I held in my hand, although it was a shocked laugh. I understood why Paloma might have been led to write a Knowledge Report, but why on earth would she send me a copy? It would be placed in her ethics folder—this much I remembered from my time in the Church—but I wasn't a Scientologist, hadn't been one in more than a decade; Scientology's protocols had nothing to do with me.

Nevertheless, as I read what Paloma had written, my world tilted and spun.

Time, Place, Form, Event, Hubbard requires in such a report, and Paloma supplied them.[3] She described our friendship while I was in the Church, discussed her role as my auditor, addressed how my parents had been virulent in their disapproval, how the Church had dubbed them SPs—Suppressive Persons—and insisted I formally disconnect from them, which I'd refused to do. She also included details of our recent talks, including the fact that I'd called Scientology a "cult" and that—this was the "knowledge" she was "reporting"—I was *writing a memoir about it.* Except for perspective (her point of view was not mine), what she wrote was neither histrionic nor incorrect. It was knowledge—her knowledge—and she had reported it.

I scanned the pages again, wondering what her purpose was. Had she sent the Knowledge Report to scare me? After all, the Church is infamous for attacking those who criticize it. Was she sending it as a warning? To make me stop writing, to shut me up?

Of course it was intended to scare me, and to shut me up. Such behavior is consistent with my experience within the Church: For years I observed Scientologists, especially those in management, employing such tactics, creating a semihysterical "us versus them" tension to keep us (for then I was a Scientologist) in fear and in thrall.

And even though I was empathetic to Paloma's need to employ every available tool to make her illness go away, I was shocked. She is smart and kind, and a writer herself; was she really willing to subject a fellow writer, and a friend, to such a thing?

But why be shocked? Paloma has been a Scientologist for forty years, weathering and justifying decades of attacks against Church practices. In Hubbard's nomenclature, she was being "unreasonable," which is, believe it or not, an accolade. When you are a devout Scientologist, no one is capable of "reasoning" you out of your firmly held beliefs (which are, of course, Hubbard's). Being called "reasonable" does not, to a Scientologist, mean "having sound judgment, being fair and sensible"; rather, it's the worst sort of pejorative: It means you are explaining things away, coming up with reasons you haven't managed to get something done, justifying behavior.[4] Paloma, being a good

Scientologist, was being unreasonable about the possibility that anything negative might be published about her church.

And this decision—to file a Knowledge Report, and to send a copy (a warning) to me—is an example of the mind control the Church exercises: teaching its practitioners, as they accept and embrace its commonsensical and useful ideas, to accept and embrace its authoritarian and outrageous ones. Scientologists willingly and of their own accord place those blinding mechanisms around their intelligences so that they can continue to believe.

I know, because I was once so persuaded. With intention and purpose, I screwed those mechanisms into place, mechanisms that filter information, massage facts, and gerrymander perspective. And in spite of ferocious doubts, I kept them there a long time.

I slid the pages of the Knowledge Report back into the envelope and headed back up the driveway thinking of the many memoirs written by former Scientologists, filled with their dreadful stories, and of the nonfiction books and documentaries that substantiate these abuses. But for me, and in my book, beyond this incident—if you can call receiving a Knowledge Report an "incident"—there was no personal outrage or scandal to relate (except for how and why I came to stay in a cult for seven years). I was never forced to sleep in a brig or scrub a latrine with my toothbrush; I was never locked in a trailer playing musical chairs with my future attached to grabbing a seat. I lost dear friends when I finally left, but I didn't have to abandon cherished family, leap an electric fence on a motorcycle, or execute a complicated escape plan, as others have had to do.[5]

Although I did lose things. Those years, for instance.

Which is how I thought of it, for a very long time.

However. Scientologists, to learn a particular skill, practice or "drill" that skill with a partner. If one does the drill incorrectly, the partner says, "Flunk." And immediately, "Start." Harsh as "flunk" may sound, there's no intended animosity; it's just a way of communicating that you're doing it wrong. The first few times I experienced it, I was startled, shocked. It's horrid to be told you've failed, and "flunk" begins with that *f* hiss and ends with that shocking *k*. But once I got over the jolt of it, I came to see its efficacy: you just get on with doing the thing you didn't do correctly the first time.

Staying in Scientology as long as I did, I felt I'd "flunked" a huge chunk of my life. As I worked on this book, I realized that, somewhat to my surprise, that perspective was changing. Also that I was finding a possible "start" in examining those lost years and what, in fact, I might have gained from them. A hope grew that the book might bolster someone doubting her own involvement in the Church to find the courage to leave. Even, possibly, that it might offer a lens to those who felt they'd tossed a decade of their own into the dustbin—a drug problem, a destructive relationship—through which to see meaning and find purpose. Perhaps not in having made those choices in the first place, but in the life we have as a result. That is, having "flunked," there is the option to "start."

All this I thought about on that walk back from the mailbox. Then I settled in again at my desk, put the envelope in a drawer, and got back to work. I was, I realized somewhat grimly, writing a Knowledge Report of my own.

A NOTE TO THE READER, AND A BIT ABOUT THE ENDNOTES

In the early fifteenth century, a MEMOIR was a "written record." From the French *memorie*, it meant a "note, something to be kept in mind," which makes me think of a to-do list, or the memos we write at the beginning of a day full of errands. The word descends from Latin's *memoria*, "memory." Only in the late 1600s did MEMOIR take on its current meaning: a person's written account of her life.

Such an account relies, of course, on memory. Memories can be vivid and precise, or they can be vague; they may change in the telling, or over the years as new information is assimilated; they can emphasize some things and neglect others. We have only to ask family members about last year's Thanksgiving to find a multitude of accounts.

I relied on memory as I wrote this book. Also my journals and research. While of course I can't recall entire conversations word for word, I do remember the spirit of them, where they took place, and certain lines of dialogue, around which I've built scenes. I consulted diaries and datebooks to reconstruct a timeline. Some people who knew me well during the years recounted here will be surprised that they are nowhere in these pages; others may be startled to find themselves represented. While I've changed some names and identifying places and characteristics, especially of friends and acquaintances from my Scientology years, I've stayed true to those people, and to those encounters.

As I've strived to tell things as truly as I can, I've also done my best to present L. Ron Hubbard's "religious technology" as it was laid out at the time I was involved with the Church, from 1982 to 1989. Since the ascension, in 1987, of David Miscavige as head of the Church of Scientology, many changes have been implemented, including the editing and republishing of Hubbard's materials. This may mean that my experience of a particular Scientology course or doctrine does not match its current iteration. When I use a Scientology phrase, quote from Hubbard's writing, or refer to Church doctrine, you will find, in the endnotes, a reference to the book, tape, policy letter, bulletin, or article where the particular quotation or idea would have been found during the time I was a Scientologist. Many of these citations are from the *Dianetics and Scientology Technical Dictionary*.[6] I also cite current official Scientology websites or sources, where Hubbard's original text has often been updated or edited.

In dozens of documents, including the policy letter "Keeping Scientology Working," Hubbard lays out that he is the sole source of his religious technology, and that no one, other than himself, may revise, rescind, or cancel any part of it.[7] If it isn't in a bulletin or policy letter, he wrote in April 1965, "or recorded on tape in my voice, it isn't tech or policy."

This is known as Standard Tech. And to ensure that Standard Tech would stay standard, Hubbard implemented various safeguards, including an injunction that practitioners never indulge in "verbal tech." In addition to such things as "altering" or "obstructing" or "corrupting" official policies (words from the document), verbal tech is defined as "interpreting [the Tech] verbally for another person." One must always cite, and show, the Hubbard-authored material one is quoting so that the person may read Hubbard's words for her/himself.[8]

Bearing in mind this injunction, I felt I needed to quote "chapter and verse" (as we say of other scriptures) of Hubbard's writing in the endnotes. However, to replicate so many of his sentences was unwieldy. For the most part, therefore, unless I offer a personal perspective, I cite the source of the given definition, quotation, or piece of Tech described. The interested reader may find further information in Scientology's online glossary or on various websites, to which I provide links. You will also find citations of books and links to websites that offer other perspectives on Scientology.

I've always been fond of endnotes, especially when authors use them to do more than provide citations, sometimes augmenting their thinking or offering a perspective on matters that fall just outside the purview of the book itself. So it is with mine. In them you'll find source information as well as details or anecdotes that may be of further interest.

I

Nothing Better to Be

WE NEED YOU TO BE A ZEALOT

Her lovely face revealing nothing about the purpose or mood of our meeting, Jessica ushered me into her office and closed the door. On her desk lay a large red book embossed with gold letters. I recognized it. It was one of a dozen volumes that contained, in chronological order, all the policy letters and bulletins that L. Ron Hubbard had written regarding auditing, Scientology's form of counseling. A bookcase behind Jessica's desk held the entire set, bound in red leather, with an inch-and-a-half gap where this one had been removed. Another bookcase held the equally large set of "admin" volumes, bound in green, which contained everything Hubbard had ever written about how to found and run an organization. Of course Jessica kept these books close to hand. As head of a Scientology mission—the "mission holder"—she would refer to them often.

Jessica emanated serenity. She wore simple, elegant clothes, black and tan and linen. Her long hair was straight and glossy. She had unswerving faith in L. Ron Hubbard's religious technology, yet even as she ensured that the mission (she called it a "Center," choosing, with purpose, a less religiously charged word) adhered to his policies, she was never dictatorial. This was generally true of the Scientologists I'd come to know in my five years in the Church. I found them reasonable, kind, ethical, straightforward, and sane. Through the Church's hermetic seal (especially hermetic in 1987, pre-Internet), whispers and speculation made their way: someone who'd done something wrong—"gone out-ethics"—had been chained for days to a toilet in a brig or forced to live in something like a gulag, eating rice and beans and doing menial labor, but these rumors had nothing to do with my own experience. Nevertheless, ever since the previous night—when, as I'd been finishing up my duties in the Center's course room, Jessica had stopped in to request this meeting—I'd been anxious.

I perched on the edge of a chair, swallowed, and swallowed again.

She took her place on the other side of the desk and, folding her hands on its glossy surface, said, "Sands. You need to be firmer in the course room."

I nodded, a little dazed, wondering what I might have done wrong.

My post at the Center was as a Course Supervisor. A Course Supervisor does not teach; she oversees the study going on in the course room—study that is entirely of materials written by Hubbard—making sure students understand what they are reading. So what Jessica was referring to might mean that I had not been absolutely vigilant as I checked a student's understanding of one of Hubbard's policy letters. Or maybe it was that student, Skip, who'd had so much trouble with the Training Routines. The previous week, he'd enrolled in the Success Through Communication course but, after just two nights, hadn't returned. I was haunted by the story he'd told me, about a weekend retreat that was supposed to have taught him how to master fear but instead seemed to have fried his brain. If I'd passed him on a drill when he wasn't ready to be passed, I might be responsible for whatever fragile mental state he might find himself in. Even though he'd come to us in a pretty fragile mental state.

"The Tech is the most precious thing," Jessica was saying, her dark eyes serious. "You know that, Sands. If we're to keep Scientology working, we must apply it correctly."

She reached for the book on her desk, opened it to a marked page, and swiveled the volume around so I could see it.

I knew it well: an HCOPL—Hubbard Communications Office

Policy Letter—written in February 1965 entitled "Keeping Scientology Working."[9]

Jessica cleared her throat. "'We have some time since passed the point of achieving uniformly workable technology.'"

She was either reading upside-down or reciting. Many Scientologists memorized, word for word, chunks of what was known as the "Tech."

"'The only thing now is getting the technology applied,'" she quoted.

"I understand," I said.

She smiled. "I'm sure you do. But I can hardly tell you to Keep Scientology Working without doing exactly what LRH says we must do if we are to keep Scientology working."

I tried to smile back, and bent my head to read the familiar words. This policy letter was the first thing you read each time you started a new Scientology course. Which meant I'd read it about a dozen times. I see now that the first sentence makes a statement as if it's self-evident—"We have some time since passed the point of achieving uniformly workable technology"—and the other steps follow from that assumption. But at the time I did not spot how this led the reader, unquestioningly, into the second step—"Two: Knowing the technology." After which comes:

> Three: Knowing it is correct.
> Four: Teaching correctly the correct technology.
> Five: Applying the technology.
> Six: Seeing that the technology is correctly applied.

I looked up from the page and again said, "I understand."

And it was true that about this far I was usually able to follow Hubbard's thinking, even if I found it awfully arrogant. He and he alone had come up with the *only* possible technology? Still, although I might not agree it was *the* only correct technology, it did seem as if it might be—my knowledge was limited—*a* correct technology. I was not in the course room to teach the Tech, but I was doing my best to make sure students understood it. I understood that "applying Tech" meant living your life more or less by Hubbard's policies and perspectives. Around this I was definitely wishy-washy: my faith in the validity of everything Hubbard had ever written or said was in no way absolute—some things actually scared me. But I did believe in the efficacy of a lot of it.

However, the next four steps of Keeping Scientology Working really troubled me, even though I'd glibly demonstrated my understanding of them—which certainly implied agreement—any number of times. They were so *adamant*. I lowered my eyes to the page.

> Seven: Hammering out of existence incorrect technology.
> Eight: Knocking out incorrect application.
> Nine: Closing the door on any possibility of incorrect technology.
> Ten: Closing the door on incorrect application.

"Sands," Jessica said. "We must, as LRH says, 'close the door on any possibility of incorrect application.' "

I nodded, wondering what door of "incorrect application" I'd left ajar. And who had noticed? Who'd brought it to Jessica's attention? The only thing I could think of was Skip. Poor Skip! How on earth could he live with the images in his head?

Jessica turned the page and pointed to a paragraph at the end of the document.

> The whole agonized future of this planet, every Man, Woman and Child on it, and your own destiny for the next endless trillions of years depend on what you do here and now with and in Scientology.

I knew the rest of this paragraph. This was a "deadly serious" activity. If we didn't manage to "get out of the trap" now, we might never have another chance. The inherent hysteria made me roll my eyes, just a bit. Humans had been on the planet a long, long time.

Which, I also understood, was part of Hubbard's point.

"If we falter in delivering the Tech in a completely standard way, Sands, we risk losing it." Jessica's voice had the slightest wobble in it. It wasn't just that her own status as the mission holder was on the line if the Center was found to be delivering anything other than Standard Tech—a terrifying idea for all involved. It was also the idea that under her watch, Scientology might not work as it was meant to work. I found this utterly noble and beautiful, even as inside the little cat of doubt I knew so well stretched a paw and yawned.

"We need you to be a zealot, Sands."

I blinked. The blood in my veins came to a halt. "A zealot?"

She nodded. My blood began to pump again. Actually, it lurched and spun as through my head roiled visions of men holding gleaming scimitars in one hand and in the other, gripped by their long hair, the bleeding lopped-off heads of women. I saw horses screaming and rearing as their riders stormed through a crowd of unbelievers. I saw a little girl, held by her ankles, whirled against a rock to smash her heathen forehead. I saw a hundred Muslim bodies impaled on sharp poles, left to writhe and die. I saw Christians opening their arms to welcome the hungry lions that, mouths agape, raced toward them across a Roman ring.

"At times you are too gentle," Jessica said.

I could only stare, caught up in the sight and sound and smell and filth of carnage in the name of faith.

"At times you allow yourself to be swayed by someone you think of as stronger than you—or, what I mean is, if you think they're smarter. Especially if that person is male."

I nodded. This was inarguable. My father. My brother. The man I'd married, Jamie, whose brilliance as a musician helped persuade me that he might also be brilliant about his chosen spiritual path, which was how I'd come to Scientology in the first place. My current sweetheart, Skye, was tenderer, but the quicksilver quality of his mind, and his marvelous sense of humor, caused me to sometimes wonder whether his thoughts might be better than my own.

Except for the volume open between us, the surface of Jessica's desk held only a photo in a frame and a small potted plant, and she ran a hand over the gleaming rosewood. "Delivering the Tech has nothing, *nothing* to do with being 'nice.' Let me remind you—you're the one who pointed it out to me—that the root of the word 'nice' is 'foolish.'"

"Well," I said, "ignorant, anyway."

"You are not ignorant. Nor foolish! So don't be 'nice.' I worry that you'd rather be liked than risk offending a student by sending him back to, say, restudy material."

Again I tried to think where I'd been lax. After taking the Course Supervisor Course I'd had to do an internship in a course room, and I thought I'd gotten pretty good at telling people to restudy their materials if I felt they had to. Hubbard's Study Tech was an aspect of Scientology in which I completely believed.

"That's what I mean by 'zealot,'" Jessica said. "If Scientology is applied standardly, we *know* it works."

I thought about Skip. I wondered if the Tech had helped him. I worried that by now he'd blown his brains out.

I thought, too, that I really needed to look up the word ZEALOT. Maybe my understanding of it was incomplete. Maybe I misunderstood it entirely.

"Okay," Jessica said. "You can go now. We're glad to have you with us—I just want to urge you toward being the most effective Course Supervisor you can be."

A LITTLE STUNNED, I left her office and headed to the course room to get ready for students who would soon arrive. A Scientologist would describe the mission's quarters, not far from Rodeo Drive, as "upstat." And the large rooms, wall-to-wall carpet, solid furniture, and a recent paint job did indicate an organization whose "stats" were "up." All of it pulled elegantly together by Jessica's taste: a vase of dried grasses and flowers on one surface, just the right number of Scientology's endless glossy publications on another.

Dusk pressed against the large course room window, even as the setting sun flushed the sky with salmon and turquoise, colors that made me think of the Southwest, and of the Anasazi. I often wondered where those ancient Native Americans had disappeared to, and why. The past summer, Skye and I had spent a few weeks in the Four Corners region. We'd visited my sister Tracy and her family before heading to various Anasazi sites to clamber in and out of cliff dwellings, imagining the lives of those who'd carried water up barely visible stone steps pecked into rock. I wanted to live in one of those states—Colorado, Arizona, New Mexico, Utah—and one night, in Taos, I'd even talked to Skye about that possibility. But, as he'd pointed out, what his life was about—Scientology, music—was in LA. And so, because I appeared to have handed my life over to what others might have to say about it, I'd returned with him to the life I had here.

Seven years before, I'd fled New York City for Los Angeles. I'd persuaded myself I was in flight toward an expansion of my acting career, when in fact, I see now, I simply could not face what had happened to my brother—the result of a terrible fall from a bridge. Just a year and a half later, almost as if I'd aimed straight for it, I married a Scientologist, in the process pretty much marrying the Church. Jamie and I'd divorced a year later, but now I was living with Skye, another Scientologist. I did not think about what had become of my brother: I understood his brain was damaged, irrevocably, but beyond that I resolutely did not go. Any ideas about what I might do with my life—act, sing, write—had scattered like marbles on pavement. At night, instead of rehearsing a play, or playing music, or even going out for a beer, I was working in a Scientology mission. Instead of composing songs or working on a novel, I studied Scientology. I'd switched theatrical agents three times, cut and even permed my hair, thinking these were the problem. They were not.

For a moment I thought about running back down the Center's stairs and heading east on Wilshire—not to Los Feliz, where Skye and I shared a house, but all the way to Grand Junction, where I'd take up Tracy's longstanding offer: if I ever needed a place to land, I could stay with her and her family.

Family. I pressed my forehead to the window's cool glass and closed my eyes.

CLAPTRAP

"And then," my father said, "and you have to understand that Barbara and I couldn't believe our eyes—right there, in the nave of that cathedral, Sands drops to her knees."

Mother nodded at the appreciative gasps that came from the Porters, who wore their tennis whites and sipped at drinks my father had made for them in blue Mexican glasses. I was sitting on the floor beside Mother's chair, chin on my drawn-up, eight-year-old knees.

"To our horror," Dad said, "and remember, she's just two years old, she starts shuffling on her knees toward the altar. Well, I'll tell you, I jerked her to her feet so hard and fast I dislocated her shoulder."

"Oakley! You didn't dislocate her shoulder," Mother said. "But he did jerk her to her feet so hard and fast he made her cry."

"Good thing," Mr. Porter said. "Don't let them get any of that claptrap in their brains—they'll never get it out."

Dad held out his hand for Mr. Porter's glass. "Another highball?"

Dad had told this story a number of times: the hushed cathedral in Mexico City, the heavy scent of beeswax candles, the three of us, as I saw it, even though my brother must also have been there, turning toward the grand and glittery Altar of Forgiveness.

"Why is it called a highball?" I asked.

"They get you high?" Mrs. Porter said. They all laughed.

"My family didn't call them highballs," she said. "We called them cocktails."

I played with the lacings of my mother's tennis shoes, looking out the windows of our living room at the mountain called Squaw Peak, and to its right, closer to us, the vast mound of granite known as the Rockpile.

My father built much of that A-frame house. He dragged beams, hammered nails, threw up plywood. My mother told of lying on the steep slant of roof, arms stretched wide to pin down the tarpaper that a late-summer Sierra wind wanted to rip away, while my father tacked it down around her. They'd graduated from UC Berkeley, schooled and worked in Manhattan, traveled to Europe, lived in San Diego and Mexico—and then, in 1958, moved to a rural valley in the Sierra Nevada to build their own home. Only as I got older did it occur to me that they'd known no one in the area; the first time they looked at the property, they'd had to ride horses up the mountain. They simply knew that they, themselves, and their children—Tad, me, Tracy, and eventually Brett (she'd be born in 1962)—were enough.

I was still thinking about Daddy jerking me to my feet in that church in Mexico. I could well imagine I'd cried. I retied Mother's laces. "Why's it called a cocktail?"

Mother put a hand on my head. "Do you remember any of that?" she asked. "The church? Lupe? How Lupe used to carry you everywhere?"

I shook my head. But I could imagine it, from details provided when my parents told these stories. Bolstered by photographs taken at the time, I knew that several years before, in the mid-fifties, as my father set to work on a new novel, my parents rented a house in Chapala, Mexico, and Mother hired a local woman, Lupe, to help take care of Tad and me. Lupe carried me everywhere, my legs and feet, in shoes that she re-whited every morning, dangling from her arms. My mother was afraid I'd forget how to walk, because Lupe never put me down. I was with her as she haggled over tortillas and avocados, as she stood on street corners gossiping with friends, and—as soon became clear—as she attended daily mass.

At some point during their time in Chapala, Mom and Dad headed to Mexico City. Dad was enraptured with the history of Mexico; he'd end up writing almost a dozen novels incorporating it. Our trip included a visit to the Cathedral of the Assumption of Mary, seat of the Roman Catholic Archdiocese of Mexico, and—these were the kinds of connections that fascinated my father, as they would come to fascinate me—built on land that had been sacred to the Aztecs. Cortez accomplished this desecration/construction in 1591, commanding that the Aztec temple be destroyed and its stones used to build his church.

None of this did I know at the time, of course. Nor do I remember being in the church, or shuffling toward the altar, or even my father jerking me vigorously from my knees. But Dad told this story often, and I understood there was a lesson here: I'd been jerked to my senses, as well as jerked to my feet.

"You did the right thing," Mr. Porter was saying. He turned his florid, round face to look down at me. I pressed my cheek against one of Mother's calves. "All religions are full of claptrap. Especially organized ones."

I was expected to nod, and I did.

Dad nodded too. "But those religions have also given the world a great deal of culture. We can't forget that."

"So much beautiful art," Mother said. "Paintings, sculpture—"

"Music," Dad said. "Especially music. 'The Hallelujah Chorus'!"

I knew this was on a record that he played loudly on Christmas mornings.

"And ideas," Mother said. "Many great ideas."

Dad nodded. "A conundrum, to be sure."

"What's a conundrum?" I asked.

But they began to talk about the great shot Mother had slammed down the alley that finished their tennis game. I headed outside to see what my brother might be up to.

•

TWO PHOTOGRAPHS OF that year spent in Chapala have fluttered with the family through the years. One is of my brother. He was given the birth name Oakley Hall III but, so as not to be confused with his father, was nicknamed Tad. In the photograph, he's dressed as a caballero: loose white pants and a wide-brimmed sombrero. He stands in four-year-old glee at the part he's playing, his feet, sheathed in heeled boots, wide apart. He grins at the camera, even then his dark eyes intense and roguish.

In the other photograph, I'm sitting on my mother's lap, holding a book. She appears to have been reading to me, and has paused: she's leaning back on tanned arms. I was a towheaded child, and a section of white-blond hair is pulled atop my head. On my feet are lace-up baby shoes, probably whited by Lupe just that morning. Even though Mother's face is angled away from the camera, it's clear she's smiling. She wears a skirt that comes just over her knees, a belt emphasizes her slim figure, and both calves are tucked back in a pose both feminine and easy. On her feet are espadrilles, laces twined above her ankles. She carries this bohemian loveliness with grace and style, without looking the least bit "stylish."

It's a quality she's had all her life. Long before ethnic clothes became fashionable, Mother was using her Singer sewing machine to rig intriguing tops out of a bit of white cotton and a yoke of exquisitely embroidered Guatemalan cloth purchased in one of the Mexican markets she loved to frequent. She used a wicker basket to carry her babies and had no problem, even in the uptight fifties, breastfeeding her children in company; she simply draped one of many colorful rebozos over a shoulder. At a time when women were still wearing girdles and nylons, she built tiered skirts that fell to the tops of her bare feet, constructing four-inch waistbands that set off her small waist. She loved silver jewelry, especially Mexican silver, and over the years purchased all sizes and kinds of crosses. Along with enormous cooking pots, a recipe for pozole, yards of colored fabric, and embroidered huipils, she and Dad carried this silver home. Five or six crosses at a time, attached to long chains, dangled from her neck. They were never a statement of religiosity. They were beautiful artifacts, collected the same way she and Dad acquired pieces of pre-Columbian art.

In her fifties, she began to explore photography, attending the Art Institute in San Francisco, then journeying to Nepal and India, taking striking black-and-white photographs of Nepalese women and Tibetan monks. She also brought back Tibetan dorgies, which look like small silver handweights and are used for prayer, and a Tibetan spirit house, which she filled with amulets and Mexican milagros and Zuni fetishes. Both my parents sought such items—when traveling, in flea markets, in hole-in-the-wall antique stores—and they were often mutually decided-upon gifts: an image of the Black Madonna painted on tin; a small wooden crucifix, Christ's spear wound red and gaping; a Virgin Mary made of black Oaxacan clay whose outstretched arms ended in palms that could each hold a candle.

Even as the walls and shelves of the family home in Squaw Valley, as well as the second house they eventually purchased in San Francisco, filled with religious totems, my parents made it clear that while they respected what these things represented, there was nothing there in which one actually *believed.*

Which meant that in our family, one did not "go to" church, although we did enter a lot of them. One "visited," as a tourist, to appreciate important cultural contributions.

And yet, on Christmas mornings, Dad dropped Handel's *Messiah* onto the record player and turned the volume knob to ten.

"The kingdom of this world," he'd sing, softly, "is become . . ."

Then, raising his voice along with the thunderous choir, he'd roar, "The kingdom of his Christ, and of his Christ! And he shall reign for-ever and e-e-ver!"

It was possible to revere the products of religion, I understood, while disdaining the practice of them.

ENTHUSIASTIC DEVOTION TO A CAUSE

A student, Julie, had arrived ten minutes early so she could claim her favorite spot near the window. I greeted her but didn't meet her eyes, certain she'd see the doubt flaring there. As she settled in, I moved about the course room, aware of the melancholy night pulsing beyond the window, and far beyond, the Anasazi ruins, the Southwest's mesas and sunsets, my sister's Colorado home, to which I yearned to return. I straightened chairs that were already straight, tidied the tidy piles of objects on the tables known as "demo kits." I usually enjoyed these minutes, quiet and settled before the three-hour bustle of the evening began, preparing for work that now and again I thought of as sacred, although Hubbard eschews the use of words that other religions have imbued with meaning. But this night I wished I could just leave—"blow," Hubbard's word for a "sudden, unexplained departure."[10]

It had never occurred to me, in the five years I'd become more and more involved in Scientology, that what was needed was for me to be a zealot. No matter how enthralled I'd been while reading Hubbard's materials or even following an insightful session with an auditor or other Scientology counselors, I'd been unable to believe, not deep down, that Scientology had all the answers. Well,

Hubbard wouldn't want one to say it that way; he would simply say he'd developed a "workable system." But you were also supposed to believe it was the *only* workable system. How could that possibly be true?

Yet I walked through every day as if it were true. I had wonderful friends who utterly believed it and trusted that I did, too. I lived with a man who, even as he talked me through my doubts, believed that I believed it. I worked with dozens of students who thought me a model of belief. But Jessica had found the hole in my psyche and wiggled a finger into that squishy place.

And the squishy place included what had happened to Skip. Had I been as *zealous* as I could have been? Was there something else I could have done, should have done? He'd come to us terribly disturbed by whatever had gone on in that "conquering your fears" seminar. After just a few hours in his company, it had seemed to me that an introductory Scientology course wasn't going to help him. I'd also wondered—a betrayal of everything I was supposed to believe—whether Scientology could help him at all.

Yet there was no room for that possibility. If the Tech didn't work, it was the fault of its practitioner: Skip, or me. The Tech itself could not be lacking. To think otherwise would be being "reasonable."[11] It certainly would not be Keeping Scientology Working.

I crossed to the bookcase, which contained various manuals and dictionaries and many books by Hubbard. I pulled out the *American Heritage*. The thing I loved most about Scientology, the thing that had done much to convince me that Hubbard was not a charlatan, was what was known as Study Tech, especially Hubbard's insistence that you define any word you don't understand. You even define words you *think* you understand.

Julie was reading. The rest of the students had yet to arrive. I flipped to the back of the dictionary.

ZEALOT: 1) One who is zealous, excessively so.

Irritating, when a definition uses a version of the word to define the word.

> ZEALOUS: Filled or motivated by zeal, fervent.

Of course ZEAL would be part of ZEALOT.

> ZEAL: 1) Enthusiastic devotion to a cause, ideal, or goal, and tireless diligence in its furtherance.

Put like that, being a zealot didn't seem so bad. What was wrong with "enthusiastic devotion"? How could one have a problem with "tireless diligence"? That's what it took to be an effective actor, an effective guitarist, singer, writer—an effective anything.

For Hubbard, "clearing" a word includes examining its derivation, essential to full comprehension. The roots of ZEAL move from Middle English to Old French to Late Latin to the Greek, *zelos*. I moved my finger back to ZEALOT and its second definition:

> 2) A fanatically committed person.

This definition began to close in on my emotional response, as did #3, spelled with a capital letter, Zealot:

> 3) A member of a Jewish movement in the first century A.D. that fought against Roman rule in Palestine as incompatible with strict monotheism.

So there was a religious aspect to it. That hadn't been my imagination.

I thought I understood FANATICAL but just to be sure leafed to the page and ran a finger down that column, pausing to confirm that the innocuous-sounding "fan" descends from FANATIC. I scanned the derivation:

faniticus, meaning of a temple, inspired by a god, mad.

I tapped my finger against the page. Interesting connections:

inspired by a god, mad

As if one necessarily leads to the other.

I could see that. The previous summer, as Skye and I had traipsed around the ruins of kivas in New Mexico's Chaco Canyon—that mysterious, compelling place—I couldn't help but imagine the strange and even violent uses to which the Anasazi might have put those vast stone circles. Or how about Greek priestesses eating laurel and spinning prophecies, or Pentecostals speaking in tongues? Just the other night Skye and I'd watched, aghast yet amused, as Jerry Falwell preached and his followers screamed and writhed.

From the Latin *fanum*, temple

So, "fanatical" had some connection to being in a temple. Becoming inspired by a god to such a degree that one became mad. Which could lead to zealotry. Yes, I could see that.

And here I was, a Course Supervisor in what could be seen (although not by most Scientologists) as a temple: rooms where people studied the scriptures of L. Ron Hubbard.

And to some degree I was being told I needed to become "mad." In order to be zealous.

"May I use that dictionary?" Julie stood nearby. "It's my favorite."

I closed and gave it to her. She held it to her chest. "Not just because it's the one LRH says has the best derivations. It's just clearer than *Webster's*." I watched as she returned to her seat and opened her course pack, a thick packet filled, as all course packs used in Scientology course rooms are, with materials written only by L. Ron Hubbard.

Looking at her bowed, zealous-looking head, I thought of a story she'd told me about recent Scientology counseling. Julie was among those taking courses at the Center who were also receiving auditing. Auditing usually involves uncovering "chains" of incidents: recalling events that are earlier, and similar, until you reach the original one that has caused the pain/grief/confusion.[12]

Toward the end of one session, Julie couldn't seem to find an earlier incident, but Jessica kept asking, "Is there anything else?" and Julie finally found it.

When she was eight, she'd peed in a swimming pool!

Her face had reddened as she told me this transgression—in Scientology, called an "overt"—and the vast relief that flowed through her once she'd gotten it off her chest.[13] "It was such a terrible overt! I was too embarrassed to even *say* it!"

I'd stared. I understood how it was an overt: "an intentionally committed harmful act committed in an effort to solve a problem" is one of Hubbard's definitions, as is "that thing which you do which you aren't willing to have happen to you."[14, 15] But a "terrible" one? I thought about having slept with not just one married man, but two of them, when I'd first landed in Los Angeles seven years before. I thought about staying in my parents' San Francisco apartment, telling them, *lying* to them, that I was visiting friends, when in fact I was there to attend a Church rally, which they would have hated.

A few days after Julie had shared her "huge" overt with me, I mentioned it to Jessica, chuckling at how awful Julie thought it was to have peed in a pool. "I can think of a lot worse things," I said—thinking, for instance, of my chronic doubt regarding Scientology.

Jessica shook her head and, almost, rolled her eyes. "That's not the incident that's at the bottom of that chain," she said. "Julie just can't confront the magnitude of what it really is. Not yet. But we'll get there."

This had shaken me. I'd liked the idea that, for some, peeing in a swimming pool might be as bad as one could get. But by now I was used to the idea that overts were pretty much at the bottom of everything; if you looked hard enough, you'd always find the bad or negative thing you'd done to create the bad/negative place you were in—or the reason that you wanted to leave the place you thought might be bad for you: such as Scientology.

As other students began to arrive and settle in with their course packs, I picked up the binder containing the roll call sheets and other student information, hoping, although I knew it was pointless, that Skip would be among those coming through the door.

He wasn't. I called roll. I assigned students to do drills. I touched a shoulder here, leaned over a table to help with a question there. But I was barely in that room. I was a helium balloon in a high corner, jerking against the paint and plaster, wanting out.

But what would I do, where would I go? I couldn't go to my parents. It wasn't just that I was in my mid-thirties. They were virulently against my involvement in the Church. Sometimes I totally agreed with them, but time and again managed to let myself be persuaded that they simply didn't want what was best for me. The shame of creeping home to them was unimaginable. Also, there wasn't just this life to worry about. What would happen to the immortal soul I'd always believed—and now, due to Scientology, was increasingly convinced—I had? The soul that would keep coming back, having to relearn and relive all the sad, violent, stupid, karmic lessons, lifetime after lifetime? Wasn't I going to find the way out, through Scientology? How could I turn my back on all this certainty?

And what if I *did* just up and leave? Everyone knew that a "sudden departure" meant that the person had done something terribly wrong. If I blew, it could only be because I'd committed an overt, something so insidious and awful that, like Julie, I simply couldn't examine it.

I actually groaned aloud. A student looked up at me. I did my best to smile.

IF GOD EXISTS, WHY IS HE SUCH A BASTARD?

My father was raised Episcopalian, my mother Christian Scientist—words that meant nothing to me when I was young, and which were uttered in a tone of voice that indicated how unimportant this background was. I'm not sure how much churchgoing went on in Dad's childhood, but the Bible was definitely part of Mother's, as even a brief inspection of Mary Baker Eddy's teachings indicates: *As adherents of Truth, we take the inspired word of the Bible as our sufficient guide to eternal life.* Nevertheless, by the time my parents met, in 1944 at the University of California, Berkeley, neither seemed to have much use, other than the literary, for what might be found on the pages of the Old and New Testaments.

And yet there was the deep pleasure Dad took in Handel's *Messiah*, and the collecting of religious images. So perhaps a residual Episcopalianism wavered in and out, as did some Christian Science. Well into her seventies, Mom told me that during sleepless, troubled nights she'd summon the Mary Baker Eddy creed she'd memorized as a child: *There is no life, truth, intelligence, in matter. All is infinite Mind and infinite manifestation, for God is all-in-all. Spirit is immortal truth; matter is mortal error . . .*

One morning when I was about eight, I told her I was sick and couldn't possibly go to school. She sat on the edge of my bed and asked, "What happened yesterday?" She didn't ask *if* something happened. She *knew* something had. I burst into tears: I'd been teased on the playground.

"You're not sick, honey," she said. "Rise above it. Get up and get dressed. You've got ten minutes to eat your egg and get out the door."

This was Christian Science at work. And though I wouldn't know it for decades, it's pretty much how a Scientologist would have dealt with the situation. These ideas took firm hold. Long before I began to study Hubbard's writings, a friend told me I was the last person in the world she'd call if she were feeling ill. "You just ask, 'What's *really* going on?'" she said. "I have respect for that way of thinking, but sometimes someone's just *sick*! You don't have to make the sick person feel worse!"

I was sad not to be the first friend she'd call were she in trouble. Nevertheless, I couldn't shake a certainty imbedded with the same adamancy that an egg is the best form of protein: Ill in body is ill in mind. And eventually I'd find my way to a religion that completely supported the idea that if something bad happens, you've created it; you've "pulled it in."

Mom grew up in California's Sacramento Delta, where her father raised orchards of peach and pear on enough land to house a literal village of Chinese, Japanese, and Filipino workers. She remembers visiting them: the cooking fires and vast iron woks, the rising aromas and the ability to feed dozens from a single pot—inspirations that stayed with her all her life. No matter how many might show up for dinner: "Throw in a packet of frozen peas," she'd whisper to me, "and get another loaf of French bread out of the freezer."

All of her childhood, her mother was ill with rheumatic fever. The week leading up to Mom's fifth birthday, the huge house was hushed, all play curtailed. On the day she turned five, there was of course no party. That afternoon her father came to find her to give her a present: a silk-lined box containing a choker of large round crystal beads.

"He must have just grabbed something out of my mother's jewelry box," Mom told me. "Even then I knew it was inappropriate for a child. It made me understand how sad he must be. It also made me understand she was dead."

Still, for years, way into college, she wondered if a practical joke was being played on her. Any day, she half believed, half hoped, her mother would return, and they'd all have a good laugh about how fooled she'd been.

Only once do I remember seeing her weep. Even in 2008, as her beloved husband, to whom she'd been married for sixty-three happy years, took his last breath, tears filled her eyes, but did not fall. I think she'd learned, that day she turned five, that it would do no good, and she did not allow herself to start down a path that would tear her heart open.

In a way, Dad, too, lost his parents when he was young: they divorced, bitterly. He spent part of those childhood years in San Diego with his father, and part with his mother Jessie in Hawaii. This may have been a reason he could seem cold at times, or might explain the rage that now and again surged through him, when he'd make rash decisions or say or do startlingly cruel things. He told far fewer stories than our mother did of his childhood. One of the few I remember is of the day he found a coin—"two bits"—on the coffee table. He ran out to buy candy and a magazine, *Boy's Life*, and when he returned, found his mother weeping. She'd planned to use that quarter to buy their dinner.

It may have been this, as well as the news available in a newspaper on any given day, that made Mom sometimes say, "If God exists, why is he such a bastard?" And Dad would nod. Sometimes they laughed. Sometimes they didn't.

"If God exists, why is he such a bastard?" Every time I heard this, I was struck by the simultaneity of possible meanings: God did not exist, which seemed in line with what I thought my parents believed. On the other hand, he might, which was confusing. And if he did, he had it out for the world he'd created.

TRAINING ROUTINES

All evening, I continued to hope that Skip would walk through the door. He'd been on course only a few nights—he'd started the week before, escorted into the course room by Ed, the Center's executive director.

"Skip is here to begin his first service," Ed had said, with a flourish of his hand, as if he'd conjured Skip out of a hat.

Skip was in his late twenties, fit and tan, with a lovely smile. But his eyes skittered, as if he was looking for something he couldn't find. I chalked it up to his being nervous about starting a Scientology course. People often were.

"After talking about it a bit," Ed said, "Skip and I think Success Through Communication is just the course he needs!"

I smiled, slightly ashamed by the charade Ed and I were playing. Success Through Communication was almost always the introductory course recommended to anyone compelled/encouraged to give Scientology a try. Five years before, newly married, it had been the course I'd finally been persuaded to take—and what it covered intrigued me, one could even say hooked me, as it was designed to do. The "comm course" dances between the pragmatic—that communicating effectively requires certain steps and that those steps can be learned—and the spiritual: that one may *have* a body, but one *is* a spirit, and that here, too, there are steps to take toward, well, being an ever-more-effective spirit. It took me a long time to understand that the communication skills the course teaches (which are real, and useful) pull one inexorably into the specifics of auditing, and thus, of Scientology.

Skip carried his shiny course pack, which Ed would have given him when he paid for the course. Even on this October evening he wore shorts, T-shirt, flip-flops. I got him signed in, went over the course room basics, and watched him open his course pack, before going to check on the other students.

A Scientology course room consists of at least two separate rooms: one used for quiet study, and another, called the "practical" room, for those parts of a course that require talking or practicing/drilling. A Course Supervisor is not there to teach. Hubbard's materials do that. Rather, moving back and forth between the rooms, I was to ensure that students understood what they were reading (or, in the case of tapes, listening to), and if they didn't, to help them find where they'd encountered a "Barrier to Study" and to get them over it.

Skip signaled to me that he'd completed the first section in his booklet. This meant that he was ready to be checked out on his understanding of the Cycle of Communication.

As Hubbard did with many of life's most obvious and common activities, he took a look at what's involved in communication and broke it down into its component parts. This "cycle" is straightforward enough: you say or ask something, the other person responds, you acknowledge the response; for example:

> Joe: Hey, Sue, shut the garage door when you leave,
>   will you?
> Sue: Sure.
> Joe: Thanks.

When I took this course myself and studied the cycle for the first time, I'd found it to be so obvious as to be almost laughable.

Yet I'd also felt a curious stirring, an inward squint of interest. It caused me to consider various moments in my life when misunderstandings had arisen over that final bit of the cycle, the "acknowledgment"—shortened by Scientologists to "ack." Silence can be used as a weapon, and interpreted in a number of ways. If Joe doesn't say "Thanks," Sue could hear "How many times do I have to tell you!" It was easy to imagine the resentment or even argument that might ensue without Joe's ack.

It was glaringly obvious. And yet, like much I was to encounter in Scientology, the obvious thing was often ignored, or simply not employed.

I asked a student, Jen, who'd completed this same course, to check Skip's understanding. She started by requesting that he demonstrate—"demo"—the comm cycle.

He seized the concept of demoing right away, as students tended to do.

"Well," he said, lifting a battery from the pile of items on the table. "This is Pete." He rustled around a bit more and selected a little metal thimble abandoned from a Monopoly game. "This is Suzie," he said, stowing it on the tip of his pinky.

Jen nodded. "Good."

He wiggled the thimble. "Hey, Pete," he made it say in a high voice, "Get milk!"

He wiggled the battery. "Will do, Suzie," he said in a low voice. He looked up.

"And?" Jen said.

Skip frowned. "Pete said, 'Will do.' He *acknowledged* Suzie, like the bulletin says."

"Flunk," Jen said, as kindly as she could.

Skip looked startled. "What?"

"You need to read the bulletin again."

"Why? Oh! Right! Now *Suzie* has to acknowledge *Pete*." He wiggled the battery. "Thanks, Pete!" he said.

Jen opened Skip's course pack and pointed to the page in question. "That's right," she said. "Suzie's ack completes the cycle. But you need to reread the bulletin anyway, and make sure there isn't anything you don't understand."

Skip rolled his eyes. He reread the page in about five seconds and passed the drill. He initialed that step as done on his check sheet and moved on to the next item, which was to read about the first training routine of the Communication Cycle, called OT TR0: Operating Thetan Training Routine Zero.

OPERATING THETAN TRAINING Routine Zero.

Those words, and its acronym, OT TR0, are packed with information.

Hubbard launched much of Scientology from Saint Hill Manor in England, and his work includes various Britishisms. He dates his writings in the British way, using day/month/year: Hubbard Communication Office Policy Letters and Bulletins (HCOPLs and HCOBs, respectively) are dated 15 Apr 1983, rather than the American month/day/year: April 15, 1983. He also begins various counts with zero rather than one; thus, the first Training Routine is 0.

Training Routines, or TRs, are designed to take students through "laid out practical steps gradient by gradient, to teach a student to apply with certainty what he has learned."[16]

And THETAN is Scientology's word for "spirit" or "soul": "the awareness of awareness unit."[17] The word was coined by Hubbard using the Greek word *theta*, which, according to him, means "thought or life or spirit."

And the all-important *Operating* Thetan—OT—is "willing and knowing cause over life, thought, matter, energy, space and time."[18]

For Scientologists, to be an Operating Thetan is the ultimate goal. However, it's a state with many demarcations, and those yearning to be OT move, for years, along what's known as the Bridge to Total Freedom. An OT III, significant stage though that is to achieve, has quite a distance to travel before becoming OT VI; even an OT VIII understands there's a lot of territory to traverse before she's totally "at cause." But one starts with OT TR0.

So in order to understand even the *name* of this first drill, there are a number of dense concepts with which a student has to grapple. This may be why, in the current iteration of the course, this Training Routine is called TR0 Be There.[19] However, since I studied these materials as Hubbard originally titled and described them, that's how I'll relate them.

The directions for OT TR0 are: "Student and coach sit facing each other with eyes closed."[20]

That's it. That is what the drill trains two people to do: to sit facing each other with their eyes closed.

Except, of course, it's a lot. Some have likened it to meditating, except that you're not focusing on breath or a mantra—you're staying conscious of what's going on in the room around you, particularly of the person sitting opposite. Over the years, I'd come to think of it as training senses other than sight in being aware. You are readying yourself for communication, but it doesn't necessarily have to be speech that arrives, or that is sent.

I asked Kolya, who'd completed a number of courses, including the comm course, to drill the TR with Skip. They settled into two chairs, facing each other.

"Start," Kolya said to Skip; he was "coach." They closed their eyes.

But Skip fidgeted. Kolya opened his eyes and said, "Flunk."

Skip made a face. "Why do you say that! *Flunk!* It's a terrible word."

I'd thought exactly the same thing the first time the word was aimed at me. "Flunk" begins with the faintly ominous *f* and ends with that harsh *k*. And it means you failed! But years ago, during my own first night on this same course, I'd heard the Course Supervisor say it often: whenever someone wiggled or giggled. And she'd said it with no inflection, no judgment, no harshness; it just meant "do it again, do it better."

I'd come to appreciate the idea: Flunk. Start. Flunk. Start. My brother had once quoted Samuel Beckett saying something similar: "Fail again. Fail better."[21]

Almost, I could hear his voice: deep, comforting. We were both living in New York then, and one day, having lost out on a yearned-for role in a play, I'd gone to him weeping. He took a deep drag from his cigarette, his brown eyes deeply kind.

"'Ever tried. Ever failed,'" he said, speaking through the smoke curling out of his mouth. "Remember what Beckett says: 'No matter. Try again. Fail again. Fail better.'"

I shook my head to fling my brother out of it. Still: *Fail again. Fail better.*

I told Kolya to go back to his own study and sat down opposite Skip.

"I know what you mean," I told him. "But it's just a way of saying something's not quite right and to try it again. You understand the drill, right?" I picked up his pack, which he'd stashed next to his chair. "Anything you don't understand?"

"Yeah, yeah, I get it. It's just . . ." He pushed his hair back from his face with both hands. "About a month ago, I did this retreat on Kauai, about confronting your fears? And supposedly mastering them? We did a lot of stuff, a lot of stuff, a lot of weird 'mind over matter' stuff." He began to scrub his head, making his hair stick up in tufts. His breath came in spurts, as if he'd just run up seven flights of stairs. "I don't know, ever since then I've got these weird visions in my head. I can't sit still. The world just pitches around."

He poured out more details about the seminar and its leader, but even though my sympathies were deeply aroused, it had been drilled into me that when I was in the course room, I was "on post." I could be kind, of course, but I wasn't to listen to a student's problems; that was for the Ethics Officer, or an auditor. I acknowledged Skip, checked his understanding of the drill, and asked Jen to do it with him. She took her place in the chair opposite, watched Skip close his eyes.

"Start," she said, and closed her own.

Skip's body tilted, straightened, tilted, as if he were on a roller-coaster ride. A few moments later, Jen's did the same. They looked like dogs chasing rabbits in their sleep, little aborted movements that were strangely terrifying.

Jen opened her eyes and looked at me with disbelief. "Umm, flunk?" she said, and I nodded and told her to go back to her own study. Feeling asinine, I checked Skip's understanding of every word in the drill. Once again I asked Jen to twin. Once again they lasted about sixty seconds. I gave Skip one of Hubbard's bulletins to read and went and knocked on Ed's office door.

"Yup!" he said.

Ed was a man I'd never taken to, although I grudgingly admired him. He seemed to me one-quarter redneck and three-quarters rogue, the roguish part undeniably charming. He was brash, a quality that could also count as directness. He seemed to care a bit too much about wearing hip clothes and using language he thought was savvy and cool, but even as I disdained what I saw as a strange eagerness, I saw how this quality might help attract upstat kinds of people to the Center. I told him what was going on.

"How about you do the drill with him?" he said. "I'll watch the course room."

As I sat opposite Skip, he leaned forward and, keeping his voice low, said, "All of us, that weekend? And there were about a hundred? We had to do a firewalk, we had to walk across burning coals. *Twenty feet.*" His face flushed a terrible red. "Twelve hundred degrees," he said. "You can feel the heat *forty feet away.*"

I didn't ask the obvious question.

"I did it." His cheeks lost color, so that the skin of his face was now a splotchy red and white. His forehead shone with perspiration. "I hardly remember. It was a blur. It didn't hurt. The guru guy told us to say 'cool moss, cool moss,' and to keep our eyes on something in the distance, whatever we did to *not look down*! I got across. But ever since I haven't been able to sleep. I can't sit still. I can't do much of anything!" His voice broke. "That's why I'm here. A person told me that maybe Scientology could *help*."

I knew I should say, *of course it can*. But my mind scanned how I'd found my own way to the Church: how I'd homed in on it, the avoidances and refusals, the plunges and graspings, the flickering doubt always present between epiphanies—which rising portcullis I slammed back down.

"Let's try again," I said.

We closed our eyes, and I said, "Start."

I need to reiterate that "all" that's required in this training routine is to sit opposite another person, both of you with your eyes closed. It's part of the Cycle of Communication (and, as I had come to see, an essential part of an auditor's training) because a person needs to be present to receive a communication, just as a person needs to be present to begin one. It seemed to me, although it had taken me a while to grasp this, that part of what the "routine" was "training" you to do was to consciously and continuously and kind of hugely include the other person. Not just what he might be saying. Not even how he might be saying it. A larger sense of that person—another spiritual path might call it an "aura." As with a number of Scientological ideas, once I understood their purpose, it seemed an excellent skill to have.

But sitting opposite Skip, I felt as if I were being spun inside a whirligig. I jerked to stay on my chair, and opened my eyes.

He was staring at me with bald longing. "I want it to stop," he said.

I nodded. I felt perspiration beading on my own forehead. "Flunk," I said, smiling. "Start."

I closed my eyes. Again the vertigo set in. Years before, I'd driven through a snowstorm so fierce that I'd no idea where the road was; at one point I was positive, even as I knew it was impossible, that I was driving the car straight *up* the whirling flakes. Sitting opposite Skip was like that, with the addition that it was violent and scary: purple-black clouds swirling by as we rattled too fast over a road full of potholes. It was visceral. Yet all we were doing was sitting in chairs. I tried to still my pounding heart and to bully my way through it. What *was* this? Could this be emanating from Skip? How was that possible?

I opened my eyes. His long eyelashes flickered and he opened his. "How can I keep the freak-out from happening?" His voice rose, his face flushed.

There was no way I was going to say "Flunk." I just nodded.

Ed kept a desultory eye on the course room while I sat with Skip for minutes, checked in, started the drill again. After a while he was able to sit for a slightly longer stretch. The sense of rushing winds wasn't quite as bad. I got Jen back in the chair opposite. After some fits and starts, they eventually did the drill for fifteen minutes. Scientology's upper courses require one to do OT TR0 for two hours in order to pass. But Success Through Communication is an introductory course and simply asks that the student do it "comfortably." Skip insisted he was "comfortable."

Still, after saying good night to the students, and as I tidied up the course room, I was troubled. I appreciated the TRs and what they offered. But what had gone on with Skip was a whole new territory. What could possibly have caused those kinds of brain waves? Ones that emanated from Skip, physically—so powerful that they affected the person sitting opposite him?

And it wasn't just me who'd experienced those sensations. It wasn't my imagination.

DANCING THROUGH LIFE

Perhaps the sorrow in their childhoods, as well as the lack of ties to either of their families, helped my parents create their famously happy marriage. Mother often said as much: in the difficult early days of marriage, there'd been no one and nowhere to return to, so they turned to each other and held on. What family she did have accused her of "dancing through life." Perhaps that's what it looked like: the move to New York City after graduating (Dad majored in political science, Mom in English), where he enrolled at Columbia and she worked as secretary to the philosopher Lin Yutang; the trip to Europe and the year spent in Geneva; the return in time for Dad to enroll at the Iowa Writers' Workshop in Iowa City, where my brother was born; the jaunt across the country to La Jolla, California, where I was born; and from there to Chapala, where Lupe whited my shoes, Tad learned to use a lasso, and our sister Tracy was conceived. Perhaps the "dancing" accusation had to do with jealousy that Dad was able to support all that traveling and a growing family on his writing alone.

And then, in 1958, came that move to Squaw Valley and the building of a house high above a wide, lovely meadow. The 1960 Winter Olympics transformed our sleepy bit of rural heaven into a destination ski resort: half that meadow was turned into ice arenas and parking lot, although we still had a National Forest as our backyard. Brett was born in 1962.

At their parties—and there were many—candles flickered, wine flowed, and from speakers placed high on the walls, music poured. Late afternoons, friends often stopped by for a cocktail or glass of wine, and I delighted in putting cheese and crackers on a plate and delivering it to the animated, laughing group around the coffee table.

Around the time I turned eight, I started a twenty-six-page, three-hole-punched booklet, the topmost hole tied with yarn, to house my collection of homonyms. I listened to grown-ups talk, and when I grasped a word that sounds the same but means something different, I'd dash to my room to record it: THERE and THEIR and THEY'RE and TO and TWO and TOO and FOUR and FORE and PLANE and PLAIN and, as the collection grew, PLACE and PLAICE, as well as Britishisms like KEY and QUAY and JAIL and GAOL. These last were favorites (once I knew they were not pronounced, respectively, *kway* and *gayol*) because they could be recorded on *two* of my alphabetized pages. Sometimes I'd bring this out to show the grown-ups, delighting in their exclamations. As often as not, these gatherings morphed into a soufflé and a salad and bread, or a casserole made out of whatever was in the pantry plus a can of enchilada sauce.

One morning after such a party, I watched Dad leaf through a dictionary; the night before guests had accused him of being UXORIOUS. He and Mother laughed and laughed at the idea that he was, indeed, "excessively fond of one's wife."

"But not *excessively submissive*!" he said, reading the rest of the definition.

Bookshelves lined most of the rooms and comprised the back of a couch my father knocked together in an afternoon; his carpentry may have been slapdash, but it got the job done. When Mother began to pursue photography, and asked for a darkroom, he chose an area under the house and handily built her one. They were proud artists: bohemians. Their lifestyle shaped not only their own lives but the lives of those around them. At least three of my friends have told me, eyes shimmering with gratitude, that visiting our house—eating and sleeping in book-lined rooms, participating in talk of art and literature around a dinner table, witnessing the relationship shared by my parents—inspired them to create lives very different from the ones in which they'd been raised. At the time, of course, I'd no idea it was unusual. It was just . . . life. What other way could it, should it, be lived?

Yet as I began to grapple with boyfriends, living spaces, career choices, and, eventually, marriage, I often thought, jealously, how lucky my parents had been, not to have parents they wanted to emulate, or whom they felt they needed to please. Once they'd figured out who they *didn't* want to be, what a vast menu of options greeted them! Even as I glimpsed that this way of thinking was problematic, I envied that they'd simply created a life they envisioned, as if they were characters in a novel, and they were writing their life.

THIS IS SO WEIRD!

Because Skip's first encounter with the Training Routines had been a little rocky, I was relieved when he showed up his second evening for roll call. Sometimes students didn't. Sometimes, confronting the reason they'd come to Scientology at all brought up things they couldn't actually face. Or a friend or family member discovered they were involved and convinced them to stop. Or they didn't like that you couldn't drink alcohol within twenty-four hours of being on course. If you studied five evenings a week, that meant a lot of nights you couldn't have a beer.

When I asked Skip how he was doing, he shrugged. "It's bad," he said, and began to study the materials that describe the next drill, TR0.

Training Routine Zero is similar to OT TR0, in that two people sit opposite one another—but in this case, their eyes are open.[22] Again I asked Kolya to twin. As I worked my way around the course room, attending to various raised hands, I heard Kolya "flunk" and "start" Skip a number of times. I stepped over to watch. Although Skip was blinking a lot, Kolya was actually squirming. He could not seem to keep his eyes on Skip's. After half an hour of this, he said he wanted to keep going with his own course. I asked another student to twin, and then another. Neither was able to do the drill for more than a few moments before dropping their eyes.

"This is so weird!" one said.

I knocked on Ed's office door. "It's Skip again," I said. "We're kind of stuck on TR0. You're a trained auditor, on your OT levels. Will you do it with him?"

He shook his head. "Just keep doing what you're doing, Sands. Don't be reasonable! Just apply the Tech. When the Tech is applied *standardly*, it always works. Always."

"I'm not sure, Ed, in this case—"

"There is no *in this case*! Sands!" Ed widened his eyes so that he looked shocked. "You know that! *Always*. Also, it's clear he trusts you."

"You're going to need to watch the course room," I said. "And I think that's a little *un*-standard, I have to say." But I didn't say it very loudly, and he didn't appear to hear me.

"I'll be there in a minute," he said.

I knew he wouldn't be, but I settled in opposite Skip anyway. His eyes were pleading, his face flushed. "Start," I said.

His was a handsome face. But the most astonishing thing began almost immediately to happen. The jawline lengthened, the eyes narrowed and then flared open like parallelograms. His cheeks bloated way out, then collapsed again. His lips pulled back in a rictus, impossibly wide. His face rushed at me, like the worst kind of nightmare, and yanked back. Skip's actual face, his eyes fixed on mine, hovered beneath these terrifying distortions. My hands slipped from my lap to grab the edge of my chair. I did not say "flunk." I couldn't speak. I held on to the chair as we rattled over spine-jarring potholed roads, going far too fast for either comfort or safety.

"Okay," I managed to get out, and dropped my eyes. We sat there not saying anything, catching our breath. My heart pounded. This is beyond me, I thought. This is beyond anything I am trained to do, beyond anything I have experienced, beyond what I understood can happen in or to the human brain.

I asked Skip how he was doing.

"Oh, that was par for the course," he said. "I just keep seeing all these weird things. It's been going on for a month. It makes me want to kill myself. I hate saying that! But it's awful. I feel like I'm crazy, but I don't actually think I am. I want it to *stop*."

I smiled. I gave him another of Hubbard's bulletins to read. Ed wasn't in the course room. I knocked on his door again. "I think this is auditing material," I told him. I described what was going on.

"We can't get him into session until he can sit opposite an auditor, right?"

"Well, then, an Ethics Officer," I said. "Lots of people don't have their TRs in when they talk to an EO—we can be freaked out, or sad, or mad, or whatever else!"

He shrugged. "Still. You know what Hubbard says: 'Flatten the process.'"

"The rest of the students are starting to wonder what's going on, Ed. And I'm not on post if I'm doing TRs with him."

"I'm keeping an eye on the course room."

But he wasn't. At one point he'd actually closed the door of his office to take a phone call.

"I think you need to try it," I said. "Something pretty intense is going on. I think getting him to talk about it, how it came to happen, would make more sense."

Ed smiled, his blue eyes, crinkling at their corners, evincing his utter understanding. "Got it!" he acked, emphatically. "However. The drill is the drill! Flatten his reaction! Go."

I backed out of his office. The whole idea of "flattening" a reaction had always bothered me. The idea was to just keep doing the thing that had caused a given reaction until the person stopped having that reaction. It occurred to me, often, that it made zombies out of people: you just wore them down until they simply didn't *care* anymore. Although I'd also seen that it was useful, and could lead to what seemed to be very real epiphanies.

Maybe I just needed to backtrack a bit. Maybe I'd allowed Skip to check off the previous drill too quickly. I set him to do OT TR0 with another student. He seemed tense but sat there, eyes closed, for another twenty minutes. I had Jen spot-check him on the TR0 bulletin. He passed. I fetched Ed to watch the course room and settled in opposite Skip.

"Start," I said.

Once again the strange swoops began, as if my body, even as it was upright in its chair, was tilting wildly from side to side. Again the body-jolting sense of driving too fast over rutted roads. Worst of all, those jeering, looming faces, driving at me so hard and fast that I wanted to jerk back, then pulling away, elongating, billowing, contracting like images in a funhouse mirror.

I stood it as long as I could, trying to get through it, to endure it, to push past it. Finally I held up a hand.

He looked down at his sculpted, brown, sandaled feet. "I want my mind back."

Ed had been watching. I think he was curious, if nothing else. "Let me give it a try," he said, and sat opposite Skip. "Start!" he said. He lasted about a minute, swallowing and blinking. "Okay, Skip." He rubbed his hands along his thighs. "Let's talk about some other options."

Skip picked up his course pack and followed Ed out of the course room. I had no idea that he wouldn't return. I thought he and Ed would talk, that he'd get some auditing or an Ethics Handling to figure out what was going on, and that he'd soon be back, finishing up that course and starting another: that Scientology would, as he hoped, help.

SAINT CATHERINE'S WHEEL

In 1963, when Tad was thirteen, I eleven, Tracy eight, and Brett still in diapers, Mom and Dad took us to Europe. My father's novel, *Warlock*, had been nominated for a Pulitzer Prize and subsequently made into a film starring Anthony Quinn and Henry Fonda. With the proceeds from that sale we sailed from San Francisco on the graceful *Oriana*, moving through the locks of the Panama Canal, touching in Bermuda, and landing in Le Havre, France, where Dad had arranged to buy a Peugeot. In that car we traveled for eighteen months: two adults, four children, food, tents, and camping equipment.

Any lodging reservations, certainly the purchase of a car, had been done via letter or, I suppose, telegraph. One way or another our parents managed to rent a house in Athens, a flat in London, and a casita on the Costa del Sur. In between those three-month resting spots, we camped: through France, Italy, Yugoslavia, Greece, Spain, and, toward the end of the adventure, we took a boat up Ireland's River Shannon, rigging our tents on its banks each night. We came to understand the thrill of a still-warm baguette with a slab of brie and another of pâté. Mayonnaise and mustard came in handy tubes. The chocolate was unlike any we'd ever tasted, and Mom let us have it. We'd pull into a campground, and as Dad and Tad put up the tents, Mom worked on dinner. I was supposed to help, but as soon as possible I'd dive into a Georgette Heyer Regency romance. Tracy raced off to organize a game with other children in the campground. Brett toddled about looking adorable.

At the beginning of our stay in Athens, we lived in a flat from which we could watch the *lumière* of the *son et lumière* on the Parthenon. One morning, Dad, who every day clacked away at his portable Olivetti typewriter, received a large envelope from the Bodley Head, his British publishing company. Out of the envelope he shook a half dozen paper rectangles, which, opened out to full size, were about the size and shape of AAA maps. Covered with small print, the huge pages listed titles and descriptions of books published by the Bodley Head, including the marvelous Puffin, Penguin, Peacock series.

"Take a look," Dad said. "Mark the titles that look appealing."

For days we pored over those lists, putting ticks by hundreds of books, before handing the sheets back and forgetting about them.

While in Athens, Tad, who'd been accepted by Phillips Academy, Andover, a college prep school in Massachusetts where he'd matriculate the following fall, worked with a private tutor. Tracy and I, enrolled at Saint Catherine's British School, wore gray skirts, white socks, and brown shoes. Stitched onto the left-hand pocket of our red blazers was the school's emblem: the wise owl of Athena encircled by the wheel of Saint Catherine.

A Saint Catherine's wheel looks like a circle of jagged spikes. It reminded me of a waterwheel, and I envisioned Saint Catherine earning her martyrdom by having to endlessly walk that wheel, except the little buckets that might carry water were instead steps as sharp as knives. I imagined that not only were they designed to cut Catherine's bare feet, but, should she stumble and fall—which of course she must, exhausted, eventually do—they'd shred her to pieces. In a curious combination of the myth of Sisyphus and what even then I saw as the existential horror of a hamster's wheel, I mentally watched her go round and round on that wheel. All the pain in the world could not shake her faith in Christ. I thought this very fine, and wondered if I could ever be so brave and so dedicated.

Lurid and violent as Saint Catherine's martyrdom was in my

imagination, it wasn't as horrid as the actual form of her torture. Much later, I learned that with the use of a blunt object—usually a heavy wheel, driven over the victim—the victim's bones were broken. Then the mangled limbs were threaded through the spokes of the wheel and the whole still-alive *thing* pulled aloft so an audience could cheer the writhing, endless, and very painful death. (For the record: Saint Catherine's faith was profound enough to cause the wheel to fly apart before she could be tortured; she was instead beheaded.)

Inside the Catherine's wheel stitched on our blazer pockets blinked Athena's owl. I understood that Athena was depicted as an owl because an owl is wise, as she was, and because an owl can not only twist its head almost all the way around, it can see through darkness—all of which I understood meant that Athena could see what others could not. I revered Athena. I wanted to be her. She had gray eyes. She wore sandals. She helped Odysseus! She flew around and did cool goddess-y things. Included in my admiration was that she'd leapt fully formed and armed from her father's forehead. This, too, seemed immeasurably fine. It would take decades to understand the patriarchy this represented, and how influential the "manning up" of this wonderful goddess—a virgin goddess, no less—would be.

This ironic conjunction of myth and image, stitched with gold thread onto the pockets of our blazers, caused a lot of parental amusement that I only vaguely understood.

Weekdays, we attended classes. Weekends, the Peugeot stuffed with picnic supplies and camping gear, we headed out to the palm and five fingers of the Peloponnese. Sometimes I pulled a shawl over my head and, handing one to Tracy, paced the hills behind our tents. Tracy followed, chanting the long slow syllables I'd taught her that sounded to me ancient and religious. We were ancient Delphic priestesses. I was entranced by mystery and ritual, the focus and activity that being a priestess, a goddess, a martyr might involve.

"Stop it!" Mother said. "It's too much like the real thing. You're scaring me."

I stopped. But, out of earshot, I went back to treading the smoky-green hillsides, chanting away.

On one of these trips, as we returned from visiting a ruin, a shepherd greeted us, waving his arms wildly.

"Kennedy bang!" he shouted, aiming a forefinger like a gun. "Jackie kaput!"

I had no idea what this meant. But from the look my parents gave each other, the world might have come to an end.

"Are you sure?" My father's voice was high and tight.

"Kennedy bang!"

That night Mom and Dad took rooms in a hotel and left us there, sleeping, while they sat in a taverna and listened to the radio. Sipping sour retsina, they heard that Kennedy had indeed been assassinated, that his assassin had been assassinated, and that Johnson was now president. Jackie was not kaput, but her dress, covered in blood, had created a rumor that, in faraway Greece, was hard to disprove.

We'd never seen our mother cry. But that week, driving along Embassy Row, where flags of all nations had been lowered so far that their vast hems swept the earth, my mother wore dark glasses I didn't know she owned, lenses so big they covered half her cheeks, which shone with wet. We were on our way to an Athens cathedral, where Tracy and I, part of Saint Catherine's choir, were to sing carols we'd been practicing for a month.

"The holly and the ivy, when they are both full grown," we cheerily caroled, while at the back of the cathedral my mother, wearing those huge and unfamiliar dark glasses, sat stunned with a grief that I didn't understand was not for a man, but for a nation, for a forever-vanished direction of culture and history.

In December we headed to Crete. On Christmas morning, in our whitewashed hotel rooms, we each woke to find, tied to the iron bedsteads, red woolen Cretan bags absolutely stuffed with paperbacks: Penguins, Puffins, Peacocks, history, romance, fantasy—titles we'd chosen months before. December 25, 1963, found us in a Cretan cove, reading, while our parents napped, the Aegean lapping at their ankles.

HE WAS KIND OF A NUTCASE

The next evening, when Skip wasn't in the course room, I figured he and Ed were tackling his demons. But he didn't show up the next night, or the next. It was a week later that Jessica called me into her office. While she hadn't mentioned Skip, I couldn't help but wonder if her concerns about my being "too gentle," about my lack of zealotry, were connected to him. So after that evening's stint in the course room, I stopped by Ed's office.

He sat at his desk amid piles of folders. Ed was not only Executive Director, he was also Ethics Officer, Registrar, Case Supervisor (the person who reviews auditing sessions), and, as needed, auditor. As the Center became more successful, others would be hired to fill these positions, but for now, Ed covered a lot of posts.

The thick legal-sized folders piled on his large desk would hold notes taken during auditing sessions, as well as write-ups regarding Ethics Handlings. According to Hubbard's ideas about ethics, "When one is ethical it is something he does by himself by his own choice."[23] So it's not necessarily about wrongdoing (although, often enough in Scientology, it very much is); Ethics Handlings may have to do with solving chronic fights with a husband, a crisis at work, a parent virulently against Scientology—for that latter reason alone, I'd sat in the office of many an Ethics Officer.

"It's about Skip," I said. Even thinking about him made my forehead clammy. "He hasn't been on course for a week. Not since that night you took him here to talk."

"Okay. And your concern is?"

"Three students, students who've passed their Training Routines, couldn't get through TR0 with him. *You* couldn't!"

Ed nodded, looking weary. I forged on. I was feeling, I realized, kind of zealous. "That facing-your-fears seminar he did clearly traumatized him. Doing the TR with him, I got a good sense of what it might be like inside his mind. I don't see how he's even walking! Isn't this the sort of thing the Tech is supposed to handle?"

"He was kind of a nutcase," Ed said. I must have looked dismayed. "Oh, don't be naïve, Sands! We're a *mission*. We can't deal with the kind of case he was evidencing. I think we routed him to the Advanced Org."

"Oh, *no*," I said. At Ed's surprised face, I scrambled to clarify: "Of course, the AO is great, but I think he came to us, to the Center, because we make Scientology approachable. AO is so vast—I mean, it takes weeks to get used to all the corridors and floors—and everyone is so *efficient*. I'm afraid he might get lost. Did anyone take him there?"

"Sands, we don't have time to escort people hither and yon."

Ashamed of my silence, I stayed silent. We both knew Ed went to great lengths to have drinks with, dinner with, and certainly to "escort" anywhere they wanted to go those who were interested in services at the Center—if they had money. But, I realized, Skip must not have been rich enough, or important enough, to warrant that kind of care.

"Will you check into it? Please?"

"I'll do that, Sands." He clicked his pen and scribbled a note.

I knew he wouldn't.

The new-carpet smell still lingered in the hallway, and I held my breath against it as I descended the stairs. I was eager to get home, to talk to Skye about it. As I unlocked the car door, a huge truck lumbered by. I had to wonder: Where was Skip? Had he made it to the Advanced Org? Would his desperation force him into that big blue building?

I doubted it.

I thought about Ed saying I was naïve for thinking that auditing might solve Skip's problem. But what about *Having the correct technology. Knowing the technology. Knowing it is correct . . .*

Was he saying that in Skip's case, it wasn't going to work?

Yet what else had he said? There is no "in this case"!

What if I—what if Scientology—actually made Skip's situation worse?

I'd end up having this internal argument many times over the next two years. But I knew that if I headed down the well-worn trough that was me doubting Scientology, things got messy. I'd no desire to land in yet another meeting with an Ethics Officer, going over and over and over how if I'd just face the fact that my parents were Suppressive Persons, and if I would just "disconnect" from them, I'd finally have real gains.

As I turned the key in the ignition of my car, I imagined Skip in his, hose laced from exhaust pipe through duct-taped window, engine running.

NOTHING BETTER TO BE

During those months in Europe, Mother took hundreds of photographs, but there's one moment she didn't capture.

Dad has decided that the tents need washing. We're camped by a lake, and he instructs Tad and me to pull them out to a distant float—the idea is that the movement through the water, there and back, after which Dad will spread them on the grass to dry, will clean them. Tad and I shove and push and drag the first of the tents out to the float. It's the tent my parents sleep in, made of yellow canvas. As I hang from the platform, admiring the tent's strange goldenness, Tad hoists himself up onto the float and, with a wild banshee cry, launches himself into the middle of the vast yardage spread out on the surface of the water. The canvas billows up around him, taking him in like a kind of shroud.

He is going to drown. I see it as clearly as I see the sun in the sky. There's no way he's going to be able to fight his way out of that tangle of heavy golden cloth.

But he's kept his arms outstretched as he jumped, and the fist of one stays above all those soggy layers. With that one hand he somehow—it seems to take hours, I don't know what to do to help—bats his way out of the swirling fabric. Looking terrified, he pulls his chest onto the float and hangs there, gasping.

"You could have died!" I say, uselessly.

"I know." Panting, he scrabbles all the way onto the float and flops over on his back. Mom and Dad have no idea what's happened. They're sitting at a little table on the shore, having wine. At their feet, Tracy and Brett splash in shallow water.

My brother's eyes are closed, his chest heaves. Droplets scattered across his skin glitter in the sun; his hair is a mass of Dionysian curls. He seems to me absolutely immortal.

IN THE SUMMER of 1964, while we were all living in a flat in London, my parents put Tad on a ship bound across the Atlantic. He'd be picked up in Boston by a friend of a friend none of us had ever met, who would drive him to Phillips Academy, Andover, where he'd enroll in a school neither he nor his parents had ever even visited. He was fourteen.

I understood even then that the high school Tad would have otherwise attended, in the small town of Truckee, ten miles away from Squaw Valley, was, as Dad put it, "lousy." There'd been some talk of boarding schools, which seemed to me a combination of a Dickensian orphanage and a jolly sleepover. Still, it's difficult to comprehend what prompted Mom and Dad to send their teenage son across the ocean alone. Precocious though Tad had already proven himself to be, he'd been brought up in a forest, playing in a creek that meandered through a meadow. He'd seldom worn a blazer, much less a tie.

But his IQ was extraordinarily high (which he'd been told); he was cocky and confident. At fourteen he'd not only flirted with the maid in Athens, he may even have joined her in her bed. These had to be among the things that allowed Mom and Dad to walk off the gangplank and wave goodbye from the dock. The decision was no doubt prompted by the time period, as well as literary examples: in many novels, children are sent to boarding school. But I've come to believe it's an example of how our parents thought of marriage.

Marriage was the priority. Children were to be cherished, given opportunities, encouraged in the direction of their ambitions and dreams, but what mattered most was the unit that was husband and wife.

However Mother may have felt about watching Tad sail away, I do know that a few weeks later, as we were camped beside the River Shannon and she was combing a kerosene-like substance called Seta-Seta through her daughters' hair to get rid of the lice we'd contracted by playing with kids on the beach in Spain, she said it was time to go home. Within a few weeks, the Peugeot, covered with tarps, was lashed to the deck of a steamer bound for America, and we trundled onboard with our luggage.

By the time that car was back across the country and we were ensconced again in the A-frame family temple, I'd become aware that ours was an unusual family. Whatever we'd been before that eighteen-month journey, we were more of it now. My parents were extraordinary people and had an exceptional marriage. My brother was precocious, brilliant, destined to go far. I was, too, of course: I was a Hall!

I did not see this as a burden. It was a mantle, a crown. It took me a long time to realize how this led me to perceive others as lesser beings. (It took me even longer to realize that many families think that they and their children are unique and extraordinary.) I just wandered through life deeply conscious that, simply because of my surname, I was to accomplish something significant.

ONE EVENING THE Porters arrived bearing their own bottle of Tanqueray, making no secret of the fact they couldn't bear to drink the Lucky brand gin supplied by my father. This led to a discussion I found fascinating: how to order more than one gin and tonic. One doesn't ask for "three gin and tonics" but, rather, "three gins and tonic."

At the end of the evening, as they departed, Mr. Porter lifted the green bottle from the counter, saying, "We're not wasting our Tanqueray on people who don't care about the quality of their gin!"

The next morning I was told they were Republicans. Along with being racist and always taking the side of business over the individual, I understood that Republicans were greedy and cared about unimportant things like designer clothes and fancy houses.

"Imagine spending so much money on a bottle of booze!" Dad said.

Other parental perspectives were increasingly clear, including the idea that "natural is best." One should wear only cotton, especially for underwear; other fabrics, made of petroleum products, make you sweat and smell. Hair should be worn long and not styled. Makeup was for loose women and to be avoided. One did not get sick. Television was a waste of time; books provided all needed entertainment. Movies didn't slot into our growing-up years, probably because the sorts of films that came to Squaw Valley were of the popular variety, rather than the art-house sort. Theater was an excellent source of culture, and now and again our parents took us to San Francisco, four hours away, to see some plays (these were precious excursions), but musicals were for underachievers. Tennis was a terrific game, but only morons watched football; they also drank beer. Wine, on the other hand, was for artists.

I shoved my whole being into these notions, donning them like the most fashionable and well-fitting of jackets. It didn't occur to me to wonder what my parents' friends, Republican or otherwise, might think of those crosses draped around my mother's unreligious neck. Of her long skirts and bare feet. Of the politics reflected by the voices of Odetta and Lead Belly, Joan Baez and Pete Seeger, which Dad blasted from the speakers. Halls were artists, Halls were bohemian, Halls were exceptional.

There was nothing better to be than a Hall.

SHE WENT CLEAR LAST LIFETIME!

Skye would be wondering why I was late getting home. Even so, I went out of my way to drive by the Advanced Org, a huge set of buildings off Fountain Avenue, painted, inexplicably, a deep blue. As vast as the complex was (it had been a hospital before being purchased in the 1960s by the Church), everything at the Advanced Org was run on the same "standard" schedule as the Center. Which meant that even if I did act on my vague plan of heading inside to see if Skip had ever checked in, there'd be no one on post to ask. The staff, most of whom were members of the Sea Org, would be sleeping.

At the time, my knowledge of the Sea Org was vague, a lack of curiosity that appalls me now. I knew that it involved signing a contract that committed you to work for the Church for very little money, and to do so for a billion years. A billion years!

I drove slowly up L. Ron Hubbard Way, taking in the vast sprawl of blue buildings and pondering, not for the first time, that if you engaged with a religion where you understood, immediately, that there were members who'd agreed to join for a billion years, you were indoctrinated into that belief system: you'd lived before, and you'd live again.

Now, now, I scolded myself—as "indoctrination" sounded like a criticism, and criticism meant you had hidden transgressions against the person or thing you were criticizing. Other religions indoctrinate their believers: Hindus are raised with the understanding that what they did in previous lifetimes dictates who they are in this one. Catholics grow up with the idea of original sin and the comfort of heaven. American Indians know the earth is to be cherished. So why, where Scientology was concerned, did it seem so manipulative? As if, once the idea of a million lifetimes was implanted in our psyches, we'd be open to and easily swallow other ideas.

For instance (a thought I had, and pushed away, often), what if the Sea Org was just a way for the Church to get a lot of worker bees? While they might be in their "berthings" now, they'd soon be back on post. By 9:00 A.M., the course room would be full of students studying and Course Supervisors supervising; auditors would be auditing and Case Supervisors supervising those sessions; Ethics Officers doing Ethics Handlings, Registrars registering (or, as it was called, regging), and, I supposed, janitors janitoring. Perhaps Hubbard's intention here, as people insisted was true elsewhere in his Church, was altruistic: to give purpose to those who otherwise might toil away in this world, day after day, without hope or purpose or meaning. Scientology did offer purpose, and it did diminish hopelessness—you were saving the planet. That is, if you believed that Hubbard's version of "saving" was real, and achievable. Which clearly some did—enough to sign on for a billion years of such an effort. And which I seemed to, as well; hadn't I signed on to work nights and, increasingly, weekends, at a Scientology mission?

Was this how they pulled you in? Would I wind up joining the Sea Org?

I shuddered. Never, ever, *ever*. I could imagine a few hours a day, for maybe a few years, devoted to the Church, but twelve-plus hours a day for not only this lifetime, but for millions of them? If you signed that contract, you not only gave up all worldly possessions; you gave them up to Scientology. Your saving accounts, your house—even, to some degree, your family. If your spouse or parents didn't approve of your joining, you had to get them to either join or accept that you had, or agree not to see them: to "disconnect."

Sea Org members lived simply. Hubbard's word is "monastic." When I imagined where they slept, what came to mind was a dreadful combination of catacombs and a college dorm. When people joined, they accepted, along with everything else, that their weekly salary would be based on their Org's overall stats, which meant that they might not be paid at all. Although hadn't I joined the Center under a similar financial arrangement? Jessica had been persuasive: We were near Rodeo Drive! We'd attract upstats! The stats would eventually be up too, and so would my salary.

As I gazed up and down L. Ron Hubbard Way, fretting about Skip, I thought about an encounter a few weeks previous, when Skye and I were out to dinner at a nearby Mexican restaurant. As we were being led to our booth, we passed a couple sitting very close together at a small table. Before them was a single wide-rimmed margarita glass with two straws. Also before them was a paperback. They recognized Skye, and as he paused to speak with them, I realized they were sharing that margarita. They turned the book over as we chatted; on its lurid and shiny cover, a humanoid held two blasting lasers. It was *Battlefield Earth*, the first volume of Hubbard's sci-fi series. I'd been told that in these volumes LRH outlined the history of the planet according to him, that they hinted at the confidential materials one could learn only at the upper levels of the Bridge (something about past lives and intergalactic wars that led to humans being imprisoned on the penal colony known as Earth). I hadn't read the book. I had no interest in reading it. One didn't waste time on sci-fi; it wasn't literary. Also I didn't want to know about the supposed history of the religion—which I wondered, even then, if Hubbard had simply invented, as an author does a story.

Skye said goodbye to the couple. "Sea Org," he told me, as we slid into a booth. "They're on 'family time'—they've got just an hour before they have to be back on post. So that's got to be a virgin margarita, and I bet it and that basket of chips are pretty much all they can afford."

I studied them, sipping my own non-virgin margarita, and realized they were reading the novel simultaneously, one waiting for the other to finish the page before turning it. By the time our vast platters of enchiladas arrived—which I wanted to just give to them—they were shaking the last of the chips out of the basket. With a cheerful wave, they headed back to their respective jobs inside the big blue buildings of the Advanced Org.

Thinking about Skip, and even though I knew that it was too late, in every way, to check on him, I pulled over and, from across the street, studied AO's sprawling structure. A few windows shined squares of light, but mostly it was dark, hulking—in a word, ominous.

But there was no reason I should find it ominous. My experiences in the Church, and with Scientologists, had been pleasant enough. So why did I feel, often, that there *was* something menacing? Why was there such relief when I was away from it all?

I knew. Where there was so much smoke, how could there not be some fire?

But I simply did not want to look at that. Not only did I want my actions to have validity, not only did I want my choice to have been a correct one, not only did I not want my parents to be right again, I couldn't face all I would lose if I left. In addition to years of hoping the wrong thing would turn out to be the right thing (a version of throwing good money after bad), I'd lose dear friendships, the man I loved, and a certainty, much of the time, that I was doing good things in and for the world. A song I'd written ostensibly for Jamie was really about the order I felt I'd found within his religion: *What a port to come to, after such a storm.* The lyrics addressed how scared and sad and adrift I'd been. *My sails lost, the steering gone* . . . I didn't want to be there ever again.

Directly across the street, two-thirds of the way up the AO's tall central building, illuminated letters twelve feet high spelled out SCIENTOLOGY. Above the letters, attached to the very top of the structure, the Church's eight-armed cross, stuffed with a thousand bulbs, spewed kilowatts into the night sky. So far, I'd been able to largely avoid stepping inside that building; I did most of my studying at Celebrity Center. But the previous year, I'd been in the course room for a few weeks, taking the Course Supervisor Course. During those weeks, one of the Course Supervisors had been unbelievably young. At one point, perhaps because I was engaged in studying her instead of my materials, she picked up my course pack and spot-checked the bulletin I was reading. As she stood next to my seat at the table, her eyes were exactly level with my own. A gleaming braid hung over either shoulder. She wore a plaid dress, belted, that made her look as if she'd stepped out of a British boarding school. Her self-possession was absolute. I was so stunned—she was all of *twelve*—that I stumbled as I started to define the word she had her finger on. "Flunk," she said, with not a whit of scold and no particular friendliness either. "Start." She handed me my course pack and walked on.

My face was hot. I seldom flunked. The student next to me whispered, "She went Clear last lifetime! Her parents are Sea Org, and she knows she was too. She attested to last-lifetime Clear when she was seven!"

I could hardly take my eyes off the efficient, sturdy little thetan-in-a-body.

"She was also Course Supervisor last lifetime!" the student whispered, and nodded at my amazed face. "At Saint Hill! She had to take the Course Supervisor Course again, here at AO, but she zipped through it—and here she is!"

"Here she is," I'd whispered, impressed, and done the math. By this time I knew that the definitions of Clear include "has no vicious reactive mind and can operate at total mental capacity."[24] She did seem to be operating with a lot of mental capacity. If her spirit had "dropped a body," as Scientologists put it, before taking up residence in another one more or less twelve years ago, that previous lifetime could have been in the seventies, when Scientology was booming, especially at Saint Hill, the foundational Org in Britain. It was indeed possible, if you believed in past lifetimes—and Dianetics—that she'd been audited to Clear in her previous one.

•

WITH SOME FURY, I started the car, pulled out into the dark, quiet street, and headed home. What if it *was* a bunch of balderdash? What had Mr. Porter called it, so long ago, when Dad had talked about jerking me to my feet in that Mexico City cathedral? "Claptrap." Good word, with that sense of being snared.

As usual, Skye had turned on the lights in the living room in welcome. The front window glowed warmly. I spurred the car up the short driveway.

"Muffin!" He stood at the top of the steps, arms raised, the golden light from the open door spilling all around him. "You're late! Everything okay?"

The first time Skye called me muffin I literally choked. Halls didn't employ terms of endearment; they were corny, used by jerks and sentimentalists. Sometimes Skye even called me babe, which had the simultaneous effect of making me feel beautifully sexy and as if I were riding pillion on the back of a motorcycle. I'd grown to love the words, the affection that washed over me as he said them. Tonight, however, I winced. If I lived with someone else, not a Scientologist, I wouldn't have to worry whether "muffin" was a good thing to be called.

"You don't have to turn on every light in the entire house," I said, slamming the car door. "They do the same thing with that huge stupid cross on top of AO. It wastes so much electricity!"

I trudged up the stairs and brushed past him. I did this all the time, taking out on Skye the anger I felt at myself for feeling outmaneuvered: There were all these reasons I should leave the Church, but I was simply unable to take that step.

And I'd just called the cross on top of the Advanced Org "stupid." Criticism = overt. What had I done wrong? There had to be something.

"Did something happen at the mission tonight? Are you okay?"

Was it Skip? Not being zealous enough?

I began to weep. I headed to the kitchen and dragged the dish-towel from the handle of the refrigerator.

"Sweetheart! You left today all happy. Now we're back to this again."

"I don't know what I'm doing! My life is a *mess*. I am. How did I come to *be* here?"

Sitting next to Skye on the couch, dabbing at my eyes with the dishcloth, I snuffled out my sorrow, or as much of it, at the time, that I could understand, or that I could bring myself to examine. By this time, I'd been in the acting companies of both the Oregon and Colorado Shakespeare Festivals; when I first arrived in Los Angeles, seven years before, I'd landed guest-starring roles on various sitcoms. While living in New York, I'd sung my songs in various venues, been part of a band. Just two years before, I'd had a summer season with Old Globe Theatre in San Diego. What had happened? My agents seemed to have forgotten about me; I never went out on auditions. For months, I hadn't picked up my guitar.

"But you're writing," Skye said. "Isn't that what you want to do?"

But the novel was hopeless. I'd described it to my father, and he'd asked why everyone had to die. But weren't happy endings corny?

"Anyway," I sobbed, "what makes me think I can be a writer? That's what Dad does. He and Tad. Or at least Tad used to." Which made me cry even harder. "I don't know what I'm doing!"

Even as Skye's eyes were sympathetic, I knew that he was utterly certain about where he, himself, stood. He'd drilled those TRs hundreds of times, and his were impeccable: He was OT III, and a highly trained, Class VIII auditor. Here was all this *wisdom*, and all these *friends*, and if I left, I'd have to leave Skye, and how could I?

I found a dry spot on the dishtowel and blew my nose. "I appreciate Scientology, and I *love* you, but I just think this isn't what I should be *doing*."

"Is it what *you* feel you shouldn't be doing? Or is this about your parents?"

Skye had asked this many times. As he'd also said, more than once, that if we hadn't met as Jamie and I were divorcing, I'd have drifted away from Scientology. "You think you want it," he said. "But I think you want it because I want it, or because you think you 'should' want it. You have to figure it out for yourself, muffin."

It took me years to see how right he was, how I tried to replace my need to do what my parents wanted with a need to do what Jamie and then Skye—and, by powerful extension, Scientology—wanted.

The phone in his study rang. It was almost midnight, and with a little grunt of surprise, he pulled his arm from around me and crossed into his study to pick it up. I sniffed, listening. It was clear from his end of the conversation that it was Katey, the Registrar at Celebrity Center and a bit of a friend, talking about the big rally at the Sheraton that Saturday, very important that all Scientologists be there. Skye and I knew about it. We'd both received, as part of the ubiquitous, continual Scientology mailings, huge glossy postcards urging us to attend this very important event: *Release of Vital New Information!*

It seemed to me that "vital new information" was always being released. It got old. And so many trees died in the making of those endless mailings.

Oops. Criticism. Overt.

"Got it, Katey," Skye was saying. "Yes, I know, but we've got other plans. I understand! We'll be there if we can."

"No!" I whispered. I *hated* those rallies. There'd always been celebrations of things like LRH's birthday, which Scientologists were encouraged to attend, though Skye and I rarely did. But since Hubbard's death the previous year, and the ascendancy of someone named David Miscavige, the events had increased in number and glitz and fervency. Staff at various Orgs were pressured into endless "regging." It didn't matter if you already had money on account—write another check, take out another credit card, you'd always need more auditing, always another course. Sometimes the Reg called to beg that we get anyone who'd expressed the remotest interest in Scientology to sign up for a course. Someone starting a course would mean a tick upward. Upstat, good. Downstat, very bad.

In one of Hubbard's policy letters about management, he writes that when someone's doing fine on their post, they shouldn't be hauled off to do work that isn't in their bailiwick. Yet here were senior members of various Orgs calling late at night with these kinds of messages, to prove something to someone higher up the chain of command. Even in my course room at the Center, I'd begun to feel the pressure: more courses completed, more pages read, more words looked up. The stats had to be up, up, up, every week, or it meant something wasn't being done *standardly*. Which meant overts. Out-ethics. If a stat was down, there was a reason: something the person on post had done, or had not done.

And, for the first time, I'd begun to have a creepy feeling that it was no longer okay to skip these big events.

Still: "I'm not going!" I whispered urgently to Skye. "I hate those things!"

He nodded and listened to another burst of talking at the other end of the phone line. "Yes, I can do that," he said. "Sure. Sure. I can make a couple of calls for you."

He hung up, and as he punched some numbers into his phone, said, "It's Thursday night. Stats are due. Katey's assigned herself the condition of Emergency, and she's on Step One of the formula: Promote. She wants to make twenty-five of these calls before midnight and asked me to make a couple for her."

As he stopped dialing and held the receiver to his ear, the phone on my own desk rang. Puzzled, I let the machine pick up.

"Hi, Sands," Skye said, grinning as his voice simultaneously emerged from my answering machine. "There's a big rally at the Sheraton on Saturday night. We've been urged to put in an appearance. Love you, babe! Cheer up!"

He hung up the phone in his study and walked across the living room to my desk, picked up my phone, and punched some numbers. His phone rang, and his machine picked up.

"Hi, Skye," he said, "this is Skye. Big rally at the Sheraton on

Saturday. Hope the music's going well, and say hi to that sweet muffin of yours!"

He replaced the receiver and spread his hands in a big shrug. "I said I'd make a couple of calls. A couple of calls I have made."

I had to laugh. I stood up and threw my arms around him.

YOU DO KNOW C. S. LEWIS WAS A CHRISTIAN?

The Church labeled my parents Suppressive Persons because they didn't want me to be a Scientologist. But what if my parents were simply . . . right? They'd been right about a lot of things. Other families might have cookies or ice cream for dessert; we were encouraged to have an apple and cheddar cheese. We were not allowed to have soda: "It'll rot your teeth." Nor were we taken to see Disney's adaptations of fairy tales.

"If his silly pictures of those great old stories get in your head, you won't concoct your own," Mother said. "That's what an imagination is for."

Even then I saw her point. I usually did. The perspectives and accompanying regulations seemed not only obvious but, simply, correct. Yet not obsessive: The page that held recipes for brownies in our *Joy of Cooking* was splotched with melted butter and chocolate. The large freezer, which Mother had painted Day-Glo sixties orange, was stocked with fish sticks and chicken potpies for the nights when she and Dad were out. Sometimes there was even ice cream, though mostly we were encouraged to put honey and raisins over the yogurt Mother made from scratch.

I wanted very much to follow these edicts; I wanted to be as good as possible. My sister Tracy didn't seem to care—she galloped on her long legs through the Valley, eating and wearing what she wanted (I was pudgy, heading toward fat, and was comfortable in things that looked like caftans). Tad, on the other hand, seemed to court trouble. A top-notch skier and an excellent tennis player, he was also a terrible sport—although throwing a tennis racquet seemed kind of splendid when he did it. He read voraciously, especially intrigued by matters sexual and violent. He didn't care about our parents' perspective on what did and did not comprise literature. Comic books may have been the work of the literary devil, but he bought them, and threw in *Mad Magazine* as well. His first summer home from Andover, he flirted with a friend of mine who was spending the night and managed to coax her—how? a grin, a dark gaze—into his bedroom. Even before he applied for a permit, he drove a car, far too fast. Marijuana was entering the picture, and he inhaled all he could; he tried all drugs, and drink too. My goody-two-shoes abstinence fueled more teasing.

One afternoon, Mother set up easels in the living room so that Tracy and I could finger-paint. The living room's windows framed Squaw Peak and the Rockpile. As we swirled paint around on pieces of butcher paper and Mother worked away at some hand-sewing, Tad clambered over the railing of the porch outside the window, yanked open the door, and threw himself on the couch.

"I could have died!"

He pointed at the Rockpile, which from that angle filled three-quarters of the window. "I was climbing up this really tricky section and I slipped! If I'd fallen, I'd have tumbled all the way down. Probably broken my neck!"

We peered out at the massive slope of steep granite and looked back at him, awed.

"My shirt saved me!" he said. "Look!"

We clustered around him, examining the tear in the corner of a shirttail, stopped from ripping all the way open by double-stitch binding. "That hooked over this piece of rock. It held me until I got my feet under me. If it had torn all the way . . . !"

Mother paled. "Don't you ever—" she began. Tad grinned, and for a moment it seemed she couldn't help but smile back. But she mastered the impulse. "—ever, *ever* do such a thing *ever* again."

He pulled my hair. As I squealed, "Mom, tell him *don't*!" he ran out of the room.

Even though I revered him, it was a relief when he headed back to Andover, although he was also in chronic trouble there: taking illegal trips off campus, refusing to wear the required tie to chapel. When he was called out for this latter offense, it turned out he *was* wearing a tie, but had arranged it under his sweater and blazer in such a way as to appear as if he was not. He reveled in the resultant fuss.

He loved rock 'n' roll, while, predictably, folk music was my métier—the albums I chose to rotate on our turntable included Peter, Paul, and Mary; the Weavers; Joan Baez; and, increasingly, Judy Collins. Dad bought me a Joan Baez songbook, and, for my fourteenth birthday, a Martin guitar (a hard-up UC Berkeley student sold it to him for $175, including its hard case). But while my parents approved of my choice of music they were concerned about my taste in literature. I was still obsessed by Regency romances, and had recently devoured C. S. Lewis's space trilogy. This made me return to his Narnia series, which I thought of as advanced fairy tales, anthologies of which lined shelves in my bedroom.

"You do know C. S. Lewis was a Christian," my father told me one evening.

"What?!"

"An Anglican. Those novels of his are all Christian allegories." He closed the tome he was reading about the history of Mexico and leaned back, arms folded behind his head. "Take that Aslan you love so much—he's just a stand-in for Jesus."

"He is *not*!" This was outrageous. We didn't *approve* of religion! How could it possibly show up in a children's book my parents sanctioned?

"Sands. He's sacrificed on an altar—"

"It's a slab of stone!"

"What do you think an altar is? But all right, a slab of stone. Aslan allows himself to be sacrificed, right? He lets himself be captured and shaved and dragged to that stone?"

"Daddy!" I could see where he was heading. It was appalling.

"You see how Christlike that is? Although, frankly—and this is very interesting—there's lots of argument about the reasons for Jesus' death. You should read Robert Graves's *King Jesus*. There's no doubt it was political. Anyway, you tell me. What happens after they tie Aslan to the rock and kill him?"

I had my chin pulled in and down, glaring at him. "The mice nibble the ropes that hold him to the slab and he gets up again."

"The Resurrection! You see?"

"Nooo! I *love* this book!"

"I'm just telling you that it's got a deeper purpose, Sands, and there are many other books that are deep too. Look at all the books in this house! Stop reading *fluff*!"

He was right, and I knew he was. Over the years I've thought many times of that conversation, which introduced me to the notion of symbols and metaphors, of deeper reading, and to the idea that there are other versions of the life of Jesus than the one gleaned from Christmas carols and Handel's *Messiah*.

Over dinner one night, Mom and Dad discussed the literary merits of the Bible, and told my brother and me that they'd signed us up for a class at a local church. If we memorized the names of the books of the New Testament, we got a free Bible. *MatthewMarkLukeJohnTheActs,* I can still say, and I remember holding, and intending to someday read, the white leatherette Bible that was the reward.

"Abridged," Dad said, sniffing in disapproval.

THE HIGH SCHOOL in Truckee had not improved, and both my sister Tracy and I, like Tad, enrolled at private ones, leaving Brett the only one at home. But not for long. Winter of his junior year at Andover, Tad dove headfirst out of a third-story dorm window into what he thought was a snow bank but turned out to be a stone bench. I didn't hear about it until a week later, when I called home from boarding school. Tad answered the phone and told me he'd been expelled.

"Expelled!"

Mom took the phone and explained that he'd exacerbated the school's fear and dudgeon about the accident by sneaking off-campus the following weekend to visit his girlfriend Dana at Foxcroft. As a result, he'd been, as they say in British novels, "sent down."

"It was very stupid of him," Mom said, "diving out of a high window! He bled all over the place! Head wounds. He had to have stitches. He was very silly, and very lucky."

THAT SUMMER, DANA, daughter of those friends who'd brought Tanqueray to a dinner party and taken it away again, moved into Tad's bedroom. My parents had no problem with their sleeping together: sex was a beautiful thing, there was no reason to forbid it. Their room was directly over my head, and their lovemaking enthusiastic. Sometimes I headed out to sleep on the living room couch.

Blair Fuller, editor of *The Paris Review* and one of a growing group of San Francisco friends who summered in the Valley, decided to make a movie using his Super 8 camera. He cast eighteen-year-old Tad as Dionysus. The plot largely consists of a naked Dionysus being chased by furies and sylphs, goddesses and nymphs, all played by our parents' neighbors and friends. Managing to escape their clutches, on he nakedly runs.

Filming took place in various outdoor venues in the Valley. In the climactic scene, Dionysus skates, barefoot, down a long slide of snow that even in midsummer could be found in a shadowed ravine high on Squaw Peak. At the bottom of that long tongue of ice, he crashes and dies. All the women, dressed in flowing black, file past his corpse, wailing and beating their breasts. In the final moments of the film, the maenads drape a respectful fig leaf over Dionysus's naked penis.

I watched Mother triumphantly track down a bottle of grape leaves on her pantry shelves, purchased a few years before when, freshly back from Greece, she intended dolmas to be something she made and served at dinner parties. She carefully unrolled the marinated leaves until she found the largest one, which she handed over to Blair to use in that final scene.

He was their eldest child. Their only son, my only brother. We adored him.

IMAGINE A PLANE

By Saturday night, both Skye and I'd come around to thinking that it might be best, after all, to attend that rally at the Sheraton. I even wondered aloud if someone might walk around with a clipboard and a list of names checking off who appeared and who didn't.

"That's ridiculous," Skye said. "Anyway, there are *thousands* of Scientologists at those things." But as he turned away, I thought he looked a little concerned.

This was new: this sense of being observed, assessed, counted. It felt like evidence of the reputation that had always surrounded Scientology—an authoritarian, thought-policing horror—which was why I had resisted engaging with it for so long, even when I was intrigued. But my studies and my friends had brought me to believe that the Church was, at its heart, full of good and kind and sane people. However. Skye and I knew that you could commit an overt by *not* doing something just as well as by doing something, so there we were, zipping along the freeway, heading toward Universal City, where the Sheraton's high-rising glass glittered with the gold and pink of sunset.

We parked and made our way through silver streamers, laminated posters, and drifting metallic balloons to a vast ballroom. Amid all the glitter and fuss, I felt like a country bumpkin. I waved at Jessica, who was there with Ed. I hugged a number of friends. I even looked around in the futile hope that I'd see Skip, loping over to tell me about the great auditing he'd had, how he was feeling so much better, that he'd be back on course soon! Synthesized music swelled, simultaneously ethereal and martial, reflecting the dramatic space operas of previous lifetimes, the possibility of which enthralled many in the Church. People shouted over the music, adding to the noise. Photographs the size of Cadillacs flanked the stage: in one, Hubbard jauntily wore his captain's cap; in the other, he stared out at the gathering crowd, stern but affectionate.

"I *hate* those huge photos," I muttered to Skye. "Like he's some kind of guru."

Skye didn't reply. He'd been a Scientologist for more than a decade, had trekked quite some distance along the Bridge to Total Freedom. Maybe LRH was a guru—after all, what was a guru but a spiritual leader who shared and taught a way to be enlightened? That we believed in Hubbard's way was, presumably, why we were all here. I looked around to see if I could spot anyone sneaking through the crowd with a clipboard, ticking off names. With so many people milling about, it did seem, as Skye had said, unlikely.

Taking up a great deal of the stage was a set piece made up of a huge *O* within which squatted a large *T*. Interlaced, they more or less created the Greek letter *theta*—θ—a reminder to all of us gathered in that huge room of the lovely meanings Hubbard attached to that word, including "reason, stability, happiness, cheerful emotion, persistence."[25] And, of course, it was there to remind us of a good Scientologist's ultimate goal: Operating Thetan! OT!

More music and swells of applause as members of the Sea Org took the stage to speak about how well Scientology was doing worldwide. White blazers sporting rows of medals, faces shining under billed caps, they pointed to graph after graph that slid across the screen: All stats up! This same event, we were told, was being replicated in a hundred upstat hotels around the world. Pictures of these palaces flashed on the screen, accompanied by waves of applause: Cairo, London, Sydney, New York City, Amsterdam. Soon, David Miscavige, the new leader of the Church, would be speaking at Flag, the "flagship" Org in Florida, and what he had to say would be beamed, live, to every other Org around the entire planet!

Wild sustained applause!!!!!

Standing at the back of the room, I clapped without enthusiasm. Skye gestured toward seats, but I shook my head. I might be present, but I wasn't going to join in.

A well-known actor took the stage. More applause, which he eventually held out both hands to subdue. He waited until the entire room was quiet. There were a few laughs, silenced. Admiration gathered. Look at those TRs! Look at the way he can control the entire room! He stood for another few moments without speaking or moving. Then he took a breath and leaned to the microphone.

"Imagine a plane."

Instantly, concocted by all of us, planes hovered. For some reason, mine looked like Howard Hughes's *Spruce Goose*, big and clunky and wonderful (albeit a failure as a plane).

Then the actor shook his head. "No," he said. "All wrong. Imagine a *plain*."

And he moved his arms in a wide gesture, showing us how vast the plain was that we were to imagine.

The planes poofed into nothing.

There was a little stunned silence, and then the whole room laughed. Look at that Operating Thetan manipulating our minds like that! More applause, and then we did as he asked. We imagined a *plain*. Mine was an endless golden field, tall plants bobbing in a breeze. All over the room, above the room, hovered thousands of plains.

Ah, the power of the word! The power of *intention*!

Which was what the actor went on to address. The power of the Tech, of the Upper Levels, the mastery they confer: to allow someone to see what and as you want them to see. To allow them to do as you'd like them to do.

I leaned down to scratch an ankle. No. No. No. I really loved that he'd played the pun on plane/plain. I really loved that he'd worked our imaginations like that. But while I could see the benefits of making people see what and as one wanted them to see, it also sounded like something that could be used in all the wrong ways. It sounded like what I feared most about Scientology, and what I liked least.

"Can we go?" I whispered to Skye. What I meant was, could we leave *all* of it?

"Not yet, sweetheart."

"This!" The actor's trained voice rang with joy. "*This* is the power of Scientology! *This* is why we train and audit ourselves and others. *This* is why we keep our ethics in and our stats up! *This* is why it's so important to fill those Orgs all over the world. Their purpose, and ours, is to deliver Scientology! To get each and every one to Clear—and I know many of us in this room are already that!" (Sustained applause.) "As I also know that many of you are already OT!" (Wild cheers.) "And what are we going to do with all the capability in this room, and in rooms just like this one all over the world, full of Operating Thetans? We are going to *Clear the planet*!"

Hoots, whistles, applause!

When I'd first read the phrase "Clear the planet," I thought Scientologists intended the planet to be cleared of humans the way a hilltop might be cleared of trees—a most disturbing idea. That mental picture had since been replaced by another, the Sherman-Williams Paint logo: a bucket tipping red paint over the entire globe, with the slogan, "Cover the Earth." That seemed closer to Hubbard's grandiose ambition.

"And how do we Clear the planet? By delivering the Tech, *Standard* Tech, to every single man, woman, and child *on* the planet!" (Wild cheering.) "And now, to tell us more about how this is going to happen, please welcome the man vested by L. Ron Hubbard *himself* to take over the Church when he died: the *leader* of the Church of Scientology, *and* the Chairman of the Board of Scientology's Religious Technology Services, David Miscavige!"

Across the large screen at the back of the stage, images began to stream, including the logos of various arms within Scientology, overlapping, brightening, fading. For the first time, it occurred to me that the new glitz and glamour at these events, and the increasing insistence that all Scientologists attend, had emerged right around the time of Miscavige's accession. The events, with all the surrounding *stuff*, had only gotten more—

—at the time I didn't have the word to describe what it was they'd gotten to be more of, but I do now: Corporate.

Corny and funky replaced by efficient and glossy.

A lot of surface gleam to demonstrate, to persuade of, vast success.

An emphasis on success, on profit.

This was all quite different than what had helped pull me to the Church, and had made me willing to hang in. It had seemed—and this had utterly surprised me, given Scientology's reputation—gentler, kinder, the word might even be folksier. But this new direction was scary.

Trumpets blared, drums rolled, the screen pulsed, as onto the stage at Flag, in Florida, strode Miscavige: tan, vibrant, gazing out at us from under his captain's cap.

It turned out that he, too, had great news for us. He, *personally*, would be reviewing all of L. Ron Hubbard's files! He'd also be taking a look at every previously published Scientology volume to make sure that each and every one of Hubbard's books was *absolutely standard*, as LRH had originally written them, down to every semicolon, every *comma*. It meant that every Org and mission, every auditor, every student, every single Scientologist would get to purchase these new books, in which every aspect would be *just as Hubbard intended*!

"Hubbard approved those books!" I whispered. "Why do they need changing?"

Skye's face had gone very still. Others around us looked equally puzzled. Everyone knew that *only* Hubbard could rewrite or reissue what he'd written. Decades before, Hubbard himself had overseen publication of the red volumes that cover auditing technology, and the green ones that cover his ideas about administration. What errors were there to be found?

And we'd all read "Keeping Scientology Working." Adamant—*zealous*—as it was, it was also very clear: Don't mess with the Tech. Hubbard's Tech. Standard Tech.

Wasn't all this being countermanded by Miscavige's proposed project? Even if all he did was move a single comma? There's a big difference between *Wonderful, Bob!* and *Wonderful Bob!* Or *Eat, children!* versus *Eat children!*

The huge room seemed to fill with a worry that could almost be smelled.

"Skye," I whispered. "Doesn't this mean you'll have to buy all new books?"

By the set of his jaw, it was clear he'd thought of this. As an auditor, he was required to own sets of both the Tech and Admin volumes. Over the years, he'd purchased all of LRH's books. To replace them would cost thousands upon thousands of dollars.

People kept their eyes lowered. They shuffled their feet. Miscavige was the head of the Church of Scientology. Hubbard had designated him as his replacement. How could anyone have a problem with Miscavige's plan?

Once again I peered around to see if I could spot a man with a clipboard, or a woman carrying surveillance equipment. It was an absurd idea. But just in case, I didn't say anything more. And I certainly wasn't going to draw attention to myself by leaving early.

AGE OF AQUARIUS

Summer 1968, when I was sixteen, the Maharishi came to Squaw Valley. His wrinkled, smiling face had been on the cover of *Time* and *Newsweek* as he'd traveled the world extolling the benefits of Transcendental Meditation.

One afternoon, my father called the family together. "I am going to try this 'TM,'" he said, in a curiously formal way. "I am going to go through the initiation. I understand it's a matter of offering the Maharishi a piece of fruit. He gives you a mantra, nothing embarrassing, and you start meditating."

I felt my universe tilt and slide. Wasn't what the Maharishi did kind of like a religion? Didn't Halls not do such things?

Dad cleared his throat. "I hear it helps lower blood pressure. And if any of you are interested, I will pay for you to get a mantra too."

Mother smiled, dubious. Tad shrugged. Tracy and Brett looked a bit confused. I said I'd like to do it.

Early the next morning, Dad and I each selected a piece of fruit from a bowl on the counter, and he drove us down the hill to the hotel in which the Maharishi and his entourage had set up for the weekend. Dad wrote the check for our initiation fees; I remember it being fifteen dollars each. Dad was escorted one direction, I another. After a quiet, candlelit wait, a man wearing a white robe escorted me to a small room where I was taught my mantra, a series of syllables repeated to me until I could clearly repeat them back. While the mantra might not be necessarily unique, I was told, it was mine, something not to be shared with another. I was told what the words meant, but forgot almost immediately. I remember those syllables, however. From time to time, I still use them.

Eventually we all came back together. There were about thirty of us. The Maharishi, his neck encircled with leis, sat cross-legged on a dais, surrounded by a lot of fruit. In a charming singsong voice, an Indian lilt inside a British accent, he told us to work toward sitting alone, silently repeating the mantra, for at least twenty minutes a day, twice a day. He spoke of the benefits, including world peace.

"Just imagine," he said, "if everyone were to do this twice a day. Would there be time for such a thing as war?" His whole body rocked as he laughed and laughed.

We all meditated together before being released into the afternoon.

It was a bit like coming out of a matinee: blinking in the surprising light of day when one expects the velvet of nighttime darkness. As I stood getting my bearings in the bright Sierra sun, I wondered if it was my imagination that I felt changed: there was Sands before she received her mantra, and Sands after it.

All that summer, morning and afternoon, I sat cross-legged on the floor of my bedroom turning that mantra over and over like a stone in a pocket. I liked knowing that elsewhere in the house my father was also sitting, though probably not cross-legged. There was no discussion of meditation attached to spiritual matters; rather, arms folded behind his head, sipping his Jim Beam, Dad talked of its beneficial effects on memory, and how he hoped it would keep him from smoking. He laughed at how much he'd obsess over the bourbon he'd get to have when he was finished with the afternoon's twenty minutes.

"I guess that's one of the purposes of the thing," he said. "You think you can't wait to have whatever it is you can't wait to have, but then your mind moves on to something else, and you realize you *can* wait, but then you realize you're thinking about the Jim Beam again, and you sneak a look at your watch and not even a *minute*'s gone by. Don't know how you do it, Sands, but then you've always been attracted to this sort of thing."

He was talking about having to haul me off my knees in that Cathedral all those years before. How I liked pretending to be a Delphic priestess. My affection for the vast mythic landscapes of Tolkien and C. S. Lewis, and, too, the fantasy provided by my beloved, derided romance novels. But I think it was also a kind of a warning: he perceived (perhaps even recognized, as I think in this we were similar) that I had a pilgrim soul, that I was attracted to spiritual matters—and, troublingly, to the trappings that might come with them.

BY 1969, *HAIR: The American Tribal Love-Rock Musical*, launched by Joseph Papp's New York Public Theater, was being produced in cities around the world. The story of a counterculture hippie commune—replete with draft dodging, dope smoking, and nudity—permeated even our distant High Sierra kingdom. Articles about it filled the magazines that flowed through the house, its music was all over the airwaves, and Dad bought the album. He already owned the Who's *Tommy*; he loved that the band used rock 'n' roll to create an opera.

I was intrigued by the lyric that addressed the approach of the Age of Aquarius. I did feel something was dawning, that something vast was about to change. Fairy tales and the worlds of Tolkien and C. S. Lewis had certainly predisposed me to a yearning to find a magic ring, walnut, skates, cape, to walk through a coat closet and find an enchanted land. Still, I was convinced that a very real power, based on love and a final, and finally effective, push for world peace, was at work all over the planet. The terrible deaths in Vietnam, the protests against war, the sit-ins on college campuses, the students' deaths in Paris, were all about to accomplish their goals. I believed, fervently, that something remarkable was about to happen, lifting us out of one reality and into another. This certainty might have been described as a hope for the Second Coming, or the Rapture. But I didn't know to think in these terms. I just felt keenly and deeply that life as we knew it was about to change.

But then Martin Luther King was assassinated. And Bobby Kennedy. And one day, while vacuuming and thinking about the work they'd been doing, now halted by their tragic deaths, I became aware that this, vacuuming, was just a moment in my life. It was a moment attached to another moment that, once lived, was gone. The roar of the vacuum cleaner engulfed me. If you filmed a person's life, I thought, just trained a camera on every minute of it, the moments of vacuuming, emptying the dishwasher, reading, would be boring. You wouldn't need or want to see the moments on the toilet or the hours spent sleeping. And yet life was made up of nothing but moments, frame after frame, like the celluloid strip that in those days made up a movie.

Standing there in the midst of the vacuum's noise that created its own immense quiet, I felt as if I were remembering something I'd once been told, that had once made sense. And I also suddenly and completely grasped: *This is life.* Nothing more. This, moment by moment by moment, is it.

And, I understood, there would be no change. The benevolent force that had been heading toward us had decided to veer away. We weren't worthy. We as a planet hadn't produced enough love to deserve the glowing *consummation.* No. Life was going to have such things as vacuuming in it—forever. Moment after moment was all it was ever going to be.

Moving the wand of the vacuum back and forth across the carpet, I thought of the cathedrals in Europe we'd visited, Dad carrying Brett on his shoulders. The shuffling and murmuring; people kneeling, foreheads pressed to clasped hands; the certainty (were they certain? was that part of their prayers?) that because—if?—there were something beyond life, there had to be something, then, meaningful about living. Displayed in those cathedrals had always been a writhing body on a cross, blood dripping from palms and feet, eyes cast up. Was Jesus asking God a question? Pleading for a sign? Seeing transformation, a vast beam of sunlight through clouds, heading toward him? I did not know, then, that Jesus' final words were *My God, my God, why hast thou forsaken me?* But even so, I'd long wondered if the depictions of his pain were intended as a mirror for the average suffering of this life—while also offering a promise of a reward to come. Jesus had endured it; he'd endured far worse! And you could too. Having faith (if you had faith) in what was waiting for you after death gave you the strength to endure living.

I turned off the vacuum. In contrast, I thought, as I coiled the electric cord, this moment-by-moment thing kind of made you appreciate *this* moment, now. You didn't wait for the end of life for solace and meaning but made sure you took care of it in this one.

Although that was kind of sad. And scary.

And, once you realized it, then what?

No wonder people turned to religion.

EDMUND, A FRIEND of my brother's, was studying photography at San Francisco's Art Institute. During the summers, he and Tad painted houses to earn money; in their spare time, they climbed rocks and, eventually, mountains. When they returned from these adventures, I cooked them dinner. Night after night, that summer of my eighteenth year, I waited on them, in my long dress and my long hair, acting out a medieval fantasy: lady to my knights. And in his rented room in the house down the hill, Edmund built a double bed; when he was finished, I joined him there. My parents made much of the metaphor.

When he and Tad and some other friends went on a three-week climbing trip to Canada, Dad told me to stop acting as if Edmund were a banished Romeo and I Juliet.

"You need to know something," he said. "There's a reason Shakespeare has Romeo in love with Rosalind as that play begins. Shakespeare's pointing out that Romeo is fickle—he'll move his affections on to the next someone who captures his attention."

I looked up, shocked. This was not the romance of *Romeo & Ju-*

liet that I knew. Was he telling me that Edmund would move on to someone else?

"The only thing that turns *Romeo & Juliet* into a tragedy is that their parents don't want them to be together." Dad shook his head, amazed at the stupidity of the Capulets and the Montagues. "If their parents weren't so bullheaded, if they just let the thing play out, Romeo would eventually tire of Juliet, just as he did of Rosalind, and move on to the next pretty face. The parents would have gotten what they wanted."

"Are you saying . . . ?" But I couldn't articulate what I thought he was saying.

"*Stop moping!* You haven't lost Edmund, he's not banished. He's gone *climbing*. And your parents happen to *approve* of him. Stop being a character in a play you're imagining."

Edmund and Tad returned safely. They regaled the family with pitches dangerous and summits mastered. But, sliding dishes into the dishwasher, I was aware that once you had a happy ending—bed built, virginity gone—what next? I find it odd, now, that I didn't think of marriage, and certainly not of children. Those must have seemed like sentimental, obvious choices, not interesting, artistic ones.

GUILT IS GOOD

As we drove home from the rally at the Sheraton, Skye sighed. "All that money."

He didn't add anything more. I didn't either. Criticism—"nattering"—usually meant you'd done something to the person or thing you were criticizing.[26] So even though we knew each other well enough to be aware we had a lot to say, silence settled over us as we sped along the freeway.

I cracked open the window. Leaning back with my eyes closed, I let the breeze flutter along my forehead and thought about our recent trip to the Southwest. I'd loved traipsing in and out of the Anasazi ruins with him, loved the colors, the landscape, and the idea that, living there, I'd be closer to Tracy. I wanted to be pregnant in Santa Fe, to raise our child there, and one night, in our ultra-funky Taos hotel room, I'd told him so.

He'd gone still. "And what am I supposed to do, muffin, bag groceries?"

He'd drawn on his cigarette and blown smoke, hard, into the air above our heads. "I need to be in a city, sweetheart," he said. "There's my music, but there's the Bridge, too. There isn't an Org within a hundred miles of Santa Fe. This is when I get really concerned about us, Sands. You don't want what I want. You want a whole different life."

That was true. It often cropped up. Yet there we were, rattling along an LA freeway, on our way back from a Scientology event. And I anchored myself yet again: I reached over the gearshift to put a hand on his thigh, and said, "I love you."

He lifted my hand to his lips, then replaced it on his thigh, keeping hold.

I did love him. I just didn't love our life. Yet I kept making our life happen. I kept living in Los Angeles. I kept being a Scientologist. *Why?*

Skye sped up our driveway and parked. Since leaving Universal City, all we'd said was his "All that money" and my "I love you." We trudged into the house, changed out of our fancy clothes, brushed our teeth, slid beneath the sheets, turned to one another, and held on.

We kept silent because of an insidious aspect of Hubbard's ideas regarding the overt, the "motivator": When you've done something bad to someone or something (or feel that you have, or convince yourself that you have), you can come to believe that it was "motivated" by something that someone or something did to you.[27] This allows you to justify other overts, as well as why you want or need to leave. Sometimes you do leave. But (and this is Hubbard's point), you are not looking at your own culpability in the matter.

A classic example: A married man is attracted to and flirts with another woman. The overt is in the flirting, acting on the attraction. The man begins to find reasons to justify his actions: he "natters," telling the woman and others how hard his wife is to live with, what a shrew she is; he finds reasons for and eventually manufactures a fight. He finds a "motivator" for his own actions. And due to that original flirtation, he may end up leaving his wife: he "blows."

A few years before, while attending American Conservatory Theater's advanced training program in San Francisco, a fellow student and I had rented a flat together. Bonny and I got along well. But one day, when my own razor was dull, I used hers to shave my legs. I didn't tell her. I now had what Hubbard dubs a "withhold" (which follows an overt). Soon I became "motivated" to find reasons to criticize her, including how selfish and thoughtless she was.

(Hubbard points out that we often accuse others of the things that we, ourselves, are guilty of. While he's not alone in this observable truth, this sort of "wisdom" made it hard to figure out when he was being, well, wise, and when Machiavellian.) Even though Bonny and I'd talked of living together the following semester, I decided I had to find a different living situation. It wasn't until I studied the overt/withhold/motivator sequence, and the often resultant "blow," that this behavior made some sense.

Knowledge of this sequence (and what is implied if you find yourself "nattering") means that Scientologists are aware when they find themselves critical of someone or something, and especially if they find they want to leave a place or a person. They tend to inspect what they might have done that they feel they shouldn't have done.

As often as not, this does lead to some useful realizations. However, it's also one of the biggest reasons it's hard to leave Scientology. When I was tempted to call it quits, as I often was, I went looking for the nefarious motive that underlay why I'd want to. And I could usually find something I'd done/said or not done/not said that was the *real* reason I wanted to "escape." If Skye or I mocked or criticized the glittering event we'd attended, the extravagant décor, the beribboned speakers, the many dollars squandered in mounting it—and especially Miscavige's troubling announcement and the outrageous amount of money good Scientologists were going to have to spend on new books—it must mean we'd committed a transgression against the group. So we stayed quiet.

This terror—that I'd be "blowing" because of some bad thing I'd done—is what kept me glued to Scientology for years. I think the fear was widely shared. When the urge came to *get out*, we'd been indoctrinated into the idea that we just needed to inspect what we might have done that would make us feel that way. There was always something. You'd write it up, have a "win," and stay on. And on.

So lying there, my head on Skye's chest, feeling his heartbeat beneath my cheek, I examined my behavior. Of course I was guilty of an overt: *Lack* of action as action. I hadn't participated. I hadn't cheered. I'd clapped perfunctorily, I'd averted my eyes from the photos of Hubbard, I'd refused to join the rah-rah nature of the event.

And perhaps Skye had committed a transgression when he'd made those "couple of calls": that little "lie" could certainly be seen as an overt.

And I'd laughed; I'd even hugged him! Chalk another one up for me.

And then there was Skip. What I could have done, hadn't done, might have done.

He'd come to us looking for help. And we'd failed him. I had. Ed had. Scientology had. If he'd managed to get in a car and find his way to the Advanced Org, he'd taken one look at those big blue buildings and turned right around to go drive off a cliff.

Oops. There went another critical thought.

I didn't speak them aloud, but I had plenty of them in seething silence. More overts.

"Guilt is good," Dad often said. I think he meant that the fear of feeling guilty makes you do the right thing. Or, not wanting to feel that you didn't do the thing you should have done, you do the thing you should do. Scientology's emphasis on ethics seemed like an extension of this idea. Most people want to be good, decent, ethical. I certainly did. Even as I was able, occasionally, to see this for the trap it was, I couldn't figure out how to wriggle out of it.

I'M ME, I'M ME, I'M ME

After we returned from the family trip to Europe, I often woke in the night to hear Mother, sleepless, pacing the house. In hushed voices, she and Dad talked about something called a "double mortgage"; both tone and attitude made me think someone had died. When Dad was tapped for the position of Writer in Residence at the University of California, Irvine, there were similar dire-sounding conversations; it took me years to understand how hard it must have been for him to face that he was no longer supporting his family on his writing alone.

He accepted the position, as he accepted the subsequent request to found and run Irvine's Master of Fine Arts program in Fiction. Except for Tracy, still in school in Colorado, the entire family now spent the academic year in Newport Beach, returning to Squaw for summers. Brett attended grade school, I a local high school. Tad, accepted into UCI, changed his name to Oak and made his way directly to the drama department, where he became a star—a pugnacious, outrageous, cocky, handsome star. His affection for loud, raucous music grew even more pronounced, and like that music, he lived hard. He smoked anything smokeable, drank anything drinkable, slept with anybody remotely sleepable-withable. He had run-ins with police. He and Dana were still sweethearts, but his dazzling sexual appetite included trysts with some of my parents' friends (we didn't know this for decades).

Between his first and second years at UCI, Tad-Oak-Tad (which was what tumbled out of my mouth when I addressed him) attended a summer training "congress" at San Francisco's American Conservatory Theater. Housed with fellow actors, he invited me to visit. We spent an evening perched on the apartment's fire escape, as they smoked and dissected what made good theater; the next day I sweated my way through African Dance class with them, and ran behind them up the stairs to a class on Shakespeare.

And it was in that room, a studio several floors above busy Geary Street, directly across from ACT's Geary Theater, that I had an inkling of what I might want to do with my life. I watched what would become familiar and beloved: an empty, battered space slowly filling with bodies that dropped themselves and their bags to the floor with exquisite ease. Cups of coffee suddenly littering every surface. People stretching, leg lifted to ear, forehead dropped to knee, upper body twisted until a vertebra cracked. Scripts to hand, being memorized. The quick roll of a head, the saying of *muh, muh muh*, the muttering of *Peter Piper picked a peck of pickled peppers*. I loved it. I wanted to be an endless part of it.

This was Scansion and Dynamics, a class usually taught by a member of the company. But that day, Bill Ball, ACT's innovative founder and artistic director, gave a lecture. A short, balding man, he commanded fierce attention. He spoke as if each word were a delectable piece of fruit. He began by reminding us about a few elements of verse—the iamb, the trochee, the spondee—which somehow morphed into a description of how honey is made, which led to a discussion of architecture as "frozen music," which somehow connected to the value of a well-trained voice, which led to a discussion of *King Lear*. I was rapt. I remember holding my clasped hands to my chest as he spoke, as if I could hold there, forever, what he was revealing.

"This *honey*," Ball concluded, "is what Shakespeare gives us to work with, to utilize as we build the architecture of our characters.

You'll find, almost always, that the music of a character's verse jangles when his emotions do. All right. Class dismissed."

I stumbled out of that sunlit studio as if I'd swallowed the most magic of elixirs. It had to do with Shakespeare, absolutely; with theater, yes; language, yes; but above all, the class offered an astonishing new road, which enticed me then and entices me still: a close engagement with *words*. In 1970, when I arrived at UCI, in part because all my life I'd been told I was "dramatic," certainly because of my brother, but mostly because of that astonishing hour with Bill Ball, I headed straight to the theater department.

BUT I WAS a chubby girl. Mom and I began to have nasty fights about my weight. One afternoon, she suggested that I try the diet drink Metrecal.

"You just drink one can for each meal," she said, "and all necessary vitamins and minerals are included."

She was making pozole for an English department party and had handed me a knife to cut up tripe, the stomach lining of a cow. I sawed away, unable to believe what I was hearing. My mother didn't want us to eat *sugar*! She'd raised us on homemade yogurt. She believed in wheat germ and whole wheat bread!

"This is an important choice you can make about your whole life, right now," she said.

"I'm me!" I said. "I'm me! I'm *me*!"

"Except this is not you," Mother said.

I closed my eyes and discovered a rage so huge it filled my entire universe with red. I blinked, startled that "seeing red" was not just a phrase. I threw down the knife and ran up the stairs and slammed the door.

A few days later, cans of Metrecal, chocolate and vanilla, each containing three hundred calories, appeared in the refrigerator. More than once, after sipping one of those cans of goo, I realized, with horror, that I'd put myself over the daily caloric limit—and I hadn't even had dinner yet. I'd give up for the day, telling myself I'd start over in the morning. I wore tent-like clothes and, when I wasn't on campus, sat in my bedroom hunched over my guitar, writing sad songs.

And then the dean of the drama department, Clayton Garrison, selected *Kiss Me, Kate* for the spring production. To my utter surprise, he took a huge gamble and cast me as one of the leads: the spunky, flirty Lois.

It changed my life. For one thing, horrified by the idea of dancing and singing in front of an audience as a fat girl, for months I ate nothing but carrots and Juicy Fruit gum, farting all the while. As I shed pound after pound (thirty of them), filling the air with cheese, I seldom slept. I lived on adrenaline. Dad fretted that I was like his mother, by which he meant fanatical; as she was dying, she'd insisted on ingesting nothing but milk and lime juice. I took this as a warning to beware some obsessive part of my nature, and, indeed, once I started to lose weight, I only wanted to lose more. I threw myself into activities that would keep me from thinking about food. When I wasn't in rehearsal or dance class or doing homework, I practiced voice, studied lines, reviewed choreography. And I began to understand that I could dance, that I could sing more than wavering folk songs.

However, in the Clan (or cult) of Hall, sophisticated people enjoy drama and opera; simple people like musicals. Other than the rock operas *Tommy* and *Hair*, the closest thing to a musical that ever rotated on our turntable was Brecht's *Threepenny Opera*. Even though the reviews of *Kiss Me, Kate* were stellar, and even though I was told that I was "made" for musical theater, I knew I wouldn't pursue it. I'd be a serious actress, playing serious roles.

OAK—MORE AND MORE he was Oak—earned his B.A. from Irvine in just two years and headed to Boston University, where he pursued a master's in fiction. Holding his example before me, I, too, chose to zip through Irvine. That astonishing hour with Bill Ball in mind, I applied to and was accepted into ACT's Advanced Training Program. Two years later, after a marvelous summer playing, among other roles, Imogen in *Cymbeline* with the Colorado Shakespeare Festival, I picked up my sister Tracy, now married and living in Colorado, and we headed across the country to attend our brother's wedding: Oak was marrying a woman named Mary in her hometown in Massachusetts.

I was twenty-three and my car was packed; after the wedding, I was moving to New York. My brother was there; that's where I'd go, too.

And so I moved into an apartment on Manhattan's East Side (five-floor walkup, tub in the kitchen) for no other reason than it was near Oak and Mary's (six-floor walkup, shared toilet down the hall). As I moved into Oak's neighborhood, I also moved into the circle of theater artists who gathered in his living room and at all-you-can-drink Sunday brunches. Drinking seemed kind of essential. Sometimes there were even empty vodka bottles amid the crumpled beer cans in Mary and Oak's trash. I was concerned but mostly dazzled. I wasn't the only one who thought of them as a contemporary Scott and Zelda.

Now and again, however, I thought about the storm that had blasted in the afternoon of their Cape Cod wedding. A late summer nor'easter, it had blown our skirts and ties and hair sideways, sent ham sandwiches whirling. Raised as I was on the meaning of signs and portents, I wondered what it might mean, what the heavens had in store for them.

I could not have imagined.

WILLS AND THINGS

Several times I called the number Skip had given us when he'd signed up for that course, but the phone just rang. I worried what it meant that Scientology hadn't helped him. I hoped he'd found something that had—then worried that I'd had that thought.

Sometimes, as I drove home from the Center, I imagined I'd just keep heading east, to Grand Junction, and accept Tracy's invitation to stay with them. As I waited to find a good time to talk to Skye about this possibility—I wouldn't be *leaving* or anything—I felt like a huge, glowing spirit, bending, like the angels in the carol, on hovering wing. It reminded me of what I'd read about suicidal people who'd finally decided on a day and time, how those around them commented on how happy they'd seemed, how content. "Just for a few months," I practiced.

One night I arrived home to find a message on my machine. "Sands. This is your father. We have something to say to you. Call."

By this time, I expected the curt tones that hovered over conversations with my parents, as if warmth or laughter might lead me to believe they approved of what I was doing. But the tone of his voice on the machine was not only cold, it was terrifying. I hadn't talked to them in months, hadn't seen them for almost a year. It was too late to call that night; I tossed and turned and in the morning drove to a pay phone. I wasn't going to have that conversation at home, where Skye could hear the betrayal that showed up in my voice every time I talked to my parents, my in-spite-of-everything-beloved parents.

"Hello?" Mother's cheery voice.

I imagined their San Francisco flat, where they spent fall, winter, and spring, with Dad commuting once a week to Irvine for his teaching duties. Summer found them back in Squaw Valley, preparing for and then running the Community of Writers. A perfect life.

"Hi, Mom!" I did my best to sound like the cheerful, successful young lady they'd once imagined I'd be. As if I had a perfect life, too.

"Sands!" So much love in her voice. "How's my darling girl?"

My eyes filled with tears. The cars rushing by looked as if they were underwater.

"I'm fine. Really fine. Just—great."

"Well, it's a lovely day here in the City," she said. "We're about to have brunch with Leah and Jerry, and then we'll go to the flea market. And how are things with you?"

I could not come up with a single specific to answer that question. They didn't want to hear, and I didn't want to tell them, about my mate, my work, my spiritual path. I certainly couldn't tell them I was thinking of leaving. What if I didn't make it happen?

"How's it going with your plan to apply to graduate school?" Mom asked.

"I don't think I'm a good enough writer," I said.

"Of course you are! You're your father's daughter! Here, he wants to speak to you."

A few inaudible muttered words. Standing in the phone booth, traffic whooshing by, I twisted the thick metal snake of the phone cord.

"Sands? Your father here." His voice was stern. "I'll be at Irvine for my Tuesday seminar. I'd like you to have lunch with me beforehand. I have something to say to you."

"Okay."

"The Beachcomber, in Newport. It's on the water, remember. Noon."

At the other end, the phone settled into its cradle, interrupting Mother's "Don't hang up without letting me say good—"

I held the cold plastic to my ear and listened to the dial tone.

THAT TUESDAY, I pulled into a parking space outside the Beachcomber. In the rearview mirror, my face looked pale and scared. I shook out my skirt, locked the car, pushed through the thick doors of the restaurant. Dad was waiting by the hostess station. He smiled when he saw me, but his eyes were unfriendly.

He ordered us glasses of wine. He raised his eyebrows when I said no thanks to one—I'd be on post that night—but didn't address it, and neither did I. Even though I'd been working at the Center for almost a year, I'd yet to let my parents know how I was earning my small but steady salary.

The talk over our fish was as spiky as the bones we picked out of them. I waited for him to tell me what he had to say, but his face was shuttered. I launched topic after topic, trying to appear smart and witty and informed:

Skye and I joined this protest about the U.S. sending arms to the Contras . . . ?

Did you read McPhee's essay in *The New Yorker* about orange trees . . . ?

Skye's rented me a piano! It was quite a scene, getting it up the stairs . . . ?

He pushed his plate to one side. "Your brother's no longer living with Tracy. Did you know that?"

I did know that. Tracy had called to tell me. It was among the things that allowed me to imagine I could stay with her. Their spare room would be open.

"He's in Chicago now. Moved to be with that woman, Robin."

That woman Robin had been taking care of him—he couldn't take care of himself. She was *supporting* him. But I didn't say anything.

Dad's face twisted. He shook his head. "Both of you with your fucked-up lives."

I looked down so he wouldn't see the tears flare into my eyes. It struck me that "fuck" started and ended with the same letters as "flunk," and had similar impact.

As the waitress set down the check, Dad said, "About this going back to school. Where are you thinking of applying?"

"Umm. The Iowa Workshop, I guess?"

"Of course Iowa. And Stanford. Do you have stories for your application? You need to get on that. Most deadlines are mid-December." He swallowed the last of his wine. "Let's go back to my office."

I followed him along the beautifully named Jamboree Road, which at the time was still bounded on either side by open fields, and onto the Irvine campus. We parked and walked together without speaking to the building that housed the English department. While he checked his inbox I chatted with the department secretary, Betty, who remembered me from my own time at UCI fourteen years before. Then, our shoes squeaking on the shiny linoleum, I followed my father down the hallway to his office.

Even during the years I was on campus, I'd rarely visited him there. He wasn't one for decorating. There were loaded bookshelves, a metal desk, wooden chairs. He motioned me into one of these and circled around to the other side of the desk. My feet reached the floor, but it felt as if they didn't. I felt squished and bent.

He looked fierce. He didn't sit.

He cleared his throat. "Do you plan to continue with your so-called religion?"

I *want* to leave, I couldn't say. I *intend* to leave. I'm going to go stay with Tracy. But I knew how much lay between the intention and the action.

"Your mother and I have been talking. There is the question, you see, of wills and things."

I blinked. Wills!

"In spite of all we've asked you to examine about the *squandering* of your talents, your education, your upbringing, your *life*, you continue to be involved with this cult."

My mind churned. Wills! A will was a plot device in nineteenth-century novels. It had never occurred to me that my parents had a will. That was not something people like my parents did, did they? Think about the future in that monetary way? Wills were for Republicans. Surely not Democrats. In any case, was there any money to put into a will? Since the trip to Europe, Mom and Dad had been broke—it's why Dad had taken the Irvine job. Also, wills meant you were thinking about dying. Were they thinking about dying?

"That religion of yours has got its claws into you, and it's clear it's not going to let go. So your mother and I have come to a decision."

I pictured her in the room with us, her blue eyes steely.

"If you continue on with Scientology, you will not receive a cent of our money."

I couldn't figure out what he was talking about. What money? I had never, once, thought about inheritance. It had never occurred to me.

"We've read what that church of yours does. Anything we give you, you'll be forced to give to them. So. If you continue to be a Scientologist, we will write you out of our will. We can't put it any more clearly than that."

I said nothing.

"If in some way we cannot foresee you do somehow benefit from our money after we are gone, and you use it for that religion of yours, you may expect *curses from beyond the grave*." His voice shook. "Do you understand?"

I did understand.

I sat there for a long minute, trying to formulate a joke about his hatred for a religion that actually supported the idea of being able to make things happen from "beyond the grave." But I could say nothing.

We did not hug or even say goodbye. He busied himself with some papers on his desk.

Back down that long hallway I walked, shoes squeaking, everything blurred with the tears I didn't want to spill out of my eyes. I waved at Betty but didn't stop. I didn't want her to know my father and I had had an altercation. I didn't want her to have any idea I was a Scientologist, I didn't want *anyone* to know I was a Scientologist. And wasn't there something pretty wrong with that?

I managed to hold back the tears until I was in my car, and then I wailed all the way north on 5, talking to the rush-hour traffic around me as if it were my parents, or a jury I was trying to convince. "I think about leaving all the time!"

The brake lights of the car ahead of me flashed, flashed again. I caught my breath with an awful realization. "If I *do* leave, you'll think it's only because I want your money!"

As the traffic moved at a clip around a long curve, I spoke aloud, "Hey, there, Mom and Dad. So I've left Scientology?" I extended an open palm to the windshield. "Now, can I have some of your money?"

The car ahead braked again, fast and hard. I slammed on my own brakes to keep from crashing. All around, tires squealing, traffic came to a halt. "Flunk, flunk, flunk!" I cried, hitting the steering wheel. "How on earth can I leave now?"

II

The Whole Agonized Future of This Planet

—L. RON HUBBARD

YOU DO KNOW THAT GUY'S A SCIENTOLOGIST?

It would take decades to understand that when my brother fell off a bridge and so massively broke his crown, I not only lost him: I lost myself. I had shaped myself around his example—in some ways, against it—for so long that when he wrecked his way, I wrecked mine. While he drank, smoked, screwed, *tried* everything, I sat in my ivory tower, meditating, writing (often sad) love songs, and drinking herbal tea. Even so, it was his lead I was following as he hacked his way through the forest, and I was grateful for that lantern glinting ahead amid the looming trees. So when he fell and damaged his brain, and I lost my brother, my leader, my model, I plunged into a vertigo that—so it seems now—spun me directly toward the Church.

The idea that Scientology might offer answers may have been planted the day I attended a seminar given by a famous acting teacher. By this time, winter 1976, my brother and friends had formed the League of Theatre Artists. Exploiting Manhattan's passion for raw, original Off-Off-Off-Broadway theater, we were going about creating it in storefronts and basements: trucking props and set pieces around the streets and even subways of New York. In that group, often spearheading activities, was Kate Kelly, a red-haired, vivacious beauty. I envied Kate's certainty about being an actor; with what sometimes seemed like conflicting interests and foci required by songwriting, theater, and writing, it was easy to worry that I was pursuing the wrong path. And Kate was always on the lookout for ways to better her craft; she studied with the legendary teacher Uta Hagen, and with Kate's encouragement I auditioned for and was accepted into that class as well. She often invited me to join her for movement workshops or acting seminars.

One morning, she phoned with such an idea. "This teacher's famous for finding acting problems," she said. "We're too late to sign up to perform a scene, but at least we can watch him work with others while they perform theirs."

We met up outside a studio on the West Side and pretty much tiptoed into the space. A palpable, almost cathedral-like hush permeated the room. The acting area was an empty square created by rows of chairs. Into this square strode a thickset man who radiated charisma. He made jokes about being a New York Greek now living in Los Angeles, how glad he was to be back "where there is *weather*!"

Settling into a chair, he said, "First scene?"

Two actors moved into the space, took a moment to get situated, and began to speak. The teacher watched for just a few minutes before getting to his feet. "Why are you talking like that?" he said to the man.

"Like what?" the actor said.

"As if you have your teeth clenched. Why are you doing that?"

The woman in the scene melted into the audience. The actor began visibly to quiver. "I don't know what you're talking about," he said.

The teacher imitated him, not unkindly, making his jaw immovable and talking through and over it. As soon as he did, we saw what he'd observed and we had not. There was a bit of laughter, flattened by a look from him.

The actor flushed. "I don't want—"

"Come here." As the teacher held out a hand, a big paw, the room seemed to darken and focus around the acting space. "It's as if someone has hold of you, your jaw."

The actor backed up a few steps, shaking his head. "It's just the fall I took when I was skiing a few years ago. I had to have stitches."

The teacher studied him. "Before that."

The room was silent. Tears pooled in the actor's eyes. Again he shook his head.

"Before that," the teacher said again.

"Just braces. I had to have braces, like we all do, when I was twelve or so."

The teacher reached a hand and took hold of the actor's jaw. In front of us the actor became a boy, and the boy let him.

"Before that." The teacher moved the chin in his hand gently from side to side. "It's as if someone has hold of you. Does someone have hold of you?"

The boy began to cry. Also to nod. The teacher released his jaw and waited.

"Just like you did," the actor finally said. He was weeping. "She'd hold my chin and force the spoon in and I'd try to keep my mouth shut because I didn't *want it*!"

The teacher studied him. "Let's be sure to talk later," he said. "Next scene?"

The acting problems unearthed in the next few scenes weren't as dramatic, but we could see they were holding the actors back in some significant way.

"That was *amazing*," Kate and I raved, as we joined the group bumping its way out of the room.

Someone next to us said, "You do know that guy's a Scientologist."

"No!" we said.

"That stuff he was doing? That's Scientology."

Horrified, Kate and I looked at each other. As one, we shrugged. "It was still *amazing*."

And it was. He seemed to have located a buried memory that not only appeared to be holding the actor back from a successful career, but that might be affecting his whole life. I don't remember being aware of this teacher's name: Milton Katselas. But less than two years later, after I'd fled Manhattan for Los Angeles, I almost immediately found my way—at the time it seemed like mere coincidence—to his acting class.

AT A TABLE in a restaurant, on a stool in a bar, sitting cross-legged on a chair full of pillows in his living room, my brother radiated brilliance, confidence, power. His friends, talented and astonishing bees, supped at the honeycomb of his light; he was the wax that held us all together. He did not smoke so much as suck his cigarettes, inhaling simultaneously through nose and mouth. He picked up a mug of coffee, which he drank black, by gripping it with an entire hand. If coffee wasn't to hand, beer was, and vodka, and, increasingly, whiskey. Mary matched him beer for beer, shot for shot.

She'd told me, early on, that she and Oak would eventually live in a New England farmhouse. I easily envisioned this: Oak churning out literary bestsellers in a cozy attic while children romped below. There'd be Irish Setters, walks through fall leaves, mugs of spiked cider.

But that wasn't the man she married.

One night, I inveigled them to come to dinner by telling them of the jeroboam of Johnnie Walker Red left as a house gift by a visiting friend. As I served up spaghetti that Mary did not eat in favor of another inch of scotch, the conversation centered around the newly formed League of Theatre Artists, which Oak had been instrumental in creating, and which included all of our friends. We were currently rehearsing a three-woman version of *Othello.*

Mary drained her glass. She and Oak were drinking the scotch like wine. But it meant they'd come to dinner. Once Mary was home from work, she liked to stay home. As I hefted the bottle, which was so enormous it was a joke, and poured them each a bit more Johnnie Walker, she said that she hated actors.

Oak stirred, uneasily. "That's not a jeroboam, it's a Methuselah," he said. Typical, that he carried the names of relative sizes of wine bottles in that brain of his. "Maybe even a Nebuchadnezzar."

I was still holding the huge bottle. "You hate them!" I said.

"Yes. *Hate* them." Her lips were pinched in fury.

The room darkened. A huge winged creature had slid through the brick wall and was hovering over us, dimming even the candles flickering on various surfaces.

"But—*why?*"

Oak, sitting cross-legged on my rug, lit a cigarette. He wore the slightest of rueful expressions. Mary leaned across the board perched on bricks that served as dining and coffee table. "Look at what they do for a living. Just *look* at it!"

"You mean *act*?"

"I mean *lie*." Her face was venomous. I thought for a moment that she might throw something. She reached for Oak's cigarette, took a drag, and almost spat out the smoke. "What they do for a living is *lie*!"

For the first time, I realized that their marriage had a terrible hole in it. And in spite of having been raised in a family where wine was often served, it was also the first time I sensed that alcohol—hard liquor—could shift a mood so quickly and palpably.

I got up and made coffee, into which they both poured more Johnnie Walker Red.

MY FIRST GLIMPSE of Schoharie Creek, the stretch of shallow water and sharp rocks that would eventually claim my brother's brain, did not seem ominous. It was just a wide, twinkling stretch of water running alongside the small town of Lexington in Upstate New York. It was crossed by a suspension bridge that led to what had once been a popular Catskill resort. The property, owned by the family of a member of the League of Theatre Artists, was now home to the Lexington Conservatory Theatre.

Oak was LCT's artistic director; its executive director was a friend from UCI, Michael VanLandingham—Vano. The "campus," as it was dubbed, had for some years been used for a children's camp, and there was already a Barn Theatre. Oak and compatriots converted an old billiard hall into the River Theatre. The company lodged in the old hotel, where two showers and three toilets were made to function. There was even a detached canteen, with not only a stove and fridge, but plates and forks and tables and chairs. Meals were cooked and served and cleared in rotating shifts. All of it just hours away from Manhattan.

I wasn't part of that first Lexington season. The Colorado and Oregon Shakespeare Festivals both called with offers; I chose Oregon. But even as I delighted in the deep text work, performing outdoors in Ashland, and working with friends I'd met the previous Colorado summer, I felt I was missing out on something big. In comparison to what my friends were up to in Lexington—creating new theater! acting in new plays!—Ashland seemed stodgy and old-fashioned. It did not occur to me that playing Cordelia in *King Lear* at the Oregon Shakespeare Festival could be seen as an excellent step in a growing career; I don't remember thinking in terms of a career. At the end of the summer, turning down an offer to stay on for Ashland's winter season, I returned to New York.

The all-you-can-drink Sunday brunches were now studded with anecdotes of Lexington Conservatory Theatre's magical first summer. The season had included my brother's adaptation of *Frankenstein*, a dark and eerie production that had been hugely successful. I heard what it took to create theater in a barn, tales of wondrous acting moments, whispers about trysts in the moonlight, laughter at the delights of "summer camp with art," and about the thunderous applause from audiences startled to find such magic in an abandoned Catskill resort.

I was determined to be part of Lexington's second season, and was, turning down offers from both the Oregon and Colorado Shakespeare Festivals. Along with other company members, I moved into the old hotel, choosing a room on the top floor; many a night, Kate and I crawled out onto the roof carrying wine and my guitar. *Home is where the heart is* . . . we sang. *The road curves on and on* . . . I edited bios for the program; devised recipes to feed dozens out of donated zucchini, brown rice, and vats of peanut butter; and acted.

The summer's productions included John Ford's *'Tis Pitty She's a Whore.* Ford's script, about a brother and sister who, Romeo and Juliet–like, cannot have each other, is full of mayhem and swordplay, violence and death. Already dismayed by the play's subject matter, I watched with dazzled horror as Oak, directing, reveled in making the production extra violent. He and his actors developed grisly stage-fights that included massive amounts of spilled blood. Oak cackled with glee as he oversaw the trial-and-error creation of a most persuasive gore, made of peanut butter, food coloring, and cherry Jell-O.

Even then—and particularly in retrospect—the violence, the blood, the glee seemed like the worst sort of hubris. A kind of purposeful taunting of the gods, until they paid attention, and flung their retort.

I REMAINED CONVINCED I was fat, even when I could see that my clothes hung off me. In an obsessive need to keep off the weight I'd lost, I created an equation of calories as money: I could "spend" only eight hundred a day. My daily practice included a jog along the East River, followed by meditation and sit-ups and leg lifts. Burning calories, I walked everywhere, all the while making incessant mental lists of the calories I was consuming, which, if written out, might look like this:

Egg 80
Toast 70
Apple 80
Carrots (2) 40
Tea w/milk 15
Banana 80
Salad w/ dressing 100
Roll 100
Wine 100

Some camera was always aimed at me, watching how I walked down a street, how I ate, what I ate, my silhouette. I was often exterior to myself, watching, judging. I wanted to be perfect—whatever that meant, it seemed possible—and perfection included being thin.

I was so chronically underweight that I stopped getting my period. I had yet to hear about anorexia, but it's clear, now, that the mental disorder had me in its grip.

Mary, too, was excruciatingly thin. And in spite of her feelings about actors, she decided to spend that second summer in Lexington. She and Oak could have had their pick of rooms in the hotel, but they slept in the lobby. Actually, they perched in the lobby, surrounded by open suitcases, scattered clothes and shoes, and overflowing ashtrays. I don't remember her ever joining us in the canteen for meals. But one day, as she and I were driving around Poughkeepsie putting up posters, I watched her cram—there is no other word for it—three cherry Danishes into her mouth. I began to wonder if she could only eat, she *would* only eat, when she was away from the theater. A Persephone pulled to the underworld of LCT, perhaps she thought she'd be trapped there forever if she accepted anything from us: a scoop of peanut butter, a piece of toast, a bed.

This self-imposed proscription didn't apply to beer. My brother's drinking was already legendary; no matter the time of day he seemed to have a container of something alcoholic nearby. Mary, too. Mostly cans of cheap beer. Sometimes jug wine. Now and then cups of orange juice and vodka. Whiskey. The dancing-in-the-fountain Fitzgeraldian delight of the early days of their marriage began to slide toward something grim.

One morning she showed up with a black eye.

What *happened*? we asked.

"Oh, this squirrel ran out in front of the car." Her once curly red hair was turning a muddy brown, and uncombed, looked like a Brillo pad. She touched fingertips to a cheekbone. "Oak had to brake, hard. I hit my face against the dashboard."

There was another conclusion to be drawn, but none of us wanted to imagine it. Although I recalled that night with the Johnnie Walker—her glittering eyes, the inch of liquor tossed like peanuts to the back of her throat, the way the energy in the room had swirled, suddenly, into something so dark. If she hated actors for lying, what did she think of playwrights, who created those lying lines?

By midwinter 1978, as things were gearing up for LCT's third season, it was clear to all of us that Oak and Mary's once heady, passionate relationship had turned ugly. Booze was everywhere. Neither showered, both smelled. The apartment stank, too: crumpled beer cans and overflowing ashtrays littered every surface. The trash container sometimes held several vodka bottles. A palpable tension seemed to surround them most of the time.

YOUR BROTHER'S HAD AN ACCIDENT

Inspired by Percy Bysshe Shelley's *The Cenci: A Tragedy in Five Acts*, Oak was working on his own version of the dark and demented Cenci legend: an infamous sixteenth-century Italian aristocrat abuses his wife and children, but, because of his wealth and power, his actions, known though they are throughout the city of Rome, go unpunished. His wife and daughter Beatrice eventually manage to kill him. The pope decides to have them publically executed, in spite of a protesting outcry from the people of Rome. I vaguely understood that the story made Beatrice into some kind of symbol of resistance against tyranny, but other than that, had no idea why Oak might be drawn to it. It just sounded like the kind of bloody, weird thing that had always attracted him. *Beatrice and the Old Man* would open LCT's Season Three.

But again I wouldn't be part of things. I'd been cast on a soap opera, *The Guiding Light*. I was ashamed of having accepted the job, believing that in doing so I'd eroded all my artistic integrity. (It's hard to believe now, but at the time, among my friends—among "serious" actors—there was a powerful ethos against accepting such work.) Even though my brother had talked me through all the good reasons to be on a soap, including the experience and the money ("You can throw some of it at the theater company"), I'd cried myself to sleep after saying yes. I comforted myself that it wasn't a running role—my character was scheduled to be part of the storyline for just eight weeks—but as I waved goodbye to my uncorrupted friends heading to Lexington, it flitted across my mind that I might be *glad* to be away from the tension-filled wire that encircled my brother and his wife and therefore, to some the degree, the entire theater-making enterprise.

Exteriors were filmed in the Bahamas, a delightful interlude, before cast and crew returned to Manhattan. We'd shoot indoor scenes at CBS studios. But I wasn't called for a few days, and wanting to see my friends, and to be there for opening night of Oak's new play, I caught a train. Oak picked me up in a hearse. Its long interior ideal for transporting lumber and other set-building necessities, it had been donated to the theater by a local company. Oak had errands to run, and he ran them driving far too fast, a can of beer lodged in full sight on the dashboard. He seemed distracted, mutedly angry. The narrow roads near Lexington were lined with tall grass, and particularly in the twilight it was hard to see very far ahead, much less around a corner. As Oak skidded around curve after curve, I closed my eyes and gave myself over to the death I was sure was coming our way. But finally we rattled across the Lexington Bridge. Across the street from the old hotel, Oak jerked to a stop and I slid from the car, amazed to be alive. Shooting gravel, he gunned the hearse up the long driveway to the theater.

I paused to take in an enormous black and red fabric poster that was strung between two trees: BEATRICE CENCI AND THE OLD MAN, A BIZARRE COMEDY BY OAKLEY HALL III. A dagger, blotched with gore, pointed to the production dates. From the tip of the dagger, a large gob of blood fell toward the phone number: CALL FOR THE GORY DETAILS.

It made me shudder. And even as I greeted friends, things felt weirdly off-kilter. A grim sensibility pervaded the campus.

In the morning, I found Oak in the strange little hut he used as a studio. He was standing, looking down at his typewriter, which was on the floor along with an array of loose pages and books and a snarl of dingy blanket. I assumed he must wrap this around himself, against the dawn chill, as he sat on the floor, cross-legged, typing. He was holding a plastic glass full of liquid as yellow as unhealthy urine.

"Oak," I said. "Is that *wine*?"

He smiled, his dark eyes full of both mischief and sorrow, and rotated the glass in the sunlight floating through a cobwebbed window. "Sauterne," he said. "Rotgut."

"It's nine in the morning!"

He shrugged and ran dirty fingernails through hair that looked as if it hadn't been combed in weeks. "I've been writing," he said, "not that it matters."

As awful as he looked, and even though his body odor was rank, and even though he was drinking at 9:00 A.M., I admired him. He was such an *artist*, for one. (True artists, I was convinced, were tortured and troubled; it took a long time to understand that one could be an artist and be settled and content.) His writing schedule, for another. He wrote every morning, rising long before dawn. Nothing ever got in the way of that.

"I'm looking forward to seeing *Beatrice*," I said, to say something.

He shook his head. "The actors hate it. I kind of hate it."

THE SHOW OPENED that night. At first I did laugh at what appeared to be a "comedy" that was clearly "bizarre," about a brother chained beneath the stairs by a wizened father who seems to like his daughter a little too much. But as the play unfolded, I shrank in my seat, horrified. The father seduces/rapes his daughter. The brother, attempting comfort, ends up having sex with her, too. Beatrice manages to kill the father she hates so much and is tortured to death for doing so. And just as we think she may have attained some otherworldly peace, as she mounts the stairs to Heaven, eager to be greeted by her Heavenly Father, we discover that He is the same father as the one she thought she'd left behind, and their terrible relationship expected to continue.

As the lights faded to final black, there was little applause. The audience filed out, somber. Kate and I remained in our seats. Finally she said, "The other day Oak told me, 'I am Beatrice.' He said, 'Except she's braver than I am. She does what I don't dare to do.' "

"What's that *mean*?" I stared at the set, bald and sad in the house lights, at the ugly nest of chains and blankets under the stairs, at the stairs themselves, which mounted to that terrible Heaven. "What does he mean? Kill his father?"

"Maybe," Kate said. "In a larger way? Maybe a sort of 'if you meet the Buddha on the path, kill him'? You know, in order to move on or something?"

I tried to take this in. Dad could be distant, self-involved, angry, but he was unrecognizable in the character my brother had put on that stage. Maybe it was about the theater company. Or Mary? Was there a message about a kind of "incest"—that we were *all* too close? But what, *what*, was the source of the terrible anger that surged through the script?

Kate put a hand on my arm. "Let's go get a beer."

In the old stable that the previous summer we'd hosed out and transformed into the company's own Blue Moon Café, I sat with Kate at a piano, singing songs that went unheard in the opening-night hubbub. Mary, who'd come up from Manhattan for the opening, sat beside Oak. She'd recently discovered she was pregnant and was managing to neither drink nor smoke, though the room was full of people doing both.

Suddenly, in the midst of the noisy hubbub, my brother's large, matted head of hair rose up. He stumbled from the table, turning over a chair. "I'm gunning for *you*, man!" he shouted. "It's *you* I'm gunning for!"

He wasn't talking to anyone in the room. He was deeply, disturbingly drunk, a person not in his body.

In the sudden silence, someone laughed. No one else did.

Oak could hardly stand. He propped himself against a table, one leg splayed out like an actor playing a cripple. He pointed at empty space. "You! Gunning for *you*!"

Bodies surged around him. Mary tried to talk him down. I moved toward him. He waved all of us away, violently. "Enough arms! I've had enough arms!"

I ran and ran and then walked, far out on a dirt road under the twinkling Lexington stars, wiping at my eyes, feeling absurdly theatrical yet utterly real.

Why that strange, violent depiction of a family? Was it our family—our father? Or was Oak talking about *God*? But what kind of God was that? And what did it mean that Oak drank so much? Why all the *anger*? What was *happening*?

THE NEXT MORNING, Sunday, a small group of us gathered on the bank of the slow-moving Schoharie. Oak plunged into the creek and came out again, shaking his long hair in a shimmering snake of sunlight and water. Squatting on the riverbank, he talked about how he loved hangovers. General laughter, largely uncomfortable. I watched as he discussed with a stage manager the best way to repair a broken prop, and, with a friend helping with a state grant, the objectives of the company. Upriver, the dark metal bridge cast its shadow across the twinkling water.

Around noon, as the actors began to gear up for the Sunday matinee of *Beatrice*, I caught a ride back to Manhattan. I was due at CBS studios at 6:00 the next morning.

Sometime after midnight, my phone rang. I fumbled across the room to pick it up.

"Your brother's had an accident," someone said, urgently. "You need to go tell Mary. This isn't news she should hear over the phone."

"Pardon?"

"Oak's in an ambulance. He's on the way to Albany General. Someone's got to tell Mary. She and Oak appear to have had a fight this afternoon, before she headed back to Manhattan, and we don't think she should just get a phone call. *Go.* As fast as you can."

I ran. Down my stairs, up First Avenue. The buzzer of their apartment building didn't work. I called Mary from the telephone booth on the corner.

It was 1:00 in the morning. But Mary picked up immediately, as if she was waiting by the phone. "What's happened," she said. There was no question mark.

She buzzed me in. I ran up the stairs. I told her what I knew. She searched for and found a pack of cigarettes and began to make phone calls. From her end of these conversations, as she lit one cigarette from the glowing butt of another, I began to put together what must have happened.

Following the ill-attended and badly received Sunday matinee, Mary had left for Manhattan—she had work the next day—and Oak went across the river to the Lexington Hotel, where he sat at the bar and drank boilermakers with a man who was visiting a friend that weekend. On the way back to the theater, he fell off the bridge.

Or slipped off the bridge.

Or jumped off the bridge.

Somehow he went off the bridge, landing on his head on the sharp rocks below. It began to rain. An emergency vehicle arrived. Lifted on a stretcher, he was taken to a local doctor's office, where a nurse said, "Shit, another DOA." Oak might have looked dead on arrival, and it's possible his heart did stop during that time, but the attending physician, Dr. Bock, who knew him, shoved a tracheotomy in his throat, shouting, "Don't you die on me, don't you dare fucking die!"

They loaded him into an ambulance. A member of the company, a friend from Irvine days, Bruce Bouchard, climbed in. The doors slammed. Sirens screaming, they raced through the rainy night to Albany.

Which was where he was now, in something called Intensive Care.

To me, Intensive Care was yellow lotion in a bottle. But Mary, a doctor's daughter, knew exactly what the term meant.

Voice trembling, she asked whoever was on the other end of the line, "Is he going to . . . live?"

I shook my head at the absurdity of that question. There was no *way* it was that serious! This was my brother! He survived, he always survived. It was just a matter of a Band-Aid! It would be like that time he almost fell down the Rockpile, or leapt into the tent spread across the lake in Europe, or landed on that stone bench at Andover. A lot of blood, maybe. Head wounds bleed! But he would be, as he'd always been, very silly, and very lucky.

Mary made more phone calls—surely one of them was to my parents—and packed a bag. I stood with her as she hailed a taxi. I waved her off and stalked the blocks to my apartment and up the five flights of stairs. As I walked in, my alarm was ringing: 3:30 A.M.

I tried to follow my workday ritual, lighting a candle and meditating. My body shook. My eyes were hot and dry. Was my brother going to *die*? Folding forward over my cross-legged position, I put my forehead to the floor. *Please don't let him die.*

I opened my eyes. For a long moment I kept brow pressed to rug, watching candlelight flicker against its woof and warp.

I took a breath. I had to get going. I had to get to work.

And what was that work? *A soap opera.*

But I could not not show up. These were the days when many soaps were filmed live. Video was still rarely used. Thousands of dollars and dozens of people's time would be wasted if I were not there, the entire production machine thrown into havoc. This had been made clear to me when I signed the contract.

Forehead against the floor, I argued with that logic. And then I got to my feet.

In a grand piece of irony, the scene we shot that day was one in which my character, Maya, finds out that her sister has drowned in a scuba diving accident.

"Don't cry, Maya," said the man playing my fiancé. But I could do no crying.

"Don't cry," he said again, a little worried.

I put my face in my hands and shook my shoulders. It was all I could do.

I didn't have scenes to shoot the following day. I headed to Albany. As I found my way to the Intensive Care Unit, I ran into Mary.

"He's doing really well!" she said.

I smiled back, hugely cheered. Of course! This was my brother!

But walking into the ICU, what I saw was a bed filled with a massive dark *thing*, a cubist painting that took long moments to form into discernable parts.

The head two and a half times its normal size. The face bloated, unrecognizable. Forehead wrapped in a blood-spotted bandage, the bandage angled in a way that made it look pirate-like, jaunty. Two Santa Rosa plums bulging out of what must be eye sockets. Protruding from his throat, which was thick as a bull's, was a tube, the skin around it bloated and bloody—it had clearly been jammed in there. Down his bare chest, from clavicle to pelvis, a bandage four inches wide seeped blood. Tangles of transparent tubing surrounded him. Tubes attached to bottles that hung from metal trees dripped something clear and viscous into his veins. Tubes running from his body, attached to every limb, to his chest, to his head, were filled with a mottled pink and gray that inched along and made me think of brain matter. A tube connected to his penis was red with blood, mixed with something as yellow as that sauterne he'd been drinking—had it been just the day before? A machine to one side of his bed, which reminded me of something used backstage to make the sound of wind, clacked and whooshed, expanding a collapsed lung.

The top of my head rose and hit the ceiling. The room tilted. As I reached toward the bed to steady myself, the tube snapped out of his throat. A terrible rattling filled the room. A nurse rushed in. As she worked to reconnect the tube to the hole in his throat, I realized he was breathing through that tube, it was the *only thing giving him oxygen*.

I locked my eyes on yet another machine that stood beside the bed, in which green lights blinked and flashed, occasionally flickering a terrifying red.

The nurse turned, ready to tell me something. She took one look at my face and pulled me into the hallway, sat me in a chair, and with a deft, gentle hand, pressed my face between my knees.

"Breathe," she said.

PLEASE, PLEASE, PLEASE DON'T TAKE HIS MIND

The man who shared Oak's room in the ICU was in a bed designed to rotate so he wouldn't get bedsores. He'd been in a car accident and was completely paralyzed. But his brain had not been injured. In the other bed was sturdy Oak, whose body, except for his smashed head, suffered little permanent damage.

I think about that man in the ICU being turned on an apparatus that held him like a chicken on a spit, all the while knowing what had happened to him. It's hard to imagine that knowledge. How you go on breathing.

Oak did not know what happened, or the extent of the damage, for a long time.

Neither did I.

MOTHER FLEW EAST on a red-eye. She had a brief layover at JFK before the flight to Albany, and wanting to surprise her, I scrambled across town, predawn, to catch a subway to the airport. Waiting for her plane, I gazed about at the sprawl of humanity readying themselves for the next step on their journeys, stunned, as I was all those days, that life could just *go on*. At the same time, I could not believe anything had actually happened. Any day, Oak would clamber over the deck railing, displaying the double-stitched binding on his shirt that had kept him from falling. He would surge out of the lake, out of the mass of golden canvas that enshrouded him. He would be *just fine.*

Mother was gratifyingly delighted to see me. As we sipped terrible airport coffee, I was glad for the grace of small talk. Until those hours in the ICU waiting room, I'd never grasped how essential the chat is that gets us through the moments until it's time for "big talk." The woman whose daughter was undergoing a kidney transplant listing every step of a recipe for meatballs; the man whose wife was dying of leukemia describing the antics of their poodle, Boo; the deep, head-shaking discussions of weather. All of us glad to be distracted, for a few moments, from what was going on with our loved ones in rooms full of ticking machines down the hall.

"Your father," Mom said, her face a terrible pale gray.

It was time for big talk.

"He said if Tad did it on purpose, he's no son of his."

"Mom! It wasn't on *purpose*! Tad—Oak—would never do that!" But I understood: Tad had failed. Even if it was an accident. Halls didn't have accidents. The fall was a metaphor—the real reason was lodged in there somewhere.

"After Mary called with the news," she said, "I went out onto the deck."

I imagined the huge shoulders of Granite Chief hunched up against a sky full of stars, and Mother standing on the redwood deck, staring up at that sparkling brilliance, thinking of her injured son, three time zones and three thousand miles away.

"And I said, I *cried*, to whatever the hell it is that isn't up there, I said, 'Take his body, but please, please, *please* don't take his mind.' "

I walked her to the gate. As she waved one last time before disappearing down the gangway, I thought of her screaming at a god she didn't believe in—a god who, if he existed, was such a bastard—screaming in massive pleading fury, *Please don't take his mind!*

That night, she called from a hotel near the hospital. When Tad had heard her voice, she told me, and especially when she took his hand, tears seeped out of eyes still so swollen and bruised that he could not open them.

"This seems to be important," she told me. "It means he's remembering, that somewhere in there his brain is working."

Of course it's *working*, I thought. He's just had a really bad fall.

She told me that Mary was handling things very well, although being very stern. "Maybe she thinks I plan to take him home, but I'd never do that. He's her husband. She's his wife. And as your father and I learned, that first year of our marriage . . ."

She related, again, what she'd told us often: how those difficult first months of marriage, when neither of them had family to which they were willing to turn, had played a huge part in forging their powerful partnership.

"So you'll not find me in the role of clichéd mother-in-law!" she said. "But it's all so awful. I need to call your father. He wants me to come home."

"But you just got there," I said, stunned.

She stayed a day and a half in Albany. She returned to Manhattan, came to CBS studios with me, to lunch with Dad's agent. That night she talked on the phone with Dad for over an hour. At dawn, we caught the subway back out to JFK, where I waved her into the plane that would take her home to her husband.

"I don't want to be in Mary's way," she said when I protested. "And your father needs me."

"But *Tad* needs you!"

She was adamant. Her son had a wife. She had a husband.

MARY CLEARLY FELT the same. She pretty much banished Oak's friends—not telling them when he'd been moved from one room to another, not even when he was moved from Albany to Boston's Massachusetts General. My affection for her had some time before morphed to a terrified admiration, and I understood why she was furious, anguished, murderous: In addition to the horror of what was unfolding in her married life (and she was far clearer, much earlier than I, about the ramifications of the accident), she was *pregnant*. But the spikiness seemed aimed at me, personally.

Part of this may have been that Oak knew early memories: that I was his sister. His mother's voice. Even friends from the Irvine years: Michael VanLandingham, Bruce Bouchard. But the pregnant woman who spent every day and night by his side? Who was she?

So perhaps I should not have been surprised when, one morning, Mary and her mother banished me.

By this time I'd spent several Thanksgivings and Christmases with Mary's family. I adored her mother. More than once she and I'd talked late into the night about her beloved Catholicism. Without apology, she spoke of God and of her religion, including that she held a blasphemous view: that heaven was here on earth.

"Why is that blasphemous?" I asked.

"Because my church teaches that we are all sinners. We must endure the travail of life, walking upright in the eyes of God, and *if* we manage to step correctly through our days and nights, *maybe* we'll make it into heaven." She smiled. "Whereas I think Jesus is saying that it's all right here, right now. *This* is heaven. It's a matter of seeing that's so. And that takes faith."

This corroborated feelings I sometimes had, when I glimpsed God, or maybe what I meant was transcendence, in golden light spilling onto a brick wall, when I was bent over my guitar with a new set of lyrics coming clear, sharing laughter with friends around a table.

So I trusted Mary's mother. I believed in her goodness. I guess that's why, sitting in her kitchen, when she said she had something she needed to say to me, I listened.

She told me that I wasn't good for my brother. That I was, in fact, bad for him.

Mary had cracked the kitchen door so she could hold her cigarette outside. She was extremely thin, except for the dome of her pregnancy.

"So," Mary's mother said, "as you want the best for Oak, you need to not visit him."

"What do you mean, not visit him?!"

"We also noticed that after your mother visited he was upset—"

"She's his *mother*! He probably wanted to go *home*!"

"*Everyone* needs to leave him alone. The theater company too. To get better."

I was on my feet, holding onto the back of a chair. "He doesn't know what's happened. He doesn't know where he is. Maybe even *who* he is. He needs people he *knows*."

Mary pulled the cigarette inside to take a drag, then pressed a cheek to the doorjamb to blow the smoke outside.

"He knows *who I am*!" I said. "He needs someone there that he *remembers*!"

This was exactly the wrong thing to say. They were aware of it too. He did not recognize Mary. I think he assumed she was a nurse.

"You'll do what's best for your brother."

"There's no way I'm not going to visit him!" But my voice shook.

I have a vague memory of hitchhiking after this. Rather than catching a ride with Mary to Boston, I must have put out a thumb. I caught the next train to New York, where I was due to shoot the soap the next morning. En route, I did not visit my brother.

IT MAY HAVE taken them a while to persuade me, but once they did, my belief was absolute: I was bad for him. I didn't visit Oak in the hospital again. Mom and Dad stayed on the other side of the country. Friends tried to see him, but mostly, Mary got her wish. We left him completely alone. It makes me tremble, now, to imagine my brother's loneliness.

That was August. Late that fall, Oak and Mary returned to Manhattan. No doubt Oak should have stayed in the hospital longer, certainly have engaged in rehab, but in the late seventies, no one knew that there were ways to rebuild a damaged brain. Once he'd recovered from reconstructive surgery, there was no reason to keep him hospitalized. All things considered, the plastic surgeons, who'd asked for photographs, did an astounding job. They even managed to retain the rather impish quality of his nose. But his eyes were set at slightly different levels. It looked as if some massive force, running along a fault line, had shifted the two sides of his face. Still, he could see. He could hear. He could talk. He could walk, and did, to purchase Camel non-filters at the corner store and measure Folgers and water into the battered Mr. Coffee. Once again he sat cross-legged on the old chair. Above the collar of his shirt, the wicked red star left behind by the trach was perfectly visible.

Nothing was irretrievably broken. Except his brain. But I didn't know that yet.

ON A SNOWY February night in 1979, Mary was rushed to the hospital to have a C-section. The umbilical cord was wrapped three times around her baby's throat. He survived. They named him Oakley Hall IV. Soon they were calling him O4.

Mary now had two children to take care of. Because Oak was like a child, a terrified one. He was convinced that huge bugs and even larger spiders were crawling across his skin, that snipers were swarming the rooftop of the building opposite, lying on their stomachs, aiming rifles into his living room. He snuck from window to window, hiding behind the frames, peering out, swiping continuously at his shoulders and back. Mary moved his reading chair so he couldn't see the building opposite. She hung a mirror so he could twist and turn and confirm that insects were not drifting across his back with long scaly legs.

His friends tried to act as if things were the same, trekking up the stairs to visit him.

Was that a cigarette in his hand? Was that a *beer*?

Well, perhaps those were just signs that he was on his way back. He'd survived; what else was possible?

I accompanied others on those visits; I never came alone. I felt terribly guilty, convinced my presence might harm him, perhaps already had.

That accusation stayed with me for decades. It dented any joy I took in being with him. It meant I lost him in two ways: to the brain injury, and because I simply didn't talk, laugh, *be* with him. The amount of time I squandered believing what I'd been told—years I stayed away from him, years in which I didn't let him know I loved him—makes me weep.

LATER THAT SPRING, Kate Kelly, with her red hair and her voice that in two seconds could rise from a hum to a note packed with vibrato, appeared on Broadway. A group brought Oak to the opening, his first theater outing since the accident.

I'd forgotten about it until recently, when a photograph jolted the evening into memory. Oak is standing outside the theater, the name of the musical, *The Utter Glory of Morrissey Hall*, visible on the marquee behind him. His face is eggshell white. His hair is lank, unwashed. He's attempting his cocky gap-toothed grin, but his eyes are full of fear.

I sense that a number of people surround whoever is taking that photo. They are all jubilant: thrilled for Kate's success and that, no matter how ghostlike, Oak is with us again!

Except it wasn't Oak. He'd changed, forever.

I think that was the moment I finally and fully understood that the brother I had known was not coming back. That damage to his brain wasn't temporary. The damage could not be undone, reversed, repaired, rejoined, healed, solved, fixed.

He was no longer Oak: driving a hearse, drinking a beer, writing a play, running a theater company.

He was no longer Tad, my older brother, always leading the way.

But who was he?

And who in the world, then, was I?

Vertigo closed in, seeping like India ink across wet paper, darkening everything with that terrible understanding.

•

I REMEMBER LITTLE of that winter and spring. One reason is that I was eating ever-smaller amounts, and though I didn't know it at the time, low blood sugar makes memory murky. I was controlling what I could control, I see now, but even I was shocked, if vaguely gratified, the day I got on a scale and peered between my toes to find that—I'm almost five foot seven—I'd gotten myself down to 104 pounds.

I began to notice that I brought my parents into every conversation. "My father says . . ." "When my mother was growing up . . ." "When my parents lived in Mexico . . ." It was as if, with Oak—brother, mentor, leader, friend—"gone," I no longer existed unless I substantiated my existence with theirs. I'd hear myself say, "My mom told me . . ." "In a letter from my dad, he . . ." and close my lips around the rest of the sentence. I stopped telling stories, as they all seemed to revolve around my family. Although this had not been the case before, I found that without those stories, I seemed to have nothing to say.

At some point that winter, I was involved in a rock-musical adaptation of *The Revenger's Tragedy*, part of what I remember as a kind of three-woman chorus. Or it could be that I was working on the show in some other capacity and, watching these women, channeled myself into them. We/they wore spangles and tights and corsets. Rehearsals were wild and eerie and immersive. Through that process, I found fellow musicians. We created a band, among other things playing a fundraiser for the Lexington Conservatory Theatre. One of the only images I hold of this time is performing my song "Chippewa Street," to which a band member added a powerful pockety percussion:

Don't know what'll happen
Don't know who I'll meet
But I'm gonna keep on walking
That ol' Chippewa, Chippewa Street

I sang those lyrics as if it were the end of my life, and maybe it kind of was. A shock wave tore through me as we rocketed to a close and the audience, as one, rose to its feet and roared.

Other than those snippets of memory, these months are encased in a bubble: no sound, no feeling. I see now the bubble was grief, or, rather, my inability to face that I had reason to grieve. I was in a vast depression, one that would last for years.

THAT'S THAT SCIENTOLOGY STUFF HE DOES

April 1979, nine months after the accident, I was out for my morning jog along the East River when I stopped, midstride.

I had to leave.

Staring out over the gray surging water, I said it aloud: "I have to leave."

I jogged back to my apartment and began to make arrangements to move to Los Angeles. In no way did this seem connected to my brother, to my inability to accept who he now was. I was following, as I saw it, my career trajectory.

And so I abandoned an apartment full of things, the cherished music I was making with that band of artists, a circle of beloved friends. The money from the soap opera, crammed into savings, funded the move. By the time my friends were again in Upstate New York, creating LCT's fourth and what would turn out to be final season, I was gone.

That final Lexington summer, Oak insisted on being part of things. Yet what was there for him to do? He might have been capable of physical labor, but his damaged brain meant he couldn't even figure out how to hammer a nail. If someone gave him a project, his mind got waylaid between step 1 and step 2. He was terrified of getting on a ladder.

What he could do was sit and smoke at one of the tables outside the canteen, telling tales no one could understand. He'd get a few sentences out and then, as if all the information that wanted to emerge just jammed up at the exit point, he'd say a nonsense word: *kakapadoodle!* Recognizing it was nonsense, he'd shrug.

At the end of that summer, members of the company moved to Albany, New York, to create a year-round theater, Capital Rep. This was a plan that, before his fall, Oak had been concocting, and he went with them.

For a while, Oak was perceived as a tragic figure, even a heroic one. I think there was hope that his brain might come back, that the work would make him whole again. But while he couldn't drink the way he once had, that didn't mean he didn't try, and the alcohol worked on him quickly, and badly. More and more he just looked and acted and smelled like a bum.

At the time, I knew none of this. I was on the other side of the country, doing my best to start again, doing my best not to think about it. I pieced it all together much later.

MY YOUNGEST SISTER, Brett, had enrolled at UCLA. We decided to rent a place together and found a charming bungalow in a warren of them, the walkways filled with glossy greenery and splashes of bougainvillea. The rent was extraordinarily cheap.

That first year in LA, 1979 to 1980, I landed decent acting work, including guest-starring roles on shows like *Lou Grant.* But my personality had undergone a seismic shift. I drank, a lot. I, who eschewed all drugs, fell in with company that snorted cocaine. It made food irrelevant, while also making me feel extremely thin and very smart.

While Karen Carpenter had not yet died of complications due to anorexia nervosa, the eighty pounds she weighed, the gasps in the audience when she walked onstage, and the possible reasons behind such an obsession had begun to draw attention. I dismissed a lot of what I heard: Karen Carpenter might be anorexic; I was *fat*. But one day, I read that it's an illness that affects young women from "good homes" who long for approval, and who fear they'll lose their parents' love if they don't live up to expectations. This rang a distant gong, but I clapped a mental hand against it. Yes, my parents expected much. But how else would they teach their children how to live not just a good life, but the best life?

More and more, I ate almost nothing all day, so I could "spend" the calories on dinner, and on alcohol. Little by little, I stopped meditating. Whatever depression I'd been in when I left New York, I sank into it more deeply now. *Leanin' into loneliness*, I wrote,

With my elbows on the bar
Sipping from a shot glass
Wondering where you are

I slid into affairs with not one, but two married men. The first I'd met at the Writer's Conference the previous summer, the whole thing stoked by cocaine. The second I came to know during rehearsals for a play, our lust ignited and then fueled by love scenes that for a month we played out on stage. As Roger and I steamed up the windows of his car, even as we took a hotel room, I assured myself I wasn't really doing what I was doing. I was aware he was married, that he had children, but the kissing was sublime, the sex immersive. For hours at a stretch I was able to lose all sense of time, of thought. I didn't want to think.

Roger was an accomplished actor, including having had, at one point, his own television series. He was a member of a master acting class that met on Saturday mornings at the Beverly Hills Playhouse. As Roger told me stories about his teacher, I was reminded of the workshop I'd attended with Kate Kelly a few years before.

When I described the way that teacher had held the actor's jaw, Roger said, "Yeah, that sounds like Milton. Milton Katselas. That's the Scientology stuff he does. 'Is there an earlier, similar incident?' He probably signed that guy up."

He laughed at what must have been my aghast face. Yes, Kate and I'd been told that, but here it was confirmed! But Scientology was a cult! Scientology hounded those who said or wrote anything negative about it. It claimed it was an actual religion—how laughable was that!—so that it could get tax-exempt status. How could that charismatic, reasonable, wise-seeming teacher have anything to do with *Scientology*?

"Lots of actors who study with Milton aren't Scientologists," Roger said. "Me, for instance! Don't worry about it!"

Milton's master class comprised a who's who of Hollywood luminaries, most of whose names I did not recognize, as I did not watch television and rarely went to movies—a revealing detail about my supposed choice of careers. Roger kindly offered to take my résumé to Milton and ask if I could join the class. Somewhat to the surprise of both of us—usually one needed to be a pretty big star, or to have taken a number of previous classes at the Playhouse—Milton said yes. I was honored, and very nervous.

The class was surprisingly inexpensive, a good thing, as, unlike most of its starry members, I was working as a waitress in a Westwood café. But on Saturday mornings, carrying a cup of coffee, I joined those sitting in the charming Beverly Hills Playhouse to watch Milton work his magic. I was not the only one scribbling in a journal when he stopped a scene to nudge, cajole, badger the actors into more truthful characterizations. Sometimes he and some of the actors seemed to talk in code, acronyms that represented a shorthand. Roger called it "Scientologeze." Other than that, Scientology didn't come up much, although one day, a woman in the class cheerfully asked me where I was "on course." When I said, "Pardon?" she said, "Aren't you a Scientologist?" My "No!" sounded as if she'd asked me if I'd like to kill her cat. But it did cause me to wonder: Why would she think I was a Scientologist? She clearly intended it as a compliment. I found that intriguing.

Acting issues are usually connected to life issues, and sessions with Milton often led actors to examine larger elements of their lives. Perhaps that's why I let Saturday after Saturday go by without performing a scene. My psyche was *fine*. I was a Hall. Halls didn't need therapy. And if anything about me *wasn't* fine—I have no memory of thinking about my brother's accident, or about my need for approval, especially parental—I certainly didn't want that examined in front of an *audience*.

Which inaction pretty much reflected my acting career. I simply could not will myself into the guise of an LA actor, those shining paragons of success who know what shoes go with which hemline, who can manipulate brush and hair dryer, who own enough tubes of lipstick to select with purpose a particular shade. None of it had to do with what I adored about theater: language, verse, the immediacy and even sacrament of live performance. Increasingly, I thought of myself as a child in a sandbox, wielding her truly-unimportant-in-the-scheme-of-things shovel and pail.

Shyly, I made a private appointment with Milton. I think, now, that I was angling to be told that he (or, perhaps, Scientology) could "fix" me. He was characteristically blunt: "The whole thing's a game," he said. "Think of it as a role. You need the wardrobe to play it. Get rid of those long skirts, to start with. Cut your hair, you look like a hippie. Wear a skirt that shows off your legs, you have good legs! Buy silk shirts, good jeans, an underwire bra."

I owned none of those things, and would do anything to avoid wearing pantyhose (hence the long skirts), which made my legs feel as if they were stuffed into sausage casings.

He must have read something in my face. "Do you even want this?"

I had no answer. Why would I cut and style my hair, wear pantyhose and push-up bras, use makeup to enhance my features, when *natural is best*?

I'd wrapped myself in a straitjacket, a natural fiber one. My agent lost interest and focus. I was sent on fewer and fewer auditions.

I was seldom in touch with my New York friends, not even Kate. I do not remember ever thinking about my brother. I examine this now with a kind of horror. How could that have been possible, when he had been such an elemental, even titanic force in my life, all my life? But so it was.

HOWEVER, ONE MORNING in our little Westwood bungalow, Brett and I received a phone call: Oak was being put on a plane in Albany, New York. He'd be landing at LAX.

As the Lexington company had gone about creating the new theater, they'd done their best to keep him part of things. But he was still drinking, still smoking, still not bathing (I shudder to think where he slept)—things that could no longer be chalked up to a droll and charismatic nature. Quite rightly, his friends felt it was high time for his family to step up. Perhaps my parents felt it was his wife's responsibility, but Mary was living in Manhattan with O4. And I was certainly MIA. We not only failed him, we utterly failed.

I don't include Tracy and Brett; they stepped up to the plate. It was Brett who picked him up at the airport, brought him to our apartment, and ran him a bath. After the water slipped down the drain, a slurry of silt remained. He hadn't showered for weeks. In addition, on the plane, terrified to be so high above the ground, afraid of falling, he'd defecated himself. Brett had to run him a second bath.

Eventually—I think we put him on a Greyhound bus—he landed in Squaw Valley, back with his parents. Mary and little O4 would eventually join him there.

I do not recall being in the car when Brett picked him up at the airport. I might have taken him to the Greyhound station; I don't know. I remember almost nothing of this whole episode. It wasn't that I didn't want to think about him. I simply . . . didn't. It's as if what smashed his brain also wiped out a portion of mine. I was still eating hardly anything. Not only does that diminish memory, it also makes one cranky—depressed, in fact. But that never occurred to me. Halls didn't get depressed. *Despair is base* is the motto of Dad's Scottish ancestors, the Maxwells. And despair *is* base. But you kind of have to *know* it is despair, in order to label it as such and do something about it.

One day, as Roger was driving and I crying, a not uncommon situation, he pulled into the parking lot of a 7-Eleven and, leaving the engine running, disappeared into the shop. Sliding back into the driver's seat, he tossed two packets of Planters peanuts into my lap.

"Eat these," he said. "Then we'll talk."

I stared in shock. Never had I equated my bouts of weeping with an empty stomach. I wanted (weepingly) to protest, but I was too hungry. I ate them. We had a good evening. The connection had been made.

Where food was concerned, it was the beginning of a long climb back to sanity. However, this effort to perfect, as I saw it, my body, was about to be replaced by a new possibility: perfection of spirit.

BRETT AND I discovered why the rent on our bungalow was so cheap. The whole lovely warren was slated to be demolished to make way for another Westwood high-rise. As Brett searched for an apartment with friends near UCLA, I looked at options in Beachwood Canyon, an area nestled beneath the hills that hold those huge letters spelling out HOLLYWOOD. At the foot of the canyon stood a marvelous if dilapidated building that took up an entire block. The hidden nature of its grounds—it was surrounded by a high stone wall twined with ivy—reminded me of a favorite childhood book, *The Secret Garden*. It was not just the sense of an elegant manor with grounds; it was also the hint of something waiting there, something that could be found only by dint of applying tender loving care.

One day, as we were driving by, I said as much to Roger.

"Are you kidding?" He practically choked. "That's Celebrity Center. It's owned by the Church of Scientology."

I twisted in my seat to stare up at its high, mysterious profile. On the sidewalk in front of it, a woman stood with a clipboard trying to engage passersby in conversation. I recognized what she was doing. While attending the acting program in San Francisco, I'd walked down Mason to get to the studios on Geary, and there must have been a Scientology headquarters nearby, as the corner was usually full of smiling people carrying clipboards with surveys that posed the question, ARE YOU REALLY HAPPY? Even then I understood that their purpose was to get you to talk about yourself, to find what you felt was missing in your life (later I'd find this was called a "ruin"), and tell you that Scientology would solve it. "Are you really happy?" Even as I veered away and shook my head—and then quickly nodded (of course I was happy!)—I pondered the "hook" that question provided. Was I?

Was anyone, ever, *really* happy?

What did "really" mean?

I thought it a very clever question.

Again I twisted in my seat, looking back at the building known as Celebrity Center. "What do they do in there?"

Roger shrugged. "Scientology, I guess. But only if you're a Scientologist—and a celebrity. John Travolta. Mimi Rogers. Karen Black. Chick Corea. Lots of people in Milton's class do things there. You could ask them."

"Too bad!" I said. "It's such a pretty building."

I CAN'T HELP but wonder, now, why I chose that particular canyon, when there are so many lovely ones in Los Angeles. But by the summer of 1980, I'd found a place nestled in those hills above Celebrity Center. Around this same time, Roger moved out from his wife and kids. Scared this would mean we were committed to each other, I broke up with him. I had one last evening with cocaine. While the experience ensured I'd never touch it again, it also offered insight into a potentially greedy aspect of my nature that appalled me. I kept the waitress job in Westwood. Now and then I dropped in to see my agent. This always created a brief flurry of auditions, and I often got called back, but I landed little actual work. I had no idea what I was doing with my life. I saw Brett rarely. I seldom talked to Tracy. Not to Mom and Dad, nor to Oak, who was living in Squaw Valley with Mary and O4. I remember feeling like a flea-bitten dog, scratching at something that tickled, bit, ached in an unreachable, unassuageable place.

Parked in Beachwood Canyon, I often found flyers tucked under my windshield wipers. Ubiquitous and irritating, they often advertised Scientology's free personality test. Others offered various goods and services; only later did I find out that they were almost all businesses owned by Scientologists, and that such flyers represent an essential part of LRH's expansion advice: "Outflow equals inflow."

One day, a coupon read, *Buy dinner and get a glass of wine, free!* The restaurant, Two Dollar Bill's, was located at the bottom of the canyon, on the opposite side of the street from Celebrity Center. Feeling both lonely and broke, I tucked coupon and journal into my purse. Having no idea how much this would change my life, I headed down the hill.

HOPE SPRINGS ETERNAL

The atmosphere of Two Dollar Bill's was funky but cozy. There seemed to be just one waitress. When she finally got to me, I ordered a spinach salad and, handing her the coupon, my free glass of wine. I opened my journal, but instead of writing, I stared out the window at the building across the street. Partially hidden behind walls and trees, bristling with crenellated bits of roofing, Celebrity Center looked like a cross between a fairy tale and a set for a horror film. Karen Black might be there. John Travolta. Actors who gave the Church credence. Milton could tell me what went on there. I could even head across the street and ask. Except there was no way I'd ever walk into that place.

The restaurant was nice enough, but the service was terrible. A sign in the window said HELP WANTED. Tired of driving to the Westwood café, I asked for an application. I didn't need to fill it out. The waitress—also acting as hostess and manager—asked about my restaurant experience.

"Great!" she said. "Come at ten tomorrow morning. We'll get you started."

By the time I was halfway through my first shift, it was clear that Two Dollar Bill's was run by Scientologists and that its organization was based on Scientology principles. These appeared to be about giving good service while also selling as many items and/or the most expensive items possible. In the world of restaurants, these ideas are not novel. As I scooped spinach into bowls and tucked parsley on the sides of burgers, my fellow waitresses told me how I was "already" so much like a Scientologist.

"Are you Clear?" I was asked.

I wanted to ask, "Clear about what?" but didn't, as I wanted to be whatever Clear was. Clearly it was a good thing. I gathered I was cheerful and organized (at least well-trained by previous waitress jobs). I wondered if one had to be a Scientologist to be Clear. Was it possible to find that state—whatever it happened to be—on one's own?

I paced the restaurant, smiling, carrying baskets of rolls and carafes of coffee, bolstered by the idea that I was perceived as Clear. But outside of that restaurant, peering down the purposeless road of my life, I felt most definitely unclear. Again and again I tried to get back to meditating. On my bookshelves, *The Gnostic Gospels* slanted against *The Dancing Wu Li Masters*; Robert Graves's *White Goddess* was piled atop paperbacks about chakras and yoga and meditation. I often dipped into these books, yearning for the knowledge between their covers, answers that might illuminate a way to believe, act, live, be happy.

My fellow waitresses suggested that I read a book by L. Ron Hubbard. "You can't judge Scientology by what you've heard!" they said, when I shook my head. "You need to find out for yourself, and the best way to do that is to read one of his books. Or take a course! Success Through Communication! It's a great way to begin!"

"No, thanks!" I said gaily, heading off to refill a coffee mug.

On Friday and Saturday nights the restaurant featured live music, often jazz. One night the combo on stage was a jazz trio. A blond, very handsome man wearing loose white clothes played a blazing solo on the upright bass. When the applause died down, the pianist and leader of the band told us his name: Jamie Faunt.

I'd never particularly listened to jazz before. After fetching customers tea and wine, I stood off in a corner, entranced by the music and falling in love with it. I also fell just a bit in love with the man making it, whose full lips worked as his fingers raced up and down the strings of the bass.

It also turned out that Jamie fell a bit in love with me. Or whatever it was made him lean across his bass during a break between songs and say to the pianist, "That's the girl I'm going to marry."

MY FELLOW WAITRESSES let me know that the members of the jazz trio were celebrities. They studied at Celebrity Center! Jamie played bass with people like Chick Corea (who'd been a Scientologist for years!) and Al Jarreau (who'd signed up for a course!).

Which must mean that Jamie was a Scientologist.

So when Jamie asked if I'd like to have a cup of tea, I was wary.

Over our steaming mugs he told me he'd recently been doing his services at AO. When I looked mystified, he translated. He'd been getting auditing at Scientology's Advanced Organization. Those blue buildings further down Fountain? Topped by an eight-armed cross?

"I just finished a major intensive." He was clearly proud of this achievement. Under a short-sleeved shirt, a bicep pulsed. His skin was luminous, pale and smooth as marble.

"An intensive?"

"A bunch of auditing," he said. "Scientology's form of counseling."

I looked around the café, wishing he'd whisper. I didn't want anyone to hear me talking to someone who used the word "Scientology" so readily.

"I'm OT III," he said.

I nodded, as if I knew what he was talking about. Clearly, being OT III was a big deal. His eyes were the color of the ocean in cruise advertisements. He was a brilliant musician. He ran a music school. I could not help but imagine those well-manicured fingers playing me as they did his bass. But there was no way I would have a relationship with a Scientologist!

A week or so later, when the trio again played Two Dollar Bill's, Jamie asked if I'd like to have another cup of tea. I said I didn't think he was the one.

"'The one'?" Jamie said, smiling. "Do you really think there's such a thing?"

I'd been teased for my belief in this, as I'd been for my certainty that it was possible to be perfect. I shrugged. "I just don't think we're . . ."

He smiled again. "Maybe not yet."

I AUDITIONED FOR a lead in a CBS movie of the week, was called back a number of times, even met Ron Howard, who'd be starring. But my agent called to say it had gone to someone else.

"I'm sorry, Sands," she said. "It would have been a breakout role for you."

I knew the capricious nature of the career I'd decided to pursue, but the disappointment churned up by this news felt connected to larger losses, inchoate and mysterious. I wept far more than was appropriate. It was hard to return to filling creamers and rolling paper napkins around a knife and fork.

A few mornings later, the phone rang in my little Beachwood apartment. "Good morning, Sands."

"Good morning, Bernard."

I was still in bed, thinking about the Peace Corps. I'd recently sent for an application. I lay back, phone to an ear. Bernard was a San Francisco lawyer about fifteen years older than I, whose attentions I wanted to appreciate. He was intelligent and generous and kind. However, even though he was in his mid-forties, he looked and moved as if he were seventy.

"Is it a good morning? You sound a bit sad."

"Well, it's a beautiful morning, anyway."

A breeze moved the leaves of the tree outside the window, causing sunlight to flicker on the bedspread. Birds wheedled. Later that day I'd be waitressing, for which focus and activity I was grateful.

"You don't sound as if you think it's a beautiful morning, either."

"I want it to be." I gave a little laugh. "*Hope springs eternal . . .*"

"*. . . in the human breast*," Bernard finished the phrase. He made a curious huffing noise. "Do you know the origin of that phrase?"

I wiped my eyes with a corner of a sheet. "No."

"It's Alexander Pope. You know that, of course."

I didn't but didn't say so.

"Here's the rest of that couplet, Sands: *Man never is, but always to be, blest.*"

An anguished wail began to twine around my heart. "Say it again?"

"Not that this is such a great thing to ponder, especially on a morning you're not feeling particularly happy. But I find it irritating that people repeat that phrase with no sense of what Pope is actually saying! '*Man never is, but always to be, blest.*'"

The impact of this phrase was enormous. The notion that we keep ourselves afloat by imagining that any day now things will make sense, that we'll be "blessed," and yet we never will be, shifted my sense of life, of living. It was Sisyphus, hoping that this time he'll finally manage to push the stone all the way up the hill—but of course it always slips from him and rolls back to the bottom and he has to start again.

And if Sisyphus does get the rock to the top of, even over, the hill, what then?

All that day, Pope's words hovered: *man never is*—and as I served salads and burgers that night—*but always to be blest*—the jazz trio once again worked its magic. Between sets Jamie found me. We flirted gently. At the end of my shift I found that my car had been boxed in. It was 2:00 A.M. The drivers were not in the café. The band was though; they were packing up their instruments. Jamie held out a hand for my keys. Backing and filling, he succeeded in edging my car into the street. As he slid out of the driver's seat, I allowed myself to adore that strong jaw, those blue eyes, the fingers that ran up and down the frets of his upright bass with such grace, such strength, such facility.

"I think I might have been a bit hasty," I said.

He gave a little courtly bow. "I'll call you tomorrow."

MUCH ABOUT JAMIE was entrancing: full lips, blue eyes, skin smooth as marble but warm. He was rock-star handsome, with a fey, elfin quality—he usually wore black Chinese slippers, which caused him to glide more than step—and he could play any instrument put before him. A wizard on bass, known in the business as an extraordinary session player, he'd contributed to the albums of major jazz artists, including Chick Corea. But as a result of that recent "intensive" of auditing, when he'd attained OT III, his epiphany was that he no longer wanted to make a living as a performer. His calling was to create a music school. He was now hard at work standardizing his courses and training teachers.

He worked really hard at this, often, I gathered, staying up all night. One day he invited me to brunch with friends. He arrived very late to pick me up, clearly having just awoken, and we joined the group long after they'd finished their eggs. I thought it terribly rude, but they seemed to find it unremarkable. I remember Stanley Clarke was there, and Al Jarreau, as well as other musicians celebrated in jazz circles but—except for Chick Corea—unknown to me.

In homage to those lost New York Sunday brunches, I ordered a Bloody Mary. By the time the waitress delivered it, I realized that no one else at the table was drinking alcohol and was tempted to pour it into a nearby potted shrub. However, except for that grave lapse, the people around the table seemed perfectly normal. Chick Corea and his sparkling-eyed wife, Gayle Moran, were lovely, smart, and accomplished. There was chat about a recent tour, and laughter about Gayle's affection for Valentine's Day.

"Wait until you hear Gayle sing 'My Funny Valentine' to Chick," a woman next to me said. "The sweetest!"

My fears began to feel ridiculous, based on negative press, misunderstandings of Scientology's intentions. Because, as the comfortable buzz of talk around the table began to rotate largely around Scientology, what they explained made sense.[28]

"Each of us *has* a body, and each of us *has* a mind." Jamie was talking to Al Jarreau as much as to me. "But each of us *is* a spirit—you can think of the body as a container."

In spite of an intense interest in matters spiritual, in spite of years of meditating, this idea, which of course is not novel, struck me forcibly. Before this, I don't think I'd particularly thought of those entities as separate from one another.

Jamie went on to explain that there are two kinds of minds: "The Analytical Mind is where we store things we're clear about. And then there's the Reactive Mind."

One of Jamie's friends added that the Reactive Mind is full of "charge," and explained, "Charge is all those unexamined memories and misunderstoods that make us behave in erratic and misemotional ways." He made a loony face. Everyone laughed.

The ideas made sense, but the language seemed peculiar: *Misunderstoods*? *Misemotional*?

"That's what's covered in Book One, *Dianetics*," a woman named Barb said.

Jamie nodded and said that Hubbard found that what he covered in *Dianetics* hadn't gone far enough. He realized there had to be something that *looks* at those images. "So LRH named the thing that does the looking, what other religions call the spirit or the soul, the thetan."

"Thetan," I repeated. The word sounded as if someone with a lisp said "Satan."

"See," someone said, "the thetan is aware of being aware."

Aware of being aware. I liked that very much. It tied in with my meditating efforts.

"The thetan *activates* the body," Barb said. She was tall and graceful and didn't look the least bit odd. None of them did. They seemed intelligent and kind.

It made me think of a painting I'd seen in a Madrid museum during that long-ago family trip to Europe. In it, people have gathered around a man whose chalky white body is naked except for a cloth draped across his loins. One pale leg dangles off the bed. He's clearly dead. His face is peaceful, but the people surrounding his body are grieving. High in the right-hand corner of the painting the artist had painted a wraith, a little white gauzy coil. Dad, holding my hand, had pointed to it.

"See that? That's the spirit, rising from the body."

Clutching Dad's big hand, I'd nodded, vaguely grasping that our bodies are activated by *something*. Scientology appeared to agree with that idea.

"I understand how the soul activates the body," I said, "but where do those two kinds of minds fit in?" I'd always figured that mind and soul were pretty much the same.

Jamie floated his spoon above the remains of eggs benedict on his plate. "Here's you, the awareness unit—that is, the soul, the thetan—looking at those pictures. *You* are looking at memories stored in your Analytical Mind"—he tapped the plate—"the ones that you're clear about. But you can't be quite so clear about ones you *react* to. You react maybe without knowing why you're reacting, or why the reaction is, perhaps, so big."

As he rummaged the spoon around in a smear of egg yolk, there was a comfortable growl of laughter at this representation of the Reactive Mind. I appreciated the "show, don't tell" nature of the demonstration—it was a writer's phrase I'd heard all my life, and in my mind, Scientology gained points for utilizing this wisdom.

Tucking the spoon under the plate, Jamie lifted it slightly, to more laughter—the spirit-spoon inhabiting the plate-body. He broke a crumb apart to show how auditing allows you to examine a buried memory that is working on you in unknown ways.

Barb hastened to add that it wasn't that auditing makes you forget.

Gesturing at Jamie's plate, she said that all those "memory crumbs" were still there, just no longer clumped together, because the memory was no longer unexamined. Auditing, she said, moves the memory from the Reactive Mind to the Analytical Mind, so there's no longer a reaction when that button is pressed.

"That's where the idea of Clear comes from," she said. "All the buttons on the adding machine have to be 'cleared' if the computation is to be correct."

This analogy to a machine, especially an old-fashioned one, was disappointing. I wanted to be clear like a mountain stream. But I thought about Milton holding the actor's jaw and asking those gentle questions. So far, none of this seemed outrageous.

"You see," Barb said, "the thetan *looks* at the memories. Good and bad. But the mind doesn't always process them correctly, and that's got to be cleared up. That's where auditing comes in. And sometimes—here's the really cool thing—you remember incidents that couldn't have happened this lifetime!"

I nodded, thrilled. I'd always wondered about past lifetimes, why some historical periods seem so much more familiar and vivid than others.

"That's because there are all these *other* lives you've lived. And you—the you of you, the thetan—*carries* those memories! Which is where Scientology comes in."

She began to laugh. "You know that phrase 'Life's a bitch, and then you die'? Well, for us, it's 'Life's a bitch, and then you live forever'!"

This was greeted by roars of laughter. I laughed, too.

I EXCUSED MYSELF to go to the bathroom, feeling a roil of conflicting emotions that would characterize my relationship to Scientology for years to come: wanting to leave, to get back to life as I knew it, no matter how mysterious and confusing, while, simultaneously, being drawn to the certainty it offered. The happiness it seemed to promise.

When I returned to the table, they were talking about something called the Dynamics. There appeared to be eight of them, and they were about survival.[29]

"But more than just survival! About living well!" Jamie smiled up at me.

I didn't sit back down. I was trying to find a moment to ask if we could leave. I would have him drop me at my apartment and we would say goodbye, The End.

The First Dynamic seemed to have to do with your relationship to yourself: as simple as hygiene, or what you choose to wear, your education, certainly your spiritual path.

"And then there's the Second Dynamic," Jamie said. "That's the one you have with your family, and of course with your spouse and your children."

I slid back into my chair. We carefully didn't meet each other's eyes. He moved his spoon to be with the knife and fork: family. The group watched with grins on their faces.

Someone else described the Third Dynamic: survival through various groups you're part of, relationships you have with friends and also through work. "Such as fellow Scientologists," someone offered. I did my best not to wince.

"Lots of groups," Jamie said, quickly. "For some of us, the group known as Jazz Musicians. For Sands, the group might be Actors."

I nodded, relieved. "I see. Like the Democrats."

An uncomfortable silence descended.

"We don't get into politics much," Jamie said. "There's too much other work to be done." At what must have been my puzzled face, he added, "On the planet. There's really insidious stuff going on. That's why we're all on the Bridge—the Bridge to Total Freedom! Because then we can save the planet."

It seemed kind of arrogant, that they thought they were capable of saving the planet (whatever that meant), although I was touched that they wanted to.

They began to gather purses and jackets, and there was a general exodus. Several remained in the parking lot, talking and smoking. I stood in their midst, as if I were one of them. Which I was not! Yet we'd been talking about important things! Issues of art! And life. And purpose. Except for the lack of white wine that should go with such conversations, this could have been a lunch around my parents' table. And here was this handsome, talented, respected man by my side. Who just then took my hand, holding it as we waved goodbye and walked across the parking lot. After a moment, I curled my fingers into his.

As we drove, the air between us fluttered, full of promise, and no little terror.

"So you got as far as the Third Dynamic," I said, to say something. "What's the Fourth?"

"Survival as a species." He grinned. "So you like the Dynamics?"

"I like how they order things. Sometimes life feels awfully chaotic."

"You'll find a lot of order in Scientology." He described the other Dynamics. They appeared to cover everything from self to family to nature to the physical universe to spirit to infinity. "Some might call that god, but we don't, usually. 'The allness of all,'" he quoted.

I was absolutely fascinated, even as I feared this might be exactly the way one got dragged into the dread cult. Who hadn't heard of the lawsuits, power mongering, bullying, financial excesses?

But on the other hand! The organization! It was so orderly! Everything could be broken down into its component parts and *explained.*

Also, just because you got involved with someone who belonged to a particular religion didn't mean you had to get involved too. One might *say* one was Christian, or Jewish, or Buddhist, or, I supposed, even a Scientologist—*was* it a religion?—but it didn't take over one's life. Especially not a Hall's life.

My understanding of the possible role of religion, especially in regards to marriage, was not just blithe. It was fantastically ignorant.

THAT'S SOURCE!

Jamie's absolute faith in what he called the "Tech" troubled me. Yet his explanations of Scientology notions were compelling. And doubts got swept under the rug when we kissed.

One afternoon, as we were having tea at the round wooden table in his kitchen, he said, "It's very important that you understand the whole overt/withhold phenomenon." He placed the emphasis on the first syllable: *o*vert.

"Do you mean o*vert*, like something that's really obvious?"

"Nope. Not an adjective. A noun." (This kind of clarity of language, common to Scientologists, I found very appealing.) He fetched a thick red book. On the cover, its title was embossed in gold: *Dianetics and Scientology Technical Dictionary.* "I shouldn't be explaining these things to you," he said. "That can lead to misunderstoods, and even to squirreling."

"Squirreling?"

He flipped pages. "Squirrel," he read. "'Those who engage in actions altering Scientology, and offbeat practices.'[30] Because the Tech is so powerful, and people see that it is, it's possible to take pieces of it and use them for your own purposes. Werner Erhard, for example. He took a few Scientology courses, read a ton of Hubbard's books, and squirreled all that into those self-help seminars he runs, 'est.' Because it's the Tech, it works, but because it's not the whole Tech, it can be damaging. That's squirreling. The way to keep that from happening, the way to keep Scientology working, is to always go to Source."

"Source?"

"What Hubbard says. He's Source." He placed the open volume before me, and leafed to the page that held the words OVERT ACT.

> **Overt act** 1. An overt act isn't just injuring someone or something; an overt act is an act of omission or commission which does the least good for the least number of dynamics or the most harm to the greatest number of dynamics. (HCOPL 1 Nov 1970 III) 2. An intentionally committed harmful act committed in an effort to solve a problem. (SH Spec 44, 6410C27) 3. That thing which you do that you aren't willing to have happen to you. (ISH AAA 10, 6009C14)

Jamie pointed. "If you want to find the policy letter or bulletin or tape these quotes are taken from, inside these parentheses is the information you need. For instance, 'HCOPL' means the Hubbard Communications Office Policy Letter you can refer to. 'SH Spec' are the tapes he recorded at Saint Hill, the big Org in England, and the numbers are where in the tape you can find that quote."

I stared. "This must have taken so much work!"

He nodded. "If you aren't able to define words—LRH covers this in the Study Tech materials—you have misunderstoods, and those can lead to overts and even blowing. This way, see, if you define a word, and it's still not clear, you can go to where Hubbard used it and read it in context. You can always go to Source." He pushed away from the table and headed up the stairs. "Let me show you something. Come on."

After a moment, I followed. Source! It sounded so totalitarian! Or so ultra-religious. Weird, in any case. My stomach churned.

The second floor, in addition to the living room and bedroom, held his study. One shelf was loaded with a row of huge red books.

Another shelf held a row of equally large green ones. There were at least a dozen volumes in each set, beautifully bound.

"The red ones are the Tech vols," Jamie said, reaching for one. "Everything LRH wrote about auditing. Also Study Tech, lots of stuff." The pages were legal-sized, which meant the volume was long as well as thick. "See, it's all HCOPLs or HCOBs—policy letters or bulletins. That's Source!"

I didn't want to touch it. The whole thing was so unsettling—and so intriguing.

But they looked really well bound. "They must cost the earth," I said.

He nodded, running a finger along the spines of the green books. "These vols have everything to do with admin, about starting and running an organization—I mean, look how Scientology is thriving and expanding all over the planet! So these are essential as I build my music school. I just bought them. And yes," he said proudly. "They cost a lot."

I followed him back down the stairs.

"So," he said, "overts! We don't want those coming between us. Because that creates what's called a withhold." He read from the *Tech Dictionary*: "A withhold is 'an unspoken, unannounced transgression against a moral code by which the person was bound.'[31] See," he said, "a withhold makes you pull away. Where there was high affinity, there's now going to be zilch, or sudden unexplained resentment."

I nodded. "You think you can't tell the person what you've done. And maybe that leads to even more transgressions—I mean, *o*verts?"

"Well done!" He looked pleased. "Then things go downhill. You feel you can't talk to him anymore, you begin to justify the original overt, you even feel it's *his* fault. That's called a 'motivator'—you come up with a 'reason' you 'had' to commit that overt. It can even lead to blowing—you feel so much guilt, you just leave! So it's always important to examine, when you feel like you need to get out of something—a relationship, a job, whatever—what you might have done to create that feeling."

My head was spinning. "Wow," I said.

"It's all about ethics. Ethics is very, very important."

INDEED, I BEGAN to realize that ethics, and ethical behavior, were an enormous aspect of Church doctrine. Even as I appreciated the order it imposed, I found it worrisome how often people in Scientology were "out-ethics." One morning I watched as Jamie dressed entirely in black, down to shiny and uncomfortable leather shoes.

"Do you have a business meeting or something?" I asked, incredulous. I'd never seen him out of his Chinese cloth shoes, much less in a suit.

As he perched a foot on the edge of a chair to tie the laces, he told me that one of his teachers in his music school had gone "out-ethics."

"What did he do?"

"You don't need to know." He rustled around in a drawer for a tie. A tie! "Since right now it's only me running my Org, I hold every post. Today I have to be the Ethics Officer. Dave has committed some overts, and he's got some motivators going. My dressing all in black will get my attitude about it across, don't you think?"

I did think.

As I also saw that one could go "out-ethics" easily. Transgressions abounded. But not just transgressions. If something went wrong—you broke a favorite bowl, you snapped a string on your guitar, you cracked your car's engine block—you'd done something to "create" it. If you looked deeply enough, what that was could be found.

This was familiar territory. I'd been brought up with this idea. You just had to look for the metaphor. A few months earlier—prior to meeting Jamie or hearing anything about Scientology—I'd still been seeing Roger from time to time, and one day I lost the key to my house. As I phoned a locksmith, I knew exactly what it meant: I needed to "change my locks," to be resolute about breaking things off with him. The cracked engine block came about because I'd allowed my parents to loan me a car when I should have purchased one for myself. I broke the bowl because I shouldn't have had ice cream. The snapped string was more complicated, but I managed to figure it out: I was working on a song I'd written about Roger even though I was now seeing Jamie; the shocking twang of that string was a warning.

So Scientology's notions landed on well-tilled soil. But I couldn't fathom Jamie's certainty that it was "the only way." One morning, as he was extolling this aspect of Hubbard's accomplishments, I laughed.

He rolled out of the sheets and sat on the edge of the bed, his back to me.

"Jamie," I said. "Religions always say theirs is the 'only way.' It's a ridiculous claim."

He turned, his face marred with fury. "L. Ron Hubbard has It. All. Figured. Out." His movements fierce, he stood, shoved his legs into his pants, buttoned and zipped.

"I'm sorry, Jamie. I didn't mean to insult you, if that's what I did. I'm sorry."

"You don't get it. Just wait until you're OT. Then you'll see the *mess* this planet's in! And how Hubbard's the only one, with *the only way*, to get us out of here."

He left the bedroom. I heard the jingle of keys and the thud of the front door. He'd rented an office for his music school, and I knew that's where he was headed.

I wrote an irate note and headed home. I was done. Forget it! He was loony-*tooney*.

But as I started my car, music from a cassette he'd given me, a beautiful melody he'd composed on the piano, soared through the speakers. As I drove home, lyrics began to form.

She's
free from her cocoon
changing with the moon
shining like the sun
Finally
you've found her

the one
but don't hold on
don't crush her wings
Butterfly

Perfect! "Butterfly" would be my way of telling him we were done. Butterfly/Goodbye!

But even as I worked on lyrics about "letting go," I thought about how we could do this. We could be a songwriting team!

I called him. His surliness abated under my barrage of apologies. Later that week, I sang him the song. It was clear he'd no idea the lyrics were intended to be about us. As we worked on fitting the words more precisely to the music, the attraction was heartily there again.

"You know," Jamie said, "we should get married."

I kept my eyes lowered. But as we kept working, strengthening a word, adjusting the length of a note, our life unrolled before me. With my words and his music, we'd compose award-winning songs. We'd perform together. We'd have a band—we'd tour the world! We'd *change* the world! We'd sing for peace and . . . well, all kinds of good things. We'd have a marriage full of creativity and friends and wine and travel and candlelight and love!

I took in the curve of his jaw, the fingers that had learned to play me well. About half an hour later, I said, "Maybe we should do that thing you mentioned."

He nodded. "Okay."

I'M NOT SURE how I broke it to my parents that I planned to marry a Scientologist. I imagine I presented Jamie's bona fides: He's a jazz musician! He's friends with Chick Corea! He runs a music school, he owns a home in the Hollywood Hills . . . I do remember that I tried a diversionary tactic by bringing in Dianetics.

"*Dianetics?*" Mother's voice had risen a full octave by the last syllable. "Sands, in the fifties, that book was a cocktail party *joke*!"

Oh, ummm.

"People sat around and did that silly exercise of asking for an 'earlier, similar incident.' 'Earlier, sillier,' is more like it. We *howled* with laughter at the things that got invented."

"Well . . ."

"Now don't go making a big mistake. You have a whole life ahead of you."

"But I love him, Mom."

"I just don't know how we could have a Scientologist to dinner."

I not only understood her concern, I shared it. Nevertheless, I held on to my intention to marry Jamie as if it were a bucking horse and I the most determined of riders. I would not be unseated in spite of knowing I could—*should*—let go, fall to the ground, dust myself off, and get the hell out of the corral. As often as I felt this, however, I also felt the opposite: This was destiny. He was the perfect man for me. Finally, the love I'd thought and talked and sung about for so long had arrived. The curve of his capable forearm, the blond hairs glinting there, allowed me to shrug away the incessant smell of cigarettes, the ubiquitous black cloth shoes, the religion that swirled through every aspect of his life.

But we fought, a lot. I obsessively watched other couples, wondering if they argued as much as we did. Did they have issues to "confront"? Did they stay up all night and "handle" (with some piece of Hubbard's Tech) whatever had cropped up between them?

The pages of my journals during this time vacillate between grave doubts, grateful musings that we'd found each other, and wondering if (as I scribbled on one page) "I'm going to have to look into Scientology." Yet I continued to have a problem with Jamie's assertion that it was the "only workable system."

I asked what he meant by "workable."

"I've told you about the Dynamics, I've told you about ethics, I've told you about Admin Tech," he said. "These are just a *fraction* of the ways Hubbard has ordered life into parts that anyone can understand—and he offers ways to *fix* things when they go wrong. No other religion does that. They rely on vague things like prayer, meditation. Do those things *work*? Maybe sometimes, but not *always*. Scientology is a *system*. It *works*. *Always*."

Around this we circled and circled, at the kitchen table after breakfast, in his car driving home from a gathering of his friends, on a beach watching happy people (were they *really* happy?) tossing a ball. I see, now, that I was arguing with the idea that I was going to have to dive in.

"You talk about the chaos, Sands, it ends the chaos."

I remembered the predawn moment in my New York apartment after I'd heard that my brother had fallen from a bridge and mashed his skull, when I'd put my forehead to the floor, praying to *something*. Ending the chaos was very appealing.

WE SET THE wedding for October. I wanted to use the Squaw Valley house, as Tracy had when she got married. I wanted to wear Mother's satin wedding dress, as Tracy had also done.

Why the rush? Mother wanted to know. Why not wait until spring, when the wedding could be held outdoors? Tracy and David's wedding had been a magnificent party. Why not do the same?

But Jamie and I were both in a strange hurry.

That summer, 1982, we headed to Oregon to visit his family and friends. We spent almost a month on that trip, and sometimes I wondered lazily if all this time away from my own friends and family, and with so much talk about Scientology, was a kind of indoctrination. Perhaps because we did some camping, it reminded me of those eighteen months in Europe so long ago, when it was just family, for months and months, and how it had solidified us *as* a family.

One afternoon, as Jamie and I pitched our tent near a lake, a terrible headache took hold. It stretched from my lower back, up my spine, and across the crown of my head—ganglia of outrageous pain. Jamie, like all Scientologists, didn't approve of aspirin or ibuprofen, and I seldom used them either—ancient family injunction—except to relieve cramps when I got my period. But I'd never had such a headache. I knew it had to do with Scientology, the pervasive thing it was becoming as we headed toward marriage. Jamie and I talked about that as well. He was so understanding, so very kind as we (in a journal I refer to it as *that fucking Scn phrase*) "handled" it.

We also visited his parents, who lived in a double-wide. They'd once had a lovely house, Jamie explained, but when he and his brothers moved out, his parents downsized. I fretted: My in-laws-to-be lived in a *trailer*? What would my parents say!

One morning, as I was helping with dishes, his mother confided, "Jamie's been a Scientologist for almost ten years. We so hope you'll pull him away, but we fear it will be the other way around."

As Jamie and I drove up the Oregon coast to visit musician friends, I pressed myself against the passenger door, wishing I could slide out and hitchhike back to Los Angeles. But I'd given up my apartment. I'd moved in with Jamie the month before.

"What is it?" Jamie said, several times. "What is going on?"

"Nothing. Stop asking! Nothing!"

He grew quite stern. "You're acting like you have a withhold, Sands. Your affinity for me is way down. Do you need to tell me something?"

The implication, of course, was that I'd committed an overt, because a withhold is what manifests after you've done something wrong. As the sour day went by, I realized what it was: His mother had criticized something he held dear. And I hadn't defended him!

I didn't want to have a withhold. I wanted to be good. So I coughed up what she'd said.

"Flunk!" he said, furious. "Major flunk!" He asked for details, "wearing his auditor's hat," as he termed it, meaning he did not interrupt or challenge or contradict. I understood this was what happened in an auditing session: getting every little bit of the overt expressed so that nothing was left to fester. It made sense. Kind of like irradiating cancer cells so they could creep no further.

That night our "affinity" was back. We laughed with his friends, crawled happily into the bed they provided, made delicious love.

"You see how getting off that withhold made things okay between us again?" Jamie whispered. "That's Tech. It works!"

I saw that it "worked." But soon after, we tangled again. And again. Back at his parents', I searched for what I might have done this time. All I could come up with was that I was nervous about Scientology. In fact, it terrified me.

"That's your parents speaking, not you," Jamie said sternly. "You care too much about what they think. It's *your* life!"

I utterly saw his point. And yet. What if I had the same thoughts as my parents, but they were still *my* thoughts? Wasn't that possible? That my concerns might be valid even if my concerns were also theirs? It was exhausting to think about.

I allowed as how their life seemed kind of lovely; what might be wrong about emulating it? Books and dinner parties and friends and laughter and wine and music . . .

"That's all surface stuff," Jamie said. "There's a lot more to life, to *really* living."

It seems like good surface stuff, I didn't say. Yet I knew what he meant: it was that Sisyphean, existential nightmarish possibility: *Man always is, but never to be, blest.*

"But Scientology *costs* so much. Where's the money go? What if there's something, ummm, *not* so good about that part of it?"

"Those are *lies*," he whispered, fiercely (his parents were asleep down the hall). "Your mom and dad are feeding you these rumors, this terrible, evil, *black* PR. It's *not* a greedy, moneymaking enterprise! Hubbard is trying to make this planet a better place for everyone!"

He'd gone on in this vein. I tried not to listen. I'd decided. As soon as we got back to Los Angeles, I was calling off the wedding.

HOW MUCH ELECTRICITY?

The next day, our final in Oregon, we visited the Delphian School, where a friend of Jamie's was the executive director. Still chafing from our fight the night before—we'd gone to sleep without resolving it, which was easy to do, as his parents insisted we sleep in separate rooms—I said, snottily, that I'd heard it was some kind of "Scientology school."

"Sure, it's founded on Hubbard's ideas," Jamie said. "But it's not like they study Scientology. They just use the Tech to help them learn."

I shrugged and stared out at the passing Oregonian green. Unexpectedly, Jamie took a hand off the wheel and twined his fingers into mine. After a long moment in which I wished I was on the deck of my parents' house, laughing over a glass of wine with them, I squeezed back. I did envy his certainty, and that of his Scientology friends. I couldn't imagine being that certain about anything.

Delphi's executive director escorted us around the school's property, describing its mission and vision. There must have been buildings, as the place was built in 1933 as a Jesuit novitiate, but in my memory it's a vast acreage of empty fields and ominous-looking wooden outbuildings in disrepair. What existed of the school so far—course rooms, dormitories, kitchen, dining and living areas—appeared to be contained within a single three-story house.

The ED's office was nestled in a corner room on the ground floor.

Its two large windows, shaded by trees, created a space that felt dim and green. Beneath the windows stood a desk, and on the desk was an e-meter.

Jamie had told me about the e-meter, the electrometer, and I knew it had to with auditing.[32] It worked like a lie detector, he said, but was "much more precise." Auditing, Jamie said, involved holding a tin can in each hand, which were connected to the meter by wires. The smallest bit of electricity was passed from the meter through the wire to the can in one hand, and the electricity then sought its way, through the person's body, to the can in the other hand. En route, the electricity, and therefore the meter, could find and read reactions—"charge"—the person might have about whatever subject was under discussion.[33]

It sounded fascinating. Still, when Jamie first explained it, I'd asked, a little horrified, "How much electricity?"

He assured me it was infinitesimal. "Just enough to detect where you've got 'charge.' Usually it's attached to fear or grief or anger. There's stored energy there, and the auditor helps you find it—the needle on the meter bumps or jumps. It's amazing to see it happen!"

So I'd heard about the e-meter, but this was the first time I'd seen one. As Jamie and the E.D. continued to discuss the enterprise the school represented, I squiggled my way slowly to and around the desk to peer at it.

It looked fairly innocuous. An oval of blue plastic, the surface of which was slanted up so as to be visible, held a couple of dials and several oval windows, one of them rather large. That must be the meter. Yes. There was a needle, relaxed completely to the left. A glowing red light indicated that the meter was on. Next to the e-meter were two silver cylindrical objects, which did appear to be nothing more than slim tin cans, including a kind of charming galvanized seam.

I reached for them. My heart thudded. As I wrapped my palms around them, the needle in the meter bumped. And in a test of everything I'd been hearing about auditing, about Scientology, about this thing called "charge," with conscious intention I pulled up an image of and concentrated my thoughts on *Mother.* It would have been the visages of both parents I summoned, as I felt they were pretty much in agreement about everything.

The needle didn't just bump. It slammed to the right.

Oh my! It *worked*!

I'd heard enough about "charge" to understand that I had some regarding my parents. And the meter could "read" that charge! It was astounding to witness.

As if the leap of the needle had been audible, the ED turned and took me in with a curious smile. I put down the cans. I didn't know, then, that he was probably examining the fact that he was going to have to report himself. He'd not been diligent, and someone, a non-Scientologist no less, had accessed his e-meter. The next time he was in session, this lapse (overt) would come up. Even if he was solo-auditing, as one learned to do on the upper levels, he'd have to write up what the meter read. His best recourse would be to report it and assign himself an Ethics Handling. This is conjecture, but knowledge of what an auditor may assess from the behavior of the e-meter's needle, and an understanding of the built-in consequences, teaches one how to think and behave.

Gestapo-ian though it is, it has its positive side: If you know it will come up in session, you tend not to tell even a white lie. You leave the stray dollar where you found it, you do not make eye contact with the attractive man, you are "unreasonable" when someone quibbles with the Tech. As my dad put it, "Guilt is good."

As Jamie and I bumped our way back down the potholed road, I said nothing. I didn't want to describe what I'd seen, didn't want to discuss this forcible *proof* of what he and his friends had been saying: the e-meter's ability to recognize areas that might inhibit one from working to one's full potential. What if an auditor and an e-meter really could help eliminate such blockages, so one could live a fulfilled and happy life? And what of Jamie's insistence about Hubbard's *altruism*? The night before I'd rolled my eyes. But as I held a hand out the open window, palm riding the summer air, I experienced a moment of vast and illuminating possibility. What if it were all true? What if

Hubbard *did* have the best possible intentions? What if rumors to the contrary *were* nothing but, as Jamie put it, "black PR"?[34]

That night, I stared out at a moon that hung like a Christmas ornament from a high branch. Okay, maybe the e-meter did help you track down moments of charge and release them, thereby making you a more highly functioning person. But what if that little dose of electricity *addicted* you to the Church? What if those wires floated some kind of elixir through your corpuscles? What if it wasn't really a desire for everyone to enjoy the state of Clear that motivated Hubbard to design the e-meter, but a far more insidious purpose?

And yet, that moment with the e-meter indicated that it was possible to explore the "charge" I clearly had where my parents were concerned. What if Scientology *was* the "only way" to release their hold, to find my own purpose, to live life happily?

I buried my face in the pillow.

THE NEXT MORNING, as Jamie's mother placed an aromatic breakfast casserole of eggs, ground beef, and cheddar cheese on the sunlit table, Jamie confronted her about what she'd said to me, about hoping I'd get him to leave the Church.

"Don't you dare try and drive a wedge between us!" he said, his blue eyes stern and cold. "This is our spiritual path."

I was horrified. Why would he bring this up? Also, it *wasn't* my spiritual path!

Even as I was touched by that "our."

His mother looked at me, her face baffled and hurt, and went back to putting squares of casserole on flowered dishes. I felt awful.

Later, Jamie and I tangled about it in the hallway: "You didn't have to tell her I told you," I whispered.

"Of course I had to tell her!" He did not lower his voice. "I will not be reasonable! Our comm lines have to be kept squeaky clean!"

Again I tangled with Hubbard's reverse engineering of "reasonable," a word that had always designated (and no matter how hard I tried, always would) a positive attribute. Sometimes, grappling with how it was so good to be *un*reasonabl*e*, I felt like I was being asked to use, *Alice in Wonderland*–like, a flamingo as a croquet mallet.[35]

When Jamie's genial-faced father peered around a doorjamb to ask if we needed anything, Jamie stomped away to finish loading the car. I stayed out of the kitchen, although I wanted to fall to my knees on the linoleum and apologize.

As soon as we'd finished waving goodbye, Jamie and I argued for a dozen miles and sat in silence for fifty more. Arms and legs crossed, I stared out at the undulating grasses through which we were passing, twitching back and forth between the strange certainty I'd reached the day before and all the fighting we did, sure evidence of our unsuitability.

What if—oh *my*!—I became a Scientologist and *didn't* marry Jamie?

I gave a ghost of a laugh.

"What," Jamie said.

"Nothing," I said, folding my arms even more tightly.

As we passed from Oregon into California, Jamie spoke. "We have a *major* ARC Break going on here."

The letters are said separately—not "arc" but "A-R-C." I understood that the term meant something like "disagreement."

"I don't know what you mean," I said, sulky. "And why all this *lingo*!"

"Nomenclature," Jamie said.

This was Hubbard speaking. I'd begun to see that words like "nomenclature," "gradient," "obfuscate," and even "crepuscular"—Jamie's use of which, early on, had deeply impressed me—were part of his vocabulary because they were part of Hubbard's.

Jamie put on the blinker and slowed to pull off to the side of the freeway. "Musicians use terms that others might not understand. Actors have a special vocabulary, right? Well, that's nomenclature. 'ARC Break' is Scientology nomenclature. That's all."

I thought of gatherings with his friends, how sometimes I could hardly understand what they were talking about, except from context.

Often it sounded like a distinct language. Language connects people, of course, binding us into a uniquely shared world, while also serving as a barrier, separating us from others. It would take a long time to realize how Scientology's vocabulary, its nomenclature, abetted such binding, and how purposeful Hubbard had been in creating it. I knew then only that the orderly aspects of the religion were deeply appealing, helping me sort through a terrible, consuming confusion. It's difficult, now, to confront how, during this search for meaning, I chose to overlook, even ignore, the larger and very troubling ramifications of this belief system. Flunk.

As Jamie would sometimes say, "Major flunk."

Jamie cut the engine, opened the glove compartment, and began to pull out various objects. He intended to "demo" the concept for me. No matter how troubled or irritated I might be with him, this always managed to move me. His desire to help, to explain, to "save," was so earnest. Also, I approved of the "show, don't tell" aspect of it all.

He held a AAA battery on his open palm. "Here's Suzie Battery, and she and Joe Pressure Gauge"—he held up the gizmo used to check the air in the tires—"have recently met. There's a lot of *affinity* swirling around them, okay? That's the A."

He placed a stubby pencil between the battery and the gauge to represent the affinity. "So Suzie and Joe talk about a lot of things. They're *communicating*." He twined a broken rubber band around the two items to indicate all the talking that was going on. "That's C. And they decide on R, *reality*: lunch at noon on Friday at the Map of Oregon Restaurant."

The map was between our seats. He slid it onto the dashboard to represent both the reality and, I gathered, the restaurant. He placed Suzie Battery on the map.

"So what they have, you see, is understanding! They *understand* that they like each other. They also share an understanding there might be a future there. For understanding, there must be all three things: affinity, *and* reality, *and* communication. It's an equation: A + R + C = U!"

Cars flew past on the freeway, making Jamie's hatchback rock in the wind of their passing. Around us stretched the late-August, dun-colored fields of northern California. He tapped the battery on the map.

"So Suzie arrives at noon on Friday at the Map of Oregon Restaurant with the reality that Joe will join her. But Joe doesn't show up at noon. He doesn't show up at quarter past. Suzie waits until one o'clock! That's how high her affinity is!"

"But not anymore!"

Jamie was describing us: I was always early; he was always late.

"And why?" he said. "Because Joe didn't show up when he said he would: *reality*." He didn't *communicate*, letting her know he was going to be late. So her *affinity* is way down."

"She's *furious*."

"That's because there's a break in *understanding*. So here's the thing. If there's an upset, no matter how big or small, it *always* means there's a problem with at least one of those three things: affinity, reality, or communication. That's an ARC Break." Again the car rocked as a semi roared past. "But Hubbard shows us how it can be solved. How do you think that happens?"

I shrugged. "They talk. Duh."

"Bingo! They *communicate*! Joe calls and tells her he was stuck on the freeway because there'd been a huge accident and he couldn't get to a phone for almost three hours!"

"That's not why you're always late, Jamie. You're late because you don't ever take into account the time it takes to actually *get* someplace—"

"*Beam me up, Scotty!*" he crowed. "The world should work like that: leave where I am and *bang*"—he snapped his fingers—"*be* where I'm going. That will happen when I'm truly OT."

Jamie's description of being an Operating Thetan made me think of Eastern religions: the yogi on a remote mountain pinnacle who knows someone's going to show up even though there's no way he could have that information; the woman who has cobras weaving and spitting at her yet doesn't get bitten; the man in a turban sitting cross-legged on a carpet zipping around above the rest of us. The yogi, the woman, the turbaned man so adept in their spiritual paths that they can "operate" their bodies and the world around them.

"Of course, you can solve the upset by finding other ways to get the affinity back," Jamie said. "Or other ways to bridge the reality gap. But usually it takes communication."

He replaced the objects in the glove compartment and lit a cigarette. We sat in silence. As someone who could be mesmerized by the metaphor—the "demo"—of just about anything, I made hay with the ribbon of pavement unspooling ahead, the tired fields on either side stretching into the distance.

"So, as I was saying." Jamie blew smoke. "What we have here is a major ARC Break. Because my reality is that Scientology works. And that is not a reality for you. And in spite of a lot of communication, it's affecting our affinity. Do you see?"

"I can't believe one religion has all the answers! It's so—*right-wing*! It's impossible!"

But for a moment I was back in the ED's office, sidling toward the e-meter, picking up those cans, watching the needle slam to the right.

"It's *not* impossible." Jamie sighed. "It's the Bridge to Total Freedom."

"And what do you mean by 'freedom,' Jamie! What do we need to be freed from?"

"Well, you won't understand all that until you get on the upper levels. When you study the OT materials, you'll get what a mess we're in. It's secret stuff. If you read it before you're on the upper levels, it'll make you crazy..."

I rolled my eyes, as I did every time I heard the idea that there were materials so upsetting that just *reading* them before you were properly prepared could make you psychotic.

Scientology's "confidential materials" did seem to be kept confidential, but little bits got through. For instance, I understood that we'd once had vast powers, now diminished. Early on, I'd even heard the name of the terrible despot who'd done the diminishing, and for a few minutes, even though I knew it was absurd, actually tested my mental waters to see if psychosis was setting in. Something called the Wall of Fire was clearly important. The rest of it? This was pre-Internet, so the Church was largely able keep those bizarre materials in hand. But I truly believe, no matter how intriguing and even useful I found some of the Tech, that if I'd known the weird details—somewhere between sci-fi and a horror movie—that you learned on those upper levels, I'd have fled. There's a reason these materials are kept confidential. You don't study them until you're indoctrinated, or so settled into friendships and community that it's hard to be the one who questions, who points out that the emperor has no clothes.

". . . and the *only* way to regain our *full potential* is to move up the Bridge so we can escape all this." Jamie threw his arms wide, taking in the freeway, cars, fields. "MEST—matter and energy and space and time? Scientology provides *the way out*."

I touched his arm. "I kind of like MEST," I said, though I knew what he was trying to articulate. "I like the sun. I like my skirt." I moved my fingers against his wrist. "I like your skin, which is pretty full of matter and energy and all that."[36]

I always surprised myself when I did this sort of thing, and I did it often: hopping back in the suitcase just as the lid opened enough for me to slide out of it. Why did I not seize these clear opportunities to leave? I think part of it, early on, was driven by a misapprehension of how huge a role Scientology played in Jamie's life. Certainly, at the time, I had no idea of the power wielded by his religion. And I wanted to not have been wrong, to not have made, ignoring the warnings of parents and friends, a mistake. I wanted, desperately, to believe in the happy-ever-after I'd chosen.

He ground out his cigarette and started the car. "Your reality and mine are far apart on this one. Our affinity helps—"

"And we talk a lot."

He gave me a look, amused but dismissive, and pulled back onto the freeway. "Yes, we communicate. But the reality is a problem. You need to explore Scientology, Sands. Once you start, you'll understand. It's the only way."

I stared out the window. It was true that a lot of it did seem to make sense. That A + R + C = Understanding, for instance.[37] That seemed kind of irrefutable. Or the connected notion that a "break" in affinity or reality or communication caused problems.[38] The idea of spirits (thetans) activating bodies. That unexplored, reactive parts of your mind make you behave in irrational ways. The Dynamics and the way they ordered a messy universe. Taking responsibility for your overts and "getting off" withholds so affinity could flow back in.

And that meter, those cans, which in my hands had definitely responded to *something*.

A COMB, PERHAPS A CAT

So in spite of blaring, honking, red-light-pulsing signals, Jamie and I continued down the road toward marriage. My parents, aghast at the abyss I was intent on throwing myself into, nevertheless cast a wide guest list, held the reception in our family home, and for the occasion rented Queen of the Snows, a Catholic church whose vast soaring windows framed Squaw Peak.

A number of Jamie's friends, in a kind of Merry Prankster endeavor, drove from LA in an old school bus. In the hubbub, Jamie's family arrived: his parents, his brothers and their wives, and Brooke, his five-year-old niece, who'd be our flower girl, all blinking as the hustle and din of creating a splendid Hall gathering swirled around them.

Was my brother there? I don't remember. I think he was back in Albany; Capital Rep was producing his *Frankenstein.* I think I'd remember him at the wedding. I'd remember his mangled, mocking face. It would have been a sweet mocking, the way he answered the phone: How clichéd it is to answer a phone, yet here I am answering it. How clichéd it is it to get married, yet here you are, getting hitched, as I once did. How clichéd it is to be a brilliant writer who dies young, yet here I am—well, not dead, but . . .

The night before the wedding, we all gathered around a long table in the Annex, a house my parents had recently purchased, just down the hill from their own. Cornish game hens were passed, wine poured, toasts offered. I picked at the tiny bones, before slipping away to the upper house, where I sat at the piano and played a few notes.

All this effort was being made *on my behalf*! No matter my parents' feelings about the groom, the wedding would be worthy of a Hall. Because they loved me, they were doing everything to support my decision.

It was my decision.

I put my forehead on the piano keys in a smoosh of dissonance. I should call it off. I should go back down to the Annex and tell them all I'm sorry. I made a mistake. Please go home. Forgive me.

Sitting there on that piano bench, I wrestled with the huge angel of certainty that told me the marriage was *wrong*. I walked back to the Annex. All eyes turned to me as I came through the door. How I wish, how I wish, I'd taken that moment to stand firm and say, "Thank you all so much for the love this represents, but I'm calling it off." But I didn't.

LIKE TRACY, AND Brett, too, when she got married, I wore our mother's wedding dress, a form-fitting fall of white satin with a sweetheart neckline, a hundred covered buttons running down its back to a small, elegant train. By the time my sisters and Aunt Joan were helping me into it, my father had consumed quite a lot of Jim Beam. Fitz, the son of some good friends, offered to drive us to the church. As he opened the car door, I realized he was actually trembling with the honor this to him represented. It brought me up short. These were supposed to be precious final minutes with my father, with my soon-to-be-ended unwedded life. I remember Fitz's eyes in the rearview mirror, worriedly taking us in—Dad and I didn't say anything in those five minutes alone in the car.

A few nights before, Dad had told me that when the priest intoned, "If anyone knows why this man and this woman should not be married," he was going to leap up and shout, "*I object!*"

But Jamie and I weren't using traditional vows. We were using ones written by L. Ron Hubbard, and there was no clause that made room for objection.

The pastor was a friend of Jamie's, Mark, who exuded vast energy and a twinkling sense of humor. An OT IV, Mark was Jamie's spiritual senior. We'd met with him to talk about marriage, including the "hats" that (according to LRH) husband and wife were to wear. Quite traditional, in many ways they described my parent's marriage: husband provided house; wife, home. I was dismissive. I knew how to do this! I had the best family in the world! It would take years, and the weddings of many friends, before I understood that such a conversation is not only commonplace, it is important.

Over his robes, Mark wore a Scientology cross, whose eight arms represent the eight Dynamics. When someone asked me, "Why a cross? Was someone crucified?" I had no answer. But it made me wonder: Had Hubbard simply borrowed that icon to make his religion more acceptable? I shook the thought away. But in my memory, as my father walks me down the aisle, that cross hangs glittering from Mark's neck, a yard long and a foot wide.

Hubbard's wedding oaths include an admonition to the husband that "girls" need "clothes and food and tender happiness and frills, a pan, a comb, perhaps a cat. All caprice if you will, but still they need them." He reassures us girls: "Hear well, sweet, for promise binds. Young men are free and may forget. Remind him that you have necessities and follies too."[39] Although it makes me gag now, to none of it, at the time, did I allow myself to pay attention.

The assembled group watched with something between horror and amusement as Jamie offered his right hand and I worked hard to push the ring onto that ring finger. No doubt they assumed Scientology purposefully used the opposite hand for its marriage ceremony. As we turned from the altar and began the walk back up the beautifully decorated aisle, I tucked my arm under Jamie's and pulled him to me in a kind of weird triumph.

Over the years I've turned this moment over and over, like a snow globe that might offer up a different image if shaken enough times. Even then, the gesture seemed to embody more than happiness at being married, in a white dress, to the man I loved. The exultation—this is *mine*!—seems more complex: perhaps to do with bucking expectations, including the books I read, the friends I chose, the shape and size of my body, even the thoughts I had.

In any case, as far as my parents were concerned, by marrying a Scientologist, and, eventually, by becoming one, I did the one, the *only* thing that could hurt them, an accusation they leveled at me for years. Only recently have I been able to examine the truth of it. Perhaps my attraction to Jamie was, in fact, attraction to something that wasn't part of the vibrant, bohemian world handed me by my parents: spirituality, even, in fact, religion. Maybe, thinking of my brother and their response to his accident—would they still love me? no matter what?—I was testing their love. Maybe the whole endeavor was a querulous demand: *Accept me as I am.*

I'm heartily sorry that was the choice I made. But I'm finally able to see why I might have made it.

IN YET ANOTHER act of sweet generosity, considering her view of the marriage, my mother not only booked us a room in a nearby hotel that overlooked the Truckee River but provided a darling nightgown full of ribbons and lace. But Jamie, unused to the amounts of alcohol that flow merrily at any Hall gathering, fell across the bed and straight to sleep. The next morning his back was out. Surly, unshaven, hungover, he evinced no enjoyment of the present-opening brunch. Much earlier than planned, he insisted we leave for our honeymoon so we could stop in Sacramento and track down a chiropractor. It was a Sunday, which made this project both tedious and arduous.

His back was out! The day after our wedding!

I'd pushed the wedding ring *onto the wrong hand*!

The metaphoric content flashed like brightest neon. Yet even though both my family and Scientology thrive on examination of such obvious connections, Jamie and I didn't speak of it. As we ordered our first dinner together as a married couple, he said no to a bottle of champagne. Even so, and even as he radiated disapproval, I ordered a glass of wine.

As forks scraped across plates, emphasizing the terrible lack of conversation, I thought of the stories my mother had told me of their wedding night, involving champagne and laughter and, of course, sex. Which only emphasized the bleak nature of our own nuptials.

It struck me that Jamie might not know the meaning of "nuptials." But I erased that thought as soon as I had it. Overt. Withhold.

The next day, Jamie slept late and woke cross. With his back still out and aching, we lay side by side in the little cabin we'd rented. He was not a reader, but, in an effort to establish ARC with my dad, had asked, if he did have to read a book, which one should it be? After flabbergasted consideration, Dad suggested *Huckleberry Finn*, which, during our honeymoon, Jamie dutifully attempted to read. Alone, I took long walks through trees dropping late-October black-spotted leaves, trying not to think about my mother's shocked voice: "How can you marry a man who doesn't *read*?"

He does read, I'd wanted to say but didn't, because the only thing Jamie read was Hubbard.

After two somber nights—we'd booked the cabin for five—we headed to LA so Jamie could get to his chiropractor. As we joined the clog of traffic making its way south, I could think of nothing to say. A horrible truth had dawned: The marriage was an error.

Although we tried for more than a year to pretend otherwise, I think we both knew it.

MY MOTHER MAILED envelopes stuffed with articles, sent to her by well-meaning friends, describing the outrages attached to Scientology. "How about *this* horror," she scrawled in her lovely, slanted handwriting along the columns of newsprint. My father sent typed postcards with ironic phrases about what he'd dubbed the "Evil Empire." At one point my mother—my yellow-dog Democrat, left-wing, liberal mother—told me: "You could have married a black man. You could have married a Jew!" Her voice rose in pitch and intensity as she outlined the increasing horrors each of these options represented. "You could have married a *psychiatrist*! But you married a *Scientologist*!"

I remember holding the phone with both hands as the room around me began to spin. Halls didn't talk like this! We weren't racist, we weren't anti-Semitic! I wanted to laugh—was she joking? But it was clear she was not. I had to sit down and, as that nurse had told me to do outside the ICU after seeing my brother post-accident, put my head to my knees.

One of the reasons I held on so hard through the bucketing difficulty of those eighteen months of marriage (among other things, Jamie, a night owl, worked at his office all night, which meant that he usually climbed into bed about the time I was steeping my morning cup of tea) was that fantasy of us as a songwriting team. I wrote a few lyrics celebrating our love (*our souls like sea and shore entwine*), and many more expressing doubt (*waking up this morning with our love in disarray . . . wonder if they'd lock me up if they could see my heart . . . don't say the magic's gone*). But it was a fantasy. Jamie had made it clear he no longer wanted to perform. Also, sometimes, when I'd sit with my guitar, working on a song, I was aware of a faint impatience. Once, when I caught a flicker of disdain cross his face, I pressed him.

"Is it because I don't read music?" I asked.

He shrugged. "Lots of talented singer-songwriters don't read music. But the music, folk music in general, isn't complicated or interesting. Jazz, on the other hand—jazz is music."

A number of fine musicians taught in Jamie's music school. All were Scientologists, all played jazz, and all, like Jamie, smoked. I began to understand that while drugs, even aspirin, were off-limits, cigarettes were fine; if you were Clear or OT, you'd never get something as mundane as cancer. And if you did, you must have done something to "pull it in."

Yet Jamie's back continued to be out. Even though we could have addressed what the *spine* in a *marriage* might be, even as it was clear that ours was very much out of alignment, we never spoke of these implications. What we did speak of was my Reactive Mind. All the unexamined incidents stored there were making me, and therefore us, unhappy. "The only thing wrong in the marriage is what you perceive to be wrong," he'd say. "We'd be fine if you were just happy."

This sentence, which came up in various forms, always served to stop me in my charged-up tracks. *We'd be fine if you were just happy.* It was my fault. It was my "case."[40]

Again and again, after a fight, or, as more and more I folded Scientology's lingo into my vocabulary, ARC Break (recorded in my journal as ARCX), I'd figure out how what was wrong, was wrong with me. I'd have an epiphany—Hubbard's word is "cognition"—take responsibility, apologize, and on we'd lurch.[41]

Those cognitions allowed me to examine ways in which I could—and did—improve aspects of my nature. These realizations led to an increasing interest in Hubbard's path. This search for spirituality was, I see now, the biggest reason I married Jamie.

All my life I'd had moments—I might be standing backstage waiting for an entrance, sitting at a brunch with friends—moments that should have been "happy," when I'd feel the bottom drop out. There'd be a writhing, tortured sensation that made me have to grip a piece of my costume or the edge of the table. Life felt meaningless. I could, I should be doing or thinking or *being* something "more worthwhile." But I had no idea what that might be.

I'd let meditating drop from my routine when I moved to Los Angeles, but prior to that, for almost a decade, I'd used the mantra given to me that long-ago afternoon with the Maharishi. But I didn't think of meditating as a religion. Religion was an opiate for the uneducated (usually right-wing) masses; it was something archaic, whose cultural artifacts one might put on a shelf or wear on a chain around one's neck. I'd no idea that a pilgrim lurked in my psyche, even though I'd long wondered, feeling traitorous, if life might be enhanced by believing in, trusting in a larger compass. So in marrying Jamie, I was groping my way toward something that had always fascinated me: the idea of religion itself.

FLUNK. START.

Eventually, as long as I didn't have to step foot into an actual Org, I was persuaded to sign up for a course, Success Through Communication. I remember it being inexpensive, $25 or so, a huge relief. It was held in a West Hollywood bungalow that belonged to the woman who was the course supervisor, Ruth. The six or seven of us who showed up were each given a little glossy book. It all seemed innocuous, even a little corny.

I read about the Cycle of Communication, I demoed my understanding, I was twinned with a man named Bob. As we drilled the first Training Routine, OT TR0 (sitting opposite another with eyes closed), I was struck by the idea that one must be ready to send a communication, as well as to receive one, with or without words. Sitting there, hands folded in my lap, I was reminded of what had caused me, over the years, to walk into churches, to read books on spirituality, above all why, for so long, I'd meditated. It was a matter of awareness and discernment, both of which, as Bob and I sat across from each other with our eyes closed for many, many minutes, glimmered and gleamed.

You could get all that by reading about Buddhism, an interior voice muttered. How about just getting back to meditating? Why sit here in this corny bungalow doing this asinine thing?

I took a breath and brought my attention back to the room in which I was sitting, and to Bob, breathing opposite. *I don't know. Be quiet.*

Ruth did not appear to notice my mental yammering, and by the end of the evening, Bob and I had done OT TR0 to her satisfaction. The hustle of gathering purses and coats and the cheerful goodbyes reminded me of the first rehearsal of a play, as you get to know your fellow cast members and the project you'll be creating together—a sense of a shared endeavor that had always held enormous appeal.

"See you tomorrow." Bob waved.

I waved back. As I drove home, I pondered that I would indeed see him the next night, and the next.

The booklet was small; it didn't seem like the course would take long, and yet—why take it at all? Jamie waxed on about how cool it was to be OT. And sure, it might be fun to soar like Superman or Tinkerbell. But what I found compelling was that so much of the Tech simply made sense. The Dynamics. The idea of overts and withholds. The idea that A + R + C = Understanding. The comm cycle. Even as I disdained the acronyms and abbreviations, even as a huge part of me wanted to sit in my parents' living room with a glass of wine and scoff, I could not deny that as I'd practiced being ready to both give and receive a communication, in whatever form, I'd become even more deeply intrigued by Scientology.

Especially in that it might offer possible answers to ancient questions: *Why am I here? What happens when we die? Is this it?* I'd always wanted a sense of a larger purpose. I'd long been entranced by the possibility that what we call "serendipity" and "synchronicity" are, in fact, much more—clues to a vast organism that includes us all. These fascinations were among those that over the years led me to read books on Eastern philosophy, to sit in the pews of dozens of cathedrals, to be grateful when a friend invited me along to Seder and I could bow my head over four thousand years of history unfolding with the salt and bitter greens. I yearned for a connection with, and a certainty about, a higher sensibility. I wanted, fiercely, to believe in a larger force, that we might be part of some vast plan that we only occasionally glimpse. Above all, I wanted, especially since my brother's accident, to figure out a purpose: why I was on the planet at all.

I parked beside our house in the Hollywood Hills and stood breathing in the faint smell of eucalyptus, thinking about a Sunday morning in San Francisco, during those years when I trained at ACT, when I'd decided to go to a service at Grace Cathedral. As the priest readied communion, he held up an actual loaf of bread. Round and, as it turned out, sourdough. Lit by rays of color pouring through a stained-glass window, it inspired me to join those walking toward the altar. With the rest of the communicants, I swallowed wine from a goblet and took a bit of that bread into my mouth. The rest of that day I enjoyed a remarkable, joyous sense of connection to everyone I encountered. Buying an apple, pressing coins into the Laundromat dryer, dodging across a crosswalk, I pulsed with wonder—had those around me eaten from that loaf? Had we shared the molecules of bread, and the colored light and prayer it contained? For the first time, I viscerally understood the word "communion." It wasn't about Christ's body and blood. It had to do with intention and interaction and love.

Leaning against my car, I stared out over the lights of Hollywood below. Scientology was an upstart crow of a religion. I wished there were a way to study what seemed interesting about it without having to "become" a Scientologist—that scared me. But it appeared to have answers. It had much to say about purpose. And it seemed to offer a bridge—there was no other word for it—across the existential chasm that too often yawned open before me.

THE NEXT NIGHT we read about TR0, the Training Routine in which two people sit opposite one another with their eyes open. Ruth paced the room, keeping an eye on us keeping eyes on each other. That was it. For minutes at a time, just looking at each other's eyes, without breaking the stare.

Again, it was a bit like meditation, when you're trying to hold your mind steady on a mantra, or on the breath, while it makes these efforts to wander away from the present moment. But in this case, in addition to dealing with your own mind, with your own thoughts, distracted by what might be going on in the room around you or the street outside, you must also take in the person opposite. After just a few minutes, that other face can go all wobbly. The nose seems to dominate, or the eyes to cross. Your own eyes water. You want to blink rapidly, or close your eyelids against the strain. An itch needs scratching. A sip of water seems vital. You must stretch, you need to yawn, you want to stop.

With a huge groan, Bob suddenly blinked and stretched his arms above his head. Everyone laughed. Ruth did too, but clapped her hands and said, "Flunk!"

By this point, Jamie had used the word with me numerous times, but I was nevertheless startled.

Bob was horrified. "What?" he said.

Ruth clapped her hands. "Start!"

Bob and I raised our eyebrows at each other, but we got back to the drill. A few minutes later, Bob opened and closed his eyes like a dying fish.

"Sands!" Ruth said. "That's a *flunk*! Call it! That's what a twin is for!"

"Umm, flunk," I told Bob, as sweetly as I could. "Umm, start."

"Good!" Ruth said.

I couldn't help but smile, and with a wicked grin, Bob said, "Flunk."

We laughed as if this were the funniest joke in the world. "Flunk!" we both said again, and, simultaneously, "Start."

Ever tried. Ever failed. No matter. Try again. Fail again. Fail better, I thought, remembering my brother quoting Beckett. But Theatre of the Absurd, which once I'd loved, seemed hollow now; the mockery existentialism makes of the idea that life can be meaningful. As I stared at Bob who stared at me, I thought of Sisyphus and his endless, hopeless task, how the stone will always get away from him and he must trudge down the hill and start again. And again. Even though he knows that he will always fail. As an undergraduate, and while shuttling props and costumes around the subways of New York, these ideas had been romantic, in a black-beret, Gauloise-smoking way. But now, in my thirties, they felt nothing but grim. I no longer wanted anything to do with an absurdist world. It was in part what had claimed my brother. I wanted life to have meaning. Which was, I reasoned, trying not to blink, why I was sitting in a tidy, orderly course room, engaging with what seemed to be a tidy and orderly and meaningful system.

Once Bob and I'd signed off on that drill, we turned to TR0 Bullbait, which involved one of us making faces and saying shocking things and telling jokes. If I (and, turn about, Bob) laughed, or "broke," we were to flunk each other, then immediately start again. We were to do it again and again until we were both able to keep TR0 going in the face of any attempt to break concentration.[42]

It seemed terribly peculiar. Why would you want to "bullbait" someone? But even as I fretted that all this might be brainwashing, I began to see a point: to really *be* with another person, when circumstances demand, not to respond with laughter or anger when someone most needs to be heard, not to allow someone to "get" you with a barb or joke when you need stay focused. And while at first I was horrified by the term "bullbait," the initial shock of the word soon wore off—was normalized. I have since read that this drill has been used in terrible, degrading ways, but that was not my experience. For me, the drill was about having buttons pushed and pushing them, purposefully, with the goal of gaining mastery over knee-jerk, unexamined reactions.

I see that I may have persuaded myself of the drill's benefits.

Over the next few nights, we covered other TRs, which taught us to communicate with intention, to listen, and of course to acknowledge.

I did not then realize that these drills train a person to master what is at the heart of Scientology: auditing. Every aspect of the Church swirls around that practice. So there's a reason that the course, Success Through Communication, is so often recommended as a first step into Scientology. The TRs "train" one in both directions: to be an auditor; and, cleverly, also to be audited. Once started, it's easy to be pulled inexorably along.

It took me a long time to sort that out.

I FINISHED THE course, and, as we were asked to do, wrote up some "wins." Which were real enough. But, in spite of strong "regging," I didn't sign up for another course.[43] A large part of my hesitation had to do with Jamie. Leaving him was never far from my mind. If I stepped further into the Church, wouldn't that cement me to him? If I left him, would I also leave Scientology, which I was actually—though I could barely admit it—enjoying?

Finally I agreed to the Purification Rundown, a kind of ongoing sweat lodge: For hours each day, while taking copious amounts of niacin, calcium, and magnesium, I sat in a sauna. My flushed, tingling skin was proof that my very cells were discharging accumulated toxins—from alcohol and drugs, from just living on planet Earth.

In the midst of the "Purif," I was called to audition for San Diego's Old Globe Theatre. To my delight and surprise, I was hired. It had been some time since I'd worked in a prestigious theater, and the career leap seemed directly connected to my work in Scientology. My faith in the efficacy of the Church, and, by extension, the worth of my marriage, was in full swing, and I took that growing certainty with me to San Diego.

Director Tom Moore created a delectable cream puff out of Oscar Wilde's *Importance of Being Earnest*, and in addition to playing Cecily in the indoor theater, I was also cast as the sweet young thing in Molière's *The Miser*, outdoors. That satisfying San Diego summer, 1982, could have been an opportunity to break away from what was, at that point, Scientology's relatively delicate grasp, and to leave Jamie—the season was three months long and the drive to and from LA a six-hour round trip.

But a profound loyalty or stick-to-it-iveness is part of my nature. In addition, I'd had so little acting work for so long, and it was easy to be persuaded that I'd landed the job because of Scientology. Was further success possible, would my marriage improve, if I kept on? So most Sundays, after the week's final performance, instead of taking a book to the beach or partying with my colleagues on the day off, which in theater is Monday, I'd drive home. I'd spend what time with Jamie I could (though he was usually in his office) and arrive back on Tuesday in time to warm up for that evening's performance.

Among the things that made me want to trust L. Ron Hubbard was his statement regarding art: "A culture is only as great as its dreams, and its dreams are dreamed by artists."[44] I wanted to share this with my parents. They would never say it in such an aggrandizing way (being artists), but once again I felt that Hubbard's views coincided with those of my family: Art is of utmost importance. Engaging in it is of utmost importance!

Yes, I thought it very fine, the way that brief sentence bequeathed both praise and duty. And in some weird need to uphold that duty, I found myself, to my horror, proselytizing to fellow cast members, in the dressing room, over coffee: a desperate need to convince myself as I tried to convince them. I know that I stunted a number of friendships, perhaps even a career—who would want to hire such a person; who would recommend to another that she should be hired?

After the shows opened, my mother came to visit. *The Importance of Being Earnest* was pulling great reviews and full houses, and it was gratifying to have her there. As she met friends and colleagues, I was reminded of what I adored about her: the way she carried off a shawl thrown over her shoulders; her bright blue eyes, so interested, so curious; her engagement in conversations that ran the gamut from iambic pentameter to local wines to the future of live theater. The tense phone calls and letters of the previous year had created a terrible animosity that the visit did much to briefly eradicate.

As she was leaving, I hugged her. "Oh, Mom, it's been so much fun to hang out with you!"

Her lovely face flinched. "What do you mean, 'hang out'?" she said. "Is that one of those awful Scientology phrases?"

I laughed, a little shocked. "Not at all! It just means, I don't know, being together, having fun. It's nomenclature used by jazz musicians."

If I thought she might be impressed by that nice big word, I was mistaken.

"We don't say things like 'hang out,'" she said. It felt like a slap.

After I waved her off—and in spite of that harsh exchange, I was raggedly sorry to see her go—I walked on the beach for hours, wrestling with that "we": we Halls, and by extension the whole cultured world "we" represented. I knew she loved me, knew she wanted the best for me. Scientology scared her; it scared me! She found things about Jamie alarming; *I* found them alarming. I should leave. *I should leave. I should leave.*

But I thought of a conversation around a dinner table a few months before, when the talk among my parents and their friends had turned to Frida Kahlo's self-portraits, and her stupendous eyebrows. "Who's Frida Kahlo?" I'd asked, and Mother had pretty much hissed, "You *know* who she is!" I realized I'd embarrassed her, and it had taken every ounce of strength to say, "No, I don't. Please tell me."

If I left Jamie, would I just be back in a world where I so often felt insufficient?

I wish so deeply I'd left anyway, and found some other method to sort out this base need for approval. But standing there on that windy beach, I realized I was having critical thoughts again. By this time I was convinced that a critical thought *always* meant you'd done something to the person or thing you were criticizing. In this case, the transgression was doubting my marriage, doubting Scientology. Even as I saw the circular nature of this logic, I gave way beneath its weight. As I examine, now, this incredibly inactive agonizing, it seems that rather than *Fail again. Fail better*, it was *Fail again, fail again, fail again*—a flunk/start not of hopeful resilience, but, rather, of stubborn perseverance.

A few days after Mom left, I stood in a gift shop turning a wine glass this way and that in light from a window. *Do I like this wine glass because I like this wine glass*, I wondered, *or because my mother would like this wine glass?*

And I scolded myself: Sands, you are thirty years old and you don't know this?

What was the solution to this astonishing lack of a sense of self? What was the reason for it? It horrified me how much I didn't know *what I wanted from my own life*. It was time, long past time, for me to figure it out.

At the moment, the religion lapping at my ankles seemed to offer solutions.

And so I headed back to Los Angeles, to Jamie, and to Scientology.

YOU COULD TAKE A LOOK AT DOUBT

Jamie had figured out why his back continued to be out.

"I'm allergic to gold!" He held up his ringless left hand. "Those chiropractic adjustments, all those dietary restrictions? No results. But when I took off the ring? Within minutes, all those back spasms—gone!"

I actually laughed out loud. He was allergic to our *marriage*?

Back I swirled into sorrow and confusion. However, the Church is masterful at "handling doubt." With the assistance of what are known as "Ethics Conditions," I talked myself out of mine again and again.

Ethics Conditions are incorporated by Scientologists into every aspect of their lives. One's ethical status is directly attached to one's Condition. And one's Condition has to do with statistics, which in turn have to do with a line on a graph, which clearly demonstrate a degree of success—or lack of it.[45]

According to LRH, everything is measurable in production, by a "stat." In a 1965 policy letter, he likens it to a typist getting five hundred letters written in a week: If six hundred are written the next week, that's an "up" stat; if the following week she writes just three hundred, that's a "down" stat. This idea can be easily applied to one's career (number of résumés sent out, number of hours practicing guitar, and of course amount of income), and certainly to a marriage:

Number of times love is made. Number of hours spent arguing. One could graph number of meals eaten together, or hours spent in bed at the same time. With any imagination at all, and a pen and a piece of paper, one can quickly determine one's "productivity," and hence one's ethical status—or Ethics Condition.

And Hubbard provides formulas to help you work through each Condition, so that you can rise from the lowest, Confusion, to the highest, Power.

So when I confessed, yet again, to doubts regarding our marriage—and, by extension, my inability to commit to being a Scientologist—Jamie sat me at the kitchen table with a pad of paper, a dictionary, and a copy of Hubbard's *Introduction to Scientology Ethics.*

"Study the Conditions," he said. "Find out which one you're in. Then just follow its formula, and you'll work out of it."

I stared at the *Introduction to Scientology Ethics*, a slim hardcover, but didn't pick it up.

"You could take a look at Doubt," Jamie said, "but it's possible you're in a condition even lower than that. So maybe start with Confusion. See if it applies."

His blue eyes were kind and full of approval. I loved it when he looked at me like that.

I picked up the book. Sturdy and well bound, its pages thick and glossy, everything about it was satisfying to the hand. This was something I'd noticed about Scientology books: They were designed for endless use.

"I'll be at the office," Jamie said. Halfway up the stairs he stopped, and practically leapt back down them to kiss the top of my head. "Love you."

His stern demeanor always softened when he engaged with the Tech. I resented how much I wanted that approbation, even as I felt myself warming beneath it. I made myself a cup of tea before opening the book, and after reading Hubbard's thoughts about Conditions in general, I took a look at Confusion.[46]

> In a Condition of Confusion, the being or area will be in a state of random motion. There will be no real production, only disorder and confusion.

There was more, but this seemed to describe my state well enough. My marriage contained little "production," and rather a lot of "disorder." Above all, I *was* confused! Should I stay married or should I not? Should I keep exploring Scientology or should I flee?

The formula to get out of Confusion seemed simple: "Find out *where* you are."

I grasped the idea behind the solution: in order to stop the whirling, the "random motion," you seize hold of one thing: *Where* are you? In relation to that certainty, everything else might fall into some kind of place.

So I touched the round wooden table, shuffled my feet on the worn linoleum, took in the dishtowel draped over the faucet, listened to the clank and hum of the fridge.

Here I am, I thought. I am here.

I APPRECIATED THAT there was a formula to help one out of Confusion—inserting order where there was chaos—and over the coming months, I applied that formula again and again to, among other things, my "wifeness." (Hubbard tends to attach the suffix "–ness" to many words—doingness, beingness, havingness, to name a few—and in frustration at what I saw as the worst sort of word-mangling, I'd looked it up. I grudgingly had to accept that "–ness" merely adds "the quality of a state of" to the noun to which it's attached, as in happiness or fastness or even marvelousness. Even so, I resented Scientologists' arbitrary/ubiquitous use of it and sometimes tried to determine what overt might lie at the bottom of that disdain—unless the disdain itself was the overt.) Trying to sort out where I was as wife—where I was as Scientologist being, for the nonce, on a back burner—I'd take in the sunlight outside our kitchen window, the well-made book in my hands, and, I have to say, the contentment that was attached to reading and applying information. For a moment I'd rise out of Confusion to—

—Treason. In this condition, Hubbard avows, if a person takes on a post and then doesn't function "as it," they will "upset or destroy some part of the organization."

Again, this made sense when applied to the "organization" that was my marriage. The "post" I'd accepted was "wife," and I wasn't functioning "as it." It wasn't just that I didn't clean house very well. It wasn't just that I nagged Jamie to come home from the office and have dinner with me. I simply didn't want to be married to him.

Did I? And if I left him, would I leave Scientology?

Of course I would! I'd have to. It was what I should do!

The world would spin. I'd be confused again. So again I'd figure out *where* I was, then push my way back to Treason and study its formula.

Treason's formula is also deceptively simple: "Find out *that* you are."

In answer to this injunction, I'd scribble pages and pages in which I might reflect that "treason" was an apt word to describe the way I compared my "wifeness," and what I felt marriage *should* be, to what Jamie and I actually had. I'd eventually find a way to put a positive spin on things: the sweet love we made, how awful it would be to uproot. I'd accept that our marriage was an "organization" I wanted to be part of, that "wife of Jamie" was a post I'd signed on for. I'd determine *that* I indeed was. And so I'd grope my way upward to—

—Enemy. In this condition, Hubbard writes, you must be a "knowing" enemy. You are "avowedly" against the organization.

That didn't sound like me (except, perhaps, in my thoughts). Still, it was easy to see that if I wasn't committed—to my marriage, to Scientology—I was being enemy-like.

I didn't want to be an enemy! I wanted to be a friend! I wanted to be good!

This formula, too, comprises one sentence: "Find out who you really are."

Just to be clear, I looked up REALLY.

"Actual truth or fact. Truly. Genuinely."

Okay. I was going to decide that I was *truly* Jamie's wife or I was not. I was *genuinely* a Scientologist or I was not.

But if I was using Scientology to decide I wasn't a Scientologist, wasn't I kind of being a Scientologist?

I wrote pages about that as well.

One of the steps of the formula to get out of the condition of Enemy is to "deliver an effective blow to the enemies of the group one has been pretending to be a part of . . ." This troubled me. A lot. I'd heard that people who'd doubted Scientology, once they'd realigned themselves with the Church, had used this step to do things like break typewriters (so the "enemy" could no longer write things against Scientology), break windows (e.g., of judges who'd ruled against the Church), and worse. In fact, pondering what might have been deemed allowable by the Church as a result of this step (murder?) usually caused me to crash back to Confusion again. However, once I did manage to climb out of Enemy I found myself in—

—Doubt!

Doubt is much like Confusion, but its formula is far more specific. Once you've wrestled through the various steps, you are charged to "remain in or befriend the one which progresses toward the greatest good for the greatest number of dynamics."

. . . the greatest good for the greatest number of dynamics . . .

Oh dear. If you were a Scientologist, then the "greatest good" would be Scientology. And wouldn't that make it possible to persuade yourself that you could do *anything*, whether or not it was "ethical" in someone else's understanding of the word, if it benefited Scientology?

This made me very nervous.

Again, it seemed impossible to use Hubbard's Technology and not choose the side that would have you using Hubbard's Technology.

Nevertheless, even as I battled with this circular logic, I perceived the benefit of the Conditions, and of Ethics and the comm cycle and ARC=U, etc. Therefore Scientology, and Jamie, won. Every time.

One of the final steps of the Doubt formula, once you've made your decision, is to "announce this fact publically to both sides."

The phone call to Jamie, usually at his office, was easy. I'd share the "win."

"Well done!" he'd say. "Now, you need to announce it to the other side. You know what that means."

It would take me sometimes days to call my parents, time enough to plunge back down to at least Treason. Or I'd get off the phone with Jamie and make the call right then and there. This meant that Mother would cheerfully pick up the phone to find me on the other end "announcing," out of the clear blue sky, the firmness of my commitment to Jamie. Or that Scientology really, really was such a great thing.

These conversations were brittle, terrible things.

IT'S POSSIBLE, IF you have your Ethics "in" and your stats "up," to rise from Doubt to—Liability. The final steps of this formula include "Making up damage done." My approach to this was simplistic and familiar: apologize. Long before Scientology, I'd offered up "sorry" at the drop of a hat (I felt responsible for that dropped hat). For the spilled wine, the stalled car. For years friends had told me, sharply, "Stop apologizing!"

Of course, to work out of Liability, an apology is not enough; an appropriate *action* is also required. Only then may you apply for "permission to rejoin the group." As far as our marriage was concerned, this might entail scrubbing out a cupboard, or not making *a single phone call* begging Jamie to come home for dinner.

Once I'd applied and Jamie had granted permission to rejoin our "organization," I was in the condition known as Danger. In Danger, the line on the graph (posted on a physical wall or in one's mind) is steeply down, but that "down" implies an "up" before the stat crashed—or, rather, something made it crash (which meant, of course, that *you'd* made it crash). Beyond Danger was Emergency and then something called Normal Operation . . . and beyond that, Power!

Even as I rarely moved beyond the frame of Doubt/Liability, I liked the logic of the Conditions. And I found something deeply engaging about sitting at a table surrounded by books and paper, reading, writing, defining words, delving.

But I was going to bed alone and waking up alone. Again I was calling Jamie at 7:00 to say dinner will be ready in about an hour! At 8:00 to say it's ready! At 8:30 to say it's ready! At 9:00 to say it's cold! And at 10:00 to cry.

And down the Conditions I'd plummet, a cartoon roadrunner leaving behind the silhouette of my spread-eagled image as I crashed through the floors of Doubt, Enemy, Treason . . .

In Scientology, this is called "rollercoastering." According to LRH, rollercoastering is evidence that someone is "invalidating" you in some way.

Jamie had long insisted my parents were the problem. They were invalidating our marriage. And therefore me. I must "disconnect" from them if our marriage was to thrive. If *I* was to thrive.

I understood this was Church policy. If family or friends have trouble with you being a Scientologist, or they criticize Scientology, you tell them you simply can't see or talk to them anymore.[47] But that idea was unimaginable. Even though it was true that when I hung up from a phone call with them, I often wept. It wasn't just the tight disapproval in my mother's voice, or Dad's jabs at the Evil Empire (eventually shortened to EE). It might be Nana Mouskouri's contralto rising from an LP in the background and all that voice represented: the family journey to Europe, the travels that seemed improbable in the life I'd chosen, parties, laughter, art, wine, friends, happiness. If you were a Scientologist (or so it seemed in my life with Jamie), you didn't travel, you didn't *have* dinner parties, because you should be on course, or getting or giving auditing. Yes, art was important, we were the ones "dreaming the dream" that would make the culture great—but only, it seemed, if we did so through Scientology.

So Jamie's claim that my parents were the problem had validity. Even then I sensed that it was my *response* to their distress and disapproval—how much it echoed my *own* distress and disapproval—that was the actual problem. But I had yet to summon the will to face that.

Finally, Jamie threw up his hands. He made an appointment for us to see someone at Celebrity Center with a terrifying title: the Ethics Officer.

THE ETHICS OFFICER

In the 1980s, the mansion that houses Celebrity Center in Los Angeles had not yet been remodeled. And though it was dilapidated, even in places derelict, its bones revealed a once gracious mansion: wide stairs, high ceilings, tall windows. As we walked through this aged elegance, a number of people strode by, wearing billed caps and white jackets loaded with insignia.

"Sea Org," Jamie said. "Signed on for a billion years."

I nodded. By this time I knew that Scientologists believe that knowledge gleaned in one life can be carried to another (it's part of what fascinated me—often Jamie's friends assured me how "Buddhist" Hubbard's ideas were). Those who joined the Sea Org were seriously committed to the idea. The Sea Org's maxim is *We Come Back.*

The name, as well as the nautical uniforms, had been launched when Hubbard, seeking to avoid legal trouble, sailed the oceans on an actual ship. The uniforms looked out of place, even silly in that elegant lobby. Nevertheless, there was a pervasive sense of bustle and purpose that struck me hard.

As I followed Jamie up the stairs, I wondered if Sea Org members had to buy their uniforms, as I'd had to do as a waitress, with the ridiculously high cost taken out of the first few paychecks. But if you were in the Sea Org, did you get a paycheck?

On a second, rather shabby floor, we walked down an unpainted corridor and sat in battered folding chairs outside a closed door. As we waited for the Ethics Officer to finish a previous meeting, I mentioned how run-down everything looked.

"When there's so much important spiritual work going on," Jamie said, "the material world just isn't that important."

Okay, but where does the money go, I didn't ask, if it isn't for a coat of paint? If Scientology was so powerful and effective, wouldn't that manifest in the "material world"? Wouldn't that include paint and decent chairs, a rug or flowers, even a waiting room?

These thoughts—and I was aware they were critical, and so was simultaneously trying to sort out what I'd done, and to whom, that I would have them—were overshadowed by my anxiety about meeting the Ethics Officer. But as often happened when I spoke with people working in the Church, among the many things that kept me engaged, our meeting was full of an affectionate, rueful understanding of the difficulties of life and life's choices. Scientologists use the word "duplicate" to convey a sense of being understood, and, at least at first, I definitely felt duplicated by the EO, Marty.

Marty looked rumpled. His jacket was draped haphazardly over the back of his chair. His shirt had been ironed, but at some distant point in the past; his hair needed combing and even a wash, but the sense was that he didn't have time to pay attention to such things—he was *helping* people. He let Jamie and me know that he'd also had a tough marriage, bad enough to get a divorce, but he and his new wife, even though they sometimes had typical problems around money, sex, household roles, were able to work things through because of the Tech.

He asked us what was going on.

"She has wins," Jamie said. "She gets excited about the Tech, and then she crashes."

Marty looked grave. Jamie leaned forward. "It's a classic case of Potential Trouble Source. She's connected to people opposed to Scientology, she's rollercoastering; she gets better, she gets worse. She's got a Suppressive Person on her lines. Probably two!"

The phrase "on her lines" made me think of a cobweb, a spider crouched in wait. But it had to do with "comm lines": those with whom I communicated.

Marty moved his concerned eyes to meet mine. "Who's invalidating you? Who doesn't want you to thrive?"

"Her parents!" Jamie said.

Marty held up a hand. "She's got to have this cognition for herself, Jamie."

Jamie sat back, fuming. "Someone who is PTS," he said, and quoted LRH (he'd showed me this bulletin a number of times): "'is connected with an SP who is invalidating him, his beingness, his processing, his life.'[48] Her parents are Suppressive!"

Marty took a sip from a Styrofoam cup. "What do you think, Sands?"

"Her mother, especially," Jamie said. "She's a *complete* SP."

I closed my eyes. "She. Is. Not."

"Well, you're definitely PTS," Jamie said. "Who else is the SP?"

"I'm not PTS," I said. "I'm just not sure about this marriage." What I wanted to say was, What if the SP is *you*, Jamie? What if the suppressive thing is *Scientology*?

"But if that were the case," Marty's voice was full of understanding, "you'd be able to work through the Doubt formula and determine that you don't want to be with Jamie."

"It's not a matter of moving a few clothes to another closet! I want to make our marriage work! If we can. Anyway, I don't even *have* my own closet anymore!"

"Let's examine the rollercoastering," Marty said. "You feel good about things and then you don't, right?" He flipped through a packet on his desk. "This is from a 1972 bulletin," he said, and read: "PTS 'means someone connected to a person or group opposed to Scientology. It is a technical thing. It results in illness and roller-coaster.'" He looked at me. "Are your parents opposed to Scientology?"

"They hate it," Jamie said.

"Sands?"

"They hate it," I said. "They hate that I have anything to do with it."

"Well!" Marty closed the packet. "That's a classic origin of the trouble that makes one PTS: You're a potential source of trouble—do you see that? Has Jamie told you about our policy?"

I didn't answer. Well aware that I was mangling the comm cycle, I avoided Marty's eyes. Instead, I looked over his shoulder, where a spider plant, badly in need of watering, hung from a hook in a macramé cradle. Beside it was a window that looked onto an airshaft. I was aware of the dead end these things represented, the dead end of this marriage, the dead end I felt sitting in this crazy place being asked to look at this crazy idea: that my parents were in any way, shape, or form "suppressive." Why was I trying to work through a marriage with a man whom, most of the time, I didn't want to be with, and who, it was clear, didn't much want to be with me? Why was I in this stupid office at all, with someone called an *Ethics Officer*?

"You need to cut comm with your parents, Sands," Marty said, and he said it gently enough that I met his eyes. "Disconnect. How can you decide if you want to be with Jamie if you're connected to people who don't like that you're Scientologists?"

"I'm *not* a Scientologist!"

A long pause quivered within those walls that needed a coat of paint.

"Well, now," Marty said. "A Scientologist is essentially one who betters the conditions of himself and the conditions of others by using Scientology technology."

Jamie nodded.

"And here we are," Marty said, "using the Tech to try and solve this problem."

"My parents are not *not NOT* Suppressive People!"

"Let's put it a different way," Marty said. "Someone who climbs in and out of Doubt is connected to someone who's against their survival."

"My parents want nothing *more* than my survival—they want my *happiness*!"

I shoved away the thought that whether I was happy seemed to have a lot to do with whether they were happy—with me.

"Perhaps they don't want you to thrive?"

"Of *course* they want me to thrive! They love me! They are wonderful, amazing, artistic, smart, loving parents. They just don't like Scientology!"

"Scientology is the only way *to* thrive!" For the first time, Marty was vehement. "Why don't you just tell them good things about it?"

"They won't listen! They don't believe it!"

Marty had his eyes firmly locked on mine. The smile was still there but something implacable too. He spread his hands wide. "Then you must stop talking to them. You must stop listening to them. You must have nothing to do with them."

"I am *not* going to do that."

Marty swallowed whatever was left in the Styrofoam cup and tossed it into a trash can heaped full with them. "I've got people waiting. Got to keep the stats up. Here's what you do, Sands. You go downstairs to the Registrar and sign up for the PTS/SP course. Right now. Start this afternoon. Take her to the Reg, Jamie."

I DIDN'T START that afternoon. In a small act of insurrection—what I see, now, was a last-ditch effort to keep hold of some semblance of myself—I refused to start until . . . *the next day*. But we did head to the Registrar, me plodding silent and resentful behind Jamie. We again crossed the lobby with its sparkling chandeliers, and entered her office, which was handsomely furnished: deep blue wall-to-wall carpet, large comfortable armchairs, a meeting table in addition to a vast, gleaming desk. Of course, I thought. This grand office, on the first floor, would be the place people came to offer up their money. Here, at the "entrance" to Scientology, things had to look as if the religion was thriving—"upstat." On the second floor, once they'd gotten you, they didn't need to have a coat of paint or clean windows.

But there went another critical thought! I must have committed a transgression!

The overt seemed to be *having* critical thoughts. Was that it? Why?

The Möbius strip of this logic took up a lot of energy.

The Reg, Katey, wore a captain's cap, a white dress shirt and navy blue skirt, and a blazer full of bars. She was delighted to meet the wife of Jamie—Jamie the celebrity, right there in Celebrity Center! Even as I wanted to sulk, I was deeply impressed by the powerful intentions at play, and found myself being weirdly polite. Jamie offered to pay for the course, but as part of my Doubt formula—"announcing the decision to both sides"—Katey recommended that I, not he, write that check.

"You have to commit to a standard schedule," Katey said, cheerfully. "You'll need to be on course at least fifteen hours a week, although lots of people study many more hours than that. You can do it in two eight-hour chunks over the weekend if you like, but the best choice is five days a week. Which time slot would you like?" She listed these off like ice cream flavors: "In the morning, you've got 9:00 to 12:00. In the afternoon, there's 1:00 to 3:15 or 3:30 to 6:00, or you can do the entire afternoon, 1:00 to 6:00—lots of people do. Or there's the evening slot, 7:00 to 10:00. Which would you like?"

I don't want to do any of it! But her cheer and resolve were completely Scientological. Even as I felt forced toward an action I didn't want to take, I admitted to a reluctant admiration that they could just *do* this. I agreed to the 3:30 to 6:00 slot, and Katey took me upstairs to introduce me to the Course Supervisor, Tim, a harried man of about forty, who pulled out a ledger and wrote my name and the time I'd agreed to show up.

"See you tomorrow," Tim said, and to Katey, "Be sure you cover the drugs and alcohol policy."

I knew it. No drugs, period, ever, not even aspirin, and no alcohol within twenty-four hours of being on course.

The next day, in a bitter, subdued fury, and purposefully late—another minuscule act of insurrection—I walked through the doors of Celebrity Center and trudged up the stairs to the course room.

Tim was busy helping a student when I arrived. As I waited for him to finish, I gazed around this place where I was going to have to spend five days a week.

Through floor-to-ceiling windows, light poured onto long wooden tables where people of all ages and types sat reading, surrounded by dictionaries and manuals and books. I thought of monks bent over their blessed work in a scriptorium. In spite of walls whose paint was peeling and ceilings blotched with water stains, it was a beautiful environment.

And, most unexpectedly, I took to it like a kitten to milk.

EVERY SORROW IN THIS WORLD COMES DOWN TO A MISUNDERSTOOD WORD

The Course Supervisor finished up with the student he'd been helping and headed toward me.

"Hello there," Tim said. "You're late. Let me show you around."

The course room appeared to in fact be three rooms. In one, people studied quietly at tables. In another, students sat opposite each other. Some had their eyes open, some closed. "This is the practical course room, where you apply what it is you're studying," Tim said. "Those students are doing what are called the TRs: Training Routines."

I nodded, proud I could indicate that I knew what those were.

At a nearby table, a student was using an e-meter while asking questions of a student opposite, who, moving the limbs of a large doll that he held in his lap, answered using a doll-like voice.

"Those two are getting ready to audit each other on Method One," Tim said, and gestured to a man and a woman sitting at another table, an open course pack between them. "And Fran is doing what's called a 'spot-check,' making sure Rob understands a bulletin."

We paused to watch. The woman pointed to a word, and Rob seemed to answer to her satisfaction. She asked something that made him spill the contents of a little basket onto the table: pennies, a ChapStick, an empty spool, a matchbook.

"That's a demo kit," Tim said.

Again I nodded, to let him know that I was already savvy about demos. Which is exactly how this noose of practice—the vocabulary (nomenclature), the drills, the sense of being one of the elect—is designed: to tighten slowly but surely around you.

"One of Hubbard's three barriers to study," Tim was saying, as we watched Rob manipulate a cork and a paperclip, "is what he calls 'lack of mass.' Demos allow us to add 'mass' to what can sometimes be abstract ideas. Let me show you the Clay Table Room."

I followed him through the busy, productive-seeming place, and paused on the threshold of a third, smaller room. Tables ran along three of its four walls. On the tables was clay. Bricks and chunks of it, which students rolled between their palms and shaped with their fingers, creating all kinds of little clay figures, gesticulating with little clay arms.

"Wow," I said.

Tim nodded. "When you have to build a concept out of clay, it becomes really clear really fast whether you understand it."

A student turned in her chair. "Could you check this out, Tim? I'm demoing 'motivator.' "

"This is Joann," Tim said as she stood. "Joann is on HQS, the Hubbard Qualified Scientologist course."

I offered a quick smile, wondering how anyone could or would sign up for a course with that name. What did it mean to become a "qualified" Scientologist? I almost shuddered.

Tim slid into the chair Joann had vacated. "Sands is starting the PTS/SP course."

"I did that one," Joann said. "It's very useful."

Leaning in, Tim began to study the array of clay figures that took up half of one of the long tables. "I see a mother carrying a little boy. He's hugging her. And now she's put him down and they're holding hands. They're smiling."

I bent to look. Joann had created a three-dimensional storyboard. First, the woman—long clay strands of hair—carried a little boy. Then they were walking, holding hands, smiling. The mother carried a huge purse.

Joann stayed quiet, chin pulled in. I gathered she wasn't to comment, but just let Tim tell the story he saw in what she'd created.

"Uh-oh," Tim said. "The little boy is reaching into the purse!"

The mother appeared to be waving at someone. Her son was taking advantage by slipping a hand into her purse. Next he held behind his back a little clay rectangle marked **$$**.

"Ah," Tim said, "now they're no longer holding hands."

"Their Affinity is down," I said. Tim shot me a glance. "Sorry," I said.

"Well, that's right. But until you're checked out on your own clay table work, you can't check out the work of others. Best thing is to take the Student Hat course, then HQS, then Method One. After that, you're fast flow. Really speeds things up."

He peered again at the clay figures. "All right, the overt's clear. So far so good. Now, let's see how you handle the withhold."

He pulled his chair to the right and leaned in to study the next scenarios. "They're looking at—are these teddy bears? And the boy is angry with his mother. Yes, that's a manifestation that often follows an overt. Good."

Indeed, the mother was pointing at a row of what could have been little bears. The boy, his mouth open and jagged (a nearby toothpick indicated how these details were accomplished), tugged at her hand and pointed to another.

"And now," Tim said, "the mother has opened her purse to pay for the teddy bear. But the boy is on the ground. He's having a tantrum!"

Joann had carved a big crying hole in the little boy's face. He was, in a kind of clay-y way, flinging around his arms and legs. The mother held hands to her ears.

"He stole the money!" Tim said. "But he's making his mother wrong because she won't buy him the toy he wants—he's 'motivating' his behavior."

In the next frame, the woman had her purse turned upside down, to show there was no money in it. A teardrop-shaped bit of clay was pasted to her cheek. The little boy was now facedown, hammering the floor with his fists.

"Pass." Tim held out a hand for Joann's course pack and signed his initials in the space allotted for it on the check sheet. Another student called him over, and as he checked out that demo, I watched Joann squish all those scenarios into one huge ball of clay that she dumped into a container full of other balls and bricks. She covered it with a plastic sheet and went to wash her hands.

"You just got a good demo of demoing," Tim said, cheerfully. "Now, let's get you started."

BY THE TIME I settled in at one of the tables, I wasn't feeling quite as grumpy. Even as I knew I was about to grapple with information I didn't particularly want to know—why I was considered a Potential Trouble Source, how my parents could be considered Suppressive Persons—I was intrigued; even, I had to admit, a bit excited.

The Hollywood bungalow where I'd completed the comm course, Success Through Communication, was, I'd come to understand, a Scientology mission. Small though it was, it established the norm: When you started a course, you were handed a packet of bulletins written by LRH. The cost of the course included the use of that packet, the services of the Course Supervisor, and a check sheet.

The first bulletin in the PTS/SP course pack would probably have been "Keeping Scientology Working"; the next covered the Barriers to Study.[49] According to Hubbard, there are three such barriers, and in his usual technical way, he identifies them, including the accompanying physical manifestations, and offers solutions. As Tim had already mentioned, one of these barriers is "lack of mass." The study subjects, particularly philosophy and religion, means grappling with abstractions. There's a reason Justice is represented as a blindfolded lady holding a set of scales; it allows us to picture the concept of "blind justice." But, as Hubbard points out, even a concrete thing, if it's never been seen or held, needs "mass." One can't learn to drive a tractor from pictures alone.

How obvious, I thought. Isn't that why encyclopedias provide images in their margins, why manuals have diagrams, and why you learn to cook using a skillet and a stove? I decided to skip all that and go directly to what Hubbard had to say about the Suppressive Person.[50] I flipped forward a few pages in the course pack.

> He or she speaks only in very broad generalities.

Not.

> Such a person deals mainly in bad news, critical or hostile remarks, invalidation and general suppression.

Nope. Well, my dad might talk about the Evil Empire. He'd certainly been tough on me as a writer from time to time, but it was he who purchased a Martin guitar for me, surprised me with a round-trip plane ticket to Paris, paid for schooling of all kinds.

In any case, the word "mainly" didn't in any way describe his "hostile remarks"—except in regards to Scientology.

Maybe I needed to put "mass" to this idea. I pulled a few items from the little basket full of them on the table and fiddled with them as I read that surrounding such a person are "cowed or ill associates or friends, who, when not driven actually insane, are yet behaving in a crippled manner in life, failing, not succeeding."

I stared at my demo—the battery that was the Suppressive Person surrounded by a safety pin stuck sideways into a cork, broken crayons piled in a sad heap, a miniature Gumby with its limbs twisted into a tortured position—and thought of the dozens of students my father had ushered into their careers, who years later still sent him news of their successes and called for his advice. I thought of the Community of Writers he'd helped create, out of which so many authors and poets launched fine careers.

I crossed the room and, whispering fiercely, told Tim there was no way any of this could apply to my parents.

"Wait, wait," he said. "Did you get checked out on 'Barriers to Study'?"

I shook my head.

"Study that first bulletin and get checked out on it. Follow the check sheet."

"I *understand* the barriers to study," I said. "But my parents are not suppressive."

"What are they?"

"They are thoughtful, intelligent, loving people."

His eyes were tired but kind. "No. I mean, what are the barriers to study?"

"Lack of mass," I said. "Umm. Not understanding a word. I don't remember the third one, but that is *not* what this is about."

"Flunk," he said, without a trace of harshness. "Study the bulletin, Sands."

Throbbing with resentment, I read it again.

"Lack of mass" I understood. I even appreciated how it might indeed keep one from studying effectively.

The next barrier was "too steep a gradient": If a student is forced into undertaking a new action without having understood the previous action, confusion results.

I tapped pen against page, remembering when I'd been introduced to algebra in the eighth grade. I'd adored it. Its combination of mystery and clean lines enthralled me. But at some point I stopped understanding what was scribbled on the blackboard; suddenly I got low scores on my homework. I remember this happening in less than a week.

Hubbard describes the physiological reactions of "too steep a gradient" as "a sort of confusion or reelingness . . ." Staring out the window into the explosion of overgrown shrubbery surrounding Celebrity Center, I remembered how swiftly I'd become convinced that, concerning anything to do with numbers, I was a numbskull. But maybe it was just that the teacher had moved too quickly through the subject.

To solve it, Hubbard suggests, just cut back to a simpler level. Again, how obvious! And I had not "skipped a gradient"!

I told Tim so.

"Let's take it one thing at a time," he said. "What sentence were you just reading?"

"It's not that I don't understand it! I just don't agree with it."

"What happens when you go past a misunderstood word?"

"I'm not misunderstanding any words!" I said. "*Supposedly* I'm a Potential Trouble Source, and *supposedly* my parents are Suppressive People."

"Sands," Tim said, and he gave a little sigh. "It's not too much to say that all of it, every sorrow in this world, comes down to a misunderstood word." We stared at each other. I imagined fights between spouses, statues being toppled, gulags, war. It suddenly seemed quite possible. "Now," he said, "you need to study that bulletin, and before you proceed further, you must be thoroughly checked out on it. I want you to pay particular attention to the third barrier to study. Am I clear?"

His eyes were still tired, still kind, and utterly implacable.

AMONG THE MANY concerns Hubbard addressed, in the stream of bulletins and policy letters issued from his typewriter in the Hubbard Communications Office or transcribed from recordings of his lectures, were those regarding being a student. There he was, laying out matters to do with mind, spirit, ethics, admin—subjects that have to be *understood* in order to be *applied*—and people weren't getting it. I can imagine him heaving an exasperated but rather pleased sigh, then rolling up his sleeves to address the "hat" a student needed to wear to be effective. That's the name of a required course: Student Hat.

All this is known as Study Tech. As I began to work with its principles, I found it deeply satisfying—in fact, galvanizing. This was especially true of Hubbard's explanation of the "misunderstood word," the third and most prevalent of his barriers to study. He suggests that going past a word you don't understand may keep you from understanding an entire subject, can even cause you to abandon a study altogether. And his notions around "clearing" words is a substantial part of what bound me to the religion for years.

At the time, I thought of words, when I thought about them at all, as a way to communicate. I remember, when I was about four, sounding out the word L-I-F-E on the cover of that magazine as I seized an understanding that the magazine's purpose was to *present life* and, simultaneously, became aware of the miraculous thing called reading. And I'd loved my little twenty-six-page collection of homonyms. But using a dictionary to look up words had never been a particular focus in our household. If I came across a word in my reading I didn't understand, I either skipped over it or went to my dad.

"How's it used?" he'd ask. I'd read him the sentence, and he'd define it.

When I wanted to know how to *spell* a word, however, parents and even teachers employed a frustrating tactic: "Look it up."

This well-intentioned effort caused me to avoid dictionaries, even to actively dislike them. They were cumbersome volumes where the pages were thin and the print small, where you looked in vain, until you were ready to weep, for PNEUMONIA, or PSYCHOLOGY, or even something as simple as acword, aukwurd, awkword, AWKWARD. Symbols and abbreviations—pl, <, LL, ë, *intr*—only added to the confusion. For almost three decades, while I read avidly, I largely defined words in and by context.

But in a Scientology course room, you are required to "clear" words and concepts you don't understand or—and this was for me the startling and fun part—*think* you understand. Anything that might muddy the waters of your spiritual and emotional and literary understanding, you clear. Not only that, you examine its derivation, its etymology.

"Have you ever come to the bottom of a page only to realize you didn't remember what you had just read?" Hubbard asks. "That is the phenomenon of a misunderstood word, and one will always be found just before the material became blank in your mind."

This was an experience I recognized. As was Hubbard's warning that you'll find yourself starting to yawn if you go past a word or concept you don't understand. I thought of the many times I'd gotten dozy while reading something like Pagels's *Gnostic Gospels*: how I'd flip back until I found a sentence I remembered having read, start from that place, read on, nod off again . . . eventually sliding the book under the bed, resolving to try again later.

"Going past a word or symbol for which one does not have a proper definition gives one a distinctly blank or washed-out feeling," Hubbard writes, adding that this barrier "establishes aptitude or lack of aptitude," and is "the prime factor involved with stupidity."

All this began to make grand, wonderful, *important* sense. It fueled my growing belief that all Hubbard wanted, what everything in his religion was devised to do, was to lift mankind out of degradation and ignorance, and onto a higher plane—into a better life.

THE TRUE SENSE OF THE WORD

Having passed the spot-check for Barriers to Study, I read what makes a person a Potential Trouble Source. The primary thing? Overts! Of course! I thought of my endless car trouble during the affair with Roger. I'd been sleeping with a married man! Lost keys? Dead battery? They made complete metaphorical sense.

This emphasis on overts, particularly for a psyche such as mine, which, by nature or nurture, was primed for blame-taking, allowed Scientology's cult-claws to sink in deeply. My epiphanies were all about being "better." Clearly I am not the only person kept in thrall by this tactic, but the employment of such an insidious and purposeful psychology—the knowledge it demonstrates, that most people want to be good, and that that desire for goodness, for being "correct," for doing what's right (even in opposition to other deeply held beliefs) will keep a vast population in line—appalls me now. I see that it borrows techniques from authoritarianism, and demonstrates a gleeful understanding and purposeful employment of groupthink. But at the time, it simply made sense: I had done something wrong. That was the answer to, the reason for, all my tribulations.

So I was PTS because of overts. But what about the idea that a Potential Trouble Source must be connected to a Suppressive Person—also known as an "antisocial personality"? Not one of the attributes connected to SPs described my parents. Certain that I understood the bulletin, I carried my course pack over to Joann for a spot check. She was "fast flow," and Tim had asked her to check me out on bulletins as I finished them.

Joann placed a finger on a word. "What's the definition of 'personality'?"

"What? How's it used?

"Flunk." She pointed to the sentence.

> The antisocial personality cannot finish a cycle of action . . . becomes surrounded by incomplete projects.

"Wait," I said, even as Joann shook her head. "Personality," I stuttered. "It's what makes a person who he is, it's the part of his character that defines his, umm, person."

"We shouldn't define a word using part of the word." She shrugged apologetically. "Flunk. You need to look it up, restudy the bulletin."

So I restudied. I defined all the uses of the word, and its etymology, considerably struck by the idea that the root of PERSON descends to us from an Etruscan word for "mask," which makes lovely sense. But how could this description—"surrounded by incomplete projects"—describe my mother, who did everything from create marvelous dresses out of ethnic material to print her own photographs in her own darkroom (full of instruments purchased by and in a space created by my supposedly suppressive father)? How could this apply to him, at the time the author of—which meant he'd *completed*—two dozen novels? Who'd hammered together much of the house in Squaw Valley? Who was a brilliant teacher of writing? I could hardly imagine the number of "cycles of action" that had been completed as he helped his many students toward their degrees. Suppressive? I looked up the word in the Tech Dictionary:

> To squash, to sit on, to make smaller, to refuse to let reach, to make uncertain about his reaching, to render or lessen in any way possible by any means possible, to

> the harm of the individual and for the fancied protection of the suppressor.[51]

I could see this described the *feelings* my parents sometimes caused in me, but they did not "squash," or "sit on," or "refuse to let reach" on *purpose*. In any case, how would doing so "protect" them? From what? They just didn't want me to be a Scientologist.

Which of course is the most important definition of a Suppressive Person. I'm sure by this time I'd heard the word TAUTOLOGY, but even as I grappled with the twists of Scientological logic, I didn't grasp that I was studying, as the *American Heritage* puts it, "a series of self-reinforcing statements that cannot be disproved because the statements depend on the assumption that they are already correct."

In any case, as far as the Church was concerned, I *was* connected to an SP, to two of them in fact, and I was PTS. Even without its Scientology overtones, the phrase "potential trouble source" was apt. I *was* trouble. The certainty I craved would arrive—and then, chimera-like, would disappear, leaving me edgy, weepy, wanting to go live a *normal* life. And just hours later, I'd be on course, defining long lists of words, in love with what I was doing.

It's hard, now, to recall whether that swooping, plummeting, exhilarating, exhausting rollercoaster ride was attached to the religion, to my marriage, or if it was simply my nature. Or if it was the depression into which I'd plunged after confronting the terrible understanding that my brother was not coming back, which had initiated that flight to Los Angeles in the first place. But as I leaf through the journals that record these swings, I see that I did not, at this point, question what I was learning. All that seemed valuable. What caused me anguish was that this knowledge, this study, was attached to *being a Scientologist*. Was there no other way to gain this information, to have—for this is what I found in those hours at those sunlit tables—so much scholarly and spiritual fun? As I defined words, made lists of others whose meanings I wanted to confirm, I began to truly love what I was doing. I see now that what I loved was the act of studying.

Also, that I loved *what* I was studying, which was not Scientology as much as it was ideas—especially regarding religion and spirituality—and, above all, words themselves.

AND MY BROTHER? He and Mary and little O4 were still living in Squaw Valley, in the Annex, the house below our parents'. Mary was pregnant again. However, not long after a daughter was born, Mary headed back east and initiated divorce proceedings. Mom and Dad hired a lawyer, but Mary's mounted quite a case against Oak's suitability as a father, and he was denied all but the most draconian visiting rights. He hardly ever saw his children again.

At which point, Mom and Dad made Oak an offer: If he could get into graduate school, they'd fund tuition and an apartment.

This is an excellent example of the denial that during these years ran rampant through the family, and certainly a misapprehension of the extent of Oak's brain damage, but at the time it made sense. It was a way for him to "start," after having flunked so badly.

And so he applied for a PhD in English at the University of California, Davis. With his bachelor's in drama from UC Irvine, his master's in fiction from Brown, his stint as artistic director of the Lexington Conservatory Theatre, and the productions of his own plays there and in Manhattan, his credentials were significant. He must have had to write an essay, at least a statement of intent, but he seems to have done it well enough that he was accepted into the graduate program. (I loved this bit of synchronicity: I was studying; he was studying!)

However, no matter how brilliant Oak may have been able to appear on paper, he was unable to find his way across the campus to a classroom, much less comprehend a syllabus. So he wandered Davis, read avidly—as he always had and always would—and never went to class. He ran into Robin, whom he'd met at the Squaw Conference before his accident, and moved in with her. Robin's sense of humor, her insouciant way of being in the world, suited him perfectly, and she gave him much needed ballast and security. But even though Robin would take care of Oak, providing love and support for the next decade, our parents never seemed to understand her vital contributions to his healing brain, and his life.

WHILE OAK WAS in Davis, ignoring class schedules, I was at Celebrity Center, adhering to mine. Jamie still worked all night and never took a weekend. We fought about it, but we managed to find affinity in the pleasure I was taking in being on course. Before getting married, we'd had a talk about my acting career—he wanted me to agree to take no work that would involve nudity, which I found laughable and off-putting in equal measure. I dismissed the entire conversation, and anything else it might have represented, as if it had never happened. He also did not want me to continue working as a waitress, perhaps because that's how we'd met and he worried it could happen again, with someone else. Instead, I taught small acting classes and a seminar on Shakespeare in our living room. Now and again I landed acting work. My agent encouraged me to go out for commercials, but I resisted; I didn't want to bite down on a piece of Trident gum in front of millions. However, the money could be really good, and I was eventually persuaded to try. I cut and permed my hair, trying to look like the girl next door, and did land a big one: Hertz. I was delighted when I found out it would air only in Europe.

But most afternoons I studied. I was persuaded by what LRH had to say about mind and spirit and their connections, and spent a lot of time delving into other forms of spirituality while clearing my ideas about this one. I was engaged by his ideas about ethics, and about the ways in which memory acts on us, and how past negative actions may be responsible for present problems. I might have gleaned this by studying Tibetan Buddhism and Jungian philosophy, while reading about Christianity and psychology, but I began to feel that Hubbard had put all that together, in a most compelling way.

Of my own accord I signed up for the next course, Student Hat, which provided hours of word-filled rhapsodic engagement, without having to think too closely about my parents' potentially suppressive natures, about my brother, about my supposed career—not even about what I was doing with these months of my life. I may have been in the Condition of Confusion regarding my marriage, and wavered in and out of Doubt regarding Scientology (even as I sat in one of its course rooms five days a week), but as a student, my Condition was not Normal, not Affluence—it was Power. I'd found something at which I excelled: study. I sat at one of those big tables, surrounded by dictionaries, studying bulletins, listening to taped lectures, reading books (all by Hubbard), happily descending into word chains when I didn't understand, or had the faintest doubt about whether I understood, any word or phrase in a definition. Sometimes this required outside readings, and I especially enjoyed using the (out-of-date) encyclopedia, as well as various manuals available on the course room's shelves. Some of those word chains, like a good Monopoly game, went on for days.

WHAT WAS SO different from that childhood resentment about being forced to use a dictionary? For one thing, and it's huge, I wasn't being "sent" to the dictionary to find out how to spell a word, which often felt like punishment for not knowing, and led me to pretend I knew things when I didn't. For another—and this was life changing—Hubbard's precise formula for "clearing a word" meant that you had to engage with its etymology.

By the age of seven I'd understood, from my little collection of them, that a *hom*onym is different than a *syn*onym. I'd been taught to spell using phonetics, so I understood that words have parts. But I don't think I knew that the prefixes HOM and SYN, even though they communicate the difference, existed prior to or beyond their English usage. I certainly didn't know that attached to other suffixes, those prefixes created other words. I found this miraculous.

Yes, I'd been birthed into and educated within the aspirations of a literary family, I held a BA in drama (graduating *magna cum laude*, words that I understood meant I had majorly good grades but not the *summa* best grades), and I'd attended an advanced training program at a prestigious acting academy. I even understood, from my study of Shakespeare, that some of our words come from Saxon roots (MUD, BLOOD, words Macbeth might use), and others were Latinate (PRODIGAL, OBSEQUIOUS, employed by a character like Polonius). I even understood that ACROPOLIS came from Greek and ABACUS from Arabic. But it had never particularly occurred to me that ACRO or POLIS might *communicate* something, that they *came from somewhere.* It was, I suppose, a version of the assumption that milk comes in bottles or butter in rectangles.

Almost overnight, language became a teeming garden of possibilities, the bouquets one can put together when one understands that CHRON has to do with time, PHILO with love, BIO with life, HYDRO with water, CARDIO with heart, TELE with distance . . . and the suffixes! –LOGY with study. –GRAPHY with drawing or writing. –METRY with measuring. –SOPHY (Sophia!) with wisdom. Like one of those children's books whose laminated pages are split in half, with the top of one animal above and the bottom of another below, which you can flip separately, creating a hybrid rabbit/tiger or cat/snake, the simplest words pulsed: TELEGRAPH TELEGRAM TELEPHONE GRAMOPHONE HYDROMETER PENTAMETER HYDROLOGY PHILOSOPHY SOPHISTRY SOPHISTICATED. I took to using a dictionary everywhere. Driving past a sign advertising DERMATOLOGIST was a galvanizing experience.

Etymology! The study of *the true sense of the word.* To me, this was the "bridge" Scientology offered, and as I stepped onto it, I found a glimmering, sacred world. Clearing a word became like the best kind of daily Christmas. I'd "save" the etymology for last: examining the root often made the whole word shimmer. Words became almost three-dimensional. I felt smarter, brighter; as if I could actually feel my mind expanding, or as if water were pushing its way through silted-up riverbeds, beginning to run, well, clear.

•

ONE DAY, I decided to clear the name of the religion itself. It actually frightened me a little. What would I find?

SCIENTOLOGY is a coined word, of course. Hubbard's Tech Dictionary had fourteen definitions (quotes from various HCOBs and HCOPLs). But now that I understood that there were parts to words, I was interested in examining those.

I understood that its suffix meant *the study of.*

And the first part must have something to with *science.*

But it wasn't science I was studying in that course room!

Or was it?

What is science, anyway?

I flipped through the *American Heritage*: "the observation, identification, description, experimental investigation and theoretical explanation of phenomena."

I chewed on that. Yes, that's indeed what Hubbard appeared to be doing, with his close analysis of life's basic principles, his codification of everything from ethics to scales of emotions to the barriers to study, not to mention the formulas he provided to work one's way out of problems and into success.

I examined other definitions, including METHODOLOGICAL, DISCIPLINE, and even STUDY, just to be sure I understood them.

And then, with the same sense of terror and awe and excitement that Eve might have had biting into that apple, I took in the root of the word—

—and looked up, blinking.

I hadn't known SCIENCE descended from Latin roots that mean *knowledge.*

Learning.

To *know.*

The beakers full of dripping liquids, the experiments with mice, the white lab coats suddenly made complete sense.

Science is about finding, gaining, proving what can be *known*!

The result of clearing SCIENTOLOGY was eye- and heart-opening. The fraught word was disassembled into a (slightly) less scary meaning. Hubbard had named his religion "the study of knowledge." Even, perhaps, "the knowledge of knowledge."

Knowing how to know.

Who wouldn't want that?

SUNNY

In Scientology, when you complete an "action"—a course, auditing, an Ethics Handling—you head immediately to the Examiner, a person whose job is to check how well or poorly these things have gone. The Examiner sits in a small room with an e-meter. You sit in the chair opposite and pick up the waiting cans. You look at the Examiner, and the Examiner looks at you, taking in what are called your "indicators."[52] These include your eyes and face, your sense of yourself, whether you're pleased (usually the case) or unhappy (rare, because it's unlikely that you'd be considered "through" with a given action until you're happy). At the same time, the Examiner keeps an eye on the meter. He's looking for a broad sweep of the needle, called a Floating Needle, or F/N.

A Floating Needle is an excellent thing. It means the current of electricity passing from the meter through your body, from the palm of one hand to the palm of the other, is, at this moment, encountering no barrier: "the charge on a subject being audited has dissipated, and is one of the indications of a process being complete."[53] The world is clean and orderly, even wonderful. (Like many of Hubbard's words and phrases, this one is also used as a verb, as in "I just F/Ned the whole evening.")

The Examiner sits with pen poised, taking you in.

You might offer up a realization: "I can do anything I set my mind to!" "I love Study Tech!" "I know how to recognize when I'm a Potential Trouble Source!"

The Examiner jots it down, notes your indicators, and tells you, "Your needle is floating." He signs and dates the sheet of paper and sends it along to whoever's overseeing the Org's folders, including yours, in which info about you is accumulating: courses you're taking, any auditing, the results of Ethics Handlings (e.g., that meeting with Marty about my parents).

I don't remember what "win" I may have offered up when I completed that first course, PTS/SP, nor do I remember picking up those cans. I'm sure my heart pounded. I'm also sure I smiled broadly, willing the meter to do whatever it was supposed to do.

When I went to the Examiner after finishing the Student Hat, however, there was no doubt about that F/N. I was thrilled. Having completed it just an hour into that day's three-hour stint, I headed directly to the Reg's office. I wanted to keep right on studying, and I knew which course I'd buy next: the Hubbard Qualified Scientologist course: HQS.

As I wrote that check, I thought of the moment a few months before, when I'd stared at the student who'd asked Tim to check her clay demo, wondering how anyone could possibly sign up for something called "Hubbard Qualified Scientologist." Yet here I was, noting the amount in my check register, intent on becoming a "qualified" Scientologist myself. On HQS, I'd learn to audit and be audited through various drills, including those called the "Upper TRs." With a "twin," I'd also do something called Self Analysis, using Book One processing—that is, Dianetics. We wouldn't use an e-meter, but we'd be on our way.

As I started in on the check sheet, a tall woman with a huge smile and a shining presence entered the course room. Sunny was also starting HQS. Tim suggested we twin.

Twinning is another aspect of Study Tech I found sensible. Instead of an entire group of people working on the same course, in the same room, on the same schedule, students studying Scientology work independently, each on their own course, at their own speed. It ensures that different levels of students, or students who can't commit to the same timeframe, can nevertheless move forward.

When you are officially twinned with someone, however, it means you're on the same course, studying in the same time slot, reading the same bulletins, helping each other through the steps on the check sheet. Until Sunny and I were twinned up, I hadn't realized how swiftly and easily this allows one to move along a course of study. And intrigued though I was with what I was learning, I'm sure that Scientology would not have carried the same weight nor provided the same joy, and I doubt I'd have stayed as long as I did, had Sunny and I not had each other as friends, models, examples. Sunny, quick and smart, with an infectious chortle of a laugh, was an extraordinary singer and musician with a burgeoning career. If someone as organized and sane and wonderful as she was doing this stuff, then this stuff was okay to do. More than once we assured each other of that shared perspective.

Among the first steps on the HQS check sheet were the Training Routines. Sunny and I sat in silence opposite each other with our eyes closed, with our eyes open, while trying to make each other laugh. We cleared words and watched each other's demos and rotated spot-checks. We had a lot of fun. We laughed a lot. We learned a lot.

ONE OF THE essential jobs of the auditor is, of course, to listen (*audire*). But equally important is that they *acknowledge*: any statement and, particularly, any realization (cognition). The importance of the Cycle of Communication became ever more clear, as did the reasons for those drills. Knowing that an acknowledgment awaits allows the person being audited (the preclear, or pc) to articulate *anything*, no matter how obvious or silly or profound. This is especially true if you have an auditor, a twin, you love and trust.

After we'd finished reviewing the Lower TRs, Sunny and I began to study and drill the Upper TRs. These routines are mobile; you no longer sit opposite another, as auditor and preclear do when "in session." I imagined these drills were designed to train one to be a Scientologist "in life," that is, not just during an auditing session or in the course room.

In these Training Routines, as with the lower ones, students take turns being coach and preclear. However, while the coach is still training to be an auditor, the student being the preclear is no longer "acting" like the one getting auditing. She is, in fact, *being* audited. In the process—it took me a long time to understand this—she is indoctrinated, little by little, into the whole idea of what auditing "should" accomplish. This gradual shift of intention never occurred to me. Realizing it now makes me shudder.

When you're being an auditor, even a student one, a Case Supervisor checks your sessions, to make sure they've gone well, to make sure your pc is "winning." I realized that the hours a CS devotes to overseeing student training is part of what you pay for when you purchase a course. As I began to perceive how many trained people were on call and in service to those on course and those being audited, the cost of these actions appeared far more reasonable. That's because I assumed all those people were being paid in some commensurate way.

They were not, but it would take me years to understand (or to face) that. Most of those with whom we came in contact, from Registrar to Ethics Officer, from Course Supervisor to Examiner to Case Supervisor, were Sea Org: They'd signed on for those billion years. I understood that what Sea Org members got in exchange for working for the Church included meals and housing and a small salary that was based on the overall stats of their Org, and, supposedly, courses and auditing. But Sea Org members worked long hours and I often wondered when they found the time to move along the Bridge. (I thought this was too bad, considering that billion-year commitment, but wondered if the thinking was that they could get to the Bridge next lifetime.)

Members of the Sea Org are allowed to marry (there is to be no extramarital sex), but for years, if they wanted to have children (or if they got pregnant), the Church required them to temporarily leave the Sea Org and work in other staff positions until the children were six years old. At that point children were usually placed in Cadet Orgs—a sort of Sea Org for youngsters—and their parents returned to work. If the parents' post was at a distance from where their child was housed, it meant they might not see him for months, even years.[54]

If Tim, our Course Supervisor, was married and/or had children, he had an hour a day of "family time" to spend with them, as well as, in theory, one full day a month. This was in the early eighties; by 1988, the Church had canceled even this minimal amount of time spent with family, saying that, "to have such breaks . . . in the middle of production has been found to be detrimental to production."[55] In 1991, the Church went further: A Flag Order (orders that are issued by top management and not intended for the larger public) stated that "the Sea Org is not set up to handle or take care of children" and "Therefore, Sea Org members that have new children will not be allowed to remain on duty . . ."[56] Those married couples that did "beget a child" [*sic*] would be sent to Orgs that were not doing well, known as Class V Orgs.[57] There are many reports of women in the Sea Org being forced to get abortions, or deciding they had to, if they wanted to remain in their posts, even though the Church itself is anti-abortion.[58] At six years of age, children—who are considered full-blown thetans in small bodies, capable of making such decisions—can also sign up for those billion years (supposedly they are considered minors, and under the supervision of their parents), and they often do.[59]

Sea Org members work an average of a hundred hours a week. Usually, their weekly pay is dependent on the Org's stats. The Church, as a religious organization, is tax-exempt, so there is no social security. There are no benefits, and certainly no insurance. Nor does the Church have a system in place for those who get old or sick. If you get old or sick or an accident causes you to be hospitalized, you must have "pulled it in."

If a person decides to leave the Sea Org, she is handed what's known as a "freeloader's debt." This is usually hundreds of thousands of dollars: the sum she owes the Church for having been housed and fed; if any courses have been taken, or auditing received, there are charges for those as well.[60]

Little of this was clear to me at the time. To know now what the children of Sea Org members went through, and in some cases still do, makes my blood run cold; the website exscientologykids.com is devoted to reaching those who were brought up under these circumstances, and reading story after story of their experiences is excruciating.[61]

While it's possible I convinced myself to see only what I wanted to see—hard-working people devoted to their posts and to the larger goals of the Church—I think that most of those with whom I came in contact felt vital to an essential enterprise, and for the most part, reading and hearing the stories of those who've left the Sea Org substantiates that understanding. It's yet another example of the forethought and ingenuity Hubbard put in to creating his religion: being convinced that you are helping to save humanity gives one a very meaningful rock to roll up the hill. There is no room for existential woe in a Scientology Org.

SUNNY AND I cheerfully drilled the various routines called for in HQS, then wrote up those sessions for the Case Supervisor. One of the drills involves the coach telling the pc to look at a wall, to walk over and touch the wall, to turn around. She then acknowledges her.

"Touch that wall," the coach says, and when the pc has done so, "Turn around," and then, "Thank you," and then repeats the command to "touch that wall." If the pc pauses to talk about something this has made her think about, the auditor's job is to listen and acknowledge: "Thank you." The pc might offer an opinion about the wallpaper; this might lead to notions about "walls" in general, which might generate thoughts about a current "wall-like" situation in the pc's life. The auditor thanks her—and tells her to touch the wall. This can go on for quite some time, sometimes for hours. The sign to end the process is when the pc has a cognition. It's usually obvious to both people when this occurs: In addition to whatever the pc might say, her "indicators" usually indicate joy or pleasure or even a shift in her sense of self.

In many blogs now available, ex-Scientologists have written that the TRs create a hypnotic state and that they are used for nefarious purposes. Perhaps because Sunny and I were so compatible, and were such good friends, this was not my experience. If anything, my awareness felt heightened, sharpened. The simplicity of the drills, as well as their repetitive nature, reminded me of the Buddhist exhortation "chop wood, carry water"; in the most mundane task can be found a life perspective. Christian sermons as well as Buddhist dharma talks are often based around this idea: Take a detail of living and turn it into a metaphor. Given this structured opportunity to observe ourselves in relation to various objects and surfaces, Sunny and I formulated intriguing realizations about space, self, relationships, life.

One day we were drilling on the top floor of Celebrity Center. Before being purchased by the Church, the building had for years suffered as a sort of transient hotel, and in the early eighties there were still entire floors that had yet to be refurbished. We were working in a room where the paint was peeling, the rug worn and stained, the furniture decrepit. It was Sunny's turn as coach. As she told me to touch various walls, I began to offer up thoughts about time and aesthetics and molecules.

"Thank you," she said. "Touch that wall."

The couch in the room was absolutely ugly. Its upholstery was a dreadful burnt orange, striped with turd-brown plaid, the pillows bunched and misshapen. Even in its glory days it had to have been uncomfortable. Over the years, the spiky fabric had acquired a faintly greasy sheen. I allowed as how it was really ugly. "Thank you," Sunny said, her eyes alight with laughter. I commented on other of its disgusting attributes, which Sunny acknowledged gravely but with a twinkle in her eye. But suddenly, in a state of wonder, real wonder, I sat down on the couch.

"In someone's eyes," I said, "this was beautiful! Someone actually thought they were creating something beautiful!"

"Oh!" Sunny was also suddenly and utterly serious. "Yes! Wow! I mean, thank you!"

This is an obvious thought. It's one I'd accepted intellectually all my life. But I'd never owned it, and it's not too much to say that I looked at the world differently after that. The recognition was not just that beauty is in the eye of the beholder, it was that there's no need to force or project one's own ideas of so-called beauty onto another. Put another way, I understood that just because it wasn't my taste didn't mean it wasn't "good" taste.

It's hard to articulate what a shift of consciousness this was. The bohemian world of the artist—the one inhabited by parents and friends—was, I believed, the "best" way to live. By extension, in a kind of cultish response, I'd come to believe it was the *only* way to live. But polo shirts and Dockers, never part of the Hall world, are considered by many to be good taste. Others' taste might run to flip-flops and shorts. It depends on context and upbringing and background. To those sliding bare feet into penny loafers, the array of Mexican silver and Tibetan turquoise my mother wove around her neck might seem excessive. And there was Mr. Porter, arriving (and departing) with his bottle of Tanqueray; according to him, where taste in liquor was concerned, my father's was dreadful.

Sunny and I beamed at each other and ran down the stairs to the Examiner.

"Your needle is floating," he said.

Sunny wrote up the session, and then we scampered back to the course room and settled in at the big oak tables to study the next bulletin, clear the next word, demo the next concept, on the way to being "qualified" Scientologists.

I began to envision that in each of these moments I was picking off a bit of caked mud that over the course of my lifetime—lifetimes—had adhered to my once bright and could-be-again shining psyche. Which began to make the thought of being audited by a trained auditor, with an e-meter, almost attractive. I still found the idea scary. But what might it be like to have that leaping needle find the dirt caked to your psyche (which I pictured as a golden orb beneath all that murk). What might it be like to get rid of all that muddy charge, so you could F/N your way through life?

EVERY FEW MONTHS my friend Marilyn and I met for lunch. We'd been in the acting company of the Colorado Shakespeare Festival during that cherished 1975 summer, and the following season we worked together again in Ashland. I loved those lunches, which usually included salad and white wine (I worked carefully around the twenty-four-hour rule). She was doing well in her career and often insisted on picking up the tab. She'd met a wonderful man and thought they might get married.

Over one of these lunches, I wept as I told her how deeply my parents disapproved of my study of Scientology.

"But *why*!" I remember her tone, and how, for the first time, I understood what authors of nineteenth-century novels meant when they used the verb "cried." Marilyn wore hats that made her look as if she'd stepped out of a painting by Renoir or Sargent, and today's was a cunning little piece of straw and ribbon, beneath which blond curls framed her face. "Why!" she cried. "Isn't it just about you trying to be the best person you can be?"

I nodded, grateful for that perception. It was what I believed, what so many of us did; it was a large part of why we stayed—and why many still do. Hubbard's purpose, his Technology, seemed so altruistic. He believed man was basically good! He had our best interests at heart! One had only to look at his many "how-tos": from effective filing systems to methods for gauging emotional states (Tone Scale); from improving the relationship between body, mind, and spirit to the one with your spouse; from getting one's stats up to getting one's ethics in; from running an organization to making a good first impression (these last include using an effective unscented deodorant, getting to one's feet upon first meeting someone, and making good eye contact). Many of Hubbard's notions seem terribly obvious, but part of his particular genius was in understanding that such tabulation is wanted, even needed. That checklist about making a good first impression, for instance. It's advice a parent gives a child, but for those who didn't have such a parent, or such guidance, it might be satisfying to tick things off a list. Clean fingernails: check. Ready smile: check. Good eye contact: check.

These systems seemed interconnected. With Scientology's help, one could rid oneself of memories and precepts and even mannerisms that might be holding one back, stride through the world with confidence, and surge on up the Bridge to an ever-expanding spiritual understanding—and, supposedly, happiness.

However, and curiously, I wasn't in fact doing any surging. I loved being on course but was still wary of auditing, even though, so I understood, that's where the *real* action took place. It was partly finances—auditing was expensive and I had no savings, and I refused to max out a credit card—but it was also a reluctance to become more deeply involved. Even as I persuaded myself of Scientology's altruism, even as I believed (as at the time I did) that those on staff were being paid a decent wage, I wondered—worried—where all the money went. It didn't manifest in improvements to Celebrity Center (though it certainly has since). Still, the idea that the Church was bilking people out of money seemed cynical—and to think so meant I had an overt. They were helping people out of unhappiness, out of unethical practices, out of misunderstood words. They were helping people *go free* (whatever that meant).

We all worked toward those aims. In the course room we were flunked (and we flunked others) for not checking out on a bulletin. No paraphrasing. Steady schedules. Inside and outside the course room we were productive, keeping our stats up. We were ethical, no overts to tangle up our psyches, to drop us down to lower Conditions. I felt as if I were part of a humming engine made up of kind souls, all of whom—from Registrar to janitor, fellow students to Case Supervisor—were devoted to this effort. I was particularly impressed with the Course Supervisor: Tim's patience and tolerance moved me. He spent fourteen hours a day, seven days a week, in the course room, devoted to creating good Scientologists.

Nevertheless, I often found myself redefining RELIGION. The word's derivation, "bind back," made me imagine a farmer working with vines, a gardener grafting the stock of one rose onto that of another.[62] Looking around the increasingly beloved, shabby course room, where fellow students leafed through dictionaries, listened to tapes, played out demos, I understood that the etymology of RELIGION describes its very arduousness.

I didn't, then, know the joys of having a *practice*. PRACTICE is a lovely word. One meaning is to work on getting better at an endeavor, as in practicing the guitar. Another is, simply, the endeavor itself—a doctor's practice, a yoga practice. Practice offered contentment. It would take a while to understand that it was what I'd had meditating all those years, and in the hours when I was working on a new song. And it's what I would have, eventually, as the practice grew stronger, in writing.

GAH

Elsewhere in the course room, students were drilling the use of an e-meter. Was I going to do that? Examine my "case," those charged-up places in my psyche? I was now familiar with the idea of ENGRAM, described by Hubbard in *Dianetics* as

> a mental image picture which is a recording of a time of physical pain and unconsciousness.

It's also "a definite and permanent trace left by the stimulus on the protoplasm of a tissue":

> [an engram] must, by definition, have impact or injury as part of its content. These engrams are a complete recording, down to the last accurate detail, of every perception present in a moment of partial or full unconsciousness.[63]

Hubbard coined the word—DIA + NETICS = "through the mind"—and claims that engrams can be relieved by processing them. One person listens to another's problem, asks about "earlier, similar incidents" until the earliest one is located, at which point the power contained in the "chain" of them supposedly disappears. According to Hubbard, the earliest incident might be found in the womb, e.g.

(an example he uses often): a fetus is hurt when Pa makes love to Ma, which turns out to be the original pain attached to subsequent incidents. Or the original engram is attached to the mother trying to abort the fetus (another example Hubbard frequently cites) using a knitting needle or by jumping off a chair.

It made me think of a story my mother sometimes told about a night just before I was born. She and Dad were driving—to the hospital? home from a party?—and they passed a car accident. The few times Mom described it, the scene was weirdly vivid to me, full of details she did not necessarily include in her telling: a tangle of red brake lights and white headlights, one of the latter aimed in an impossible direction, up to the sky instead of straight ahead. No ambulance had yet arrived. People had pulled over to help or to gawk, and silhouettes of cars and bodies, flickering in what light there was, lined the road. Dad slowed, then slowed further, as they realized the reason for that mangle of steel and bodies, the reason for that headlight skewed at the sky: Two cars had crashed, head on. As they inched by, Mom covered her eyes. But not so that she wouldn't see. She covered her eyes because she did not want me, the baby in her womb, to witness the carnage.

Hearing this story, I was touched by what a motherly act it was, protecting the forming mind of an unborn child.

But I'd also wondered: How could it be I wasn't there—and of course I wasn't; I wasn't born—when all those details were so startlingly vivid?

In order to help the pc find those engrams, the hidden mental-image pictures attached to them, and to clear them, Hubbard collaborated on the development of the electropsychometer, the e-meter.[64] The analogy to the "clear" button on an adding machine now made sense. Again, from *Dianetics*:

> Before a computer can be used to solve a problem, it must be cleared of old problems, old data and conclusions. Otherwise, it will add the old conclusions into the new one and produce an invalid answer . . .

Many people who practiced Dianetics had real gains. Quite a number attested to Clear (a state in which, Hubbard writes, one has "no vicious reactive mind and can operate at total mental capacity").[65] Clear is perceived as an ongoing state; once you attest to Clear, you don't slip back to being "unclear." Nevertheless, life will offer up new problems to solve and new miseries to be grappled with, and even people who'd gone Clear wanted more auditing. In addition, quite a number of practitioners didn't find relief when they located that first incident, not even if they found it in the womb. Some found themselves coming up with incidents that took place in *previous* lifetimes.

Even in the midst of a growing excitement about these ideas, I was conscious that they might be cleverly implanted. When, in the course room, you overhear an e-meter drill that asks someone to say how many epochs ago, to the power of ten, an incident happened, you can't help but wonder if you've had millions of lifetimes, and if one can, indeed, carry knowledge from one lifetime to another. It isn't that outrageous an idea. Many Eastern religions believe in reincarnation. If you count the actual number of bodies + souls on the planet, probably more people believe in the idea than don't. But it also began to dawn on me that that was an awful lot of lifetimes through which to process earlier, similar incidents. Could one ever *really* be Clear? Wouldn't there always be *something*?

Still, the idea that with or without a body—and *between* bodies—the thetan, the "you that is you," might carry images from previous lifetimes to the one you're living now, and that by exploring ancient anguishes, one might make sense of current troubles, was deeply appealing.

ONE NIGHT, IN the midst of my travails with Jamie, I had such an experience. Over dinner with a Scientologist friend, Jen, I confided my sorrow regarding his chronic lateness, how he was never home for dinner, my yearning for the kind of marriage I simply didn't have.

I began to weep, and after offering various bits of advice, none of which comforted me, Jen asked, "Is there an earlier, similar incident?" She slipped the question easily into our conversation. Even as I realized this was Dianetic processing, another episode with a previous boyfriend came immediately to mind. I told her about it, but was still emotional (or, as Hubbard calls it, "misemotional"). She asked the question several more times, which led to other memories. Suddenly I found myself crying even harder and shaking my head at something I called "impossible."

"Tell me," Jen said.

It took a while for her to convince me to share the memory that was now as real to me as the dinner we'd just finished eating, but eventually I offered it up.

I shivered on a dark road in what I thought might be Ireland, clutching a shawl around myself against a biting wind, waiting for my husband, who was, as he always was, at the village pub.

My cognition, as Jen talked me through this memory, was that I needed to stop weeping and wailing. I needed to *do* something.

Which of course applied to my relationship with Jamie. Jamie, like the Irish husband, might come grumpily home for the night. But he wasn't going to stay home, or *create* a home, not in the reliable way I craved and felt I deserved.

That conversation helped me sort out something I clearly needed to do: Sixteen months after our wedding, in early 1984, Jamie and I agreed to divorce.

As these things go, it was a friendly one. However, in working through its details, even as I severed ties with the man who'd introduced me to the Church, I wove myself further into it.

There is no doubt that the memory of that Irish marriage, waiting for the boorish drunk who never came home, abetted the decision. Had I concocted a fiction (the root of that word is "to form") that paralleled my current situation and allowed me to face the truth that I could not—would not—be married to a man who was never home? Perhaps. Yet the memory of the wind cutting through that shawl, how it froze the tears against my face, the utter anguish and helplessness I felt as I stood in the darkness on that high bleak road is still as physically present as yesterday's efforts to prune a rosebush. It was uncovered during what seemed like simply a deep conversation with a compassionate friend. Above all, in the process of examining it, I'd been able to finally come to a necessary decision.

I saw, more and more, what Jamie meant when he said, "Scientology *works*." And yet. And yet. There were always misgivings. Something about it felt *wrong*. But maybe it was just my overts. What I'd done, not done. There was always something.

I DIDN'T WANT to tell my parents I was divorcing Jamie.

Because they'd expect it would mean I'd also be leaving Scientology.

And I found I didn't want to.

Especially in the delight I'd been finding in study, I'd glued myself to it. How could I possibly explain the pleasures of a spiritual path to those who felt that adherence to any religion was suspect? In any case, to them, Scientology wasn't a religion. It was a cult.

But that spring, on their way back to Squaw Valley from a visit to see friends in the Southwest, my parents' travel plans included a layover at the Los Angeles airport. They proposed that I meet them there for a glass of wine.

Driving to the airport, I held close, as if it were an amulet in a pocket, what it was I had to tell them. Even then I think I glimpsed that the upcoming conversation would be an important battle regarding my sense of self.

As I found parking, a plane roared into the sky, lifting hundreds of lives to other places, as it had just dropped hundreds of lives into this one. Airports, like train and bus stations, are spots where transitions take place. It seemed to me most appropriate that this conversation would occur in this space between spaces.

As I locked the car, watching the plane's contrail dissipate, I pondered the contradiction (turning over in my mind that word's components, as I'd started to do: CONTRA, "against" + DICERE, "speech") of my parents' affection for the symbols of religion and their disdain for the practice of it. The images of Virgin Mary and Buddha, the collection of silver crosses dangling around my mother's neck, the spirit house from India filled with Native American fetishes and Mexican milagros. Or how, during that family trip to Europe, Dad had pointed out the escaping spirit in the painting of the deceased man, and how they'd introduced me to the joy of churches: their high or painted ceilings, the muttered prayers, the aroma of beeswax. And while it was true my father had jerked me from my childhood knees in that Mexico City cathedral, it was he who'd taken me to that cathedral in the first place. It was he who'd written that check so we could receive mantras from the Maharishi. Wasn't this something, on some level, that we shared?

The cathedrals of Scientology were called Orgs. The scripture I studied was called Tech. When I felt I'd transgressed, I did not go to confession, I wrote up Conditions formulas. There was no way I was going to convince them Scientology was a religion. But—and I took a deep breath as I stepped into the freezing conditioned air of that mighty airport—perhaps it was possible, if we really had the Affinity I thought we did, and we used the Communication skills so prized in the family, I could persuade them to at least appreciate my Reality, and we could achieve Understanding. Even if all we did was agree, and I prayed we could do so agreeably, to disagree.

I was so naïve.

I FOUND MY way to their gate, as in the eighties one could still do, and greeted them as they came off the plane. Their cherished faces beamed at me. I had to shift my eyes from the love and even pride that radiated there.

It was early afternoon, and Dad steered us to the airport's Mexican restaurant. They ordered glasses of the house white. I ordered tea. It was Saturday and I wouldn't be on course the next day, so I could have had wine, but I wanted to keep my head.

We talked of their trip; they'd been visiting a writer in Santa Fe. We talked of the play I was rehearsing, which would open in about a month. We talked of Tad (more and more, he was, again, Tad) still living in Davis with Robin.

"He's not attending classes," Mom said. "I wish he'd just come home, or find someone else."

But Robin is taking care of him, I didn't say. I didn't want to argue. I needed every bit of their affinity to accept the reality that I was about to communicate.

"That accident," my father said. He said it with vast bitterness, and it struck me that there were circles under his eyes I'd never seen before. It wasn't just age. They looked almost as if he'd been slugged, the pouches almost black. He made a terrible face. "Lobotomized himself." He looked at his watch and ordered another glass of wine.

It was time. I gripped that imaginary amulet in my pocket and took a deep breath.

"I'm divorcing Jamie."

Pleasure flickered across their faces.

"But," I said, "I'm not leaving Scientology."

They looked at each other. "So the Evil Empire's got you," Dad said.

I held on to the edge of the table. "I know you think it's a cult—"

"Of course it's a cult!"

"Some people see it that way." I kept my voice steady. "But that's not a fair representation. It's just Black PR—I mean, negative propaganda—I mean, bad publicity . . . It's trying to do such theta—good—things on the planet, I mean in the world, it really is . . ."

They looked at me with disbelief.

"I'm learning so much. I mean, the funny thing is, it, the Church, the Tec—" I stopped before I actually said the word, all the bits of nomenclature that had become part of my vocabulary rising up and replacing the words that I should use. "The funny thing is, it's what's allowed me to understand that marrying Jamie was an error, that choice was . . . Scientology—" (I could hardly say the word out loud, and even then wondered what that meant). "What I'm learning has allowed me to see that, I mean, how you were right . . . about that."

"Tell us one thing this church of yours is 'giving you,' Sands," my father said, using quotes. "What are these 'good things' it's doing 'on the planet'?"

I told them about dictionaries.

They stared in stupefied silence.

"You know about dictionaries!" my mother finally said.

"No one ever taught me how to look up a word—"

"Of course we did!"

"Who needs to be taught how to use a dictionary!"

"Well, I think we do have to be taught, Dad. I mean, I never really knew about etymologies and—"

"Of course you knew!"

"No, I didn't—"

My father slammed his hands on the table and stood. "Gah!" He looked as if he had just opened a container to find rotten, stinking beans. "Sands, what have they talked you into! Of course you know how to use a dictionary! Of course you know about etymologies. Of course you know how to *study*! You graduated *magna cum laude*. You're our *daughter*. What a godawful waste of your life! We've got to catch our goddamned plane. Thanks so much for the send-off."

"Mom! Dad!" I ran after them down the corridor. I wanted to tell them, I wanted them to see, that a passion for learning and for study and for *words*, while no doubt genetic, had been unfolded, had been *given* to me by the religion.

Mother turned to look at me before they re-boarded. Her face was drawn and sad. She did not wave. Dad did not look back.

I stood watching them disappear into the tunnel. As far as they were concerned, my brother and I had both lobotomized ourselves.

IMAGINATION?

A friend of my parents, author/editor Blair Fuller—cofounder of the Community of Writers, the man who years before had filmed that madcap *Dionysus and the Maenads*—came to town and offered to take me to lunch.

"There's a café on Franklin, across from that Scientology center," he said over the phone, using the word easily. "Shall we meet there?"

Blair was as close to an uncle as I'd ever had. Even as I wondered if he'd been sent by my parents to "save" me, I was glad to see him, and happy to meet at Two Dollar Bill's; it was convenient to Celebrity Center, where I'd be on course later that day.

The waitress led us to the same window table where three years before I'd sat and wondered what went on inside the walls of that lovely, shabby building across the street. And now I knew. Now I referred to it as "CC."

As the waitress took our orders, Blair and I were both aware, I think, that if this lunch were to include my parents, a bottle of white for the table would have been de rigueur. But I'd be on course later that day, and Blair was in AA. He told me that he was sorry to hear that Jamie and I were divorcing. I nodded. I was waiting for the lecture, and when he lifted his bag onto his lap and pulled from it books by L. Ron Hubbard, I pressed fingernails into closed hands, readying myself.

"So," he said, indicating the books: *Dianetics: The Modern Science of Mental Health*, *Science of Survival*, and *Introduction to Scientology Ethics*. "I've been reading some of what Hubbard has to say."

I took a deep breath, prepared for an onslaught of negativity.

"He's got some intriguing notions, absolutely," he said. "In fact, Dianetics has a lot in common with psychotherapy, which Hubbard seems to understand—he actually appears to think it will *replace* psychiatry!" He laughed. "And this Tone Scale he outlines in *Science of Survival*? That's interesting, makes a lot of sense."

He'd actually *read* the books?

"However, he holds perspectives that are downright racist: that Japanese war brides are known to have a 'sweet smell,' for instance. And it's disgusting that he thinks a solution to making the planet a better place might be to get rid of those who are 'low' on his Tone Scale." He tapped a hand on the pile of books. "Still, there's a lot to consider."

I was stunned. Blair had not invited me to lunch to scoff. Not to deride. Not to insist I leave, nor to regale me with horrors. No. He'd *read* some of Hubbard's books. He'd come prepared to talk about Hubbard's *ideas*.

"Did you know the first version of *Dianetics* was an article published in a magazine called *Astounding Science Fiction*? He started as a science fiction writer. But I'm sure you know that."

I shrugged, still wary. I'd tucked this into the mental pocket where I put things I didn't want to consider. (It was getting very full.) In the forties, *Astounding Science Fiction*, which liked stories that dealt with pseudoscience, had published a lot of Hubbard's work.

"His stuff was popular, sold a lot of copies," Blair was saying. "Hubbard expanded one of those pieces into *Dianetics*." He read from the cover of the paperback. "A 'modern science of mental health.' Astonishing thing to claim."

Blair had "gathered"! He'd researched Hubbard, and Hubbard's life! It was more than I, or, as far as I knew, many of my Scientology friends, had done.

The waitress set down our salads. "Oh, *Science of Survival*!" she said. "That's the book I'd want on a desert island. You guys must be Scientologists!" I tried not to wince.

"Hubbard knows his Latin well enough to coin a word," Blair said, as she left.

"'Through the mind,'" I said. "I love that—the derivation stuff."

"Good to know one's Latin!"

Words tumbled out. How fun it was to get caught up in chains of words and derivations. The idea of *knowing how to know*. Hubbard's theories about study.

"You've read *Dianetics*," I said, "so you know that the auditor asks, 'Is there an earlier, similar incident?'"

"That's basic psychology. The idea that a current problem might be based on an unexamined previous one. Freud actually posited that there might be what he called 'chains' of memories embedded in the subconscious."

"He *did*?"

"Well, he was speculating. This was back around the turn of the century. He wondered that if one got at the earliest memory, the chain of them would be relieved. But it sounds as if Hubbard codified such a method, and then, with the help of the e-meter, made it easier to get at those memories. However, I'm not clear about how this connects to Scientology. *Dianetics* is a self-help book. But Scientology calls itself a religion."

"Well . . ." I wondered how far to go. "As he says in *Dianetics*, some of those earlier, similar incidents can be traced back to the womb. People found that ridiculous—"

"But that was in the fifties!" Blair shook his head. "These days, women don't drink alcohol if they're expecting. And I have a friend who every afternoon during her pregnancy played recordings by Mozart with her tummy close to the speakers so her unborn baby might be influenced in some way. Maybe he became a composer."

This was the way people around me talked all the time, and not just about what went on in the womb. Recently a friend had described her two-year-old daughter doing pliés while holding on to the edge of the bathtub, then stretching a leg along it, pointed toe and all—surely she'd been a ballerina in a previous lifetime?

"All to say," Blair said, "it's no longer revolutionary to think that what happens in the womb influences later behavior. But I still don't see how that's connected to religion."

Outside, on Franklin Avenue, traffic whizzed by. Across the street, the second-floor windows of the course room twinkled. In about an hour I'd be on the other side of those windows, studying. And here I was talking with one of my parents' friends about the spiritual path I was treading with the kind of interest and ease one might discuss the current exhibit at the Getty.

"Well," I said, slowly. "What if the earliest/similar memory isn't from a few years ago? What if it can't be found in childhood? What if it can't be found in the womb? What if it's found, I don't know, say, in the trenches of World War I—what's that?"

"Imagination?"

We smiled at each other. His blue eyes were as kind as could be, but it was clear we'd arrived at a Grand Canyon of possibility that he could not and would not leap across.

I stumbled my way through an explanation of how Hubbard's "science of mental health" might have become a religion: that the only thing that might traverse lifetimes would be—were one open to the concept—the soul. "So let's say there's that memory in the trenches of World War I, and when the auditor asks about an 'earlier, similar incident,' what comes up is, I don't know, something that happened during the Crusades, and before that, something to do with the Hittites?"

"And before that, something to do with a spaceship."

We looked at each other, long and steady.

"Maybe a spaceship," I said. "I'm just making this up, okay? I haven't done a lot of auditing. But maybe the fight with your wife reminds you of the time you blasted a planet to smithereens—the same guilt, the same remorse, times a thousand."

He looked startled and then laughed. "Pretty hard to apologize!"

"Exactly! And so maybe that's the 'earliest memory' on the chain of them. And the person understands that the fight with his wife won't clear up because he hasn't been able to confront this horrible time when his 'blast' wasn't just a nasty comment, but killed a million people. And he has to take responsibility, and maybe he sees that the impulsivity that killed all those people comes from the same source as that blast that made his wife cry, and, I don't know, he decides not do that anymore. It's about being a better person."

"Maybe." Blair shook his head. "Although it also sounds like a way to make you feel guilty about everything."

I nodded. This was undeniable.

"Also grandiose," he said. "No doubt a lot of people come up with the 'fact' that they were Lincoln. Madame Curie." He shook his head. "It's certainly self-involved, yes?"

Also undeniable. I nodded. "Yes. I do think about that."

"You believe this, Sands?"

"All my life I've felt powerful connections to certain time periods: Elizabethan England, ancient Greece. What feel like *memories* get aroused, vivid ones, with sounds and aromas and dialogue. They feel very real. I've wondered about this for years, long before I ever heard of Scientology."

"But no doubt you've read excellent historical novels about those periods. Good authors persuade us we're *there*. That's what good writing *is*. Or movies."

"Yes. Still, a lot of people on this planet believe in reincarnation."

"True," Blair said.

I leaned forward. "I fret about what I'm doing. It seems loony when I look at it from my parents' perspective, and certain things about the organization really bother me. But when I'm *doing* it, it makes *sense*. I've had so many discoveries, I've met people with good minds and hearts and intentions, people I like and admire. So then I wonder, is my doubt *my* doubt, or is it that Mom and Dad's opinions seem, I don't know, *better* than mine? Their approval matters so much! I worry that I'm seeing through their eyes. What about *my* eyes?"

"I think it's great you're exploring," he said, putting the books back into his shoulder bag. "It's exactly what someone your age should be doing."

This comment caused some part of me to zoom upward and hover above the table. The gaze I remember giving us was both fond and rueful. There was Blair, sixty-odd years old, trailing love and kindness and sorrow. He'd had problems with alcohol, he was twice divorced. Opposite him was an eager-to-please thirty-three-year-old who was, from his perspective, "doing what she should be doing" by examining spiritual, even intellectual options before settling into life. How grateful I was, and remain. He took the time to explore things by which I was intrigued, as if, because I found them intriguing, they might indeed be so.

"How's your brother?" he asked. "I saw him after the accident, in New York City."

This would have been when Oak and Mary were still living in the six-floor walk-up in Manhattan, before he was flown to California, before Mary joined him in Squaw Valley, before she took the kids back east and filed for divorce, before he'd tried to go back to school. How good of Blair, and how typical, to have made an effort to see him.

"Those hallucinations," Blair said. "About being shot at, the bugs and spiders he thought were crawling across his back? That was the DTs, you know. *Delirium tremens.* I mean, imagine drinking so much and then being forced to go cold turkey like that."

I'd never considered that, and told him so.

"Those are classic signs. Where is he now?"

I caught him up with what details I had. As we left the restaurant, I couldn't help but wonder what might be different if my parents had read Hubbard's books and given my choice similar scrutiny, rather than depending on what newspapers and friends had to say. I was aware that, due to the past hour and a half, I was examining, and not in a knee-jerk, defensive way, what Blair had presented: that while there was worth to be found in Hubbard's writings, there were also claims he made that were ridiculous, unsubstantiated, disgusting, and just plain *wrong*.

While it took me too long to act on that understanding, that conversation was part of what helped me eventually do so.

"You're looking well," he said as we hugged goodbye, "except for the grief about your parents. But *I* don't worry about you. I'll let them know."

"It won't make any difference."

He nodded. "But I'll try."

WHAT IS TRUE FOR YOU IS TRUE FOR YOU

As Jamie and I began to make arrangements to live apart, a friend, Constance, told me that she and her husband were also dissolving their marriage. In a fortuitous equation, Joel moved in with Jamie for a few months while I moved in with Constance. Eventually, as our respective divorces solidified, she and I rented a house together.

Constance's black coils of hair and huge dark eyes made her look like an image slid from a Grecian urn. Quirky and brilliant, one of an increasing number of friends who made it "all right" to be a Scientologist, she introduced me to the smart and kind Skye.

Like Jamie, Skye had attained OT III. But there the similarities ended. Jamie was blue-eyed and blond; Skye, not much taller than I, had eyes the color of espresso; his hair, tightly coiled ringlets, a deep black. Jamie made a living from his music school; Skye, a highly trained auditor, made some of his income counseling. Jamie was a superb bass player who sometimes composed music along jazzy lines; Skye, a marvelous wordsmith and songwriter, was in the process of creating a rock 'n' roll persona, Skye Stryder.

Another important difference: I agreed with Skye's politics. This was a huge relief. Jamie and many of his friends either opted out of the political process altogether, calling it pointless when there was so much to be done on the spiritual plane, or they were so far to the nutsy, conspiratorial right that their thinking melded into the nutsy, conspiratorial left.

Skye was withdrawing from a previous relationship, and although Jamie and I were separated, we had yet to divorce. Highly conscious of the ethics surrounding the situation, Skye and I were careful in our coming together, taking our time. But eventually, and formally, Skye asked me out to dinner. Afterward, we drove all the way to Ventura and back, streaming through the darkness of Highway 101. In his guise as Stryder, he was in the midst of recording some tunes, and the songs soaring out of the tape deck filled the car with sound and image. We could have been in a spaceship en route to another planet, sighting the occasional lights of other ships cruising the universe.

Part of the spaceship imagery had to do with what I was picking up from my studies, augmented by films that emerged during these years: *Star Wars*, *E.T.*, *Close Encounters of the Third Kind*. While I had no idea what was revealed to those who attested to OT III, I understood there was a Wall of Fire that had to be . . . confronted? permeated? leapt through (like tigers in a circus)? However, all those lifetimes, often on planets other than Earth, seemed to imply travel between universes, as one might fly from San Francisco to Melbourne. This sense of vast space, a teeming darkness filled with possibility, was further influenced by hearing Skye's plans. Stryder, dark and lithe, was destined to be a world-famous star. And through that rock 'n' roll medium, Skye, dark and lithe, with the hugest of helping hearts, would manifest his desire to improve the lot of man. He would do this as an Operating Thetan. And once he'd done his work on this planet, this lifetime, he'd head out into the universe, without a body, to continue his heartfelt Scientological labors. In both modes he was heading for the stars. But above all this he yearned—and he yearned with a ferocity I found dazzling and terrifying, foreign and desirable—to *connect.* Returned from that Ventura spaceship ride, lyrics burbled up onto the pages of my journal:

> *There where the highway enters the sky*
> *where the dusk is just turning to night*
> *the doors of the world stand ready to part*
> *and your path lies beyond, into flight*

He'd explored a number of Eastern religions before throwing in his lot with Scientology, and his interpretation of OT seemed Buddhist to me: an alignment closer to Siddhartha than L. Ron.[66] He longed for that connection with everything above everything.

> *Out here we're driving the 101 Highway*
> *heading toward the Mountains of Mars.*
> *There's a place up ahead where the doors are ajar—*
> *Will you stride all alone to the stars?*

One night into a relationship that would last five years, and which when it ended I'd mourn for another five, I nailed what I found entrancing, as well as the dilemma that, in spite of an engulfing love, we'd be unable to solve.

I'D SWALLOWED JAMIE'S injunction that I not return to waitressing as if it were a piece of Hubbard policy, and even after we parted company, I sought other sources of income. But I was broke most of the time. And then Vano—Michael VanLandingham, once executive director of the Lexington Conservatory Theatre—moved to LA. Vano was working for a film production company, angling toward becoming a producer himself. He asked to read what I was writing and praised a short screenplay I'd adapted from a story. He suggested I become a story editor, that grandiose term for the gofers who drive from production company to production company, picking up scripts, books, articles, essays, even newspaper headlines, which they read and précis in search of material that might make a breakout movie. Once I factored in the driving, the reading, and developing the synopses, the pay was dismal, but it involved reading and writing, and I could do it on my own time. Desktop computers were just beginning to replace typewriters, and Vano loaned, then gave me, my first one. To some degree, it felt as if in Vano I had a bit of my brother again.

As, financially, I lurched along, the husband of my friend Marilyn ("Isn't it about making you the best person you can be?") offered me a job. He was building what would become a hugely successful agency, representing writers and directors, and he needed a temporary secretary. I was entirely wrong for the job, but in his generous way, he kept me on for months, and was kind about giving me time off for the occasional audition. As summer approached, and with it the Community of Writers, he might, if asked, have even given me those weeks. But I'd come to hate the prickly quality of time spent in Mom and Dad's company, and the job gave me a pretext. So even though Hall children were expected to show up and help with the Conference, for two years in a row, I skipped it.

This meant that for two years I also didn't see my family. Tad was living with Robin in various Midwest locales. I'd attended Brett's graduation from UCLA, but stayed barely aware of her subsequent move to San Francisco. Tracy, still in Grand Junction, had two sons whom I'd hardly ever seen, and had expanded a house I'd never once visited.

It didn't occur to me that I was doing exactly what the Church encouraged. Slowly but surely, I was disconnecting.

SKYE AND CONSTANCE expanded my circle of Scientology friends, each of them smart and funny and kind; ours was a cherished and tightly knit group. All were on course and, in addition to various day jobs, were pursuing careers as artists. Constance was acting. Martin and Sallie ran a recording studio. Roo was a stunning vocalist. Paloma, a highly trained auditor, was a writing coach. My beloved course twin, Sunny, was building dual careers as a jazz vocalist and voice teacher. Delph and Wyatt were at the time the only parents in our close circle (the rest of us, although we were in our thirties, appeared to be fairly clueless that time might run out on that enterprise; I think this was attached to the idea that hindrances offered by the physical world—such as aging eggs—did not apply to Scientologists). Wyatt played sax in a popular band; Delph, a fine artist, took those skills with her when she hosted parties and made meals. Once, when I was exclaiming yet again over one of her dishes, she leaned in, eyes twinkling, and said, "Sands. Here's the secret. Ready?"

I nodded, intrigued. She'd been studying Scientology for years. Maybe in addition to other matters, there were keys to cooking to be found there.

"Butter!"

These friends made Scientology fun. We talked about it at parties and over coffee; we used its precepts to sustain our friendships, to help each other solve problems and heartbreaks, and to assist each other toward our goals.

And most of these friends were at least Clear, if not on their OT levels. In addition to doing well in their careers, they seemed to weather quite well, without being robotic, problems that could be upsetting or even devastating: an audition that didn't go well, a breakup with a boyfriend. They might get angry or cry; it wasn't that their emotions were suppressed. But they knew they could process it, by themselves or with an auditor or with a friend trained in Scientology: put the experience where it needed to be and move on.

I observed, however (snottily), that OT though some of them were, the material world sometimes got in their way. They had engine trouble. They came down with colds. They had marital difficulties. Quite often they weren't attaining their stated goals. Skye, for instance. As an OT III, why didn't he have the rock-star career he longed for?

Skye explained that the state of OT couldn't be attained quickly. Like playing the violin or becoming a ballerina, it required time and practice and focus. "It might not even happen this lifetime," he said. "Look how many lifetimes it took us to get into this mess."

He was talking about OT's confidential materials, which, I gathered, revealed that Earth was some kind of penal colony. Sure, I thought. And Earth is also heaven. It's all here, right now. But my OT friends sadly shook their heads at the notion. That was clearly not the case. Earth was not just a prison; it was hell. And only through Scientology could we effect an escape.

Indeed, it was becoming ever more obvious that even though a Clear no longer has a Reactive Mind, it (the non-gendered thetan) still has a billion lifetimes in which "charged" experiences remain uninspected. These memories lie on the Whole Track, defined as "the moment-to-moment record of a person's existence in this universe in picture and impression form."[67] Like a movie, in other words, which could be slowed down and inspected. This reminded me forcibly of the realization I'd had long before—one that had seemed almost as if I were recollecting something once learned—while vacuuming the carpet in the Squaw Valley house: that life was a series of images we could scroll through like a reel of celluloid. Except Hubbard's version included riding in spaceships and blowing up planets.

So if an OT didn't manifest OT abilities, the reason was obvious: It still had case to work through. Looking at the Bridge from that point of view, it didn't look like a bridge, or even a ladder. It looked like an endless runway from which the plane would never lift. How was it *possible* to defuse the horrors and sorrows accrued over *billions* of lifetimes? I understood that you didn't have to look at every single incident to be clear of them; you just no longer had a reaction when those buttons were pushed. But in a billion lives, wouldn't there be a lot of unexamined buttons?

So even though I was putting money "on account" toward a block of professional auditing (at the time, a twelve-and-a-half-hour "intensive" cost $2,500), I continued to be reluctant. Maybe because what little I did hear about the upper levels seemed bizarre. Something about psychiatrists having lured us to Earth, that idea of a penal colony, that Wall of Fire, and something about having been stuffed in volcanoes?! And blown up?!?

I wasn't supposed to know.

Also, it's clear to me now, I didn't want to know.

MY NEXT COURSE, Method One, offered a comforting degree of the familiar, studying (twinning with Sunny), and the intriguing: auditing. We'd also be introduced to the e-meter.

This meant that Sunny and I had to understand watts and volts. Mini-studies like these cause the shelves of Scientology course rooms to hold an eclectic collection of manuals, how-to books, various kinds of dictionaries, and at least one set of encyclopedias (at Celebrity Center in the eighties, woefully out of date). Most books I consulted regarding electricity used the analogy of a faucet with spigots, and of course I had to explore ELECTRIC: "derived from amber, as by rubbing," from the Greek *electron*: "amber."

When Sunny and I felt we had a handle on it, we began our e-meter drills. A piece of wood about a yard long and eight inches high was placed on the table between us, as would be the case when we actually took each other into session. The board is there so that while pc and auditor can see each other's faces, the pc won't be distracted by anything the auditor might be doing, which includes adjusting various knobs, all while noting the questions she's asking, the behavior of the needle, and the pc's responses.

We studied how to plug in the cans to the meter and how to make sure they would "read" properly. Using a large doll or a teddy bear as the "pc," inventing silly but fun scenarios, we drilled how to make sure the pc doesn't have a "present time problem": a fight with her husband, an overdrawn account, an overt she's sitting on, "any worry that keeps a pc out of session, which problem must exist in present time, in the real universe."[68] Called "Rudiments," these also include making sure the pc's had enough sleep and enough food and that she's not too hot or too cold (indicated through the skin, which touches the cans and is therefore responsible for the meter's reaction).[69] Hands might also be sweaty, or dry, which can be solved by using a bit of lotion. In a bulletin, Hubbard refers to Vaseline's Intensive Care, and Proctor & Gamble can thank him for steady sales. As Hubbard mentions the product specifically, many Scientologists consider it "standard"; no other lotion will do.

Those bottles of yellow lotion, stashed around the course room, caused my thoughts to flicker to my brother and how clueless I'd been, before his accident, about the meaning of that phrase: "intensive care." How truly strange, I'd muse, to name a lotion after a room full of wires and blood and woe. And then I'd shake him out of my brain.

It's difficult to imagine, and unbearable to recall, not only that I so thoroughly kept my thoughts from him, but that I never got in touch. It took decades to understand how my rush to Scientology was, in part, a way to make sure I wouldn't damage him (as Mary's mother had warned). Above all, it was to fill the hole created by the loss of his huge and vital presence, and, odd method though it was, to find the identity he had for so long provided.

SUNNY AND I read theory and demoed and drilled and flunked and started and read and demoed and drilled again. We learned to record the sessions on legal-size paper folded in half, lengthwise, providing a long, narrow surface, so as one writes, one's hand doesn't have to travel across an entire page. We learned to work the various dials with one hand while noting the time, questions, needle action, and answers with the other—we also learned the shorthand for recording these. I was reminded of learning to start a standard shift car on a slope: how what at first seemed an impossible combination of feet and gears and clutch and brake and accelerator became movements I could accomplish without thinking. While I never became that adept at using the e-meter, it did become easier.

And then, one day, it was time for one of us to take the other into session.

And what we did in those Method One sessions was to clear words.[70] For someone like me—in love with study, wary of the e-meter—it was the perfect introduction. These days, it's easy to find articles on the Internet that prove that the e-meter is nothing but a piece of *Wizard of Oz* gimmickry. But in my own experience, especially clearing words, the meter seemed almost clairvoyant, and working with it was often thrilling. I could feel, inside my body, what the needle on the meter would be registering. The rising anxiety when I didn't understand a definition, the need to define another word in the process of clearing the first one, and, especially with abstractions, the grapple with comprehension. I could feel the increased puzzlement (charge) that would be making the needle rise and rise, and I knew that Sunny would be adjusting various knobs to keep the needle on the dial. And then, as definitions were found, derivations explored, words used in sentences, as we made our way back to the original word that started the chain, I could literally feel that anxiety blow away, replaced by understanding and a swooning sort of delight.

When it was my turn to audit Sunny, I witnessed these manifestations: the "mass" that accumulated as the word under examination became complicated with other words or concepts. And when the word was fully cleared, the realization reached, I saw what was called a "blow down": the needle moving so fast—dropping, as charge dispersed—that it was hard to adjust the knob fast enough to keep it on the dial.

Turn and turn about, we took each other into session. When our needles floated, we'd head to the Examiner, and whichever of us had been the auditor would write up the session and place it in the other's folder, which then went to the Case Supervisor, who'd review the session. He might note where the auditor had handled something poorly (flunk); this would mean a bulletin needed to be restudied, or a drill practiced—which, as twins, we'd do with each other—before going into session again (start). Or the Case Supervisor would indicate that we'd done a good job: VWD. Very Well Done.

We lived for those scrawled VWDs.

At some point, Sunny landed a singing gig that took her out of town for an extended period. I continued on with a new twin, Mark. Our sessions didn't have the same magic, but they were still useful and fun. I'd had the realization—cognition, epiphany—that I guessed was the End Phenomenon, the E/P, of the auditing process at least a dozen times before I finally offered it up. I knew that once I said it aloud, I would be done with the course, and I didn't want to be. But one day, after a marvelous trek through the deserts of ancient Palestine, clearing the word ISRAEL, I could no longer hold it in.[71] When Mark told me, "Your needle is floating," I said what I'd known for weeks: "If you have a dictionary—dictionaries, encyclopedia, books, manuals—and you know how to clear a word, you can figure out *anything*. You can learn, and therefore *do*, anything you put your mind to."

I now know this is something one should get from a basic liberal arts education, but I didn't know it then, and it hadn't been the product of my own education. The Examiner confirmed the F/N, and I'd indeed had the End Phenomenon. Mark received a VWD. A few days later, he offered up a similar cognition. We were done with Method One.

EVEN IN THE midst of this largely satisfying time, however, doubts arose. Often I was outraged, *outraged*, that one could only study Scientology in a Scientology course room. Other religions had books you could read; you didn't have to *be* a Buddhist to understand its precepts; you didn't have to be baptized to learn about the Trinity or to explore the metaphors attached to Jesus' death and resurrection. Of course one could buy Hubbard's books—but the *study* of the Tech had to be done under the auspices of Scientology. That was Keeping Scientology Working!

But then the other part of my brain would mutter that if you were a *practicing* Buddhist, there were texts to read and various forms of meditation to practice; if a Catholic, you not only studied the religion's precepts but engaged in its forms and traditions. Was there really such a difference? If you were committed? And also, there were so many *forms* Buddhism had taken over the centuries—was one better than another? How could you possibly know? And Catholicism's excesses had spawned Protestantism—and there are a multitude of ways to be a Protestant, not to mention ways to worship Christ/be a Christian. Whereas LRH was all about making sure Standard Tech *stayed* Standard. That there was and always would be only *one* Scientology.

So why, then, did I feel myself so held in thrall? So *stuck*?

These feelings might be stirred by a commercial featuring the Parthenon, a phone call from my sister Tracy in which she described a camping trip, a brochure announcing that summer's Community of Writers. At these moments, the decent-seeming bread of my days became so much cardboard. I should be writing a book, acting in a play, creating an album of my songs, having intellectually stimulating discussions (all with attendant travel and wine and parties), and to hell with examining, every *minute*, how my soul was doing. To hell with the horrid sensibility, which kept rising, that I had handed over the reins of my life.

Here arose a different sense of "Flunk. Start." Doesn't everyone at some point, I'd ponder, doubt what they're doing with their life? Isn't that doubt just a moraine everyone has to cross from time to time? Wasn't this a common existential mantra: *Why am I doing what I'm doing? Should I be doing something else?* I'd talk myself around the edges of this while continuing to do what I was doing; eventually there would be reasons, and on I'd lurch. In this case it wasn't a sense of doing something incorrectly that was the flunk and the intention to redo it correctly that was the start. Rather, it was that I might as well stay on the road I was walking; to leave it would force me to start over so completely that it was literally unimaginable. So I talked myself not so much into "start," but into "keeping on."

Also (I further persuaded myself), a religion that insists one know the *true sense of the word* must honor the value of the word—mustn't it? We weren't just *allowed* to look at other books and articles—even (supposedly) those that disparaged the Church—we were *supposed* to. "What is true for you is what you have observed yourself," begins one of Hubbard's most quoted maxims. "And when you have lost that, you have lost everything."[72]

So he says. Yet, in fact, we were discouraged, deeply, from such scrutiny. Such books, articles, television investigations were, we understood, full of nothing but lies and distortion, Black PR created by Suppressive Persons whose sole and evil purpose was to squash Scientology and all the good it was capable of doing. Reading or watching any of it would be "enturbulating" (Hubbard's descriptive word that means "cause to be turbulent or agitated and disturbed").[73] I was not the only one who'd mentally quote *what is true for you is true for you*, a truncated version used by many, as I jerked my eyes away from a banner headline of an essay about the Church. I'd learned that even reading the opening sentence would send me into a spin.

I think it was about this time that I came to understand that David Mayo, L. Ron Hubbard's personal auditor, had been "declared": he'd been formally labeled a Suppressive Person and forbidden any future association with Scientology; if other Scientologists were in touch with him, they risked being declared themselves. This information rocked even my protected little lagoon. Even I'd heard of David Mayo. How could the man who audited Hubbard be an SP? But so it seemed to be.

And he'd left the Church!

And not only had he "blown" (was that really what had happened?), he'd used his vast experience with the Tech to start a splinter organization. He was a *squirrel*! Could that be true?

Further rumors: Mayo was so highly respected, and the charges seemed so trumped up, that when he left the Church, a huge chunk of other Scientologists left too.[74] *Really?*

There was nowhere to go with these questions. No one to ask.

Asking would probably lead to having to see the Ethics Officer. I turned eyes and mind away. What is true for you is true for you. *Whatistrueforyouistrueforyou.*

And so it was, that in spite of knowing that where there was so much smoke there must be fire, in spite of dire warnings and terrible estrangements from those I loved most, I continued to persuade myself that a belief system so based on words, and the truth to be found within them, must be, at its no-matter-how-controversial center, good. I was so attracted to the *study* of the religion that even the understanding that I was, thus, *binding* myself to it, more and more tightly, did not deter me. Delving into words in this intimate way made me feel as if I was doing with my life exactly what I should be doing.

And in this way I became a convert to Scientology, words that, like RELIGION, I defined again and again, to assure myself of their meaning.

CONVERT: To change to another form, to persuade to adopt a religion, from words meaning "to turn around."

SCIENTOLOGY: The study of knowledge, knowing how to know.

In spite of the often-seething doubt, I came back to this again and again: I was turning around. I was learning to know how to know.

HE HAS SIMPLY MOVED ON TO HIS NEXT LEVEL

Skye and I laughed. We kissed. We talked. We sat outdoors in Malibu with glasses of wine, watching sun dip below waves, shivering deliciously in the breeze off the water. We held hands. We peeled shrimp and licked the grease from our fingers. We drove, listening to his songs. We sat cross-legged on his bed, knees touching, and talked some more. We found new levels of lovemaking. We farted, and howled with laughter.

All these things require *bodies*. Why would we not want them?

But bodies, so I understood, were what kept us trapped on this Earth. Bodies got in the way of being OT. In *Scientology 8-8008*, Hubbard writes that an Operating Thetan is "completely rehabilitated and can do everything a thetan should do, such as move MEST and control others from a distance, or create his own universe." "Rehabilitated" implies a fall from some previous grace/ability—probably that stuff to do with psychiatrists and volcanoes that I wasn't supposed to know. But: "create one's own universe"?

Skye explained that it didn't mean, say, starting a Big Bang of one's own—"although it could," he said, "if you were powerful enough. Look at it this way. Jamie's 'creating a universe' with his music school—do you see that? And I am, with my dreams for Stryder. And you've got various universes: your songwriting, acting, your novel. And we have one, in being together. It doesn't have to be a space opera, 'creating a universe.'"

He made it seem both romantic and sensible.

But in what may have been a reflection of the collision between his transcendent dreams for Stryder and the reality of creating a relationship, over the next two years we lived in six different places. I did not apprise my parents of these shifting addresses. The few times we visited, they put up a fence that was barbed and fierce. When Skye was out of the room, Dad might say, "He's awfully enthusiastic about the Dodgers, isn't he?" and I'd be reminded that only peons like such sports—why couldn't he be enthusiastic about tennis? As comments flew about a particular novel, Skye would look mulish, underscoring the fact that he hadn't read the book under discussion. Always, I came away from these visits doubting my love. And was he really *that* great a songwriter? Why wasn't he more successful? Etc.

In Scientology, this phenomenon—when someone else's perspective makes you feel that what or who you respect or love is perhaps neither respectable nor lovable—is known as "Third Party."[75]

It can be subtle: You're telling a friend about a trip you took with your husband, and how he refolded the map every time he consulted it. This had amused you; you'd found it endearing. But your friend shakes her head and says, "Golly! He sure does have to control every little thing, doesn't he!" and laughs. You do, too—but your pleasure in what you saw as a quirk begins to shift. You notice that while he was kind enough to empty the dishwasher, he's arranged the cups on the shelf with their handles pointing the same direction, which makes you think about that "control" thing. Later that night, when he asks, not for the first time, that you please screw the cap back on the toothpaste, you find yourself saying, "What's with all the controlling behavior?" And then you lie side by side in bed fuming or even fighting. Usually also at work here, if you subscribe to Hubbard's system, is the overt/withhold/motivator phenomenon.

For Skye and me, the Third Party comprised my parents. Yet I could see through their eyes. And through their eyes, I saw that Skye was in his late thirties without a career; instead, he'd devoted a decade of his life to ~~a cult~~ Scientology. And there were other matters, things my parents didn't know, as I didn't tell them: he dyed his hair, covering the gray to look younger for his Stryder persona; he'd not yet sold or published a single song; he didn't have a band—if he didn't perform live, how was he ever going to *become* a rock star? But I seldom let myself think these things, as they were critical, and meant I had overts. I loved Skye, but—like Scientology—I could not see there was a way to leave him/it without it meaning that I was a bad person.

What an insidious and invidious way to keep people in thrall.

EVENTUALLY, ONCE WE'D finally rented a house together, Skye began to figure out ways to get me the auditing that would move me up the Bridge, and supposedly solve my chronic sorrow. (The narcissistic nature of these investigations makes me roll my eyes now. Also, and obviously, focusing on what was wrong simply made things seem more wrong.) For a while, he audited me. As long as a Case Supervisor was in place—and through Skye's work at the Advanced Org, we had one—couples could do this: in Scientology, just as stats could be "up" and ethics might be "out," in this case the exchange would be "in."

But what was that exchange? How could I possibly repay someone who was helping me with what I was increasingly convinced was my immortal—lifetime after lifetime!—soul?

Also, even though Skye was a trained auditor with excellent TRs, it was hard to share with him what he could see "reading" on the meter, which included aspects of my past and, especially, my parents' opinions. So he and our friend Paloma, who was also highly trained, arranged an exchange: she'd audit me, he'd audit her, and I'd do . . . *something*. I'd no idea what, but was assured the right thing would show up.

Which didn't help the feeling of "out-exchange," as Scientologists term it. I labored with a sense of diminishment: I was a lesser citizen of the spiritual world. My acting career wasn't one—I just got work now and then. I worked haphazardly on a novel. When I had extra cash, I headed into Martin and Sallie's studio to record a song. Yet here, too—I think because I'd swallowed Jamie's notion that folk wasn't really music—I deprecated my efforts, especially in comparison to what I saw as Skye's brilliant lyrics.

One night I said to him, longingly, "I just wish I could knock your socks off. About *something*!"

A little later, the table cleared, the contented hum of the dishwasher launched, I snuggled in beside him on the couch to watch Joseph Campbell and Bill Moyers talk about myth. At one point I offered up some comment about the program. Suddenly, he pulled up both feet, yanked off his socks, and threw them across the room.

"Look at that!" he said, with a gesture of wonderment. "You just knocked 'em right off."

Our laughter was a saving grace. And much else was wonderful: his kindness, our loving hours in the dark. But I also wept, too often, about that sense of inadequacy, my chronic doubts about what I was doing with my life.

Clearly I was depressed. I think, now, that the loss of my brother exacerbated a pre-existing tendency, and, as I never processed any of the grief attached to losing him, I settled ever more deeply into that depression. Yet I've no recollection of thinking or talking about it. Not even when I started those auditing sessions with Paloma.

I'd fixated on the idea that Scientology would solve not only an existential miasma, Scientology would solve *everything*. Just by being *in* it, you were supposed to be happy (whatever that was). I had yet to comprehend that it is possible to take control of one's own thoughts, that it isn't just a lyric that encourages us to "look on the sunny side of life." Instead, I see now, I simply waited, quite passively, for Scientology to "fix" me.

•

AND THEN, LATE January 1986, L. Ron Hubbard died. Rumors circulated. Not so much about his death, which within twenty-four hours was widely known, but about the future of Scientology. A hundred of us gathered in the courtyard of Celebrity Center, thousands more assembled in the Hollywood Palladium, to watch a televised event.

The camera held steady on an expanse of stage. An enormous *O* glowed from a screen behind the podium. In the middle of it, an equally large *T* spread its wings. A sweeping bridge, white and gold, started from a physical foot in the middle of the stage and then—*tromp l'oeil*—joined the screen and disappeared into a gauzy pink-gold distance. I'd become accustomed to (and able to be dismissive of) the corny seventies-style publicity used by the Church. This was a new and rather impressive advertising elegance. There at Celebrity Center, all around me, a sigh of satisfaction rose into the nighttime air. That angelic OT symbol, that tangible yet gauzy bridge, served as both reminder and nudge: Even with its founder's death, Scientology would keep on. And we, its practitioners, must also.

I felt a guilty disappointment. I kind of hoped the Church would just, well, close.

Someone introduced someone who introduced someone who told us that the new leader of the church, granted that post by L. Ron Hubbard *himself*, was David Miscavige!

Greeted by minutes of applause, a short, fit, very tanned man strode to the podium. Although I'd heard his name, this was the first time I'd seen him. He looked impossibly young to be the new leader of the Church.

As the applause died away, Miscavige looked down at his notes. Gravely, he told us that L. Ron Hubbard had completed the work he'd set out to do and had moved on to "his next level of OT research."[76]

"This level is beyond anything any of us have ever imagined," Miscavige said. "This level is in fact done in an exterior state, meaning that it is done completely exterior from the body. At this level the body is nothing more than an impediment, an encumbrance to any further gain as an OT."

The idea that one can be outside one's own body looking at oneself—"exterior"—is a known phenomenon; I'd even experienced it myself from time to time.[77] But I wondered what kind of "cause" over his death LRH could possibly have had. I understood he'd been ill for years, living in a trailer, hiding from government probes, while some trusted minions ran the organization on the principles he'd so carefully laid out. Had he demanded, *Beam me up, Scotty*–like, "Die, body"?

Our heads were cocked back, mouths slightly open, to take in the screen. Around us people murmured, several wept. "Thus at two thousand hours Friday the twenty-fourth of January, A.D. 36," Miscavige intoned, "L. Ron Hubbard discarded the body he had used in this lifetime for seventy-four years, ten months, and eleven days."

I couldn't help the smallest shake of my head. This was certainly a transition, as Hubbard "discarded" his body, but had he really "moved on to his next level"? Would he, in fact, do it in an "exterior state"? Was this a level others should aspire to attain?

I also wanted to protest Miscavige's use of "A.D. 36." That didn't mean *Anno Domini*. No. Those initials stood for After Dianetics.[78] I thought Hubbard's grandiosity in equating the publication of *Dianetics* as a date to restart time, likening it to the birth of Christ, was ridiculous—and appalling. Standing there, listening to a woman behind me weeping, to the vast stretches of applause that greeted Miscavige's statements, I felt like a fraud.

Miscavige was quoting the *Technical Dictionary*'s definition of BODY:

> . . . an identifying form or non-identifying form to facilitate the control of, the communication of and with, and the havingness of the thetan in his existence in the MEST universe.[79]

Miscavige looked at his audience, which meant he was looking at the camera, which meant he appeared to be looking directly at me. He laid out another of Hubbard's definitions with special import: "*The body is a physical object; it is not the being himself,*" and added: "The being we knew as L. Ron Hubbard still exists; however, the body he had could no longer serve his purposes. His decision was one made at complete cause by L. Ron Hubbard."

His decision was one made at complete cause by L. Ron Hubbard. What did that mean? Why was it parsed that way?

I wondered who'd found Hubbard's body. Had Hubbard been solo-auditing, as those on their OT levels do, and had he gone "flying" in some way? Had he been peaceful? Restless, haunted by transgressions committed in the name of his Church? Had he died believing in his life's work? Had he died a charlatan?

Why was I wondering that?

"He has simply moved on to his next level," Miscavige said.

His expression, while solemn, looked to me as if he'd eaten something delicious.

A photograph of Hubbard filled the screen and faded away, followed by another, and another. More applause, minutes of it. Someone else arrived at the podium to tell us that the Tech was still the Tech. New levels were to be released, ones LRH had been working on, the ones that had allowed him to let go of "this lifetime's body," levels that would take us all the way to OT XII! (*Applause.*) In the meantime, we were to be assured that the Tech would continue to be delivered in the most Standard of ways.

In spite of these assurances, I felt a curious excitement. Maybe the religion might just shutter its windows, like a business that had run its course. Perhaps I could then persuade Skye to live somewhere other than Los Angeles, a life uncomplicated by the demands of our religion. We could be—this is how I thought of it—free.

But that isn't what happened. And once I realized that Scientology was going to continue to continue, I continued too. Sometimes I thought of the Chekov play *Three Sisters*, in which we hear the continual cry, voiced by one and then another of the sisters, that everything will be solved if only they could get to Moscow; we watch as years pass and they never ever do. And while I still thought of Samuel Beckett's "fail again, fail better," more often I recalled his play *Waiting for Godot*, in which two characters have the same exchange of dialogue numerous times, accompanied by a never-changing stage direction:

> VLADIMIR: Shall we go?
> ESTRAGON: Yes, let's go.
> *They do not move.*[80]

I WASN'T CURRENTLY on course, but I was getting auditing with Paloma. As I zipped around freeways as a story editor, transcribed tapes, taught acting classes, worked on stories and on the screenplay with Vano, I was aware of troubling rumors floating down from the upper echelons of the Church about people who'd held powerful positions being suddenly demoted. But none of it seemed to have anything to do with our lives.

During this time, my journals reflect an increasing engagement with the act of writing. An ecstasy rises from those pages. Perhaps part of it was that I wrote in cafés while sipping a cappuccino or a glass of my beloved chardonnay—the oaky, old-fashioned California kind, sunlight in a glass—and "sketched": about Skye, about Scn (as I abbreviated it), my parents, conversations with friends and their children, observations of the world around me, and about the miracle of word following word, of a sentence making sense out of itself even in the writing of it. I was in a chronic state of wonder at the process.

Still, a magazine cover from the time summed up my attitude toward the work I was doing with Vano: two chimpanzees hammer away on a typewriter over the caption, *Is Anyone in L.A. Not Writing a Screenplay?* So far we'd come up with Driver, the owner/operator of his own semi, and Eva, on the run from a bad relationship. She'd be hitchhiking; he'd pick her up. In a lonely stretch of countryside, the semi would crash and . . . *something* would happen.

Vano often had to cancel our meetings. Not only did he have pressures at work; his health was deteriorating. A mutual friend told me it had to do with his kidneys—he'd been an alcoholic for a dangerously long time. We were nowhere close to finishing, much less selling whatever it was we were concocting, and I was often in a low-grade panic about finances. So in the fall of 1986, when a woman who was planning to open a Scientology mission not far from Rodeo Drive asked to meet with me, I was ready to hear what she had to offer.

BECAUSE, YOU KNOW, YOU DID JUST TURN THIRTY-SIX

Jessica was serenity itself. Her clothes were simple and elegant, taupe and black. As we toured what would be the mission's quarters, she explained why the Bel Air/Beverly Hills area was an ideal place to launch such an endeavor. Its clientele would include those who were educated, well-heeled, secure in their jobs—and perhaps beginning to wonder if there might be more to life. It would be a "feeder" to the larger Orgs, but she would not use the word "mission"; she planned to call it a "Center," a word less fraught with religious overtones. And she asked if I would come on board as Course Supervisor.

The Executive Director, Ed, told me that at first my weekly take-home pay wouldn't be much; for the time being, the course room would be open only in the evenings and on Saturdays. We'd each be paid a percentage of the mission's earnings (a substantial tithe appeared to go to the larger organization). But as the Center grew, our salaries would as well. The Center would pay for my Course Supervisor Course, which I'd take at the Advanced Org. I'd be "on post" by January 1987.

I admired Jessica. She and Ed were persuasive. I believed in Hubbard's Study Tech. The money would be steady. I'd have time to write.

These must have been the reasons it seemed like a good idea, and why I said yes.

AS I WALKED into the big blue buildings of Scientology's Advanced Org to start the Course Supervisor Course, my heart leapt about like a tethered frog. The secrecy surrounding the upper levels was a palpable force in those shabby corridors and rooms, through which Sea Org members strode with even more force and purpose than those at Celebrity Center. But it wasn't just the proximity to Operating Thetans and whatever that supposedly mind-bending information might be. It was that by stepping into the Advanced Org, I was plunging into Scientology in a way I'd so far managed to avoid. Terrifying possibilities hovered, including a fear that somehow they'd "get" me, in their implacable, Scientological way, to sign up for the Sea Org.

I'd also by now heard about a nasty thing called the Rehabilitation Project Force (an Orwellian phrase if there ever was one, though that doesn't seem to have occurred to me at the time). Scientologists were sent to the RPF when they'd gone—or were perceived to have gone—out-ethics. Members of the Sea Org who tried to leave the Church might wind up in the RPF. A Registrar whose stats crashed several weeks in a row (which could only be an indication of overts) would be assigned to the RPF. Someone who'd had an affair with someone else's spouse. Someone who'd squirrelled. I was aware that a number of those who'd once been close to LRH were now in the RPF; after Miscavige assumed Church leadership, he'd discovered that all this time, these trusted minions had been committing overts, and they had to be "rehabilitated." In addition to having to perform menial, even demeaning labor, I understood that those in the RPF were fed rice and beans and given Ethics Handlings to help them confront the reasons they'd landed there. Then they had to scratch their way back up the Conditions: from Treason or Enemy to Liability, "making up damage done" every step of the way. People whispered that this took months, even years. *Years!*[81]

The names of the Conditions, which, when applied to marriage or to one's career, seemed like useful metaphors, suddenly took on grim implications. I kept my head down, terrified that these OTs, with their advanced states of awareness, would be able to perceive my misgivings. Was the thrum of doubt in the pit of my stomach audible?

And it was while I was there, working on my Course Supervisor Course, that that twelve-year-old girl picked up my course pack, pointed to a word, and at my "ummm," said "Flunk." And the student beside me whispered that she had gone Clear last lifetime, when she had been a Course Supervisor at Saint Hill.

Saint Hill was the British Org in East Grinstead where, in the sixties and seventies, LRH taught and recorded lectures and wrote hundreds of HCOPLs and HCOBs—basically putting Scientology together. As I watched what appeared to be that big thetan in a little body tour the course room, I did the math. It was possible. If she'd worked there, and then died, she could have come right back; born in the mid-seventies, she'd be about twelve now.

I leafed through the dictionary to find the flunked word, remembering a long-forgotten encounter. In the summer of 1974, waiting to hear if I'd made it into the second year of the American Conservatory Theater's acting program (the number of students was whittled from fifty to twenty-five), I'd spent a few months in Europe. I flew into Paris, worked for a few weeks in the bookstore on the Left Bank, Shakespeare & Company, sleeping on a shelf/sofa under the poetry books, before, traveling with a friend, crossing the English channel. On the bus to London, we met a couple whose eyes were bright, faces shining. There was a discussion of past lives, a topic that even then pulled me like metal to magnet. As the bus drew to a stop, they urged us to alight too, to come with them.

"You'll love it!" they said, grinning with ease and happiness. "We promise."

I'd been very tempted. I thought for months about the choice I'd made to stay in my seat as they swung off the bus. What if I'd gone?

What might I have found? Might it have been that yearned-for closet that opened into Narnia?

Sitting in that course room, watching that wee Course Supervisor spot-checking another student, I wondered if it had been East Grinstead where that bus had stopped, if the couple had been Scientologists, and if they'd been heading to Saint Hill. Staring across the course room at the girl's gleaming braids, I wondered if she might have been there as a student—even as a Course Supervisor—at that very time.

Sometimes it felt as if Scientology had been coming at me, or I at it, for a long time. Which made me think of my brother: all those falls over the years, those near-death moments, as if the big one, the one that mashed his brain, had been just lying in wait.

IN THE AUDITING I was doing with Paloma, I was put on various "rundowns."[82] One of these, as I recall, was a series of processes designed to handle how often I felt I was exterior. Although going exterior—when the spirit of you separates from the body of you—can be deemed a good thing, it can also be debilitating. If you're hovering outside your body and can't or don't come back in, it's hard to be in life.

Exterior was something I felt I did, or had, or was, however it might be phrased; it seemed part of how I interacted with life. Self-conscious might be another way to put it. I often watched myself, as if I were both camera and subject. I was seldom able to just *be*. The problem might dissipate over a glass of wine, when (paradoxically) I could be present: laugh, enjoy, be part of things. But sooner or later, I'd feel a terrible tug. I'd mentally move to the outskirts of the gathering, the event, assessing, judging, thinking I should be doing something other than what I was doing. Often, I found reason to leave.

Paloma and I ran such incidents. There was also an attempt to handle a chronic sense of invalidation. I processed Skye's disappointment that I wasn't OT, Jamie's dismissal of my folky music, how I felt

I never measured up to my parents' expectations, Paloma asking again and again, trying to find the root cause, "Was there an earlier, similar time you were invalidated?"

One day, as I was going on and on, blah blah endless blah, Paloma pulled a sheet from the portable file box she carried into session. This meant she was going to ask a series of new questions, run a new process. But the question wasn't about someone invalidating me. It was: "Was there a time you invalidated someone?"

The way she asked the question made me understand that the process wasn't always about invalidation. It could be asked about someone hurting you (you hurting someone), or taking something from you (you taking something), or even, in examining previous lifetimes, killing you (you killing someone). Immediately I saw its purpose. If you'd "pulled it in," you yourself must have done something to *create* that particular flow coming your way. In a word: karma.[83]

But when I'd talked my way through that series of repeated questions, in the process having the (obvious) realization about how my invalidating others had led me to be invalidated, Paloma posed another question: "Was there a time others invalidated others?"

This question opened up a vast array of options, and more realizations, but it was the fourth question that I found utterly enlightening: "Was there a time you invalidated yourself?"

I actually started to laugh. In the long run, who else could?

This is an example of the sort of thing that kept me willing to trust the Tech (I later found out these are called the Quad Flows).[84] Perhaps because I already believed that things going awry were the result of something I had or had not done, these questions made sense. But a bigger, more useful truth began to glimmer: Whether I could (or should) take responsibility for everything that happened "to" me, what I could be responsible for, what I might control, is how I feel about it. The perspective took too long to land, and came in a poisonous package, but it's very useful.

•

ONE AUDITING SESSION revealed that my father and I had quite a friendship, back in the 1870s. We were cowboys, working cattle up and down the Territories. One night, sitting by the campfire, the cattle spread out over acres of range around us, he took a sip from his tin mug and told me that he was thinking about being a writer.

I didn't hear "writer," I heard "rider."

"You already are one," I told him.

He said no, he was not, and I said yes, he certainly *was*.

He stood up and yelled, "I am not a writer!" and I stood up and yelled, "You sure as hell are too a rider!"

We got into a ferocious tangle, shouting across the fire at one another, stomping off to sleep, freezing, our bedrolls far from the firepit's glowing coals rather than be proximate enough to even hear each other snore. It wasn't until the next morning, after we'd saddled up and were slogging along the edge of a creek, that we realized one of us meant "rider" and the other "writer." Then we laughed long and loudly, making some of the cows bolt.

The overreaction we had to each other is what's known in Scientology as a "wrong indication." According to Hubbard's theory, this can cause a person to introvert, and if the wrong indications persist, or are not cleared up, can even cause psychosis.[85]

My father and I died together that lifetime. In a duel, a gunfight. I think it was over a woman. We both got off one shot. It was curiously low-key and rather dignified.

Paloma and I ran a lot of incidents about my dad in those auditing sessions. We'd known each other in a lot of lives, in all kinds of relationships, in which there was often, as in that cowboy friendship, an all-too-obvious competition.

According to me. I remember being pleased with that writer/rider pun. The cowboy lifetime could have been inspired by my father's novel *Warlock* (it takes place in the Old West). I might have been moved to all that Western imagery and action by McMurtry's *Lonesome Dove*, which I'd recently read. I fretted about this a lot, that what I was "remembering" was my imagination, or a conflation of memories and scenes from books and movies. I mentioned my concern to Skye.

"I think about that too," he said. "But here's what I figure. If the story, invented or real, allows you to get to some truth about yourself, and allows you to figure something out about the way you've behaved in the past and the way you want to change that behavior in the future, what's wrong with that? Maybe that's all auditing is: a way for us to examine the self we don't want to be, and invent a better self we can work toward being."

He gave me one of his impish smiles. "It's also possible, of course, that whatever it is you're remembering *is* a memory. A real one. There is that possibility."

"ARE YOU AND Skye thinking about a baby?" my sister, Tracy, asked in one of our rare phone calls. "Because, you know, you did just turn thirty-six."

I used birth control. But (amazingly) it wasn't until Tracy asked that question that I became aware that the sand in the hourglass for that particular endeavor was running thin. In our little group, we seldom spoke of children. Perhaps because it would get in the way of the careers we were supposedly building. But I think it was more the idea that Scientologists were not limited by such Matter-Energy-Space-Time concerns. As OTs, one could command a body to do what needed to be done—or something. Delph and Wyatt were still the only parents in our midst, although Paloma, almost fifty, spoke of adopting a child, and eventually did.

"How are we going to do that, muffin?" Skye said, when I broached the topic. "You can't stay committed to Scientology for more than a day at a time. How could we bring a child into that confusion?"

By which he meant, of course, that if we had a child we'd raise him/her as a Scientologist. It was a horrifying idea—and wasn't that another sign I should *get out*? But once again I examined the transgressions that would make we want to leave, which led back to that Beckett-ian mantra: *Shall we go? Yes, let's go. They do not move.*

I dropped the subject.

Even as I worked on the screenplay, stories, a novel, it was increasingly clear how much I simply didn't *know* about writing. In a desultory way I sent away for information about graduate programs. I even talked to my father about attending the program he ran at UC Irvine. He told me that my writing was good enough to be accepted into his program.

"It *is*?" This stunned me. He'd recently sent a padded envelope containing three paperback romance novels, the 10¢ thrift store stickers still attached, with a note to say that perhaps my style was suited to the genre. I was horrified and ashamed. At the time, I understood that any kind of genre writing meant, simply, *bad* writing; romance, above all, was "fluff." I promptly dropped off the books, unread, at another thrift store.

"Sure. And I'd be happy to have you."

I tried to imagine talking about writing with peers, my father looming over the table.

"Although," he said, "it's probably not such a great idea. Might cramp your style." We both laughed, very hard. "But we're glad to hear you're working on your novel."

I shrugged. I had yet to tell him I was working at a Scientology mission.

"Anything to get you out of the clutches of the Evil Empire, right?"

"That's right." More laughter, which faded. "Love you, Dad."

"We love you too, Sands."

I hung up the phone. I would have to tell Skye I'd talked to my father about the possibility of going to graduate school. Otherwise I'd have a withhold.

•

ONE AFTERNOON NOT long after that call I stood looking out our large front window. The sun shining on the wood floor warmed the soles of my bare feet. A breeze tossed the leaves of trees lining the cul-de-sac. But I realized I was missing my family. Brett was engaged to a man I'd met just once. Tracy now had a baby daughter, Emma. Oak was living with her and her family in Grand Junction while Robin looked for work in Chicago.

Standing there, the wood warm beneath my feet, I decided to go to the Conference. In addition to seeing family, the lectures and panels would be good for my writing. And when the week was over, I'd head to the Southwest, spend time with Tracy, and research my screenplay.

That night I told Skye my plan. I asked if he might be willing to join me.

And to my surprise and delight, he said yes. Jessica was supportive. I was prepared to quit the Center if she said no, and perhaps she sensed as much. She gave me a month off-post.

In August I headed to Squaw Valley. The bustle and work of getting things launched was as it ever had been: the family plus many helpers scurrying about: Each year, the office, the workshop spaces, and the stage for panels and lectures have to be erected newly.

Oak—Tad, again—had already arrived from Grand Junction. He seemed, simply, happy. I didn't know, had never seen, this side of him. I remembered him as driven, intense, brilliant—never *happy*. His face still looked as if someone had taken a sledgehammer and slammed it under one side of his chin: One eye sat higher than the other. Yet, however lopsided the grin might be, the mischievous gap between his two front teeth was still there. It was still his grin.

Among the staff members that 1987 summer was a writer I'll call Max, who'd just published a well-received first novel. In his long arms, his mandolin looked like a toy, but his fingers flew over the strings, sparkling and twining notes around my voice and guitar. All kinds of attractive possibilities hovered there. But I was with Skye. And Max was married—albeit, I gathered, unhappily. I'd been there, done that, and still felt awful about it. I focused on the music we could make that really was, simply, music.

As a way to end the intense, supercharged week of the Conference, my father, years before, had come up with the idea of a "talent show" featuring the participants and the august writers who taught them engaging in skits, songs, poetic rewrites and interpretations, and other literary folly. Indeed, Dad dubbed the event "The Follies." Most years, I organized and emceed, and for more than a decade, it was the only time I played any music: sometimes a tune of my own, and always a song to end the Follies that everyone in the Conference sang together. That year, with Max and the other gathered musicians, it was "Amazing Grace."

Afterward, Max gave me a hug, the only time we touched.

"Next summer," he said. "We'll work up a duet for the Follies!"

I nodded and turned away. Skye was my sweetheart. We were heading to the Southwest; we were going to travel! Together!

ANASAZI

A Pueblo word, ANASAZI means "the ancient ones. Ancestors."

But it also means "enemies of our ancestors."

This discrepancy fascinated me. I felt that in the tension between those two definitions hovered the truth of what had happened to them. Why, having occupied the Southwest for hundreds of years, had the Anasazi moved into hard-to-access cliff dwellings, and then . . . disappeared?

The mystery was compelling and complete, and Skye found it as intriguing as I did. We clambered into those cliffs. We hiked through sere landscapes to peer at petroglyphs. We meandered through museums, where I scribbled notes that seemed essential to the story I was building. We climbed in and out of kivas, marveling that during the same centuries that Europeans were lofting cathedral spires into the sky to reach the Father, Native Americans were digging deep into Mother earth to honor the Place of Emerging. We kept our tent flaps open so we could gaze at the night sky, thrilled that six hundred years before, the Anasazi had walked this land and lived their lives in relation to those same rotating stars.

For the first time in my relationship with Skye, I was leading the way. I felt a jolt, a surge of energy: This is *me*! I shared my research, introduced him to places I'd read about—and I could put up a tent! It helped a lot toward the wish I had to knock his socks off.

We stayed for a few days in Grand Junction with Tracy and David. Tad was still in Squaw Valley, cleaning up after the Conference. He'd return in a few weeks and would then head to Chicago to join Robin, who'd finalized a job. At one point, as Tracy showed me the writing hut he'd built out of cinderblocks, I tearfully confessed to the doubts that plagued me.

"Well, you're welcome here any time. If you ever, you know—" she spoke with care, respectful as she always was of my choices "—want to take a break."

Borrowing their bikes, Skye and I headed to the Canyonlands. We took in Moab, Durango, Santa Fe. Mostly we camped; now and again we booked hotel rooms that I don't know how we paid for. Skye must have used a credit card. One of those was the Rocking Horse Inn, in Taos, where our lovemaking was so lush that I was sure I'd be pregnant. I told Skye so, and that I wanted to live here with that baby, walk barefoot on terra-cotta tile, plant trees I'd see grow to maturity.

Which is when Skye said, "And what am I supposed to do, muffin, bag groceries?" And added, "You don't want what I want. You want a whole different life."

I saw what he meant. But unhappy as I was in the life we led in Los Angeles, I could not imagine leaving him, could not imagine life without him. I appeared to have handed over every bit of will to him, and to the Church.

And so we made our way back to LA. I picked up my duties again at the Center. I checked in with beloved friends. In my datebook, for each weekday morning, I printed in block letters, WRITE. And many mornings I did sit at my desk. But my stories seemed obviously and stupidly autobiographical. The novel, started back in New York, was stalled. While I didn't want everyone to die—alcohol, drugs, accidents—any other ending seemed saccharine. Graduate school seemed most unlikely; how would I ever get accepted? There was the screenplay, but Vano had other things to think about. He'd undergone a kidney transplant, with pain so monumental that all he remembered was screaming for someone to please, *please* kill him, *now*. He spent three evenings a week on dialysis. Sometimes I drove the hour to see him and sat through a few of the eight hours it took his blood to cycle through one of those stainless steel machines, but we seldom talked about writing. Once he said to me that I should turn the screenplay into a novel.

"I mean it," he said. "Except for the name Driver, it's pretty much all yours anyway."

I was aware of a vast hollow in my psyche. It wasn't fair to blame Scientology, yet there was no way to get around the fact that it had a lot to do with where and how I was spinning out the days of my life. I was desperately unhappy.

But wanting to leave just meant I had overts. I was so tired of looking for them—and always, *always* finding them.

AND IT WAS about that time, one October evening, that into the course room Ed brought the young man who looked like he spent his days on a surfboard. Skip started Success Through Communication, but there were those complications of sitting opposite him drilling the Training Routines, which student after student couldn't maintain, his talk of the firewalk, those looming funhouse-mirror faces when I attempted TR0 with him myself. Ed taking him into his office. My attempts to find out where he might have landed.

The way the whole episode shook my faith in everything I wanted to believe Scientology represented. How it opened up a reason to leave—thoughts I hid from myself as soon as I had them.

Tracy telling me I was welcome any time.

The meeting with Jessica regarding my need to be a zealot.

The death of LRH. The ascension of David Miscavige.

The increasingly rah-rah nature of Scientology rallies. The growing sense that we "should" attend them all. The rumors of havoc in the Church's upper echelons.

The conversation with my father regarding "wills and things." Even if I could have mustered up the energy to leave, I didn't know how I possibly could, if the leaving would be construed as being attached to my parent's money.

And so, winter of 1987 trudged into spring of 1988. Skye and I remained stalled on what I'd taken to calling "the marriage and kid thing." Sunday afternoons, finished at the Center, I'd race off to write in my journal. Into that three-hour slot before the twenty-four-hour rule kicked in, I squeezed a glass or two of wine. I loved those hours of writing, the world I entered as I indulged in them: sunlight chattering through leaves in an outdoor café, murmured conversations from the tables nearby, and the scribble scribble scribble of pen against good paper.

Vano was still on dialysis. The prognosis was bad.

One June afternoon, Sunny and I met for lunch. She was now OT III and her singing career was on the move; she was engaged to a man named Ron and was moving to Michigan to be with him. I stared at her in wonder. She managed, she always had, to incorporate the benefits of Scientology into her life without it taking over her life. How did she do that?

Sunny heard me out, eyes full of sympathy.

"Well, sweetie," she said, "I mean, look at it! You don't have an acting career, which is what you came to LA to do. You're not writing songs, or singing, which you love. You're estranged from your family. You don't like living here. Skye's a sweetheart, but he doesn't want to get married or have a child—"

"He might," I said, "but I'm so wishy-washy about Scientology."

"My darling Ron isn't a Scientologist, and I'm marrying him. Just look at it! All your stats have crashed! You need to solve this!"

That evening, I told Skye I was going to go stay with Tracy.

Just for a month or two, I promised. At the end of the summer, after the Conference. I'd work as a waitress. I'd work on my new novel. I wasn't *leaving* . . .

He was cautiously supportive, but the news came at a bad time for

Jessica. She'd discovered that Ed had been enjoying not only drinks and dinner with potential recruits to the Center, but, in a misguided attempt to create affinity and reality, he'd been snorting cocaine with them.

"He's off-post, needless to say." Jessica's lovely face was disgusted and sad. "There are a lot of overts to pull. He thinks he's in Enemy, but it's probably Confusion. He's got a lot of work to do before he's allowed back on-post."

I couldn't imagine his being back at all. "I'm so sorry, Jessica."

"It won't be fun finding your replacement. I hope the time will be well spent." But she looked wary. Going to Colorado to work on my novel could hardly be considered zealous.

Max, who lived nearby, called with an idea for the summer's Follies, and dropped by a copy of what he had in mind: a medley recorded by Waylon Jennings and Jessi Colter that included "The Wild Side of Life," a man lamenting that his woman had left him, and a riposte, "It Wasn't God Who Made Honky-Tonk Angels." I listened as I packed.

I was packing a lot of things for what was going to be, supposedly, just a few weeks.

The Conference was its usual jumble of literary fun. And Max and I, making eyes at one another as we sang, skated terrifically close to what the lyrics of "The Wild Side of Life" outlined. We hiked. We talked. I wanted to believe we were well suited. I thought it nothing but fortuitous that my Colorado foray to stay with Tracy was in place. Before us a future began to shimmer. But our lips did not meet. Our hands barely touched. I convinced myself I was committing no overts. He was married. I was with Skye. We'd eventually let these good people know our plans.

Feeling virtuous, I returned to LA to finish packing. I was taking so much stuff to Colorado that I needed a roof rack. As I watched Skye attach it to the top of my Honda, I thought what a good man he was. But I was not deterred.

The day before I was due to leave, Max and I met in Santa Monica for a walk on the beach. We still did not touch, but more vague promises were tendered. That evening, I walked in the door to find Skye in his study tuning his guitar. I took in the mass of black ringlets that framed his face, hair that he dyed, in his guise as the ever-young Stryder, to cover the gray. All that pretense! So unlike Max's genuinely balding pate!

I knew this was a critical thought. I knew I was finding a "motivator" for having walked along the beach with Max.

"Good day?" Skye asked.

"Good," I said, noting critically—and noting that I was noting critically—the psoriasis that sometimes plagued him. "A walk with a friend."

Skye tightened a string, plinked it, plinked it again. "That sounds nice," he said, smiling at me with affection.

And with that smile, he missed the withhold: The "friend" was someone with whom I was pretty much imagining a whole new life.

In a sudden swirl of anger I dropped my purse next to my half-packed suitcase and went to the kitchen to make dinner. As I banged around pots and pans, I wondered how I could be such an awful person, at the same time noting the dirty coffee maker, which was always dirty because Skye *never cleaned it*, eyeing the broken cup rack that Skye *still* hadn't fixed. Even as I assured myself that my critical thoughts were *justified*, I noted that I was doing exactly what Hubbard points out that we do when we've committed an overt.

To hell with Scientology! I was in love!

That night I lay as far on my side of the bed as possible, actually placing one bare foot on the floor to keep from tumbling out. I listened to Skye breathe, appalled at myself. I was leaving for Grand Junction the very next morning. This was an *overt*! I had a *withhold*! Could it be I was *blowing*?

I had all the motivators, the ways to justify my actions. Nevertheless, I wondered if it might be possible to tell him what I was doing—cough up the overt and the withhold—and *still do it*.

•

THE NEXT MORNING, Skye helped me cover the load on the roof with a tarp and bungee cords, which, like the roof rack, he'd purchased. I was in anguish. I poured us coffee and took a deep breath and said, "That walk yesterday? With that friend? His name is Max?"

Skye looked up. "Is there something more you want to say?"

I began to cry. "I don't know. I just don't like this life! I love you so much—"

"What?! What are you *talking* about?"

"—but Max just offers this whole other way of living. In the country. Playing music together." I wailed, "There's nothing to tell! I swear! We haven't *done* anything."

"Who the hell is *Max*? You haven't *done anything*? Except *imagine your life with someone else*!" Skye lurched out of his chair and picked up the phone. "I don't want to hear about it. But you're going into session with Paloma. Today, if she can do it. I don't care if you're leaving for Colorado! You're not leaving for Colorado with a bunch of overts on your head. You know about blowing. You'll never be back!"

But that's exactly what I want, I didn't say. I didn't know what I wanted. Except: no overts.

Paloma moved her day around to take me into session. We'd been auditing in the Advanced Org, and as we walked down the dilapidated hall (oops, there went another critical thought, but really, why not just a coat of paint? Where did all the money *go*?), she carried my auditing folder and the case that held her e-meter. Skye had outlined what was up, but she evinced no attitude. This, after all, was exactly why one drilled those TRs.

She set up the meter on the other side of the board that hid the motions of her hands from me but over which I could see her face and she mine. She attached the wires to the cans with the little alligator clips that seemed so makeshift. (Why hadn't Hubbard designed some *aesthetic* way to connect cans to meter!)

Another critical thought.

I rubbed Intensive Care into my hands. I forced my thoughts

away from memories of my brother in the ICU, all those tubes running into and out of his body.

As always, Paloma was firm, practiced, and authoritative. She began to pull the overts and withholds. Time, place, form, event. I offered up every last smidgen of what I'd done or even thought about doing.

But I still wanted to go to Colorado.

My needle floated.

Skye didn't ask what had gone on in session. He strapped the last of the bungee cords into place. We hugged for a long moment.

"I love you so much," I told him. "I'll be back," I said, wondering if I was lying.

He gave me a sealed envelope, watched as I opened and read it.

Play this one with infinite care. There is much at stake.

Typically, his caution was not about the future of our love, but that of my soul.

Jaw set, he stepped back. I rolled down the driveway, waving. He stood still, one arm held up in farewell. I waved and waved until I'd turned the corner. I was crying.

"But," I whispered in tortured triumph, "I've done it."

BINDING BACK

That last-minute auditing with Paloma made me pause, though, in my rush to Max's arms and what I felt that would solve. I asked him not to be in touch for a month.

Tracy and David folded me into their house and into their lives. They had room; Tad was now in Chicago with Robin. This brought a little pinch of memory, how often I had followed where my brother led. And now, in accepting this sanctuary, I was doing so again.

I loved every aspect of the house and the children, the air and the space, and, even though Grand Junction was definitely a city, the sense of a small town it offered. I wrote in the mornings and waitressed most afternoons and evenings. The writing went in spurts and starts, but I was doing it most days, from which huge satisfaction emanated. I took pleasure in hanging out the laundry on the crisscrossing lines in back of the house, standing in the autumn sun, pinching the pins over Nico's shirts, Emma's diapers. Whenever I had a few days without work, I headed south to the Four Corners, where I tromped around doing research for my novel.

It was my novel now. I wrote Vano a letter, thanking him for that encouragement, giving him updates on what was now happening with Driver and Eva. I did not hear back. He was dying, although at the time I didn't know it.

Arranging to meet friends of friends of friends—whites following the way of the People, Native Americans willing to talk to a white woman—I drove deep into Navajo territory, carrying the requisite gift of a carton of Marlboros. Sometimes I spent nights with a friend in Durango and took day trips. On longer pilgrimages, I pitched a tent and slept with the flaps open so I could see the stars. These treks to Canyon de Chelly, Mesa Verde, Chaco, gave me a feeling of adventure and personal power that I began to realize I'd dropped from my life and which were essential to my sense of self.

Chaco Canyon, which could be reached only by driving endless slow miles over rain-rutted roads, was the most mysterious and compelling of all the Anasazi sites. It had once been a vast city. But many rooms in the numerous buildings, of which only rubbled walls remained, appeared to have been used not as living quarters, but for storage. In them, archeologists had discovered pots full of corn and beans. Wide roads led in like spokes on a wheel to this central place. Elsewhere, kivas were sized to hold a dozen people, but Chaco's kivas were vast. A hundred people would have been able to congregate in just one of those circles of stone.

I began to wonder if Chaco had once been a gathering place, like Teotihuacan, near Mexico City. Perhaps that was the reason for the wide roads, the stored food, the huge kivas: to accommodate pilgrims who trekked from all over the Southwest. Prowling around, I noticed troughs running alongside several of the kivas, wide and deep enough to accommodate a doubled-over person. These tunnels—which they could have once been, before the covering rocks fell away—ended in the place known as the *sipapu*, in the Pueblo culture known as "the place of emerging." I imagined how someone dressed as something magical, something *other*, could have scuttled through the tunnel and then—emerged!

I'm a theater artist. I know how stage magic can be created. Could such an "apparition" be designed to force or sustain belief? Persuade to some idea? I hated that I would wonder such a thing. I wanted the Anasazi to be perfect, wise, their intentions clear as running water. I felt my mind flip to my own religion. I flipped it right back.

And yet. What was with those huge, corporate-style meetings? Or the "purges" rumored to be going on in the upper echelons of the Church?

Hot and dusty, I clambered around the ruins in Chaco Canyon, thinking of a shocked, whispered discussion I'd overheard between two longtime Scientologists, about the changes being implemented by Miscavige. In addition to his decision to edit and republish LRH's books, there was what he was doing to people who'd been close to Hubbard, some of whom had *lived* with Hubbard.

Pat and Annie Broeker, for instance. During Hubbard's final years, the Broekers had been his caretakers. I'd gathered that Annie had been pretty much the conduit from "the old man" to her husband, and Pat the conduit to the Church offices. Hubbard had dubbed them Loyal Officers #1 and #2. Indeed, there was so much trust in them that the expectation was that Church leadership would naturally be bequeathed to Pat Broeker.[86]

But following Hubbard's death, both of the Broekers were declared SPs.

How could Loyal Officers #1 and #2 be *suppressive*? People murmured. Very quietly. Were the Broekers, after decades of being Hubbard's most loyal friends (if Hubbard had friends), somehow responsible for his death? Yet hadn't we been told that he'd *purposefully* "dropped this body"? That he'd been "at cause" and had "simply moved on to his next level"?

Then the rumors changed. Annie had been sent to the dread Rehabilitation Project Force, Scientology's gulag.[87] And Pat—of course a member of the Sea Org—had left the church. *He'd left the Church!*

Squatting next to my tent, poking a fork into the collection of vegetables cooking over the single-burner stove, I thought about Scientology's upper levels. Yes, the OT materials were *supposedly* confidential, but maybe those bits of information were leaked purposefully, to create intrigue. Something about a despotic ruler (whose very *name* could cause psychosis), who, billions of years ago, had shipped "humanoids" to planet Earth. That much appeared to be covered in Hubbard's sci-fi novels. But then there were other rumors. This fellow (Xenu—I'd heard the name, and as far as I knew, hadn't gone psychotic) stuffed them (us?) in volcanoes (??) and blew them up with an H-bomb (!?!). Was that the Wall of Fire one confronted when one became OT III? I'd vaguely gathered that those quadrillion particles of blown-up humanoids attached themselves to *other* quadrillion particles of blown up humanoids—at the *cellular* level, where engrams are supposed to lodge. Was the idea that we might confuse others' engrams with our own, or even take them on *as* our own? Was that the rest of the Bridge to Total Freedom? With all those cellular selves mixed together, how could you *ever* figure out your own true self?

Or was that the lesson—some lovely Eastern notion that we're ultimately all one? But that didn't feel like Hubbard one bit.

I sat at a picnic table with my supper as the sun descended, pulling on a down vest against the shadows creeping across the canyon's vast floor. That we'd been marooned here, on this penal colony, was connected to psychiatry. Psychiatrists were the ultimate evil (another instance where the tenets of my upbringing intersected with those of Scientology). Once psychiatrists got hold of you, Hubbard said, they'd persuade you that you needed therapy forever, and you'd never break free. But wasn't that exactly like the Bridge to Total Freedom, which more and more didn't look like a bridge at all, but, rather, a road to nowhere in particular? Was Hubbard just doing what he said bad people did: accusing others of what they, themselves, are guilty of, in order to obfuscate what's really going on?

Carrying toothbrush and towel, I headed to the primitive Park Service bathroom. In any case, I'd heard enough to know that psychiatrists had condemned us to live in this terrible place, Earth, hamsters on what I saw as a flaming wheel. Scientology was the only way to break free. And once free, so I gathered, we could join the squadrons of OTs whizzing (body-less) around the universe introducing the Tech to other planets. The Freedom Police, I had oxymoronically named this collection of beings, imagining them slamming molecule-less batons into disembodied gloves.

I zipped myself into my sleeping bag. I didn't want to leave Skye, and my friends, and the pleasures of study. But Hubbard seemed to have sabotaged the sensible and useful aspects of Scientology with this loony sci-fi storyline. Had he just decided his religion had to have a creation myth, the way it needed a cross?

I WONDER NOW if the rumors of those purges, the weirdness going on at the upper echelons of the Church, affected my experience of Chaco. Because even in broad daylight, the cañon seemed spiked with evil, fraught with the odd, the violent, the eerie. Perhaps being in that desolate place, scrambling around in the hot, dry air, was why, for the first time, I let myself examine those bits and pieces I'd picked up about the upper OT levels. At night I felt as if spirits, ones that did not wish anyone well, hovered around my tent. As I zipped the flap closed against these imagined intruders, which I did even though I loved being able to see the moon and stars, I thought about the Mayan civilization, whose ruins lay far south. That culture, deep in Mexico, had peaked in 900 C.E. A hundred years later, the historical record of the Anasazi begins. Pondering the Mayans' violent sacrifices, I wondered if any of that—like the seashells and feathers of tropical birds that had been found in Anasazi ruins—could have made its way across the thousands of miles separating the two cultures.

So maybe, as I scribbled in a note to Vano, Driver crashes the semi, Eva in the front seat beside him, in some magical zone near Chaco Canyon they have no idea they've entered. Whisked back to the 1300s, as thousands of Anasazi pilgrims are converging, Driver and Eva are swept up in the tumble of the faithful, as they are then caught up in various rituals, which only they can see are spurious bits of religiosity. Driver, tapped by a head shaman, finds the Native American part of him intrigued. But Eva manages to persuade him that mixed in with Anasazi wisdom are terribly unsavory elements, and that they should leave. Somehow they manage to break free of the alluring Anasazi zone, taking what's useful and leaving behind the weird. Eva finds herself pregnant with Driver's baby. Now a family, they start a new life.

The connections are obvious to me now. But at the time I didn't see how completely this reflected my confusion and yearnings regarding Skye and Scientology.

As I ventured further and further afield, into territory rarely visited by the average tourist, I pondered religion and its "binding" nature. So many religions, all convinced theirs is the only way. Why this need for larger meaning? I believed absolutely that something inhabited the body—soul, spirit, thetan—and that death came about because of the departure of that thing (EXPIRE's roots are "out" + "spirit"). But belief systems only come about due to just that: belief. Faith. Well, and practice. Study. You have to do the thing, know the tenets; above all, you have believe in them. Catholicism, yoga, Transcendental Meditation, Buddhism, Scientology.

Clambering into dozens of cliff dwellings, places extremely difficult to access without the help of ladders or hard-to-discern footholds pecked into stone, I thought about how many people, within so many religions, were bound—had *agreed* to be bound—by, say, the idea of a pantheon of gods. By the idea of a single god. The idea of a savior. Of Nirvana. Of a Bridge to Total Freedom.

In spite of the intellectual, empirical world in which I'd been raised, which dismissed, even denigrated much to do with spiritual yearning, I'd always been attracted to ideas about mind and soul; one of the reasons I kept on keeping on with Scientology was that it seemed to encompass various systems that had long appealed to me. There were Eastern concepts of karma, including Hinduism's ideas regarding reincarnation and Buddhism's lack of a god to worship. My mother's Christian Science was represented: spirit could rise above and control body. Hubbard didn't mention love, which seemed essential to Christianity, but then, LRH belonged to a generation that didn't talk much about such things. Still, if one looked for it, it was there. Between the vaulting authority embodied by Standard Tech, the caretaking (mothering) involved in auditing, and the epiphanies to be had when applying ethics (confession, if you will), I could envision the stern Old Testament God and his Christian intermediaries, Mary and Jesus. Over the years, I'd sat in dozens of churches and cathedrals, breathing in forms of Christianity along with the aroma of incense and beeswax, trying to comprehend all the blood that had been spilled in the insistence that theirs (so many theirs) was the only God, their way the only way. One of the things I appreciated about Scientology was that even though one was supposed to believe it was the only way, no one—so far, anyway—had gone to war over it.

Out of breath from my scramble up a particularly steep cliff face, I looked down and across the sere landscape stretching into the far distance. That the Anasazi had moved into these cliffs toward the end of their time in the Four Corners, just before they disappeared, made it seem as if they'd been afraid of something. Protecting themselves from something. What—who—had made them do that? The Ancient Ones? Or the Ancient Enemies? And if they were enemies, why? What had they done? And *what* was going on at the upper levels of the Church?

I thought about Skye a lot. I thought about Max less and less.

I was unaware of how obsessed I'd become with an ancient religion while being so ambivalent about my own.

BACK AT TRACY'S house, lying in bed, I tried to imagine Max beside me, tried to envision the lovely life we'd lead, as he twined mandolin notes around the songs I'd pluck from my guitar. I hugged it to me as if it were a vast amount of fabric, what you might find in a wedding dress or an enormous tablecloth. But more and more the image felt like a tarp that's been left too long in the rain and sun, shredding even as I tried to salvage it. I wanted to be grateful for the catalyst I'd hoped he'd be, "saving" me from Scientology, but I had to face that while we'd been concocting all these fine plans, I was with Skye and Max was married, with a daughter. I was full of overts. I could hardly bear to look at it.

I began to face how horrid it must be for Skye, alone in the house. He'd asked me not to be in touch, so as not to open the wound caused by my leaving, and so had no idea whether I was or was not creating life with another man. When Max wrote a lovely letter exactly a month after I'd put the moratorium in place, I demurred. A few weeks later, I wrote to Skye, apologizing. The Conditions haunted me. Enemy? Treason? How would I ever make up the damage done?

He wrote back, cautious. Scientology was a constant in his life. That wasn't going to change, and wasn't that friction making me unhappy? Yet how could he tell the woman he loved that she should leave what, as far as he was concerned, was the *only* way? The familiar chasm began to yawn.

I loved where I was and what I was doing, but I couldn't live with my sister the rest of my life. I missed my friends. I missed Skye. I told him I was coming back.

I can't bear to relive the convoluted reasoning I used to justify this decision.

Flunk.

BUT THERE WAS a start, of sorts. Skye was east with his family, and after a brief, terrible Christmas with my parents—I still remember Mom's cry, "You'd *escaped*!"—I headed to LA and, waiting for Skye's return, looked into graduate programs. I managed to meet the application deadlines for Stanford and Iowa.

I did not return to the Center. Instead, I went back to waitressing. It felt good to step away from such deep engagement with the Church. At least I'd accomplished that, I told myself, quietly. While I doubted I'd be accepted into a graduate program, I held that hope there like a flickering candle. It would provide distance. And after that . . . ?

I arrived back in LA just in time for Vano's memorial service. I hadn't known he'd died. Almost I didn't attend, and I did arrive late. Maybe because his death was too much of a reminder of Oak's almost death. Vano had been good to me, and I wished I could have done more for him. As soon as the memorial was over, I fled.

Skye returned. And there we were, once again holding fast to each other in the night. His dreams for Stryder had faded. He was pouring all that passion into a novel. He wrote every day, hard and fast, on an electric typewriter. And at long last, I found a way to be helpful: as an editor. Years of scribbling in journals, listening to panels at the Conference, poring over *New Yorker*s—dazzled and inspired by the writing in those glossy pages—paid off when I looked at the work of others.

My own novel disintegrated. My research had led me to a dreadful comprehension regarding the Ancient Ones, the reason for those cliff dwellings, why the ancestors of the Pueblo had been known as "enemies": High-ranking priests of the Anasazi had become a ruling class, wielding vast power and creating widespread fear. They began to eat the others. Perhaps, in the enormous kivas of Chaco Canyon, the cannibalism was even ritualized. They boiled brains in the victims' own skulls and slurped them down.

First the People took to the cliffs. And then they simply disappeared.

It did not occur to me that this phenomenon—members of a religion eating their own—might be happening in my own church.

FOR THE MOST part, the shallow Scientology waters in which I waded reflected little of the frantic movement deep in the organization. While I knew that Miscavige had created something called Religious Technology Services, and that he'd appointed himself Chairman of the Board, I only vaguely understood that the RTS had oversight regarding *everything* to do with Scientology. (Not until I was checking citations for this book did I realize that includes the republishing, and thus the ownership of copyright, of all of Hubbard's writings.)

But there were, nevertheless, rumors of purges, of people being "declared" as Suppressive or sent to the dread Rehabilitation Project Force. Or now and again a story about someone trying to escape, and being caught and brought back into the Church.

I did my best not to think about it. It was easy to do. There was no Internet. As sealed off as the Church kept itself, it was almost impossible to know what was going on. If a reporter did manage to dig in—and at the time there were award-winning exposés in the *Los Angeles Times* and on *Dateline*—avoiding them was just a matter of turning a page or changing the channel. Every now and then I felt a rumble of some terrible truth about myself, as if a massive semi were passing by, shaking my windows and even my boiler room.

However, those months with Tracy and her family, the steady writing, the solo adventures into Anasazi country, seemed to have restored something important. I worked on my music. I kept to a writing schedule and rethought the novel. I'd keep the Southwest. But there'd be no time travel, which had been Vano's idea. If Eva—renamed Maud—found her way to the Anasazi, she'd determine what they had to teach her about herself and her quest, now.

THAT SPIRITUAL STUFF DOES MATTER

Auditing sessions begin by the auditor running "Rudiments": determining if you've had enough food and rest and that you're not otherwise distracted.[88] It's hard to concentrate on the auditor's questions if you want to weep over the fight you just had with your husband, impossible for an auditor to correctly read what's going on with the meter if you've stolen money from your business. Sometimes talking through these problems won't result in a floating needle, and the auditor may need to ask about earlier, similar incidents. Sometimes such chains can take up an entire session.

One day, back in session with Paloma, it became clear that a vast sorrow was attached to one of these rudiments; it wouldn't clear up. Once again I was crying about never being *good enough*, about having so much "case," about the lost years of my life. The crying got worse. We could not sort through it. Paloma reached for a different sheet. She checked the meter and met my eyes.

"Has someone given you a wrong indication?"

I thought about the fight about "rider" versus "writer" that I'd supposedly had with the thetan who in this lifetime was my father. I started wailing.

Paloma, watching the meter, said, "What's that?"

"I don't *know*," I said.

"There," she said, as the meter's needle clearly ticked in some way. I shook my head, intrigued in spite of myself. "There," she said again, and repeated the question, "Has someone given you a wrong indication?"

A thought zipped through me.

"Yes, that," she said. "What is that?"

I shook my head. "It's ridiculous!"

"Tell me." Keeping an eye on me, one on the meter, she was writing fast.

"I . . ."

But it was preposterous.

She smiled. Her dear freckled face, the red hair pulled back from it. "You can say anything, Sands. You know that."

I nodded. Of course. But not this.

She waited, eyes alert and focused and infinitely gentle.

"I'm Clear," I said.

She wrote, adjusted the meter. Her TRs were excellent. She did not agree. She did not disagree. She did not find it preposterous. She simply waited for what else I had to say.

"I have been for years—"

I couldn't say the next part. But she kept that steady gaze.

My body began to tingle, wave after wave surging through my veins, and I knew I was "blowing down."[89] A blowdown is often visceral, and this day it was exceptionally so: The top of my head prickled, as if energy were rising through the hair follicles; my scalp felt as if it might detach from my skull and rise beyond the ceiling. My skin seemed to pulse with heat. It was as if decades' worth of electrical charge was radiating through every pore.

"That's it," she said. "Yes, here we go, here we go." She adjusted the meter, adjusted it again.

"It was last lifetime," I said.

I thought about that twelve-year-old girl who'd flunked me in the AO's course room, who'd been a Course Supervisor last lifetime and who'd picked up those duties again as soon as she was able. About the British couple talking to me about past lifetimes, who'd swung off the bus in East Grinstead, perhaps bound for Saint Hill. Was I just making this up? Was this just some absurd, desperate effort to be something I felt I needed to be?

Paloma waited, steady as an ocean liner forging through high waves.

My body continued to feel as if it were radiating light. Images and memories flickered, ones I'd thought about but never put together. A couch in a Hollywood bungalow. The spindly legs of a Danish-style coffee table. Mangled wreckage. A single skewed headlight, lighting up a field to the side of a road. The sad epiphany, had so long ago while vacuuming the carpet in the Squaw Valley living room, that all of one's life could be likened to a spool of celluloid, how I'd stood there remembering that idea as if someone had told me of it.

"I went Clear on Dianetics," I managed to sputter out.

"Go on."

The story spilled out: After *Dianetics* was published, in 1950, I'd done a lot of Book One processes with a friend in the living room of a bungalow in West Hollywood. I'd attested to Clear in March of 1952. (I was aware of swiftly doing the math: I was, after all, born in April of 1952. It was *possible.*) Not long after, on a rainy night, I got into a car with a couple of friends and on a road near San Diego was killed in a head-on collision. I detached from my body—went exterior—and floated up above the wreckage, quite frantic to be back on Earth and not leave, not now, when I was just getting used to the idea of no longer having my Reactive Mind. From my location above the highway, I saw that in one of the cars, inching by the red lights and strewn bodies, was a couple. The man was driving. The woman, who was covering her eyes with both hands, was pregnant.

This is, of course, the story I remember my mother telling: she and Dad passing that terrible head-on collision, Mother covering her eyes so that what was in her womb wouldn't "see," wouldn't be affected by the tangled metal and the bodies and the blood.

I swooped over to the car and wedged my way into my mother's belly.

"And the spirit, the thetan that is Tracy," I sobbed, "the spirit that is my sister Tracy was already curled up in there."

Paloma's eyes flicked to the meter and back to me.

"And I nudged her out! I told her, 'It's your turn next time.' And she went! Just like that, she went."

I wept and wept. Largely because of how absurd, how *impossible* it was. Also a vast sorrow that I'd managed to make my way back to Dianetics this lifetime, only to find that Hubbard's early ideas had developed into the reviled cult known as Scientology. Above all, I wept for what I'd done to Tracy. Was my action of bumping her out of our mother's womb the reason she'd never felt part of the family, something she'd several times told me? And which had led, at least in part, to her pulling away? Was this the reason that I continually felt so guilty? Talk about an overt! The thetan known as Tracy had always been one of my closest friends and staunchest supporters.

"And it's just like her," I cried, "to just go like that. No fuss. She just—left."

Paloma and I tracked through the maze of memory surrounding my having gone Clear, then having died and gone exterior, the frantic looking for a place to reenter this world, the anguish attached to kicking my sister out of our mother's womb (I'm not sure how this happened, I just "moved in"). But what seemed to be the correct indication was that I was Clear. My needle floated. As I left the building, I felt as if *I* were floating, that the glowing orb that was me in my body also surrounded it, about eighteen feet high: an enormous light-spilling grin. It was something.

HOWEVER, A FEW weeks later, helping a friend record a demo tape, I couldn't get a series of notes in a harmony right. As I tried again and again, aware that money was flowing down the drain, I felt my mind seizing up, gripped by three equally powerful vises.

#1: I would ruin the recording session if I didn't land these notes.
#2: How could I be Clear if I let this reactive nonsense get in my way?
#3: Had I wanted so much to be *perceived* as Clear that I'd concocted the improbable scenario regarding my sister?

Years before, when I was about seventeen, I'd talked a lot about how much I wanted to be a writer, and one afternoon my father looked up from the book he was reading.

"Do you want to *be* a writer, Sands?" he said. "Or do you want to *write*? There's a difference." He skewered me with a look over the top of his glasses and went back to his book. I resolved never to talk about "being" a writer until I had a publication that proved I was one. Maybe it was like that with Clear. Did I want to *be* Clear? Or did I just want to be *known* as Clear?

Could a doubtful Clear even *be* Clear?

I thought about calling Tracy and apologizing, but how could I, when the whole thing was so *loony*? There was no way to check the "accuracy" of this memory, just as I would never ask my father if he remembered a fight with a fellow cowboy around a campfire. I was clutched within a reality that was only mine, and that of fellow Scientologists.

And the act was so *horrid*. If I had concocted it—stitched it together out of a story told by my mother, influenced by that twelve-year-old in AO's course room and a sense that I "should" be up the Bridge—why would I come up with something so dreadful? Why something so complicated, so *mean*, that engendered so much guilt?

Maybe so I could feel I deserved their anger? The ultimate overt?

To explain why I joined Scientology in the first place?

To satisfy those expectations?

Look! I'm Clear! I'm special! I'm extraordinary!

•

ONE SUNDAY AFTERNOON a few weeks later, Dad called. The previous summer, doing research for a novel, he'd taken a trip down the Grand Canyon, and he was planning to do it again. As he described aspects of that first trip—the rafts, the food, his fellow travelers—I couldn't figure out why he'd called, why he was telling me this, what dreadful thing he might be leading up to. He spoke of a dawn in the Canyon, the sun's rays sliding down the high walls to gild the river, the sight of it like the sound of an organ with all its stops pulled out. Holding the phone with both hands, I waited for the bomb of what he'd called to tell me.

"... which is all to say, Sands." He cleared his throat. "It's all to say that that spiritual stuff does matter. I can see that it does."

"Pardon?"

"Any news from Stanford or Iowa? No. It's too early. But any day now, I imagine. We look forward to hearing that news. Here's your mother."

Wait, I wanted to say. Come back. Say that again.

That spiritual stuff does matter. What had he meant? Why had he said it?

But the moment was gone.

I wonder what it was like for Dad that Sunday morning, before he lifted the receiver and punched in my number. I'd long wondered if we shared a spiritual tendency: his affection for Handel's *Messiah*, our mantras from the Maharishi, the fact that, so long ago, he'd taken his family to that Mexico City cathedral at all, even though he'd hauled me from up from kneeling on its floor. It's taken years to perceive that his acknowledgment of my quest, communicated in that precious phone call—his completely unexpected approval of *having* a spiritual path—helped me leave behind the form in which I was seeking it.

LATE MARCH 1989, I pushed open our front door over the usual assortment dropped through the mail slot: circulars, flyers, menus, and the endless parade of Scientology promo that used up a million trees a year (critical thought) because stats always had to be improved, and stats were improved by outflow, outflow, *outflow*. From Skye's study came the steady sound of typewriter keys. On the floor, shining in sun that beamed through the living room windows, lay a long white envelope. I dumped my purse and bags on the couch and picked it up, taking in the return address.

The Iowa Writers' Workshop.

Slim, the envelope. Holding a single sheet of paper.

A rejection, then. I tore open the flap.

It was a letter from Frank Conroy, Director, pleased to offer me a place in the Workshop. Apologies that he couldn't, however, provide a scholarship.

I had been accepted to the *Iowa Writers' Workshop*!

In my head I was screaming—not entirely from joy. But I didn't make a sound. I sank onto the couch, aware of blood looping, looping, looping through my veins. Holding the envelope in one hand, the letter in the other, I stared at the opposite wall.

I could leave, I could leave, I could leave.

Something about the silence alerted Skye. The threshing stopped. He emerged from his study. "You okay, babe?"

I handed him the letter.

He scanned it, lifted his eyes to mine. He tried very hard to look delighted.

THAT SUMMER I took another pilgrimage, as I'd come to call them, to the Southwest, delving into the idea that some of the Anasazi had terrorized others, but mostly giving myself the gift of research, coupled with travel, that I loved so much. I spoke with medicine men and, carrying a carton of Marlboros, found my way through the deserts of New Mexico to the hogan of a woman named Annie, with whom I spoke for hours. I'm not sure what I was seeking, but in those wonderful weeks, I found some form of it.

And then it was time to head to Iowa. When someone intends to be off course or away from an Org for any length of time, Scientology has an extensive process one follows to ensure that you're not blowing. It's called "routing out," and I did every step of it, faithfully. I didn't want a withhold to sully the waters of my going. When thoughts flickered that once I was in Iowa I might be able to *stop being a Scientologist*, I banished them. They never read on an e-meter. My needle floated.

Part of routing out of my Los Angeles life was helping Skye with the final draft of his novel. Here, too, I wanted to leave everything squeaky clean, convincing others as I convinced myself that there was absolutely no reason I'd not be back. I deeply wanted to balance the exchange I felt I owed him before I left—whatever that leaving might be.

Finally, car packed, I headed to the Squaw Conference and sat in a haze of delight among a community of writers I felt I had finally joined. I listened to lectures and scribbled notes and at the end of the week set out across the deserts of Nevada and Utah, over the Rockies, veering north on 80 to Nebraska, crossing that endless state where NPR and even music were hard to find on the radio. I grew so bored that I listened for an hour to a litany of the price of hogs and corn. For the first time in my life beyond *Hamlet* I heard the word "glean": "Farmer Haverford has finished harvesting," said the radio announcer. "Those in need are invited at dusk to glean his fields."

Glean! The word was familiar to me only as one that Gertrude uses in a request to Hamlet's schoolmates, Rosencrantz and Guildenstern: to "glean what afflicts" her melancholy son. I pulled over and fetched the dictionary out of its box in the backseat.

> GLEAN: 1) To gather grain left behind by reapers.
> 2) To collect bit by bit.
> From Late Latin *glennare*, prob. of Celt. orig.

I placed the *American Heritage* on the seat beside me and pulled back onto the freeway. Without Scientology I might not—no, I *would* not—have packed a dictionary in my luggage. Nor would I be pondering the fascinating geographical paths a Celtic word might have taken to be adopted into Late Latin. I certainly would not have stopped my car in order to look up a word. Nor would I love the act quite so much.

That much at least I could keep, surely, even if I managed to jettison the rest?

But I pushed the thought away. I was Clear! I was a Scientologist!

III

After Such a Storm

MODERNISM?

In the groups of young, articulate students sitting around long tables in the University of Iowa's English Philosophy Building (where in those days the Workshop was held), even when we headed to the Mill for the after-workshop beer, I felt like an oddity. Not only did I fear my peers' reaction should they find out I was (had been? It was still a question) a Scientologist; I was also working as a waitress. Nights when my peers might be at the Foxhead sipping beers, I was at Café Pacifico, serving them. Above all, I was a good fifteen years older than most in the Workshop. I didn't feel older. But I envied, viscerally, that most of them had spent the previous four years of their lives studying writing. Scientology may have kept me "on course," but I hadn't been examining literature or artistic movements, nor any ideas other than those put forth by Hubbard. Sixteen years before, I'd earned a BA in acting. The subsequent two years at ACT had given me cherished training in voice, scansion, movement, historical acting styles, but had done little to augment understanding of the literary kind. Conversations at the Workshop tables leapt and smoked about me. At one point I wrote in my journal, "Modernism?"

By the age of thirty-seven, I'd filled more journals than I was years old, listened to dozens of lectures on writing, thrashed my way through parts of two novels and a number of stories, but had never studied creative writing. I didn't know what I was doing.

And my peers let me know that. Sometimes they were kind. Sometimes they were not. Often it was excruciating. But I was a sponge, taking copious notes. For the first time I had a glimmer of how purposeful one needs to be. With every sentence. Every word.

It meant a lot when, in response to a second story, my first-semester workshop leader James Salter said, "This is a huge improvement." I knew it.

In calls and letters to Skye and Roo and Sunny, I appeared to be a Scientologist, but in mid-October I wrote to Skye, "I'm aghast at the closet I shut myself in for *seven years* . . ." I didn't mail that letter. I was still sorting, sorting—I found I used Scientology principles all the time—but I was obsessed by what I had missed. This, *this* was *life*! That I was on a campus, a beautiful one, with a river that looped its shining way between ivy-covered brick buildings, only emphasized all I'd rejected. For *years*. The reason I'd been unable to commit to the Church was now so obvious. And how often Skye had tried to make me see that!

Late that fall, following another agonized phone call, he tried again, in a letter.

> I get that there are many things that matter to you, but their assigned values are at odds with mine, and equal, sometimes opposite from each other . . . Keeping your parents happy is of the same value as keeping Skye happy. Having an academic, intellectually stimulating life is as important as Scientology. What is VITAL. Then what is important. Then what is nice. These delineations that can't be imposed by others or by "shoulds" . . .

I was dismissive. Of course having an intellectually stimulating life is as important as Scientology! It's *more* important!

It took years to understand the wisdom of what Skye was asking me to examine.

Also, there it was again: Skye wanted my *survival*, far beyond this single life, far beyond simply our love for each other. And so I persuaded myself that no other man would ever care so much. There'd be no other with whom I'd laugh so hard, with whom I'd share such friends, with whom I'd make such love. Having allowed him—forced him—to become everything to me, and even knowing that sooner or later we'd have to part, I could not bring myself to sever that spiritual umbilical cord.

SECOND SEMESTER, STILL paying very high out-of-state tuition, I approached the secretary of the English department to inquire about the university's creative writing correspondence course, currently taught by someone who'd graduated the Workshop years before.

"You have parents who can pay your tuition," she said. "And I'm sure they'd be happy to."

"I'm *not* going to ask my parents for money!" I did not add that they would not, in fact, be "happy to." As far as they knew, I was still a Scientologist.

"Nevertheless, they can afford it. Just ask them."

I shook my head. I kept waitressing and took out another student loan.

The ethos of the Workshop under its director at the time, Frank Conroy, reminded me of some of Degas's ballet paintings: a *régisseur*, in charge of keeping a choreography intact, stands with what looks like a long whip, ready to slash at the calves of ballerinas who execute their movements less than exquisitely. This patriarchal idea, that only through pain can lessons be properly delivered, permeated the talk around those tables.

Nevertheless, I felt the only way to become a better writer was to place myself, that second semester, under Frank's famously caustic tutelage. And he was as tough as his reputation. Among other things, he didn't appear to care what his students might have to say. He didn't seem to subscribe to the idea that it's in articulating an opinion about a piece of writing that a writer learns what's ineffective in her own work. He'd let about three of them (I can hardly say us, as I felt so alien to that group) say what they thought about a given manuscript before launching into his own perspective—sometimes positive, usually a screed.

Frank actually liked my first manuscript, an excerpt from the novel. But he flayed the second one. His lecture regarding all that was wrong with it went on and on and on and on. Afterward, instead of heading to the Mill for an after-workshop beer with those I could no longer even pretend were my peers, I found myself in a stall in the ladies room in the basement of the Iowa City Mall. I was not a writer. Frank had pointed that out. The Workshop had only admitted me at all because they figured my father—the *real* writer—would cough up the needed dough. I had no need to stand on my own two feet; my parents could do it all for me. Why had I ever thought there was any point in trying to make my own way? If I'd just led their life, the life they'd told me to lead, all would be well.

Just the previous summer my mother had told me: "If I had your talent and beauty and resources, I'd have made *such* a life for myself. You've squandered all of it."

Sitting in that stall, at such a low point, in such a low, dank place, I shivered violently. I had to leave. But where? Not LA. Nor Squaw. There was no "home" to go to. I didn't want to be on the planet at all. There was no place for me on it.

I don't know how friends figured out where to find me, but they did.

Come to the Mill, they said. I can't possibly, I said. I can't sit among real writers when it is so clear I am not one. They took me to a hole-in-the-wall, George's, where they bought me a beer and a hamburger, blood sugar I sorely needed. They made me laugh at the critique Frank had given, at the froth that sometimes showed up in the corners of his mouth when he spewed his perspectives; we talked books and authors until I could stand up from that table knowing I could get up the next morning, that I was a writer, that I would keep on writing.

Spring break, still smarting from that workshop, I headed to the Southwest, wondering if the Hopi tribe would take me in. Maybe I'd just veer off the road, disappear into a mesa, crawl into a cliff dwelling, join the Anasazi, wherever they'd wound up. Skye flew to meet me and we stayed for a few days with my brother's old girlfriend Dana, a fine artist, who lived outside of Durango.

Dana was sympathetic but bracing. "Sands!" she said. "That's what master of fine arts programs do! They yank your engine asunder, strew the parts all over your garage, and leave you to put it back together again."

I didn't believe I had an engine, much less one to be yanked asunder. But I was bolstered by the notion that maybe, eventually, I might put one together.

In the end, I learned a lot from that workshop with Frank. And it gave me a powerful purpose, although it took a few years to manifest: I'd be an effective teacher, but a student would not feel, as a result, that her only recourse was to get off the planet.

STILL I COULD not sever the cord to Skye, which meant I stayed connected, tenuously, to the Church. Fall of my second year in the Workshop, he and I took a last trip together, to England, winding up on the Isle of Wight. A storm lashed the island, and I'd left my raincoat on the plane. (PTS! Overt!) We walked in spitting rain, splashing into pools unlit by the intermittent streetlamps. Cold and miserable, we retired to our hotel room with its two narrow beds and climbed together into one of them. Wind rattled the tiny window, rain splattered. He warmed my freezing feet between his calves before we turned to each other for what we did not know would be the final time.

The next morning, back on the ferry, we squabbled about Scientology. The wind blew our hair around our sullen faces. I watched him walk to the stern of the ferry, where he gazed at the seething braid the boat left in its wake. Then he pulled a hand from his pocket, looked at what he held there, and threw whatever it was into the ocean. He returned, his face pinched. We sat in silence for the rest of the cold, blustery ride.

Dawn the next morning, we shivered in a parking lot outside Oxford, where we were catching our respective airport shuttles. His plane, to LA, was taking off from Gatwick; mine, to Chicago, from Heathrow. There in the darkness, confronted by the looming separation, we began to talk, heading back toward each other yet again.

Which, given our history, is no doubt what would have happened if we'd ridden in the same bus to the same airport. But, our breath coiling and dissipating, Skye and I hugged goodbye. With a last squeeze of our gloved hands, we mounted the steps and found window seats, holding our faces close to the glass, frosting the panes. My bus revved and exited the parking lot, his followed. Even as we headed in different directions, we waved and waved.

It would be the last time I saw him.

What he'd thrown into the ocean was an engagement ring.

AND NOW MY own trek across the coals began. I'd found The Way and was, of my own accord, leaving The Way. Those thoughts froze my brain, my blood; even worse was the terror that I'd again find reason to return. I'd told Skye we couldn't be in touch. In spite of deep urges to call him, I never did. I thrashed through the days and nights. Especially nights. It was as if I were back in the Center's course room, opposite Skip, jolting too fast over rutted roads, taking corners at dizzying speed, faces and options leering and receding. In spite of consuming deeply steeped cups of chamomile tea, which helped me slide into sleep, I'd wake within hours to continue the lurching, horrifying journey on a road that looped through a wilderness of lost life. My soul was damned if I stayed with Scientology and damned if I left. I surfaced from troubled dreams aware that my features were creased into an expression of aversion, as if I'd smelled something acrid and was trying not to breathe. This nightly mien created furrows around my mouth, as if I'd smoked for years.

As I breathed and breathed, tossed and turned, mashed a pillow into yet another shape, sometimes I thought of Antigone's effort, countermanding her uncle Creon's edict, to bury her dead brother—to scatter soil over him—so his soul could rest. Otherwise his spirit would roam the land, anguished, moaning, searching. What kind of earth could I place on my own soul, I wondered, so that after my death I wouldn't haunt friends and family forever? Would I be a large, white, comma-shaped thing, the bottom of me trailing into invisibility, wending and howling my way through tilted gravestones by night? Would I be Antigone herself, locked in a cave to die?

I laughed, sardonically, and recalled a derivation, unexpected and incredibly apt, found on course one day when I'd been checking the differences between **IRONIC**, **SARCASTIC**, and **SARDONIC**. **SARDONIC** descends from the name of a plant that grew on the island of Sardinia which, when ingested, "produced facial convulsions that resemble horrible laughter."

"I miss all that!" I whispered into the darkness. "I miss the words!"

You can still look up words in the dictionary!

Sitting up, I pressed the heels of my hands into my eye sockets until shimmering patterns pulsed. I often had these warring conversations with myself.

Scientology hardly has a patent on dictionaries, Sands. Hubbard didn't invent the idea of looking up words. He didn't invent the idea of ethics. He's certainly not the first to talk about our being comprised of body, mind, and spirit. People have been finding their way to God, many ways to God, for millennia.

I lay back again. Did I *want* to find my way to God? Anyway, what did that mean?

We're trapped on this planet, Sands. We've got to get free, spiritually free!

That would be Jamie speaking. Skye. Yet the Buddha said suffering was caused by attachment. So freedom was attached to being unattached. But here I was, attached, *glued*, in spite of myself (in *spite* of myself!), to Scientology. Which, paradoxically, was supposed to *free* me from the shackles of this MEST-y planet. Free from the hell of Planet Earth, free to stride, zip, flash through the universe . . .

Rolling over, pulling my forearms under my chest, heart pounding, I pressed my face to the mattress.

I liked the idea of being at one with God, at one with the entire universe. I envisioned this as the particles of my being enfolded into a larger one, my soul's light part of a vast radiance. Not the Rapture. Not one's body rising like a rocket, arms and hands and stockinged toes pointing straight down, eyes lifted toward the Light. No. The corporeal part would be dropped; we were talking pure spirit here . . .

Thetans, do you mean?

I pulled the pillow over my head.

Every religion has its form of soul, Sands! Hubbard does not have a premium on spirit!

I curled into a ball. If you attained real OT abilities, you were flashing around the stars with a *purpose*. It wasn't just play. You were to take the Tech with you, bringing it to all those other planets. If you marched all the way to the end of that Bridge to Total Freedom, you were expected to—it was expected that you'd *want* to—pick up the laser, the sword, the billy club, and don the uniform of what I'd dubbed the Freedom Police. As a member of this spiritually evolved cadre you'd stalk (body-less) the universe, carrying the (molecule-free) wand of Tech, bringing its benefits to all the beleaguered, fucked-up planets and life forms that didn't know they needed it.

But I didn't want to do that.

I couldn't be a zealot.

Because I didn't *believe*.

Even though I'd spent *seven years* trying to persuade myself I did. Seven *years*.

But if I was wrong (*you aren't wrong!*) (*but what if I am?*), what would happen to my soul?

An image rose up, not quite a dream. I seemed to be—not be in, but be—some kind of old-fashioned, many-masted sailing ship, and I was sinking. Drifting down through green-blue water.

What was that about.

A lapsed Catholic friend, chuckling, had told me that on her deathbed she'd probably call for a priest, "just in case." Would I? Blind, hobbling, would I find my way back to an Org?

I sat up in a whoosh of sheets and blankets, staring into darkness, willing a blazing certainty, a *truth*, to smite me. I was reading about Buddhism, trying to sit at least once a day, following my breath. But at times the practice seemed terribly lonely. What little I knew about Judaism was intriguing, but didn't you have to be born one, or at least marry one? The cathedrals and rituals of Catholicism had always been attractive. Rebecca Lee, a friend in the Workshop, had loaned me an engrossing paperback called *Hidden Christianity*; I could explore Gnosticism. Another friend had told me he thought Mormonism had all the answers, until he realized he'd have to marry his girlfriend for not only this life but for the rest of time.

With a moaning laugh I turned on the light. Utah was arid but beautiful. Maybe I'd do well as a sister-wife. Or move to the Navajo nation, braid feathers in my hair. Or become a Poor Clare, live in a cloister. Ask another Workshop friend, Karen Bender, how one converts to Judaism. Could one have a bat mitzvah at thirty-eight? I felt like an adolescent—maybe that ceremony would usher me across the threshold into true adulthood.

You're squandering your life, Sands. Were I living your life, I'd be doing such a better job.

I wanted to take a serrated spoon to the inside of my mind, scrape out its innards as one does half of a grapefruit. Shut *up*! I scrubbed my head, hard.

Silence, for a moment. But the murmuring started up again. You're not going to go back, Sands. You know that, so stop wasting time thinking about it.

But if I'm wrong, am I dooming my soul to everlasting wandering?

That was an average kind of night. (Ancient edicts of family, coupled with those of Scientology, meant that it never occurred to me to try a sleeping pill.) An image from the movie *2001* sums it up: An astronaut heads outside the spaceship to repair HAL, the computer that's the brain of the ship, which has gone berserk. HAL, aware of the astronaut's intentions, severs his oxygen line. Grabbing at his throat, the astronaut falls away from the ship. His limbs flail but soon enough grow still; the camera lingers on the lifeless body swirling endlessly into black and empty space. That was me.

IT DOESN'T MATTER

I continued to probe Buddhism. There was no question that the simple but arduous act of breathing with awareness was helpful. But even as I steeped three bags of Sleepytime tea for twenty minutes, drinking the bitter brew right before bed and crashing into sleep, a few hours later, my mind would begin to rev: jeering, badgering, mocking, blaming.

After one of these bouts, a particularly severe one, I forced myself to do some research. A few years before, I'd closed eyes and ears against a book that had been published with the descriptive title: *L. Ron Hubbard: Messiah or Madman?* Now, resolute, I headed to the Iowa City Library. I located the call number, climbed the stairs, entered the stacks—

—and stopped dead.

I raised both hands. Behind me, someone was aiming a rifle at the back of my skull.

Heart thudding, I waited a few moments before turning to confront the sharpshooter that I knew was (even as I was certain he was not) lurking behind the shelves.

Of course there was no one there.

This had nothing to do with the religion I'd personally known. Being *in* Scientology hadn't felt particularly traumatic, but leaving it certainly did.

I was tempted to head back down the stairs empty-handed. But I located the book, checked it out, and pretty much swallowed it whole. It was hopelessly one-sided. But it also iterated awful things about Hubbard and the Church, and provided plenty of backup for those claims, which helped support my decision to stay away—even as, day after day, I found myself reviewing that decision. Like some awful worm, Scientology had wiggled into my psyche and sunk its hooks deep.

Eventually I found my way to a small Iowa City Buddhist sangha. I joined the group for 6:30 A.M. meditation. I sat with them in the evenings and for weekend retreats. My mind jibbered. It jabbered. Buddhism calls this, perfectly, Monkey Mind. It crooned, it comforted briefly, then it berated. It scratched its underarms, smacked huge lips, picked lice from its hair, before leaping nimbly along a branch to jabber at me some more. Why was I sitting cross-legged on a cushion when I could be studying the Way, the Truth, the Light at an Org? There was one just three hours away, in Chicago (I'd checked). I could be on course every weekend. I could demo concepts. I could look up words. I could be *certain.*

Except I couldn't be. Or wouldn't be. I'd done all that. I'd done it again and again.

That image of the many-masted sailing ship kept rising up. I—my soul?—was drifting down through green-blue water, sinking toward the ocean floor. The feeling wasn't frightening, just terribly final. Also curiously peaceful as the ship settled: fish flitting about among the still-upright masts. I wasn't quite clear what the vision meant, but it appeared again and again, the boat nestling into sand at the bottom of the sea.

That second year, I was hired to teach the university's creative writing correspondence course. My stint as a Course Supervisor had bolstered a natural avocation, and writing critiques on all those manuscripts allowed me to develop and hone skills I knew were serving me well. I made lovely friends in the Workshop, to two of whom I actually "confessed"—as if I'd been a murderer rather than a pilgrim—my churning anguish. (They were surprised; they said it wasn't visible.) It's hard to imagine, now, when so many books have been published by those leaving Scientology, when there are blogs and YouTube videos and interviews and articles, how inured we are to the word "Scientologist," how normalized it has become. At the time, hearing it caused people to draw back, as if by simply being in my vicinity, they might "catch" what had infected me. Often (and even now) there was a shocked intake of breath. It was a deep solace to talk with friends who appreciated the search my time in the Church represented, and who did not appear to judge that choice.

One of these was Karen Bender, whose writing I quite admired. I knew she was Jewish, and, intrigued, asked about it, especially her ideas about marrying someone who wasn't part of her religion.

"I might date a man who wasn't Jewish," she said, "but I can't imagine marrying one. There's so much we share! So much . . ." She was almost speechless with the magnitude of it. "History. Intention. Purpose. Without having to talk about it!"

I nodded, glumly. Her religion was so old! Although at one point, it, too, had been new, and had been considered bizarre. Imagine, in ancient polytheistic Mesopotamia, the idea of worshipping just one god!

Another member of the Workshop, Rebecca Lee, young enough to be my daughter, wrote stories I found amazingly mature and sophisticated. Wise beyond her years, through her flowed a wide stream of tranquil spirituality. Her father was a Lutheran minister, and she shared with me advice he'd given a parishioner struggling with a life-changing decision: "Maybe you just don't have enough information," he'd said. "That's why you can't make a definitive choice. But the information will come. And then you will know what to do."

But how could I possibly not have all the information I needed?

And so it was that early one Saturday morning, I watched myself with astonished horror as I rose and dressed and drove through pelting rain to Chicago's Church of Scientology. I said I needed to talk to the Ethics Officer.

"Of course," the Registrar said, struggling to keep her TRs in the face of what I imagine was a gaunt and startling apparition. Within minutes, minutes when I held on to my chair with both hands to keep from walking back out, I was in the office of the EO, stumbling my way through the litany regarding my chronic doubt. He told me I needed to review the PTS/SP materials. *I know all that!* I didn't say. Instead, I settled in at a table in the course room, momentarily comforted by the "standard" nature of it all. Nearby lay Hubbard's *Technical Dictionary* and the *American Heritage*, full of definitions—derivations!—I might want to clarify. Words like SUPPRESS and SUPPRESSIVE, meanings I already knew. POTENTIAL and TROUBLE, and SOURCE, even RELIGION. Also on the table was a basket of batteries, marbles, rubber bands, paper clips, waiting for me to demo what I already understood. I put my face in my hands. Flunk. *Flunk.*

That night, I stayed with friends of friends. Sue was a Scientologist; just two days before she'd returned from two weeks at Flag, the "flagship" Org in Florida, where she'd attested to OT VIII. Her husband Joe was not a Scientologist, but he'd looked after the three kids while she was gone, and seemed to have done so happily. I thought of Sunny, who'd moved to Michigan to marry Ron, a non-Scientologist; they'd conceived within days of their wedding. She, too, was continuing her OT levels. Sunny and Ron, like Sue and Joe, were figuring out life without both of them having to be mired in the religion. Why couldn't Skye and I do that?

Sue's kitchen was huge, with paned windows and glass-fronted cupboards that ran all the way to high ceilings. Crocks stuffed with implements lined scarred wooden counters. A bag of bagels and containers of cream cheese spilled across one surface. Cheers emanated from the living room, where Joe was watching a ball game, sipping a beer. I'd been offered one but declined; I was due back on course in the morning. Carrie, nine years old, ran in, sawed a bagel in half, smeared it with peanut butter from a jar she left open on the counter, and ran out again.

"Homework!" Sue called.

Beyond the kitchen was the mudroom, full of dripping raincoats and umbrellas and rubber boots in five different sizes. Joey hopped in, riding a nonexistent pogo stick, asked for juice, and, carrying his tippy cup, hopped out again.

Sue began to cry. "I can't bear it," she said. "I just want to go back!"

"Flag?" I asked, and she nodded, holding a dishtowel to her face.

"I just want to live there! It's so pure. Everything is so full of light, everyone's OT, it's like floating in an ether of kindness and ethics, and it's all so clean and upstat. And here I am with so much MEST. I mean *look* at it all!"

She waved at the crowded counters, the cupboards stuffed with dishes and cans and boxes, the refrigerator where magnets held Joey's drawings and recipes and a photo of Hubbard.

"We're all so stuck. How do we ever escape this planet where we're so *stuck*!"

"Mom?" Heather, the eldest, came in wielding a taped-up hockey stick. "I *have* to have a new one! I don't know if it'll last one more game. Oh, Mom, stop *crying*!" She leaned the hockey stick up against the mudroom's doorjamb. "What's for dinner?"

I slept, or rather didn't, in Heather's room and in the morning headed straight back to Iowa City. I couldn't imagine a life as stuffed as Sue's cupboards were—rubber boots, children, tippy cups, hockey sticks, cream cheese—but all of it struck me as so *wonderful*, every particle of it! Matter. Energy. Space. Time. The huge conundrum. Yes, it was messy. Ugly. Complicated. Things disintegrated or exploded. Items got lost or broken. Time had this nasty way of marching on. And yet weren't M and E and S and T responsible for some of life's greatest pleasures? Children, books, orgasm, peanut butter, chardonnay? What was this intense need, which I'd felt for as long as I could remember, to feel I was "above" the "pettiness" of an earthly life? How about *enjoying* it? Why, to me, did being *in* life, just doing it, just *being*, seem like a lesser mode of existence?

•

START. I RETURNED to my meditation pillow. When a celebrated Buddhist roshi visited, I signed up for the retreat, and for an individual consultation. During the retreat, we sat in a circle, and my pillow wound up beside his. I'm sure I was distracting. I could not settle physically, much less mentally. When we took a break, before walking meditation, he looked at me with kind, assessing eyes. Then he lowered them again, crossing his hands into the opposite sleeves of his black robe.

Somehow I got through the eight hours, and the next day sat and walked for another eight. Those of us who'd signed up for individual meetings with the roshi would have them that evening, in the house of one of the members of the sangha.

This woman kindly instructed me in what I would need to do as I entered the space, before I put my question before the roshi. A gesture of Namaste, bowing over pressed-together palms (*the Buddha nature in me honors the Buddha nature in you*); turning in a circle and another Namaste (*the divinity in me recognizes the divinity in you*); prostrating myself three times, laying my whole body facedown, arms outstretched. Only then could I sit before him.

It's this religion's form of "standard," I told my mortified self, as I lay with my face pressed into the carpet, then rose up to do it a second time. It's necessary for *form*, for ritual, *every* religion has these things. I laid myself out fully a third time. We—I mean Scientologists—sit opposite someone else for two hours with our eyes closed! Scientologists write up Ethics Conditions. Scientologists rub lotion into their palms before picking up cans attached to something like a lie detector. What could be stranger than that?

Taking a deep breath, I bowed over my palms in a final Namaste—*the light in me perceives the light in you*—and sat cross-legged before him. I told him the way I felt torn in two.

He kept his face lowered, though his eyes were open. He was sitting on a black *zafu*, a meditation pillow, itself atop a square *zabu-*

ton—words that were, I told myself, Buddhist nomenclature just as "ARC" and "overt" are Scientology's. A fanlike pattern on the red and blue Persian carpet, like his silence, stretched between us.

I knew what I wanted him to say, but he did not say it. He did not say: You must probe more deeply into being a Buddhist. Buddhism is the only Answer, the only Way.

Instead, he raised his bottomless eyes to mine. "It doesn't matter," he said.

It doesn't matter!

I put a hand to my heart, puzzled, agonized, horrified.

"There is a way," he said, "but it can only be your way."

My mind batted against the windows closed against the wintry day beyond.

"If Scientology is your way," he said, "then you must return to it. And if it is not, then you must not."

I KNEW HE was right. He'd said exactly the right thing, the wisest possible advice. Scientology would *never* have left the choice up to me—it would have told me where the "only" answer resided. This strengthened my (sleepless) resolve.

I began to understand the ship settled on the bottom of the sea. There was no way to unknow what I knew. The reading, the questioning, the knowledge I now held, had caused my belief in the Church to sink. It would not float again. I was still terrified I'd return—look how often I'd vacillated!—but the vision told me I would not sail back into Scientology's harbor. I'd done it so many times, and it had led me to this: shut into a cave and left to die, like Antigone. A kind of death in life.

Yet I was bereft. By leaving the Church I was considered a Suppressive Person, and, not wanting to bring trouble to my Scientology friends—friends who were a huge reason I'd lingered so long and found it so hard to go—I did not communicate with them. I knew they'd have to have Ethics Handlings, would need to write Knowledge Reports; perhaps assigned the Condition of Enemy or even Treason (by being in touch with me, now an "enemy" of the Church), they'd have to write up overts and work their way back up the Conditions. These were aspects of Church policy that had always troubled me. But now, in my anguish, they outraged me and helped bolster my efforts to leave it behind.

I had to face, moreover, that in a matter of months, I'd earn a master of fine arts degree. And then what? And how could I possibly be considered a "master"? I'd published almost nothing. And anyway: Did anyone ever "master" an art?

I looked up the word.

Among MASTER's twenty-odd definitions are 1: one who has control over another; 7: one who defeats another; and 16: an original from which copies can be made. Also 12: a worker qualified to teach apprentices and carry on the craft.

The word descends from the Latin *magister*: "chief, head, director, teacher."

This I understood. Writing *was* a craft. I liked teaching. Also it was clear that critiquing others' manuscripts honed one's own writing skills. I started to look for teaching jobs, taking anything, paid or unpaid, that would help build a résumé. I signed up for the university's Arts Outreach program.

Now, in my datebook, "CC" and a bracket outlining several hours no longer meant being on course at Celebrity Center, but the time allotted to grade the correspondence course. "AO" did not indicate something I'd be up to at the Advanced Org, but a day spent on Arts Outreach. Two times a month I crawled into a car at 4:00 A.M. with other sleepy grad students from various disciplines to drive across the snowy hinterlands of Iowa. Late afternoon, having taught all day, we headed back through wintery darkness, sometimes arriving home after 9:00 P.M. I'd drop my bags full of teaching material to the floor and fall into bed.

For winter break Mom suggested I stay with them in their San Francisco flat. It meant sleeping on their floor, but both grateful and ashamed, I accepted. We appeared to have reached a détente. Strategies, put in place in their wills, limited what I'd receive in the event of their death. I never asked what they were. I did not talk about Scientology. Nor about Skye. If querulous questions about these began to emerge, as sometimes, after glasses of wine, they did, I left the room.

My appearance startled everyone. I was very thin. The lack of sleep had etched new lines. Circles under my eyes were purple-gray. I did my best to rally, but misery hovered, as dust rolls around Pigpen in *Peanuts* cartoons. I held Hunter, Brett and Louis's baby, all he'd let me, trying not to think about all I'd made a choice away from having, year after year.

One Sunday the family met at a Marin County flea market. Mom and Dad wandered off to look at some artwork. Brett and I headed down an aisle of jewelry stalls. I carried Hunter, and we paused to look at a collection of silver earrings.

"Oh, isn't this so precious!" The woman behind the counter beamed. "Mother and Baby and Grandmother!"

Brett and I looked at each other, horrified. I might be ten years older, but did I really look old enough to be her *mother*? She started to protest, but I shook my head. "It's what I've done to my life, Brett. No one else did it. I did it. I just need to walk it out. I'll meet you back at the car."

I didn't walk it out that afternoon. It would take years to walk it out. Nevertheless, something was beginning to take shape in me: an understanding—it was a phrase of Skye's—that this was *a spoke of the wheel*, and the wheel would turn. The wheel always turns.

BY LATE SPRING, about to graduate the Workshop, I'd accrued some teaching experience but few publications. What to do, what to do. Well, I loved study. I trotted across the Iowa River to the low-lying buildings of the theater department. I could actually imagine being a "master" in that art. Maybe I could land a job teaching acting, and write in my spare time. Erik Forsythe, chair of the department, was willing to apply my past experience and training so I could earn that second MFA in one year instead of the usual three. I spent that summer in Iowa City, acting in a very satisfying repertory season.

Robin and my brother had recently moved from Chicago to Ohio, and they journeyed across three states to see me in those plays. Tad was writing; years later I'd find out that he'd won a local playwriting contest. But even though they drove all that way, I made hardly any time for them. That terrible pronouncement made by Mary's mother years before—that I was bad for him—still held sway. For years, I spent hardly any time alone with Tad, did not speak with him in any substantive way about his accident, nor about Scientology. I could not confront that mangled face and the tragedy it represented. Still mourning who he'd been, I was not yet able to love who he'd become. When it was time for them to leave, I waved them off with a distressing, hateful sense of relief.

That fall, settled into the satisfyingly encompassing theater program, I was headed through town on the way to class when I passed a storefront that had been empty for some months. I literally jumped backward.

Hanging above the front window was a large and familiar blue-and-white *S*.

Scientology! In Iowa City?

It had *found* me!

Black crows seemed to wheel and shriek as I ran down the block and around a corner. Heart pounding, I slowed to a walk. Surely I'd just conjured the icon that represented so many years, so many friends, so much pleasure, and so much anguish. On my way home, I walked to the corner and peered around the edge of a building.

There it was: that large super-serifed *S*, marine blue and gleaming white.

I crept down the opposite sidewalk. Visible through the window, angled this way and that, were shiny, lurid covers of books by L. Ron Hubbard. Beyond, in a brightly lit interior, stood a table. No one sat there. But there were dictionaries. A little basket that would contain batteries, a clothespin, some pennies, a pencil stub.

There was no doubt about it. A Scientology *mission* had plunked itself down in the middle of Iowa City.

A slim dark-haired woman—probably the mission holder, probably also wearing the hats of Auditor, Case Supervisor, Ethics Officer, maybe even Course Supervisor—came into sight, heading for the window. Re-angling a book, she peered into the street. Unexpectedly, I was moved. I knew how much intention, how much effort, how much compassion for humanity, how much faith that mission represented. Also how much money.

That enormous *S* felt like a mirage, manifested out of a convoluted need. But—and it took me weeks to let myself truly examine this—I was not tempted. I wouldn't go see the Ethics Officer, nor take my place at that table.

Relief surged.

About six months later, the mission folded. Once again a sign in the window said FOR RENT. But that big *S*, disappeared, did not turn out to be objective correlative in a carefully constructed novel. The claws were in deep; there was more extricating to be done.

SPIT HAPPENS

A thick envelope arrived one day from Sunny. She was happily married, living in Michigan, she wrote; in addition to a schedule full of gigs, she was teaching voice at a university. Every few months she flew to Flag or Los Angeles to continue her OT levels. The envelope held photos of her toddler. In one, his grinning lips were coated with pureed carrots, more goo spread all the way up an arm that waved a baby spoon. Splotches of orange almost covered the letters on his bib that spelled out SPIT HAPPENS.

I understood it was a play on the phrase "shit happens." But to a Scientologist, that idea is outrageous—*sacrilegious*. It was as if Sunny had purposefully misquoted a piece of Tech. Nothing, absolutely nothing, just *happens*! You're *always* responsible. How could Sunny—Sunny the sturdy Scientologist!—let her child wear such a bib? It sent an entirely wrong message!

It took an astonishingly long time for me to smile at the photograph, so involved was I in sorting out its ramifications.

The summer after I earned that second MFA, in theater arts, I stayed in Iowa City, teaching for the Iowa Summer Writing Festival, until the Squaw Conference, after which, at my parents' invitation, I lived for a few months in their lower house, the Annex. I meditated morning and evening, walked and worked on my novel during the days, cooked them dinner at night. On Saturdays I drove four hours to Marin, spent the night with Brett and Louis and Hunter, sat Sunday sangha at the Green Gulch Buddhist Retreat, listened to the dharma talk, and drove back again. Buddhism, during that time, was as essential as breathing.

On one of these drives, all four lanes of Interstate 80 were closed by a terrible accident. Along the median, ambulances, sirens muttering and occasionally howling, worked past the veritable parking lot of cars. It brought to mind my own supposed death in a car crash, last lifetime: how I'd flitted above the wreckage and jammed myself back into a body. Even as I wondered if I'd concocted that whole episode, I could feel spirits zipping desperately overhead, seeking ways to return.

Cars rolled forward a few yards, paused. Up ahead, a siren began to yowl. As the sound of it faded, I found myself pounding the steering wheel.

"I am not responsible!" I cried. "I did not cause this!"

Over the years, I'd become convinced of the molecular power of thought, but until that moment hadn't realized how much I believed that if I, personally, pondered or prayed or *thought* and certainly acted the right way, the butterfly-wing flap of my actions, my *intentions*, could prevent everything from car accidents to famines. Growing up with my mother's Christian Science had buttered the pan for what I found in Scientology, which had prepared me for aspects of Buddhism, all of which had been given a generous sprinkle of Chaos Theory. Not only could what I did or did not do be linked to my breaking a bowl or getting a flat tire; it could be linked to the broken bowls and flat tires of strangers. It was not only my thoughts, of course; people the world over had to be clear in their thinking and motivations, which was why Catholic nuns prayed, Buddhist monks meditated, think tanks of scholars and artists and scientists met in Saigon, Oxford, Delhi to ponder, purposefully, peace and the environment. But my actions, my *thoughts* were part of this web. I was as certain of this as I was of the steering wheel in my hands. It seemed, suddenly, an awful burden. Not to mention, it began to occur to me, an egoistical one.

The line of vehicles inched by the four-car pileup. Men in bulky yellow uniforms prowled the accordioned wreckage. Police cars pulsed red-blue lights, tow trucks flashed amber ones. The ambulances were gone. There was no question that death had visited here. But how, *how* could I possibly be responsible for this accident? What did the word ACCIDENT mean, if not "a lack of intention; chance"?

But I didn't believe that. What I did believe is that everything is connected. If you feel too ill to go to school, it's because of the bully on the playground. If you have a headache, it's your psyche warning you to *take a look*. If your car overheats on the way to visit your parents, it means they make you steam, and you should not be visiting them. If you fall off a bridge . . .

As traffic began to speed again, I thought about the goo-covered bib announcing SPIT HAPPENS. As soon as I got back to Squaw Valley, I found Sunny's phone number. She was out. I left a message, wondering if she'd call back. I was, after all, an SP.

But she phoned the next morning. Without much preamble, I told her about the incident on the freeway.

"How can that be my fault?" I said. "It's crazy to think it is!"

"No, it's not," she said in her warm voice. "Our thoughts do have power. We both know that."

"It feels horridly egoistical."

"Being—having—that kind of cause is what OT is all about. Not about causing car accidents, of course. Unless one's an evil operating thetan. But being at cause like that."

Beyond the windows of the Annex, a rushing wind made the pines sway. The sky lowered, gray and grim; a storm was coming in.

"Not that one has to be a Scientologist to have those abilities," she said. "There were operating thetans before Hubbard came along—they just weren't called that, and there are those who get there without the Tech. He just made achieving those abilities more certain."

She wanted to let me know she wasn't proselytizing, she wasn't trying to haul me back into the boat. I loved her for it.

"It feels self-aggrandizing," I said.

"That's one way to look at it, sure. But most people wouldn't dream of taking that kind of responsibility."

"Sunny, I feel responsible, or rather, to blame, all the fucking time! I'm vacuuming and the rubber belt breaks, and it's *what overt did I commit to pull this in?* Or my sister's moody and I wonder what I did to make her be that way, or I stub my toe and immediately the thought is, *now, what did I do to create that . . . ?*"

"I know exactly what you mean." She sounded weary.

"My dad would say solipsistic." I remembered a day he'd talked about a self-involved student, his voice dripping with disdain: *Beware solipsism.*

"What's that mean, solipsistic?"

"Hold on a minute." I fetched the dictionary, which still traveled with me everywhere. As I flipped through its pages, we both laughed.

"Oh, I miss you! I miss us!" she said, with the wonderful slide of tone, throaty and fluty, that is directly connected to her singing ability. She was talking about being on course, drilling TRs, clearing words, those times of laughter and epiphany.

"SOLIPSISM," I read. "It's a philosophical term: 'the theory that the self is the only thing that has reality or can be known.'"

"That doesn't sound like it means 'selfish,'" Sunny said. "It sounds as if you can't really know anything except what you, yourself, perceive. What's its derivation?"

". . . *solus*, 'alone.' Plus *ipse*, 'self' . . . 'alone self/self alone.'" My voice was blocked with tears. "I do feel terribly alone, Sunny. Terribly. But mostly *responsible*. All the time, for *everything*. But how can that be? It feels disgustingly self-involved. Selfish, selfish, *selfish*!"

"Don't *do* that!" Sunny almost shouted. "I don't know how this *shit* about being selfish got imprinted on your brain, but get it out of there! It's not true. It was *never* true."

The wind slid along the house. The sky was a gray ceiling—it would be freezing out there. Times like this I wanted to go back so badly, to have the certainty, and the fun.

I hated saying goodbye. "We'll talk again, soon!" she said.

I think we both knew we wouldn't. For an hour we'd managed to create an oasis around ourselves, but the conversation might come up in her next session. Since she was on her OT levels at Flag, she'd be "sec checked"—security checked—each time she started a new round of auditing. SEC CHECK: that phrase, with its hissing *s*, and harsh *k*s, reflects the nature of what it is. Security checking pokes and prods, queries and grills everything a person might have done, said, *thought* since their previous auditing. If Sunny's needle so much as flickered—and it might, because she'd said things like "Not that one has to be a Scientologist to have those abilities," and had sounded so weary with "I know exactly what you mean"—she'd have to cough up this talk with me. She might be assigned a low Ethics Condition, have to write up our wonderful talk as an overt. She'd done me a big favor by staying on the phone with me as long as she had.

THAT IMAGE OF the ship settled at the bottom of the sea made me 99.8 percent certain I'd never return to Scientology. But the .02 percent scared me. I'd found reasons to return so many times—what might make me do so again? Also, that I'd gotten involved with the Church in the first place, the life-dreams I felt I'd mangled by staying as long as I had, and the loss of dear friends—an entire community—by leaving, settled me into a depression so vast I'd no idea I was in one. It was just what life looked like. I watched people laugh and thought them pathetic: They had no clue how sad life really was.

When a man I'd met in the Workshop invited me to live with him in Vermont, I leapt across the country, hoping he and his lovely daughter would provide the family and purpose for which I so yearned. When that proved untenable, after a few more zigzags I wound up in a town nestled in the Sierra Foothills of Northern California. I began to put together a life that involved Vipassana meditation, African dance, creating theater, writing, freelance editing, and teaching. I told almost no one about Scientology, trying to pretend those years had never been.

But a profound shift was under way, a result of that moment on the freeway and the subsequent conversation with Sunny.[90] I found myself, more and more purposefully, working to rid myself of the "I" trained into me by Scientology, itself an echo of the four-year-old me prancing about looking for approbation. I began, with increasing consciousness, to think and to speak in terms of "we," "us"—a larger compass. Although it took a while for the spectrum of these ideas to radiate into place (and I'm still learning), I felt I'd stumbled on some essential truth, an understanding vital to being on Earth, part of humanity, living this life.

THE LOSS OF NAMELESS THINGS

Eventually Brett and her family moved to that same small town in the Sierra, as did, for a while, our sister Tracy. So did my brother. He and Robin had decided to go their separate ways, although they remained good friends. Tad (I slalom still between calling him Tad, in the family, and Oak, when talking of his work in theater or his writing) met a wonderful poet, Molly Fisk, and they moved in together. He was at work on a book called *Alf & Me: The Autobiography of Alfred Jarry*. The title made me laugh: the *auto*biography of a writer who'd died a century earlier. The project was perfectly absurd, totally Jarry, totally Oak. The manuscript was a mess, but I thought I could see a way to make it work.

Once a week, after accepting a cup of coffee, he'd sit cross-legged on the floor of my study to read what I'd worked on since our previous meeting. It often occurred to me that, at least where writing was concerned, that damaged brain of his was in pretty good shape. He knew every word of his manuscript, and the order in which they appeared. Sometimes he'd read over a suggested change and nod, but just as often he'd look up and with a smile say, "Let's leave it the way it was."

For the first time since the accident, I was able to see him as he now was. And I loved that person. He was witty, incredibly droll, wise and compassionate. We laughed a lot. He was fully cognizant of what had happened to him: *Alf & Me* was not only Jarry talking about his life, but Oak talking about his. Working together on his book felt magical, certain, right, precious. I felt I was doing some of the most important work of my life. Even as he sat on the floor, his back against the couch, and I sat at my desk, I imagined our actual locations in space were reversed: He sat cross-legged on some celestial pillow and I was prostrate before him, face down, arms wide, pleading for forgiveness. He never indicated in any way that there was need for such a thing, but I prayed that he'd understand and forgive that for the previous fifteen years I'd practically denied his existence.

IN 2000, I finished the novel, the Anasazi still well represented but no longer central. *Catching Heaven* received a generous advance from Ballantine and lovely reviews. I'd become an affiliate artist with a local theater company, where I acted and directed and for which I wrote two plays. I met a wonderful man and we purchased a house together. I did a lot of freelance editing. I taught in the English department of American River College in Sacramento; and creative writing through extension programs at UC Davis, various conferences and festivals, and around my own dining room table. I began to pick up my guitar sometimes and now and again even wrote a song. I never, ever talked about Scientology.

They were good years. They were also very busy ones: an effort, I think, to "start"—certainly to make up for—the massive, irretrievable *flunk* that was, I felt, the years I'd devoted to, squandered on, the Church. Years when people build careers, create marriages, have children. I did my very best not to think of it, and, although it took a long time, succeeded. And so I spent a decade of my life pretending a decade of my life hadn't happened.

During those years, except for meditating, I avoided anything that even hinted at religiosity, declining invitations to fire circles, to Celtic gatherings (I was fascinated by anything to do with the Goddess, especially the Black Madonna, but rituals of any kind made me nervous), even to exploring the enneagram, which felt vaguely cultish.

I could not listen to music. Of any genre. It moved me too much. In the car it was NPR, all the time, or silence. I wadded up my pilgrim soul in a bunch of old newspapers and shoved her deep away.

AND THEN, ONE day in 2004 I Googled myself to check if my bio was yet loaded onto the website of a writer's conference where I was scheduled to teach. And with horror I watched the first link that loaded onto the screen, even before the link to my own website:

Scientology Courses taken by Sands Hall

Aghast, heart pounding, I clicked. There they were: the names of the courses I'd taken in the seven years I'd tried to pretend had never been.

A surge of hot, prickly shame consumed me as I realized that anyone who might go online looking for me or my website would find this information.

But to my utter surprise, this was followed by vast relief: *I don't have to hide it anymore.*

In fact, *it isn't that big a deal!* Why had I thought it was such a big deal?

I closed my eyes as what felt like the clearest, most aromatic and refreshing of winds blew past. It was a "blowdown"—I recognized it even as I didn't want to use Scientology's language to describe it: that rush that follows an enormous realization pulled out of the garbage that's been piled on top of it.

I poked around the website, gingerly, as if something might leap out and seize my wrist and haul me into its workings. To my surprise, it wasn't full of gushing accolades; it wasn't promoting Scientology. Rather, it was pointing out how many people who took a Scientology course, or got some auditing, didn't *stay.* The Church's supposedly million-strong membership actually comprised, the website claimed, those who'd made brief forays into and out of the religion. Enrollment was not, as the Church claimed (as it had always claimed), increasing, but decreasing. Graphs and stats supported these observations.

One of the stats had to do with the percentage of those who'd left the Church not long after achieving the state of Clear. There was no attempt to explain the statistic, but it was tacit. I thought of the promises Hubbard made regarding Clear ("has no vicious Reactive Mind and operates at total mental capacity") and then those regarding being OT ("willing and knowing cause over life, thought, matter, energy, space and time"). First, you were going to achieve that state when Clear. Then when OT III. Then OT VIII. Now OT XII. No doubt some, turning Clear and then finding there was still "case," and then examining the long and very expensive Bridge that lay ahead, might begin to wonder if it actually led anywhere.

The website offered links to blogs of those who'd left Scientology, and this was the first time I glimpsed that a massive exodus from the Church was in process. Links to newspaper articles describing the insidious actions of David Miscavige. Links to YouTube videos of Sea Org members discussing their decisions to abandon their billion-year contracts. Links to interviews with some of the highest officials in the Church, who, after being "declared" as Suppressive Persons and exiled from the Church, decided to tell their tales. Links to the official website of Scientology. Links to the works of L. Ron Hubbard. The entire *Tech Dictionary* was a PDF one could download. In the anonymous world of the Internet, it was impossible to stop people from scanning and posting anything they might have in their possession. Which meant that Scientology—the Tech—was available to *anyone*! The thing I'd always wished were the case, and which Hubbard had tried in so many ways to keep from happening. Now people could read about Scientology—not just its outrages, not just LRH's published books, but its private "scripture"—as easily as they could read about Hinduism or the tenets of the Lutheranism. I had to laugh. The Church would no doubt be finding ways to pull down those posts as quickly as people put them up, but they must be *furious*.

Suddenly, I was astounded that I'd managed to leave when I did, that I'd managed to leave at *all*. I'd spent seven years banging against the walls of a mental prison that I, myself, had constructed—ten, if I counted the hell I'd flung myself into upon leaving. But some of those telling their stories had handed over most of their *lives*: twenty, thirty years. They'd abandoned parents when they joined, and lost husbands and wives, sometimes children and always friends, when they left. Some, born into the Church, had lost entire childhoods to Scientology.

I let the cursor hover over one of those YouTube links, tempted.

But I still wasn't ready. I closed the website, and closed my computer.

MY SILENCE REGARDING Scientology included my parents. On the one hand, they'd been right, hadn't they? And, mulishly, I didn't want to have that conversation. But the silence was also internal. I couldn't bring myself to scrutinize why I might have been drawn to the Church in the first place. I couldn't, yet, examine that if it hadn't been Scientology, something else might have bumped me off the course of my supposed goals. It was convenient to blame what I saw as my lacks and losses—career, husband, children—on Scientology.

And then Philip Sneed, artistic director of the theater company that had produced my plays, opted to produce one of my brother's, finished just before his accident in 1978: *Grinder's Stand*, about the mysterious death of Meriwether Lewis. In the sort of brilliant insight that Brett often has, she suggested that a friend, filmmaker Bill Rose, might take an interest in Oak's story, with the production of this play as a starting point.

Bill Rose did. His quest to tell it eventually took him east, to Lexington, where members of the original company met with him as he filmed the theaters, the hotel, and of course the bridge. He spoke with those who'd known Oak then and those who'd come to know him since. He walked a tricky tightrope as he edited his way through hundreds of hours of memories, anecdotes, interpretations. And he chose to make a film not about the burdens of expectation placed on a seeming prodigy, nor about a son battling the ghosts of a successful father, nor about parents and a sister who'd basically abandoned son and brother. Even as the film touched on these issues, Bill let the statements of family and peers speak for themselves, leaving the viewers to establish their own perspective. It was deft, kind, and brave to choose such a nuanced perspective. *The Loss of Nameless Things* went on to dazzle a number of film festival audiences and to win an array of awards.[91]

And it was during my own interview for that film that I began, for the first time, to examine the vertigo that twenty years before had swirled in around the loss of mentor, colleague, friend, brother. As the camera whirred, as I responded to Bill's thoughtful questions, a different version of that leap to Los Angeles began to unfold. Was this part of what had caused me to abandon all I'd created in New York City? The sudden deep indulgence in alcohol, the cocaine, the sleeping with married men? And the draw of a religion that offered so much order? For the first time, I glimpsed what I might have been looking for, and why I'd gone searching.

IN 2003, WITH friends gathered from everywhere, Mom and Dad celebrated sixty years of marriage. A few weeks later, Mom suffered a stroke. In the hospital, the left half of her face slack, barely intelligible, she mumbled her way through a sentence in which she told me that the stroke had been a result of hubris.

"Hubris?"

"That big sixtieth anniversary party. I knew we should never have celebrated our happy marriage so openly. We made the gods jealous. They had to punish us."

This made ancient, complete Hall sense. A stroke is a metaphor. There is always a way to make catastrophe one's own fault. As Dad would say, "Guilt is good."

GUILT. Like other Old and Middle English words whose spellings have changed but whose meanings have not—words such as SWORD (*sweord*), BLOOD (*blōd*), MUD (*mudde*)—*gylt* means what it always has: "being responsible for an offense or wrongdoing" and "remorseful awareness of having done something wrong."

HUBRIS, on the other hand, comes to us from the Greek: "overbearing pride, arrogance." From which attitude must come, of course, a fall.

FALL, too, comes to us from Middle English: *fallen*, *fell*, descending from Old English. If we examine the phoneme *phoi-*, we see the word comes not only from FALL, but from BEFALL, indicating the idea that a fall "happens" to one.

Like spit.

But along with my mother's milk, I'd swallowed that a flat tire, a stroke, a fall from a bridge *doesn't* just happen. You create it. Call it egoism, narcissism, solipsism, hubris, guilt, Potential Trouble Source: You are responsible. In this fertile ground, no wonder the vines of Scientology had taken such fierce hold. No wonder it was so hard to yank them out.

MOM RECOVERED FAIRLY well from her stroke, but Dad's health began to fail. They moved to a house in the Sierra foothills, close to Brett and me, and we transferred their medical records to local doctors. I accompanied Dad on those office visits.

CARDIOLOGIST: "someone whose study is the heart." I mused, wondering if, without Scientology, I'd ever have made those connections, or cared so deeply that they were there to make.

UROLOGIST: "one who studies the body's nether tracts." NEPHROLOGIST: "one whose study is the function and diseases of the kidney." The task of an EPIDEMIOLOGIST I had to look up when I got home: "the study of what is upon people." Other things that were upon Dad included high blood pressure and cholesterol. His systems were simply, one by one, failing.

During these outings, Dad often expressed his gratitude. I told him I was deeply glad to be able to help. I believe we were having a much deeper conversation than that dialogue might indicate, and that a lot of forgiving was going on, in both directions. Sometimes I thought I should tackle, straight on, why I might have been attracted to Scientology—beyond the spiritual order that for a while it really did provide—and if we might even be able to laugh at how his "wills and things" lecture had backfired. I thought about bringing up that phone call when he'd told me "that spiritual stuff does matter." I tried to conjure the future: Would I be sorry, when he died, that we hadn't had the conversation, and could never have it? But I loved the peace we'd come to, and I chose not to disrupt it.

Eventually, we landed in the office of an oncologist. I hadn't known, before I looked it up, that ONCO is blood, and its doctor one who studies what might be in the blood: CANCER, named after the crab whose scuttling movement the illness emulates.

And one afternoon, during a visit to his GP, we were told that hospice needed to be called. Dad looked as shocked as I felt.

"You mean it's come?" He shook his head. "It's been a good life," he said. "A very good life."

As I negotiated the curves back to their house, he said, "I'm not going to fight this any longer." He meant it.

That afternoon, he was able to recite to the hospice nurse each of his medications and their dosages. Four days later, he was dead.

The nurses tried to warn Mother, encouraging her to say goodbye. She angrily dismissed them; they were being "morbid." Her husband would never leave her.

And when he died, in their bed, she did not cry. That night, she brushed her teeth. Her white hair a tangle around her face, feet bare beneath a long flannel nightgown, she climbed in beside him, pulled the sheets up over their shoulders, and curved herself around his chilling body for one last night.

PILGRIMAGE SEASON

Spring of 2008, a few months before Dad died, I'd landed a position as a one-year visiting professor of creative writing at Franklin & Marshall, a small liberal arts college in Pennsylvania. When I told him—and I'm so glad he was still alive when the news came—he held up both arms in a beautiful gesture of shared triumph. As I headed east that fall, so did my brother: moving to Albany to live with a sweet woman named Hadiya, whom he'd met during a screening of *The Loss of Nameless Things*. Brett and Louis built a cottage for Mother on their property. Tracy, remarried, was living in Arizona.

I'd taught creative writing for years, but seldom in an academic setting. As I constructed my syllabi—taking great satisfaction in conceiving what I wanted students to take away from each course, and into the world—I knew that I was employing Hubbard's Study Tech, especially the balance of theory with practice. For years, in my teaching, I'd used my experience as Course Supervisor, my knowledge of the Barriers to Study, but as I plunged into those intense semesters I was very aware of it: employing chalk, eraser, water bottle to make the abstract visible. Staying alert for the yawn, or the sudden lack of interest, that might signal a misunderstood word.

Halfway through the fall, the college invited me to stay another year, and, eventually, for many more. On one of my breaks, I headed to Albany to visit Tad and Hadiya. Their apartment was above a

Laundromat; they received a reduction in rent for making sure the floor was clean, the vending machines stocked. They both had tales about the lowlifes encountered there.

"He's a lot kinder to them than I am," Hadiya said.

Tad took a deep drag and blinked, smiling, through wreaths of cigarette smoke.

"He's a bodhisattva," Hadiya said.

I knew what she meant: He was happy. Nonjudgmental. He served as an example to those who came in touch with him and were willing to learn. He had flunked, massively—"ruining" the brilliant writing career he seemed destined for—but had accepted it. And here he was, living with a wonderful woman, taking joy in his life, working on a novel. Start.

A few years before, I'd contacted a good friend, Steve Susoyev, writer and publisher, about taking on his book, *Jarry & Me*. I now sent him the most recent draft.

ONE SPRING MORNING in 2010, as I was wrapping up the semester, Sunny called. We were still in touch—a few years before, we'd even met up in Chicago for a couple of days. At that time, I'd expressed my concern that she might get in trouble for seeing me.

"I don't let the Church dictate who my friends are!" she'd said, and once again I'd been impressed by the way she was able to balance Scientology, in a rational way, with the rest of her life.

But this day, her voice on the phone, usually so full of light and bounce, was flat: "I'm leaving the Church, Sands."

The story she told was horrifying. The previous month, she'd flown to Los Angeles for some auditing. She was OT IV, and she felt like an Operating Thetan: she had a happy marriage, a thriving family, a terrific job at the university, and her singing career was soaring. But she was plagued by physical problems: two frozen shoulders and a rebuilt knee, the result of a skiing accident.

"I was OT!" she said. "I was supposed to be immune to physical injury! But it never entered my mind to question the validity of the Tech—if there's even such a *thing* as OT. Of course I didn't! There was simply something wrong with me."

So, feeling great about her life, certain the Tech would handle her physical problems, she flew from Michigan to California. Upon arrival, she was regged to buy $5,000 more auditing, although she already had hours "on account." She was also persuaded to "donate" a further $5,000 to the International Association of Scientologists.

All in all, in just twelve days, she spent $23,000, putting it on a credit card that the Registrar persuaded her to open—behind her husband's back.

"I allowed the Reg to convince me that it wasn't an overt because it was about getting up the Bridge," Sunny said. "You know, the 'greatest good for the greatest number of dynamics!' What was I *thinking*! I don't have secrets from my husband!"

For the next two weeks, she spent 9:00 A.M. to 10:30 P.M. each day in the Org, in and out of session. She wasn't sleeping well, due to worries about that secret from her husband, not to mention fretting about how she'd pay back that money; nevertheless, the auditor took her into session again and again. By the time she climbed back on the plane to head home, she was hallucinating, limping, almost unable to see. It would take her almost a year to recover.

"It's a pile of *bullshit*, Sands," she said. "It's all, *all* about money. That's all they care about. I owe so much on those cards! But I am out of there. I am done."

"Oh, Sunny," I said, fielding a combination of emotions. Perhaps oddly, I wanted Scientology to work, at least for some. Wasn't that possible? But the fears I'd had, the reasons I'd left, felt completely validated.

"I'll tell you something," she said. "Once you start looking online, there's *so much* information! So many people have horrible stories! Stories much worse than mine. And there's *such* a support system! How did you do it? When you left, the Internet didn't *exist*! You had to go through it *all by yourself*!"

I shook my head, remembering those endless awful nights.

"I'm taking all my LRH books to the dump," Sunny said. "Did you know I had to buy all my books, all over again? *Everything.* Because they were 'new and improved'! Miscavige's so-called Golden Age of Tech."

I remembered that meeting at the Sheraton, many years before, when Skye's face had gone so still at the idea that he'd have to buy all of his many Hubbard books again.

"The sales pitches came in from *everywhere*," Sunny was saying, "from Orgs and missions all over the *country*. I finally bought them in self-defense—they *hammered* me into submission. I thought the hounding would stop, but no—they insisted I buy back-up sets! They were *relentless*. Anyway. I'm driving to the dump with those books and I am *personally* throwing them in."

It was easy to imagine this, her tall body and long arms hurling book after book over a fence, and I smiled. But a silence hummed down the line. I didn't say, *Don't do something you'll regret.* I didn't ask, *What if you get pulled back in and have to spend thousands of dollars to buy all those books again?*

But she answered: "I'm done, Sands."

"Are you?"

"I am. I so am. And I can't tell you what a *relief* it is! To just *live my life*! Remember when we had that talk about solipsism? Being self-involved? Well, that's Scientology! *Get up the Bridge!* Which is all, *endlessly* about me—*me me me me*. Always something *else* to do, or something you've done, or didn't do, or should have done, or need to do, something more to be, to have, to *buy*—always *more*. I'm so excited to just be *in my life*, without worrying about my next step! I'm determined to wring that *bullshit* out of my brain."

And she did. Sunny read everything she could find by those who'd left the Church. She emailed me links to blogs, videos, articles, by ex-Scientologists. At first I deleted them. I wasn't interested in rehashing the anguish. But certain things began to catch my interest, especially the mystery surrounding Hubbard's death and David Miscavige's meteoric rise.[92, 93] Ironically, considering how often Scientologists throw the term around, Miscavige appeared to be a bona fide Suppressive Person. Yelling and punching were the least of it. His violence was both overt and insidious: He put people in command of an area, then questioned every step they took, wouldn't sign off on things they'd accomplished, and when the assigned tasks were not completed, meted out blame and punishment. Miscavige and the Church deny these accusations, but they've been well documented.[94]

Because of Miscavige and his policies, many of which flout Hubbard's, and many of which alter Standard Tech, thousands have left the Church. But they've taken the Tech with them, forming something called the Free Zone, as well as a group known as the Independent Movement. The Indies label the Church "Corporate Scientology" (or *$cientology Inc.*). They call themselves Scientologists but study and audit outside of official Orgs. Can Standard Tech *be* standard if delivered outside the fortress Hubbard set up to safeguard it? Indeed, it seems as if one can proceed up the Bridge paying the kind of rates charged by an excellent therapist. As far as I could tell, there seemed to be no hard "regging," no vast sums of money demanded for future services, and above all—was it possible?—no blind mindset. Where the Free Zone and the Indies are concerned, Scientology appeared to be not remotely cultish. I found myself glad that the good things Hubbard developed could now be found and studied the way one might take a seminar in a subject one found interesting, or attend a weeklong retreat.

Night after night, a single light shining over my desk, I scrolled through blogs and links and articles and videos, putting together my own history in relation to what I found there. Only then did I realize that while I'd been troubled by aspects of the Church for years, it had been soon after Miscavige's sudden ascent to power that I'd decided, finally, I *had* to leave. And part of what made me *get out* had been observing that increasingly corporate mindset, and the way people seemed willing to follow Miscavige's changes so blindly. This is ironic, of course, considering the authoritarian mentality of the

Church under Hubbard, but most of those years I managed to stay unaware; under Miscavige, I found it impossible. A further irony is the ease with which those within the Church seem to accept Miscavige's changes to the Tech. I can't help but wonder what happened to Keeping Scientology Working.

The blogs, reactions to the blogs, and reactions to the reactions, written by heartbroken parishioners, sturdy Hubbard-ophiles, angry ex-Scientologists, as well as current Scientologists (it was always clear when one of these weighed in), revealed not only why they'd left but the reason they'd stayed so long: all they'd loved, all they'd *believed* in. As I read, I felt a loosening around my heart. I began to unpack my pilgrim soul out of the box I'd put her in, blew the dust off her wings. I held her in the palm of my hand, loving her, until she warmed back to movement. I hadn't realized that I'd kind of killed her, in the decade following my departure from Scientology, resisting any form of spirituality besides the most austere forms of Buddhism. I had a series of blowdowns, those moments when charge releases and the spirit is ecstatic to let it go.

It's been a pilgrimage season, I heard, and picked up my guitar. *We have been finding our way.*

WHO NEVER LEFT HER BROTHER FOR DEAD

My students, encouraged to examine the roots of words, know that ESSAY comes from the French "to try," from the Latin "to weigh out," ultimately from "to set in motion." I tell them, as in individual conferences we discuss their essay topics, that the *idea* of trying is reason enough to begin. To attempt. To set in motion and see what one might discover as word begins to follow word.

For years, teaching my Myth & Fairy Tale course, even as my students and I discussed how we must all, as do Hansel and Gretel and Snow White, go "into the woods," and there learn a lesson, I did not apply this to my own situation. Nor, as we moved into mythic territory, as we explored Joseph Campbell's ideas of the hero's journey (especially how, as heroes of our own lives, we must at some point traverse an underworld), did I view my own journey in this light.[95] Among other essays, I assign Campbell's "The Self as Hero," in which he writes, "a good life is one hero journey after another."[96]

"This will be useful," I told my students. "Remember it as you endure difficult times. Hold on to the knowledge that a trek through these dreary landscapes—be they woods or underworld—can lead to insights and understanding!" So I spoke, fervently, but still I could not see how to apply this to my years in Scientology. Even as I lectured how the insights gained in such a dark, unhappy place can be the elixir, the boon with which one can return from darkness, I could hardly glimpse how that might be true for me. "Simply holding in our minds that there are lessons to learn while we're in the underworld," I'd say, feeling like a fraud, "can lead us to find them."

I spoke with enthusiasm and with certainty, but, regarding my own Scientological trek, I'd think: That's different. Those were just wasted years. Still, perhaps because I lived with those ideas for semester after semester, I finally allowed myself to imagine that Campbell's steps on the hero's journey might be applicable to my own pilgrimage, begun so many years before: The Call to Adventure. The Refusal of the Call. The Crossing of the Threshold. The Tests, the Ordeal. The Road Back (which took so long). The Return to the ordinary world. The Transformation. And—was it possible?—the resultant awareness, that which could be considered the Boon, with which I may have returned.

Which led me, finally, to my own attempt, my own "essaying," my own "weighing out." I jotted notes: That moment when I Googled myself and found myself "outed" as a Scientologist. The questions Bill Rose asked, and the insights they unfolded, as he made his documentary about my brother. I backtracked, oh so gingerly, to Los Angeles: Jamie, Skye, Jessica's talk about being a zealot, Skip's firewalk and my increasing sense that the Church had abandoned him, Dad's "wills and things"; circling, in the midst of it, to childhood in Squaw Valley, camping in Europe, Tad's jump into the shroud of golden fabric—all of which led to New York, and eventually to that July 1978 phone call regarding my brother's fall.

I *weighed*. I *essayed*. I *set in motion*. I started writing.

LATE FALL OF 2010, I received a padded envelope, the return address Tad's in Albany, my F&M address scribbled in his hasty, almost unreadable handwriting. Inside I found a volume, slim and beautiful:

Jarry & Me
The Autobiography of Alfred Jarry
by Oakley Hall III

Our dear friend, writer and publisher Steve Susoyev, did a beautiful job producing the book, including its cover: the classic photograph of Jarry on a bicycle. On the dedication page I found, as I expected to find, as for years she'd been Oak's staunch and loving companion:

For Hadiya.

But there were two other dedications as well.

Dedicated to Oakley Hall,
Oakley Hall III's father.
He died,
After living well.
Bless him.

And, completely unexpected:

With gratitude to Sands Hall,
Oakley Hall III's sister,
who never left her brother for dead
even when he looked and acted the part,
and whose enthusiasm inspired him
to finish this book.

Yet I had left my brother for dead. For almost fifteen years. That he could think this, that he could forgive, made me sink into a chair and weep.

Three months later, on a freezing Sunday morning in February, my cell phone rang: Hadiya's name on the screen. Deeply into my work, I almost didn't pick up. I was writing so much about Oak/Tad that it felt as if we were talking every day, but I realized we actually hadn't spoken in some time.

"Hadiya!" I said.

There was a long pause. "Sands," she said. "He's gone."

I stood up from the table.

"A heart attack, they think."

No.

Hadiya had been visiting her son Sharif and her granddaughters for the weekend. She did this regularly, and when she did, she and Tad talked often. He hadn't called on Saturday, or she hadn't received the call, which worried her, but cell reception at Sharif's house was spotty. Sunday morning, when Sharif drove her back to the apartment, they found Tad lying in the mudroom. Their cat Homer was dozing beside him. Hadiya thought Tad, too, was napping, and wondered why he'd chosen to do so on the mudroom floor.

But then she saw that his outstretched hand had a bluish tint to it, and she knew.

"He was *dedicated*," the coroner told me. In the pockets of Tad's tweed jacket he'd found three lighters and two and a half packs of Camel nonfilters.

That weekend I took the train up to Albany and went with Hadiya to pick up Tad's ashes. His eyeglasses and a pile of books—he always had several going at a time—were still on the armrest of the couch. We left them there, and placed the pot of ashes in the spot where he would have been sitting, reading, looking at us now and then over the tops of his glasses. Now and again, Hadiya bent over at the waist and keened. The cat dozed in the mudroom, on the spot where Tad had fallen. Sometimes the wind rattled the windows. From time to time one of them, shockingly, fell out of its casement.

"Hello, Tad," Hadiya said, as she replaced it.

That night, friends arrived, bearing food and wine and comfort.

My own grief took me as I drove from Albany up to Saratoga to stay a night with Kate Kelly and her husband Bruce Bouchard, old friends from Lexington Conservatory Theatre days. That drive, under a flat gray winter sky, was one long wail.

We held a memorial in Nevada City. Friends and family gathered in a small theater; we placed the box containing Dad's ashes under Mother's chair so he could be with us. We held another memorial in Upstate New York, on what had been the campus of the Lexington Conservatory Theatre. Amid the boarded-up theaters and the old hotel, company members gathered to tell stories of those precious years. The sun was setting as we scattered some of Oak's ashes, and the heavy particles glistened as they floated into the grass, the flowers, the water of the Catskills.

Letters and notes and emails streamed in, many of them referring to particular moments with Tad, with Oak, many confessing to the cigarette they'd bummed and the important talk that took place as they smoked companionably on a deck, in a backyard, on a theater's fire escape.

We held yet another memorial during the Squaw Conference. As friends and strangers shared moments of grace experienced in his company (many while smoking a cigarette), it was clear that the lives he touched were everywhere.

AFTER SUCH A STORM

Halfway through the following semester, riding the momentum to finish a draft of this manuscript, I cancelled everything except my teaching duties and, one day, knew I was done. It was shaggy, but it was complete.

Late that afternoon, after teaching, I scrolled Facebook's newsfeed, and a familiar name floated by: Jamie Faunt.

Jamie!

I scrolled back until I found it, a post made by Martin, in whose studio, so long ago, I'd recorded songs: *Does anyone know if Jamie Faunt's memorial service is still on for Sunday?*

I stared, shocked.

Memorial service? Jamie—dead?

He'd been on my mind for months, of course; they'd all been, as I'd worked on the book. Skye, certainly, also Martin, who with his studio and musical talent had been so supportive of my music, and his wife Sallie; Delph, who threw such great parties and used butter in her cakes; Roo, with her gorgeous voice; Paloma, who'd seen me through so many hours of auditing. I'd thought, often, of Jamie's full lips and sculpted cheekbones, the almost clichéd rock-star beauty of him. The way his bicep pulsed as he played his bass. The way he insisted Scientology was the only way; how I laughed at that assertion until I'd been drawn to it, come to agree with it, come to believe it so much that even after we divorced, I stuck with the religion for another five years. Seven years altogether, not to mention the three it took to leave it behind.

Dear Martin, I wrote in a private message. I'd no idea about Jamie. Might you have details?

Happened back in August, he wrote back. Heart attack, I gather.

I returned to Martin's original post to see if anyone had answered his question.

Sunday at noon. At the Pavilion, Celebrity Center.

A little dazed, I put the computer to sleep and headed home through a late October afternoon, dusk taking its time to fall over Lancaster's tree-lined streets. I fetched my guitar and a down vest and sat on the porch, working on "Pilgrimage Season."

We've crawled through caverns
We've been kneeling down in shrines
The road has been dusty and stunning and long

Suddenly it was as if a huge paw descended onto my shoulder. *You must be there for that memorial. It is time to see them, to see them all.*

I shook my head. Stared at the guitar in my arms. Then pretty much leapt to fetch my phone. That hand on my shoulder urged me forward: *Paloma. Start with Paloma.*

In session and out, Paloma had heard me wrestle with my doubts. She was the one who'd listened—TRs in—as I offered up that I'd gone Clear last lifetime. Over the years she'd tried to keep in touch, but I'd stayed distant, afraid of that effort of hers to connect.

But in an old address book I found her name, dialed the number.

And so it was that within twelve hours of reading of Jamie's death, I was on a plane to Los Angeles. Paloma and her husband offered a lovely arrival dinner; the next morning she and I enjoyed a long walk in which we talked, as we always had, about our work. I shared that I was writing a memoir.

"About Scientology!" she asked, a frown on her lovely face.

"And about my family," I told her. "Which was, in a way, its own kind of cult."

I was laughing, but she looked shocked. "What do you mean?" she said, and I told her that both worlds had made me feel as if I were superior to those not in them; both felt special and made me feel special; both had exerted tremendous authority over what I felt I should and should not do with my life; both persuaded me that my own ideas might not have validity unless backed up by theirs; both involved a veneration of sorts; both had created a terrible dependence; and from both it had proven difficult to unyoke myself.

"I'm grateful for a lot," I said, "including what was learned, although that's taken a while to sort out. But I had to find my own way."

She was still frowning.

"Maybe we shouldn't talk about this," I said. "When you start your next auditing, you'll have to answer all those security questions. I don't want to make trouble for you."

"I don't let the Church dictate who are and who are not my friends," she said.

We walked on in silence for a bit. "I'm glad of that, Paloma," I said.

She nodded. "But maybe don't mention the memoir to the others."

We were joining the others for the memorial, meeting Delph and Wyatt at their house, where Roo also joined us (she'd stopped doing Scientology, which I'd only recently discovered). Together we drove to Celebrity Center, where we'd meet Martin and Sallie. Even as I was happy to be with these old friends, the idea that I was purposefully heading back into the belly of the whale that had swallowed and held me for so long made my heart knock.

As we walked toward the building, I looked up at the fifth floor, where Sunny and I had done our Upper TRs, where I'd had that epiphany about beauty. I wanted to linger, to take it all in, but suddenly there were Jamie's brothers and their wives, down from Portland, exclaiming, "Sands! We can't believe you're here! Brooke! Look who's here!"

A woman with blond hair turns. She looks so much like Jamie, except stunningly beautiful rather than outrageously handsome, that I catch my breath. The high cheekbones. The full, sensual lips. The blue eyes, which fill with tears at the sight of me. It is Jamie's niece. When she was four, she'd been our flower girl. Now she's all grown up.

"We're performing one of your and Jamie's songs," one of Jamie's brothers says. "For the memorial."

He smiles at my astonished face. Yet working on the memoir has pulled me back to singing and songwriting again. It also seems exactly right.

Friends and family share funny anecdotes and touching ones. A letter is read from Chick Corea. I am invited to speak, and I do, quoting lyrics I'd written about Jamie:

My sails lost, my steering gone
The winds of chance the only form
What blew me to your harbor's peace
What a port to come to
After such a storm

"Jamie introduced me to Scientology." I pause to take in that I am actually standing in Celebrity Center, surrounded by Scientologists. "Which," I say, "only slowly revealed itself as much of the port I felt I'd come to, *after such a storm*. And Scientology *was* a port. But then . . ." It's important to state exactly where I stand. "I chose to float my boat back out into the ocean again."

There's a shift in the room, comprehension. I feel it. No one will try to get me back. They know I am done.

A jazz trio plays some of Jamie's tunes, as well as the song we wrote together, "Butterfly." His brother reads my lyrics before they launch into it. As he takes a solo on flugelhorn, I smile ruefully. In spite of my hopes that we'd be a world-changing songwriting team, Jamie and I wrote just two songs together, "Butterfly" and "After Such a Storm." Yet I feel him turning somersaults in the air above us, delighted to have us together again, no matter the circumstances.

In her typical way, Delph has swiftly organized a small gathering, and back at their lovely home, as she and Wyatt serve salmon and roast chicken and cake (with lots of butter), I am stunned by who's assembled. Roo and I, no longer involved in the Church. Paloma, who, along with Delph and Wyatt, are sturdy Hubbard-ophiles. One friend is redoing the Purification Rundown. Another has just returned from Flag, having completed OT VII.

We're all together, and the room is full of nothing but love.

The friend who's just completed OT VII tells me how deeply it's made him want to invest in helping other musicians create their dreams. As the months go by, I will watch, via Facebook, how he goes about doing exactly that. I think of the long-ago conversation with Skye, about whether memories of other lifetimes (and at that level of the Bridge, the memories of the endless Body Thetans that have attached themselves to you) are "true," which makes me ponder an aspect of auditing that seems to me quite positive: a person who aspires to goodness will come to useful realizations. In spite of knowing, now, all the excesses and horrors of the management of the Church, the endless demands for money, the seemingly fraudulent uses to which all that money is put, I think: If that's one of the powers of auditing, well, good for it.

I catch a red-eye back across the country, rolling my suitcase into my office in time to pick up my teaching materials and walk across campus to teach Myth & Fairy Tale.

TREASURE

My mother is increasingly frail but still full of wit. As I help her out of the car one day, she asks, eyes twinkling, "Where did nimble go?" During the times I'm with her, I often bring my guitar. Among the tunes we sing together is "Pilgrimage Season," which ends:

Maybe it's just that the trees have grown
Maybe I've finally found my way

I don't sing the final, implied rhyme, wanting the ambiguity of finding a *way*, as much as finding a way *home*, but in her sweet, quavery voice, Mother always sings the final word.

One night, as I am putting her to bed, she asks, as she often does, what I'm currently writing. I tell her again: a memoir, and speak with affection about my years with Skye.

She nods. "He was such a nice man."

I stare in shock, remembering the fraught conversations, the cold, awful way my parents locked him out. "Yes, he was," I say.

Another afternoon, she asks again, and I tell her about the conversation in Dad's office, when he told me I'd be written out of their will if I stayed in Scientology.

"We would *never* have done such a thing," she says. "Never!"

I keep going with the story, lightly, describing the drive back up the freeway, and how I'd cried aloud, "How can I leave now!"

"Oh!" She looks stricken. "We never thought of that."

And we both laugh.

WE'RE HARDWIRED, I think, to aspire. To want to be better, to have or do more. Success. Love. Health. Wealth. Happiness. In his Bridge to Total Freedom, Hubbard, in all his weird twisted genius, created a way for people to satisfy—or believe they could—that deep-seated human need. If you earnestly believe that a given lesson, experience, process (especially a repetitive one), is going to improve something about you, or allow you to discover something useful, you will usually have such an epiphany. It seems to me that Hubbard built his church around this idea. He also built it around the idea that people are willing to pay a lot for such improvement, willing to pay a lot for a certainty that their lives have meaning. Some are willing to pay by dedicating their lives (starting with this one) to that effort.

Like all religions, Scientology can plug that gaping existential hole that at some point yawns open in most lives. From one view, this seems manipulative, clever and calculating, to exploit our human yearning in this way. From another (and I'm aware this may be greeted with derision), it can be seen as benevolent: to give us what we long for. I had sturdy, life-changing realizations doing Hubbard's processes. I can finally accept that just because the "win" took place via Scientology practices does not lessen the power of the lesson learned.

But then I think of Skip—his twitching eyes, the nightmare visions that rolled palpably out of his consciousness—and of the Church's indifference. That stunning lack of compassion is what finally allowed me to comprehend that Upper Management seemed interested only in those who were upstat: those who succeeded, whose successful (celebrity) status could be used to "spread the word"—spreading the word, particularly, to those who are able and willing to pay for services. Scientology offers no scholarships. The very idea, to those steeped in Church dogma, is laughable: If you can't afford Scientology, you are not in spiritually good enough shape to deserve it. Among the things I often noted but blinked away were how few people in the course rooms—in Los Angeles!—came from any world other than white and middle-class; how my Church didn't show up, as other religions did, after tornadoes and fires and hurricanes with soup and clothes and succor and materials for rebuilding. No, people who find themselves in the path of a tsunami have brought it on themselves. There is no room in the Church of Scientology for such downstats.

I recall the derision in Hubbard's books (not, I hasten to say, among my friends) for those who were gay, and for those who chose to marry a member of another race. Skip was an enormous chunk added to that pile of evidence that in my mind had begun to mount against the Church, which I could no longer ignore. I think that's why those nights sitting opposite him remain so vivid. And why, as I began to sort out my pilgrimage into and out of Scientology, I needed to begin with him. He was, though I did not know it at the time, the galvanizing force that finally not only allowed, but required me to leave. I wish I could thank him. I hope, with all my heart, that he found his way to some kind of serenity.

FOR YEARS I thought of my time in Scientology, the shame attached to the woods/underworld where I spent so much time, as unique. I was not able to see it as simply a version of a journey taken by most of us at some point in this life.

But as I began to write and, finally, to speak openly about that "squandered" decade, I heard from many who'd taken (or been led into) detours from their own expected lives. Often these were shy, whispered conversations, as they confided their own shame, what they perceived as their own "flunks": the decade in the terrible marriage, the years lost to Oxycontin, the time in an ashram agreeing to and participating in sexual coercion, the transgender child whose transition tore apart not only the family but a cherished religious community. We've all had to take careful, sometimes very difficult inventory to determine how those years and those experiences led to where we are now, and that for better or worse (and it takes time and tinkering and perspective to find that "better"), we wouldn't be who we are without having had those years and learned those lessons in our particular underworlds. That is, after darkness—*because* of darkness—we determine how to start again.

My brother and I both flunked. His version was awful; mine, in the end, fairly mundane. He fell off a bridge, damaging his brain; I clambered along one that, for a while, torqued my mind. But we both returned, in our own ways, bearing insights we hoped to pass on. He learned to be content with this moment, now. Once I was able to accept him as his new self, instead of wanting him to be the old one, I saw it all the time: in the way he'd take a drag of his cigarette and give a slow smile. Sometimes it was sad, a dark understanding of his fall, in every sense of the word; it came with a shrug, but it was also wise, and accepting. He knew he'd been racing for extraordinary, and that, arms outstretched, he'd leapt toward that dazzling trapeze—and missed. He missed, and he fell. He came to know all that, and moved on to live the life he did have.

I sidled along Hubbard's Bridge, whose initial sound structure turned, increasingly, to gossamer nonsense. After I finally managed to leave, I rejected all of it, for years. But as I began to write in earnest—as writing became a practice—I became aware of how the work at those sunlit tables in the course room taught me to love scholarship, how it was there that I first learned the magic that is contained in the roots of words. I am endlessly grateful for the gift of that three-dimensionality, which surrounds what I do, as I write, sing, act, direct, edit, teach. As I sit at my desk, all kinds of volumes to do with words, with spirituality, with history, with myth and religion—especially books that combine those subjects—are within arm's reach.

•

I'VE NOW READ that Hubbard didn't invent Study Tech, and it's possible that, like much else comprising his religious technology, he borrowed the ideas, codifying them as his own. Nevertheless, the idea of "knowing how to know" sticks with me. If, in my classrooms, I see someone yawning, I circle back to make sure I've defined my terms. I demo concepts. I try not to "skip gradients," and it's clear to me when I have. As part of various assignments, students are asked to look at the derivations of words; many find this tedious (and tell me so), but I continue those assignments for the few who write in the semester's evaluation form, or come to tell me personally, that this sometimes-arduous work has shifted the way they study, and/or their entire relationship to language—even, for some, the understanding of why they are in school at all.

Most religions, and certainly philosophy as a subject, are organized around ethics. Even as I condemn what appear to me to be the Gestapo-ian ways Hubbard's Ethics Conditions are used by the Church (particularly in the upper echelons of management), I appreciate that, while a Scientologist, I was asked to engage with these ideas so thoroughly. I doubt that I would have done so otherwise. Nor would I have understood how much knowledge and appreciation of ethics may shape our actions.

That the soul is "aware of being aware" continues to be a very useful idea, especially in relation to mind and body. It's an idea shared by many religions, but I grasped it as a Scientologist. I'm glad that thetans are genderless, that unlike, say, Buddhism's enlightenment, it's possible to go Clear (if that is an actual state) in a female body. That said, women in high positions in Scientology are addressed as "sir." And I am horrified that children as young as six are considered old enough to agree to join the Sea Org. Considered full-fledged thetans in a young body, they are encouraged to sign their entire lives away on a dotted line (not to mention the billion further years the contract mentions).[97] This is child abuse, pure and simple, but it is protected by the Church's religious status. Also deeply disturbing is the Sea Org policy regarding pregnancy.[98] I met wonderful people in the

Sea Org, and it breaks my heart to imagine what happens to them as they get old or perhaps infirm (what did they do to "pull that in"?) or simply want to retire. For them there is no retirement; there is not even Social Security. The Church raises millions of dollars a year, and due to its status as a religion, it pays not a penny in taxes. (The Church hounded and flummoxed the IRS until the IRS capitulated; the IRS is now reluctant to come after them.[99]) Instead, they cleverly invest in significant pieces of real estate all over the world.

As my knowledge grew regarding these base aspects of Church management and policy, which seem deeply and purposefully evil, it tainted in almost irredeemable ways the good things that can be found in Hubbard's religious technology. It took me decades to appreciate that in those years I thought of for so long as squandered, I did learn much, and that there is much to be grateful for.[100]

And so I ask my students to examine the roots of the word POET, as I know they'll be at least surprised and perhaps delighted to know that it descends from "make"—and that they are, when they're writing, *makers*. Their delight is palpable when they see from the roots of OXYMORON (*oxy*, "sharp" + *moron*, "dull") that the word itself is an oxymoron. Examining the roots of PHILOSOPHY lets them know that its literal meaning is "love of wisdom," and then they define SOPHOMORE. It's great to see them look up, blinking, as they realize that there's a point in learning when we're all "wise fools" (*moron*, again, + *soph*, "wise"). They know that NOUN comes from "name," VERB from "word," and that the name of the reference volume that I hope they'll all keep using, THESAURUS, descends to us from the Latin for "treasure."

And, of course, that ESSAY comes from "try; to set in motion."

Just start. Especially after a flunk.

Fail again. Fail better.

AFTERWORD

DISCONNECTION

As I began to finalize this manuscript, I wrote to Skye, asking if he'd like me to change his name. He now lives on the other side of the country, about as far, geographically, as one can get from LA, and, by extension, from Celebrity Center and the Advanced Org. He'd written a kind note after seeing the documentary about my brother, and a congratulatory one when I sent him a copy of my first CD (a few of the songs were written in his company, back in the day), but otherwise we have not communicated.

For about a week I did not hear back. Then an email arrived, not from him, but from one of those Scientology friends with whom I was now back in touch. The subject line was "Flunk. Start," and it was CC-ed to those who'd once been our precious circle. Skye had clearly let them know about the memoir. I was disappointed; I'd wanted to contact each one personally.

"You know if it is not positive," the email said, "you are cutting the line to us."

I did know. Indeed, as the book moved toward publication, I'd stopped being chummy via email and on Facebook. It felt fraudulent. Since the memoir criticizes Scientology, I knew that as far as they were concerned, I could no longer be considered a friend; in fact, because of that criticism, I would now be a Suppressive Person. It wouldn't be me "cutting the line"; that would be their choice, but I understood why, as good Scientologists (as Paloma had been when she wrote that Knowledge Report), they'd have to.

All this was not unexpected, and so did not make me angry, but it did make me sad. Part of the sorrow was that I was already wondering if it was wise to publish the book. I'd begun to fret about the Church's possible reaction. I was no Leah Remini, who, using her celebrity status, has effectively attacked and revealed—through memoir and television—the Church's underbelly; nor was I a Marty Rathbun, who'd worked in the upper echelons of the Church and, after leaving, spilled management secrets in his memoir and his blog; nor was I one who'd made it up the Bridge, able to leak confidential data.[101, 102] Still, would the Church, objecting to the memoir, come after me? One of the steps of the Enemy Formula, in Hubbard's Ethics Conditions, is to "strike a blow at the group one has been pretending to be a part of." This has justified, for Scientologists, every kind of harassment. Was I damning myself, in a horridly ironic way, considering how long it took me to extricate myself from the Church, to endless engagement with its most reprehensible aspects?

For two weeks I actively wondered if I should call my agent and say let's not publish; it's not worth it.

And then, early one morning, I had a dream—a waking dream, really; I was aware of having it, even of creating it.

I am lodged within a small vertical cave. My feet are crammed into the narrow space that is the bottom of a stone fissure that widens as it rises into a kind of V, the top a little broader than my shoulders. About a foot above my head, a thick slab is settled into place that closes off any possible exit. I am aware—not panicked yet, but a dreadful understanding is growing—that I have been interred. Buried alive. Shut up. In stone.

I can only stand, or rest upright, or slide into a sort of fetal position at the bottom of the V. In fact, I realize, the cave is vaguely the shape of a uterus, except that there are no portals—not to either side, nor at the bottom. Is this some kind of birth, then, or some kind of death in birth—a miscarriage? Like Antigone, I'm shut into a cave. But unlike Antigone, no one has done it to me. There is no one above that slab over my head—which seems only recently to have been put into place (it occurs to me that it is I who's put it there)—who would hear me scream, if I decided to do that, or who would respond if I did.

As I ponder scraping my fingernails hopelessly against rock, or yelling uselessly for help (hopeless or useless, I know that I will try, as to give up seems a horrible way to spend the days that will pass until I die of hunger or dehydration), I think about what this dream/vision means. Why am I manifesting it? What is its message?

Is it that, if I publish the book, I immure myself in an endless battle with the Church of Scientology? That the repercussions of publishing will be so awful that I will feel as if I've shut myself into a kind of cave for the rest of my life?

Or do I consider the Church's totalitarianism so vast, so successful, that I am considering pulling the plug on publication, shutting myself up in this sarcophagus rather than risk the repercussions of criticizing it? I am struck, too, by the message of patriarchy represented by the stone uterus, its aridity, its lack of entrances and exits. If I *don't* publish the book—if I allow the terror to keep me small, keep me from using my voice, keep me silent—do I condemn myself to being shut up in this dreadful place, a death in life?

It's in telling the dream to a friend and hearing myself say "shutting myself up," "being shut up," that I get the pun implicit in those phrases. I realize what the dream is asking me to examine, forcing me to confront: *Shut up.*

I laugh aloud at the realization, and something powerful shifts in me. No. I won't.

Later, I look up the etymology of SHUT: from Old English *scyttan*, it means "to put (a bolt) in position to hold fast." SHUT UP is probably a shortened version of "shut up your mouth." I won't shut up my mouth. Even though:

If it is not positive, you know you are cutting the line to us.

The Church denies that it encourages "disconnection" from those who are critical of Scientology, but I am certain these friends will, indeed, cut the line.[103] I'm also certain they will not read the book. While I have, indeed, changed their names and identifying characteristics (in addition to protecting their privacy in a general way, I don't want the Church coming after them for having been friends with me), I understand. Even though Hubbard says "what is true for you is true for you," it's difficult, if you're a Scientologist, to read anything negative about Scientology. Not only because it might make you doubt, but because the next time you're in session, the fact that you read/heard/saw anything against the Church will come up, and you will have to process *why* you read/listened/watched. What transgression made you willing to remove the blindfold, even for a second? And there will always be something. So one learns to continue on, mental fingers held to mental ears, keeping out anything negative so that you don't have to go through that again. It's a swiftly learned lesson; processing such "lapses" can be wrenching, in addition to expensive.

This is one of the biggest reasons I had to leave Scientology. Exactly this: that I could not think as I wanted. That I could not read what appealed to me. That I corralled and controlled my curiosity because, if it took me into territory that might make me question, that might make me think, that might make me doubt, that might make me *critical*, I would have to go, again, down a terrible rabbit hole—when I think about it, a rabbit hole made of stone with no exit except *what I had done.* I was touched when those old friends decided they could again be in contact with me, an "apostate," but even then I knew that it was possible only because we'd tacitly agreed not to talk about the Church. Which in and of itself is fine; many relationships include agreements that certain topics—politics, e.g.—are off-limits. But though I deal as fairly as I can with the doctrines of Scientology, and acknowledge all it gave me (indeed, there may be those who attack the book for not being harder on the Church, who will insist that the things I found effective are so much psychobabble), the book is an advisory: not so much against the Tech, but against the organization that holds it.

So I do sound a warning: If you are in, if you are tempted, get out as quickly as you can. Because you will soon be in thrall, wearing blinders of the kind I had in place for years, the kinds those friends (soon to be not my friends) still wear. If there is anything more damning, I don't know what it is. This is what authoritarian regimes demand. It's been tried at various times in our own democracy: muffling the press, limiting what can be read and seen and heard, damning critical reports as false or fake, punishing those who don't agree, turning a blind eye to excesses and wrongs for fear of repercussion from those in power.

SPIRITUALITY IS THE vast vessel that holds religion in its multitudinous forms. The Latin etymology of SPIRIT—*spiritus*—is "breath."[104] In*spirat*ion (originally used of a divine being imparting a truth or idea) can be imagined as that intake of delight that comes with a realization; and things ex*pire* when they run out: a passport's dates, or a body's breath. I appreciate that we can be di*spirit*ed, with the sense of the drooping flag of a soul that word summons, and I've long been intrigued that the plural of the word is used for hard liquor, as if those fermented and distilled elixirs create a life force that may suffuse, inhabit, and even take over a body.

And religion organizes around spirit: the holy version inherent in many systems of faith as well as the incorporeal one that each of our bodies, while alive, houses. In all the forms in which religion may be found—in all of its guises, in all the ways it binds—its essence is similar: a belief in a purpose, in a function higher than our mere selves and the lifetime we're embarked upon; and that something called love, and the largely male constructs by which it has been labeled, permeates our existence.

I yearned for a path that would reveal those truths, and for a while, with Scientology, felt I found it. What I actually acquired, in that seven-year dance with the Church, is an awareness of spirit that permeates my days, and a way to interact with words that is deeply satisfying. This is perhaps best illustrated by a moment in class the other day, as I introduced an incoming class of first years (no longer called "freshmen," perhaps because "freshwomen" sounds really odd) to the idea of a liberal arts education. I spoke to the root of LIBERAL, from the Latin, *liber*, "free," drawing a distinction between the political sense of the word, which tends to mean "the party in favor of government action to support social change," and its educational sense: intellectual enlargement.[105] Part of what they'd be doing in the course, I told them, would be reading essays whose authors often contradict each other (sometimes nastily) and that the point of assigning such readings is to have them understand that just because it is written does not make it true. And that part of their task, as students at a liberal arts college, is to find their *own* point of view, which may or may not align within those of the authors they read, their parents, their friends, their classmates, their professors.

Liber descends from the idea of a free man—one who had time for such pursuits—and it's easy to see the monumental antipathy that could have built against those who were noble but extravagant ("free from restraint"); indeed, that very aspect of the word probably gave rise to the hues of meaning that slide from qualities most would find admirable—open, untrammeled—to those that sound increasingly dangerous: unbridled, unchecked, licentious, no doubt the meanings understood (and intended) by those who use the word as a pejorative.

Such tramps through the landscape of language give me unbounded joy. It's ironic that I was introduced to these ideas while involved with an organization whose stated goal is freedom but that places such barricades to independent thought. Still, it's the gift I carry with me: words, and the animating principle within them—their etymological souls, if you will—which offer such deeply satisfying ways to observe and engage with the world.

ACKNOWLEDGMENTS

Sometimes I imagine composing an essay called "The Ethics of Rewriting a Memoir: Who Am I This Time?" The changes between the first shaggy draft of this manuscript and the book you hold in your hand are many, and the realizations had while doing those revisions profound. Along the way, a number of friends read sections and a few the entire manuscript and offered useful and sometimes essential perspectives. Leading the list is my beloved Bostick Trio, who encouraged me as I began: Christine Hemp and Lisa Schlesinger. Other essential insights were offered by Caridwen Spatz, Marilyn Jones, Rachel Howard, Laurie O'Brien, Kerry Sherin Wright, Joy Johannessen, Maggie McKaig, Diane Fetterly, Kelly Dwyer, and especially Steve Susoyev, not only for his fierce encouragement and editorial skills, but also for the example he provides of honesty, generosity, and deep loving kindness. Also freelance editors Beth Rashbaum and Roger Labrie, and attorney-at-law Lois Wasoff. And as the book neared its current form, I am especially grateful for very valuable ideas offered by Michael Mungiello.

And where would I be without my sterling editor at Counterpoint Press, Jennifer Alton? It has been a privilege to work with such an insightful reader and thinker. I am grateful to everyone at Counterpoint, beginning with founder Jack Shoemaker, who decided to take on the book in the first place. And I am grateful to each and all of the talented and committed people who shepherded this book into print, and into the world, including the terrific publicity and marketing team headed by Megan Fishmann and Jennifer Abel Kovitz, and including Lena Moses-Schmitt, Sarah Baline, Dory Athey, and Dustin Kurtz; also deep thanks to Miyako Singer, Nicole Caputo, Olenka Burgess, and superb copy editor Oriana Leckert (any remaining errors are my own). And special thanks to Wah-Ming Chang for her fierce and generous editorial eye. There are astounding hearts and minds gathered at Counterpoint, and I'm more than a little stunned, and deeply honored, that *Flunk. Start.* found its way to this great publishing company and its stellar team.

Further thanks:

Franklin & Marshall College has been supportive in innumerable ways, especially the Provost's Office and my beloved English department. Special gratitude is due to my wonderful colleagues; and I want to particularly acknowledge Judith Mueller, and the innovative director of the Philadelphia Alumni Writers House, Kerry Sherin Wright.

Sunny Wilkinson, jazz singer and teacher extraordinaire: I met her in a Scientology course room and thought I'd lost her when I left the Church. When she, too, decided that Scientology was not for her, our precious friendship sprang back. Sunny asked me not to change her name, and I am grateful for the support her decision represents.

Those friends from my years in Scientology: Although their names are changed, they know who they are (although I doubt they'll read the book). That they were so dear and wonderful is a large part of why it took me so long to leave. I understand why Paloma wrote that Knowledge Report, weird though it was to receive. I love her for her faith, as well as in spite of it.

Sunny also helped me reclaim my (singing) voice, and in that regard I also want to thank the brilliant Maggie McKaig and Luke Wilson, who were instrumental in helping me find my way back to my music. I am also deeply grateful in this regard to Randy McLean. Also to Murray Campbell, Louis B. Jones, Elena and Saul Rayo, and

Caridwen and Gregory Spatz. Exceptional and beloved musical companions all.

A number of warriors, beginning with Tony Ortega and his blog, *The Underground Bunker*: For decades, Ortega has written critically about Scientology and given many who've departed the Church a place to read information, share stories, express outrage, and find peace. Lawrence Wright for his superlative book, *Going Clear.* Mark "Marty" Rathbun, Mike Rinder, Jenna Miscavige Hill, and Astra Woodcraft, for their books and blogs. The many who've found their way out of the Church and dared to write and speak up about it, including Leah Remini, in her Emmy-award winning series, *Scientology and the Aftermath*, which does such essential work in exposing the Church's outrageous policies and practices.

Mary: Who lived with and loved Oak during the tumultuous years of the theater company, and endured the aftermath of his accident in ways that can hardly be imagined. Also their children, OMH IV and Elizabeth, with much love.

The women who were so good to my brother: Dana Ivers in his younger years, and, following the accident, Robin Campbell, Molly Fisk, and Hadiya Wilborn. Thank you for the sustaining love and help you offered, not just to him, but to the family.

For many reasons, which they will each know: Cat C. H. Bill H. Amy T. Jennifer E. Sarah S. Paul E. Mitchell K. Marjorie M. C. Kabi H. Marci N. George C. Kim C. Alison P. Lynne C. Clare H. Philip S. Nancy C. Frances S. Elizabeth S. Katie B. Amy M. Peggy H. Lisa S. Amy M. Matthew B. Monica C.

And the cherished women who have taken such good care of our mother: Pabby, Jacquie, Judy, Genna, Alika, and Viki.

The artists and friends who helped create the Lexington Conservatory Theatre: for your support of Oak and of his vision, and for your loving efforts to care for him when he fell.

Special thanks in this regard to Steven Patterson and John Sowle, who were so deeply supportive during Oak's final years in Albany; who hosted his Lexington Memorial, on the grounds of the theater and in their beautiful home; and who honored his memory by producing *Grinder's Stand* at their Bridge Street Theatre, in Catskill. No one could ask for better friends than these two wonderful men.

Bill Rose: for his excellent documentary, *The Loss of Nameless Things*, and for the questions he asked during our interview, which were so unexpectedly helpful in getting the wheels rolling on what became this book.

The man I call Skye: One could not ask for a sweeter sweetheart. The wrench of leaving him caused a deep and peculiar anguish. For the first time I understood what up to then had been merely a literary trope: that religion can stand in the way of love. I thank him for his efforts to understand the troubled woman who landed in his life.

Jamie's wonderful family: I'm glad I got to see them again at his memorial service, and that Jamie's piano has found the perfect home.

My beloved sisters, Tracy and Brett: For years, they had a rather erratic older sister. I am deeply grateful for their love and support and faith that I'd sort it out. Also their partners: the extraordinary writer and thinker Louis B. Jones and the warm and wise Jim Chumbley.

My parents: For the extraordinary childhood they offered, and for the life they led and gave us. My heart twists, now, imagining their heartache and wrenching sorrow at the choices I was making. I'm deeply glad we came to a peace about that. A few years ago, I told my mother I was feeling sad that I'd devoted so many years to the Church, and she said, "Well, it's part of what made you who you are, and that seems pretty good to me." Yes.

The Community of Writers at Squaw Valley: Founded by my parents and friends, this conference has nurtured writers for five decades. Brett Hall Jones, Louis B. Jones, Lisa Alvarez, and Andrew Tonkovich sustain and strengthen that original vision. I am deeply grateful for all the Community has given me over its many years.

Spirit guides: My wise therapist: Ginger Konvalin, who's helped me toward many vital comprehensions. Eileen Jorgenson, who so often offers the perfect insight and instruction exactly when needed. MaryAnn McDonnell, Elena Rayo, and Tynowyn for their sagacity.

Two Yoga studios: Wild Mountain in Nevada City and West End in Lancaster, as well as just a few of the yogis and teachers who offer so much inspiration, physically, mentally, and spiritually: Graham Hayes (who also designed my website), Amanda Dozal, Seren Rubens, Rachael McGrath, and Cynthia Kilbourn.

Tom Taylor: who lived with me during a number of the years when I was trying to pretend the previous ten had never happened. His love and support meant the world to me then, and still do.

Dear friend and fellow writer Christine Hemp: Our exchanges regarding writing and spirituality and relations and friendship are utterly sustaining. I cannot sufficiently express the vital nature of this comradeship, and how grateful for it I am.

My marvelous agent, the brilliant and generous Michael Carlisle, who is also my steadfast friend. My gratitude for his belief in me and in my work is beyond words.

Finally, my brother, Tad/Oak, who for so long held the lantern in the forest, lighting the way.

BIBLIOGRAPHY

BOOKS

Campbell, Joseph. *The Hero with a Thousand Faces.* New World Library. Novato, CA. 2008.

Campbell, Joseph. *Pathways to Bliss.* New World Library. Novato, CA. 2008.

Headley, Mark. *Blown for Good: Behind the Iron Curtain of Scientology.* BFG Books. New York, NY. 2009.

Hill, Jenna Miscavige, with Lisa Presley. *Beyond Belief: My Secret Life in Scientology and My Harrowing Escape.* HarperCollins. New York, NY. 2013.

Hubbard, L. Ron. *Dianetics: The Modern Science of Mental Health.* Bridge Publications, Inc. Los Angeles, CA. 2007.

Hubbard, L. Ron. *Introduction to Scientology Ethics.* Bridge Publications, Inc. Los Angeles, CA. 2007.

Hubbard, L. Ron. *Dianetics and Scientology Technical Dictionary.* Bridge Publications. Los Angeles, CA. 1982.

Note: The citations within parentheses, which I include with any definitions taken from the *Tech Dictionary*, indicate where one may find the source of the quoted definition, e.g. policy letters or other documents written by Hubbard, or recordings of his tapes and lectures.

Ortega, Tony. *The Unbreakable Miss Lovely: How the Church of Scientology*

Tried to Destroy Paulette Cooper. CreateSpace Independent Publishing Platform. 2015.

Remini, Leah. *Troublemaker: Surviving Hollywood and Scientology.* Ballantine Books. New York, NY. 2015.

Wright, Lawrence. *Going Clear: Scientology, Hollywood, and the Prison of Belief.* Knopf. New York, NY. 2013.

SELECTED WEBSITES AND BLOGS

Glossary of Scientology & Dianetics Terms (*Scientology Glossary*): www.whatisscientology.org

Hill, Jenna Miscavige, and Astra Woodcraft. www.exscientologykids.com

Official website for Hubbard's Study Technology: www.studytechnology.org/index.html

Official website for Scientology Courses: www.scientologycourses.org

Official website for Scientology's Religious Technology Center: www.rtc.org

Official website for the Church of Scientology: www.scientology.org

Ortega, Tony. *The Underground Bunker.* www.tonyortega.org

Rathbun, Mark. *Moving On Up a Little Higher.* www.markrathbun.blog

Rinder, Mike. *Something Can Be Done About It.* www.mikerindersblog.org

Scientology Handbook: www.scientologyhandbook.org

ENDNOTES

FOREWORD: KNOWLEDGE REPORT

1. KNOWLEDGE REPORT: Hubbard, L. Ron. *Introduction to Scientology Ethics*. "Knowledge Reports."

Also HCOPL (Hubbard Communications Office Policy Letter), 22 Jul 1982, revised 9 Aug 2000: "Keeping Scientology Working."

2. *Ibid.*

3. A link to the current online form for Knowledge Reports is available at Scientology's Religious Technology Center's website, www.rtc.org/matters/intro.html (accessed July 31, 2017).

4. REASONABLE/UNREASONABLE: Hubbard, L. Ron. *Modern Management Technology Defined*. Bridge Publications, Inc. Los Angeles, CA. 1976. Reprinted 1986.

See also the discussion on Mike Rinder's blog: "Scientology and Reason." *Something Can Be Done About It*. March 25, 2017. www.mikerindersblog.org/scientology-and-reason (accessed July 31, 2017).

When I first encountered these usages, I reacted quite strongly to what I saw as the most blatant kind of Orwellian "newspeak." But a friend explained it to me thus: "It makes sense when you break down the word 'reasonable,'" she said. "'Reason' plus the suffix 'able.' One of the definitions of 'reason' as a noun is 'a cause, or an explanation, or a justification for an action or event.' And 'able' means things like 'capable of, or having a tendency to, or given to.' So if you look at the word in that light, to be reasonable is, indeed, 'being capable of justification.'" This degree of engagement with words impressed me and assisted me in coming around to this point of view. And I have since been struck by the value of the perspective when, for example, someone clearly inebriated, with a baby in her car, tries to assure you that she is not too to drunk to drive.

5. Such reports can be found in, respectively: Lawrence Wright's *Going Clear: Scientology, Hollywood, and the Prison of Belief*; Jenna Miscavige Hill's *Beyond Belief: My Secret Life in Scientology and My Harrowing Escape*; and Mark Headley's memoir, *Blown for Good: Behind the Iron Curtain of Scientology*.

6. The edition of the *Dianetics and Scientology Technical Dictionary*, from which I provide sources for a number of the definitions and quotations used in this book, was published in 1982—the latest edition I was able to find. The *Tech Dictionary*, as it was casually called, appears to be no longer in print, and its exhaustive contents appear to have been replaced, under Miscavige, by a far less comprehensive *Glossary of Scientology and Dianetics Terms* (a title I've shortened to *Scientology Glossary*), available at www.whatisscientology.org. Where appropriate, I quote that glossary and/or provide a link to it, or to other Scientology websites where, at the time of this book's publication, such information could be located.

7. The documents in which Hubbard outlines his ideas are often policy letters or bulletins issued from the Hubbard Communications Office. Their acronyms are, respectively, HCOPL and HCOB. In this case, it's a policy letter: HCOPL 7 Feb 1965: "Keeping Scientology Working" series.

8. HCOB, 15 Feb 1979, reissued 12 Apr 1983. "Verbal Tech: Penalties."

WE NEED YOU TO BE A ZEALOT

9. HCOPL 7 Feb 1965: "Keeping Scientology Working" series. Subsequent quotes are from this policy letter.

Note: This PL has been quoted by other authors:

Lewis, James R. *Making Sense of Scientology*. Oxford University Press. New York, NY. 2009 (p. 92).

Kent, Stephen H. *From Slogans to Mantras: Social Protest and Religious Conversion in the Late Vietnam Era*. Syracuse University Press. Syracuse, NY. 2001 (pp. 153–4).

ENTHUSIASTIC DEVOTION TO A CAUSE

10. BLOW. *Tech Dictionary*: "v, slang. 1) unauthorized departure from an area, usually caused by misunderstood data or overts" (HCOB 19 Jun 1971 III). Mark Headley uses this term in the title of his memoir, *Blown for*

Good. It was used by Lawrence Wright in his profile of Paul Haggis in the *New Yorker*: Wright, Lawrence. "The Apostate." February 14, 2011. www.newyorker.com/magazine/2011/02/14/the-apostate-lawrence-wright (accessed July 31, 2017).

11. See note 4.

12. Hubbard, L. Ron. *Dianetics: The Modern Science of Mental Health.*

13. OVERT. *Tech Dictionary*: 1) "An overt act isn't just injuring someone or something; an overt act is an act of omission or commission which does the least good for the least number of dynamics or the most harm to the greatest number of dynamics." (HCOPL, 1 Nov 1970 III.)

Scientology Glossary: "a harmful act or a transgression against the moral code of a group. When a person does something that is contrary to the moral code he has agreed to, or when he omits to do something that he should have done per that moral code, he has committed an overt. An overt violates what was agreed upon. An overt can be intentional or unintentional."

14. OVERT. *Tech Dictionary*: 3) SH Spec 44, 6410C27.

15. OVERT. *Tech Dictionary*: 4) ISH AAA 10, 6009C14.

TRAINING ROUTINES

16. TRAINING ROUTINES, TRs. *Tech Dictionary*: HCOB 19 Jun 1971 III.

Scientology Glossary: "practical drills which can greatly increase a student's ability in essential auditing skills, such as communication."

17. THETAN. *Tech Dictionary*. The entirety of this definition reads: "the awareness of awareness unit which has all potentialities but no mass, no wave length and no location." HCOB 3 Jul 1959.

Helping me to understand this term was Definition #3 in the *Tech Dictionary*: "the being who is the individual and who handles and lives in the body." (HCOB 23 Apr 1969) And also Definition #9: "the person himself—not his body or his name, the physical universe, his mind, or anything else; that which is aware of being aware; the identity which is the individual. The thetan is most familiar to one and all as you." (Aud 25 UF)

The definition in the *Scientology Glossary* includes a discussion of why Hubbard developed his own words for various parts of his religious technology, including that which most religions call the "soul": "The term soul is not used because it has developed so many other meanings from use in other religions and practices that it doesn't describe precisely what was discovered in Scientology. We use the term *thetan* instead, from the Greek letter *theta* (θ), the traditional symbol for thought or life. One does not *have* a thetan, something one keeps somewhere apart from oneself; one *is* a thetan. The thetan is the person himself, not his body or his name or the physical universe, his mind or anything else. It is that which is aware of being aware; the identity which IS the individual."

See also: "Basic Principles of Scientology." www.scientology.org/what-is-scientology/basic-principles-of-scientology/the-thetan.html (accessed July 31, 2017).

18. OPERATING THETAN. *Tech Dictionary*: 2) SH Spec 80, 6609C08. This is just one of several fascinating definitions of this important term. For instance, #3: "an individual who could operate totally independently of his body whether he had one or didn't have one."

The *Scientology Glossary* makes a further distinction: "a state of being above Clear, in which the Clear has become refamiliarized with his native capabilities." (SH Spec 66, 6509C09)

19. TR0 Be There. "Communication." www.scientologycourses.org/courses-view/communication/step/14.html (accessed July 31, 2017).

20. OT TR0. *Tech Dictionary*: "A drill to train students to confront a preclear with auditing only or with nothing. The whole idea is to get the student able to be there comfortably in a position three feet in front of a preclear, to be there and not do anything else but be there. Student and coach sit facing each other with their eyes closed." (HCOB 16 Aug 1971 II).

See previous note: *Scientology Online Courses*: Communication: TR0 Be There.

21. Beckett, Samuel. *Worstword Ho: The Complete Short Prose of Samuel Beckett.* Ed. S. E. Gontarski. Grove/Atlantic. New York, NY. 1995. Excerpts from "Nohow On," copyright © 1983 by Samuel Beckett. Used by permission of Grove/Atlantic. Inc. Any third-party use of this material, outside of this publication, is prohibited.

THIS IS SO WEIRD!

22. The name by which I knew this drill, TR 0, has been changed to TR 0 Confronting. www.scientologycourses.org/courses-view/communication/step/15.html (accessed July 31, 2017).

HE WAS KIND OF A NUTCASE

23. ETHICS. *Tech Dictionary*: 5) "ethics is a personal thing. By definition, the word means 'the study of the general nature of morals and the specific moral choices to be made by the individual in his relationship to others'.

When one is ethical, or 'has his ethics in,' it is by his own determinism and is done by himself." (HCOB 15 Nov 1972 II)

See also: The Scientology Handbook. "Improving Conditions in Life." www.scientologyhandbook.org/conditions/sh10.htm (accessed July 31, 2017).

See also the entirety of Hubbard, L. Ron. *Introduction to Scientology Ethics.*

SHE WENT CLEAR LAST LIFETIME!

24. *Dianetics.*

IMAGINE A PLANE

25. THETA. *Tech Dictionary*: 4) *SOS* 2, p. 12.

GUILT IS GOOD

26. NATTER: *Tech Dictionary*: "sometimes pcs who have big overts become highly critical of the auditor and get in a lot of snide comments about the auditor. Such natter indicates a real overt." (HCOB 7 Sept 1964 II)

27. MOTIVATOR. *Tech Dictionary*: 1) HCOB 20 May 1968.

See also "Integrity and Honesty." www.scientologyhandbook.org/integrity/sh9_4.htm (accessed July 31, 2017).

HOPE SPRINGS ETERNAL

28. The following conversation was my first introduction to Hubbard's view of the mind, and I have done my best to replicate it as I remember it. For more information regarding the Reactive Mind, see *Dianetics*, and/or "What Is the Mind?" www.scientology.org/faq/background-and-basic-principles/what-is-the-mind.html (accessed July 31, 2017).

29. DYNAMICS: See: "The Dynamics of Existence." www.scientologyhandbook.org/dynamics/sh2_2.htm (accessed July 31, 2017).

THAT'S SOURCE!

30. SQUIRREL. *Tech Dictionary*: 2) *ISE* p. 40.

31. WITHHOLD. *Tech Dictionary*: 1) SH Spec 62, 6110C04.

See also the *Scientology Glossary*: "an unspoken, unannounced transgression against a moral code by which a person was bound. Any withhold comes *after* an overt."

HOW MUCH ELECTRICITY?

32. E-METER. *Scientology Glossary*: "short for *Electropsychometer*, a specially designed instrument which helps the auditor and preclear locate areas of spiritual distress or travail. The E-Meter is a religious artifact and can only be used by Scientology ministers or ministers-in-training. It does not diagnose or cure anything. It measures the mental state or change of state of a person and thus is of benefit to the auditor in helping the preclear locate areas to be handled."

33. CHARGE. *Scientology Glossary*: "harmful energy or force contained in mental image pictures or experiences painful or upsetting to the person, which is handled in auditing."

34. BLACK PR (black propaganda). "Public Relations." www.scientology courses.org/courses-view/public-relations/step/handling-rumors-and-whispering-campaigns.html (accessed July 31, 2017).

35. Carroll, Lewis. *Alice's Adventures in Wonderland.* Macmillan & Co. London, UK. 1865.

"The chief difficulty Alice found at first was in managing her flamingo: she succeeded in getting its body tucked away, comfortably enough, under her arm, with its legs hanging down, but generally, just as she had got its neck nicely straightened out, and was going to give the hedgehog a blow with its head, it *would* twist itself round and look up in her face, with such a puzzled expression that she could not help bursting out laughing: and when she had got its head down, and was going to begin again, it was very provoking to find that the hedgehog had unrolled itself, and was in the act of crawling away: besides all this, there was generally a ridge or furrow in the way wherever she wanted to send the hedgehog to, and, as the doubled-up soldiers were always getting up and walking off to other parts of the ground, Alice soon came to the conclusion that it was a very difficult game indeed."

36. MEST. *Tech Dictionary*: 1. a coined word, meaning matter, energy, space and time, the physical universe. All physical phenomena may be considered as energy operating in space and time. The movement of matter or energy in time is the measure of space. All things are mest except theta. (Abil 114-A)

37. ARC. *Tech Dictionary*: 1) LRH Def. Notes.

See also *Scientology Glossary*: "a word coined from the initial letters of *a*ffinity, *r*eality, and *c*ommunication."

38. ARC BREAK. *Tech Dictionary*: 1) LRH Def. Notes.

A COMB, PERHAPS A CAT

39. See Broxan, Nadine. "For Mrs. Cruise, Perhaps a Cat." November 12, 2006: p. 9. www.nytimes.com/2006/11/12/fashion/weddings/12field.html?mcubz=0 (accessed July 31, 2017).

40. CASE. *Scientology Glossary*: "a general term for a person being treated or helped. It is also used to mean the entire accumulation of upsets, pain, failures, etc., residing in the preclear's reactive mind."

41. COGNITION. *Tech Dictionary*: 3) "Something a pc suddenly understands or feels. 'Well, what do you know about that.'" (HCOB 25 Feb 1960)

FLUNK. START.

42. TR0 BULLBAIT. "Communication." www.scientologycourses.org/courses-view/communication/step/16.html (accessed July 31, 2017).

43. REG: REGGING: REGISTRAR: *Basic Dictionary of Dianetics and Scientology*: In Scientology, the person who signs people up for Scientology services.

44. "And its dreams are dreamed by artists." www.whatisscientology.org/html/Part06/Chp21/pg0388.html (accessed July 31, 2017).

YOU COULD TAKE A LOOK AT DOUBT

45. CONDITIONS (ethics). *Tech Dictionary*: BTB 12 Apr 1972R.

See also "Improving Conditions of Life." www.scientologyhandbook.org/conditions/SH10_1.HTM (accessed July 31, 2017).

46. Hubbard, L. Ron. *Introduction to Scientology Ethics*. Subsequent quotes regarding the Conditions are from this book.

47. DISCONNECTION. "There is no Scientology Disconnection policy that requires Church members to disconnect from anyone," the Church's website states. "Attitudes and Practices." www.scientology.org/faq/scientology-attitudes-and-practices/what-is-disconnection.html (accessed July 31, 2017).

However, among other contradictions, Hubbard writes, "To fail or refuse to disconnect from a suppressive person . . . is supportive of the suppressive—in itself a suppressive act. And so it must be labeled" (HCOB 10 Sept 1983).

See Mark Rinder's blog for a helpful discussion of this: "Disconnection." *Something Can Be Done About It*. June 8, 2016. www.mikerindersblog.org/scientology-disconnection (accessed July 31, 2017).

In addition, Leah Remini thoroughly examines disconnection in her series *Scientology and the Aftermath*, which Lindsay Denniger explores in her post "What Is Disconnection in Scientology?" on *Bustle.* February 28, 2017. www.bustle.com/articles/197533-what-is-disconnection-in-scientology-leah-reminis-docuseries-explores-how-it-can-change-a-family-forever (accessed July 31, 2017). Remini's program won a 2017 Emmy for Outstanding Informational Series.

THE ETHICS OFFICER

48. PTS. *Tech Dictionary*: 2) SH Spec 63, 6506C08.

EVERY SORROW IN THIS WORLD COMES DOWN TO A MISUNDERSTOOD WORD

49. BARRIERS TO STUDY. "The Technology of Study." www.scientology handbook.org/study/sh1_1.htm (accessed July 31, 2017).

All quotations to do with study are taken from this source.

See also "Study Technology—Study Tech." www.studytechnology .org/index.html (accessed July 31, 2017).

50. Hubbard, L. Ron. *Introduction to Scientology Ethics.* All quotes regarding PTS/SP are taken from this book.

See also, "Overcoming the Ups and Downs of Life." www.scientology handbook.org/suppression/sh11_1.htm (accessed July 31, 2017).

THE TRUE SENSE OF THE WORD

51. SUPPRESS. *Tech Dictionary*: SH Spec 84, 6612c13.

SUNNY

52. INDICATORS. *Tech Dictionary*: HCOB 20 Feb 1970.

53. FLOATING NEEDLE. *Scientology Glossary.*

54. See Jenna Miscavige Hill's *Beyond Belief: My Secret Life in Scientology and My Harrowing Escape.* The niece of David Miscavige, Jenna was encouraged to join the Sea Org at a very young age; her story is compelling and deeply troubling. In partnership with Kendra Wiseman and Astra Woodcraft (both also raised as Scientologists), Hill cofounded www .exscientologykids.com, which provides a forum for people who have left the church as well as for those still within Scientology who are looking for information.

55. Tony Ortega presents a copy of the letter that canceled the one-hour-

a-day family time on his blog, *The Underground Bunker.* August 27, 2014. tonyortega.org/2014/08/27/the-document-when-scientology-canceled-family-time (accessed July 31, 2017).

56. Flag Order 2 April 1991 "Children, Sea Org Members and Sea Org Orgs."

57. *The Underground Bunker.* Ortega, Tony. Septempter 3, 2014. tonyortega.org/2014/09/03/sea-org-document-dare-to-have-children-you-get-sent-to-scientologys-version-of-siberia/ (accessed September 12, 2017).

58. See Leah Remini's *Scientology and the Aftermath*, Episode 5. A&E. 2016.

59. See Note 54.

60. See Lawrence Wright's *Going Clear: Scientology, Hollywood, and the Prison of Belief.* Also the blogs of Tony Ortega: *The Underground Bunker*; Marty Rathbun: *Moving On Up a Little Higher*; and Mark Rinder: *Something Can Be Done About It.*

61. exscientologykids.com: The website's administrators are Jenna Miscavige Hill, niece of David Miscavige and author of *Beyond Belief: My Secret Life in Scientology and My Harrowing Escape*, and Astra Woodcraft, who joined the Sea Org at a young age and left when the Church pressured her to have an abortion (accessed September 12, 2017).

62. *Religare*, "to bind back," is what many dictionaries offer as the root of the word RELIGION. Sarah F. Hoyt suggests that *religare* was the etymology St. Augustine favored, but that Cicero suggested that the word had, instead, to do with *relegare*: "to go through, or go over again, in reading, speech or thought"—as indeed one does when one studies a religion. Hoyt, SF. "The Etymology of Religion." *Journal of the American Oriental Society.* Vol. 32, No. 2, 2012 (p. 126). www.jstor.org/stable/3087765 (accessed July 31, 2017).

GAH

63. ENGRAM. *Tech Dictionary*: 1) HCOB 23 Apr 1969.

Scientology Glossary: "a recording made by the reactive mind when a person is 'unconscious.' An engram is not a memory—it is a particular type of mental image picture which is a complete recording, down to the last accurate detail, of every perception present in a moment of partial or full 'unconsciousness.'"

64. The "electropsychometer" appears to have been originally designed by Volney Mathison. But Mathison and Hubbard quarreled, apparently about the use to which the meter would be put, and Hubbard put

the idea to one side. But by the late fifties, LRH had developed his own version of the e-meter, patented in 1966 as a "Device for Measuring and Indicating Changes in the Resistance of a Human Body." "The Story of the E-Meter Part I." (n.a.) *Scientology Books and Media.* June 21, 2014. scicrit.wordpress.com/2014/06/21/the-story-of-the-e-meter-pt-1-the-inventor (accessed July 31, 2017).

65. CLEAR. *Tech Dictionary*: 5) HCOB 2 Apr 1965.

Scientology Glossary. ". . . is a person who no longer has his own reactive mind and therefore suffers none of the ill effects that the reactive mind can cause. The Clear has no engrams which, when restimulated, throw out the correctness of his computations by entering hidden and false data."

WHAT IS TRUE FOR YOU IS TRUE FOR YOU

66. Buddhism teaches that "attachment" or "obsessive desire" is the source of all suffering. Scientology, on the other hand, encourages what Hubbard calls "havingness." A high degree of havingness is a clear sign of a successful Scientologist. This might mean a mansion in the Hollywood Hills with a great view, or an excellent career. Havingness is more than a synonym for affluence, however. One of Hubbard's definitions in the *Tech Dictionary* is "the result of creation" (SH Spec 19 6106C23), and the *Scientology Glossary* defines it as "the concept of being able to reach. By *havingness* we mean owning, possessing, being capable of commanding, taking charge of objects, energies and spaces." Buddhists learn a great deal about humility, about overcoming ego, and indeed, a very lack of self; Scientologists are engaged with self, to be, to do, to have across all the Dynamics.

67. WHOLE TRACK. *Tech Dictionary*: HCOB 9 Feb 1966.

See also *Scientology Glossary*, TIME TRACK: "the consecutive record of mental image pictures which accumulates through a person's life. It is a very accurate record of a person's past. As a rough analogy, the time track could be likened to a motion-picture film—if that film were three-dimensional, had fifty-seven perceptions and could fully react upon the observer."

68. PRESENT TIME PROBLEM. *Tech Dictionary*: 4) PAB 142.

69. RUDIMENTS. *Tech Dictionary*: "the reason you use and clean rudiments is to get the pc in session so you can have the pc 1) in communication with the auditor and 2) interested in his own case." (HCOB 19 May 1961)

70. WORD CLEARING METHOD ONE. *Tech Dictionary*: 1) "by meter in session. A full assessment of many, many subjects is done. The auditor then takes each reading subject and clears the chain back to earlier words and

or words in earlier subjects until he gets an F/N. (HCOB 24 Jun 1971). 3) The result of a properly done Method One word clearing is the recovery of one's education." (Aud 87ASNO)

71. ISRAEL. One day, when Mark and I were (once again) clearing RELIGION, I realized that ISRAEL appeared to be the name of someone in the Bible. Who was that? And why had his name been given to a nation?

For years I'd marveled at the postage stamp–sized piece of land out of which has arisen three world religions—Judaism, Christianity, Islam—as well as a whole lot of war, and that the worst kinds of violence, destruction, and torture have been and still are wielded in the name of an abstraction central to those religions: god. But it had never occurred to me that the name of that piece of land might mean something, might come from somewhere. I was, in fact, a bit horrified that it had never occurred to me to wonder about this.

Mark hefted the dictionary open so I could read about ISRAEL: not only the definition of the country, but the definition attached to someone named Jacob.

ISRAEL: "The descendants of Jacob: The Hebrew people, regarded as (according to Judaism) the chosen people of God by the covenant of Jacob."

I told Mark we needed to take a look at COVENANT and at JACOB.

He'd been raised in a churchgoing household, so he knew the story of Jacob wrestling with the angel and renaming himself, but I did not. I cleared JUDAISM and then found the shining fish that is at the root of ISRAEL, the Latinized form of the Hebrew YISRA'EL:

yisra: "he who fights or contends with" + *el*: "a deity."

Thus, ISRAEL: "He who contends with God"—as Jacob wrestled with that angel.

But it's also translated as "God has striven" or "God has saved." (In other, later, dictionaries I found that *Is* + *Ra* is presented as a conjoining of the Egyptian deities Isis and Ra, which would not only considerably predate the Jacob story but could indicate an altogether different notion of an androgynous god, rather than the masculine one shared by those three religions that erupted out of Israel.)

At about this point I realized that even in the *roots* of words a point of view could be discerned, as "He who contends with God" means something considerably different from "God has saved." (Similarly, a root that combines "contending" + "God" is quite removed from one that proposes that *Is* + *Ra* + *el* is an androgynous deity.) I sat in wonderment, contemplating the idea that a nation that called itself a name that, translated, means "contending with God" might have something to do with the violence that for well over two thousand years has emanated from that tiny piece of land tucked at the top of Egypt.

It occurred to me that *He who contends with God* also has to do with the Jewish tradition of questioning, of which, by then, I was aware.

Mark and I clambered back up the word chain, clarifying how the Catholic religion requisitioned that word—CATHOLIC means all-embracing, or universal—by replacing its lowercase *c* with a capital one, reminding myself what it was that Protestants were protesting, and pausing again at the root of RELIGION, that sense of binding. Then we blinked at each other, stunned by that marvelous trek through the deserts of ancient Palestine.

"Your needle is floating," he said.

72. PERSONAL INTEGRITY. "Basic Principles of Scientology." www.scientology.org/what-is-scientology/basic-principles-of-scientology/personal-integrity.html (accessed July 31, 2017).

73. ENTURBULATE. *Tech Dictionary*: Scn AD.

74. Ortega, Tony. "The Saga of David Mayo." *The Underground Bunker.* April 13, 2013. tonyortega.org/2013/04/13/the-saga-of-david-mayo-scientologys-banished-tech-wizard (accessed July 31, 2017).

HE HAS SIMPLY MOVED ON TO HIS NEXT LEVEL

75. THIRD PARTY LAW. *Tech Dictionary*: "the law would seem to be: a third party must be present and unknown in every quarrel for a conflict to exist." (HCOB 26 Dec 1968)

76. Miscavige's speech following Hubbard's death, January 27, 1986. Video: vimeo.com/12375370. Commentary and partial transcript: Ortega, Tony. "30 Years Ago Today." *The Underground Bunker.* January 30, 2017. tonyortega.org/2016/01/27/30-years-ago-today-l-ron-hubbard-discarded-the-body-he-had-used-in-this-lifetime/comment-page-1 (accessed July 31, 2017).

Also interesting: video and transcript of Pat Broeker discussing LRH's "final" level (when Hubbard supposedly purposefully "dropped his body"), including notation of the physical discomfort Broeker appears to feel as he describes these matters: Lerma, Arnaldo Pagliarini. (n.d.) www.lermanet.com/exit/death-transcript.htm (accessed July 31, 2017).

77. EXTERIOR/EXTERIORIZATION. *Scientology Glossary*: "the state of the thetan being outside his body with or without full perception, but still able to control and handle the body. When a person goes exterior, he achieves a certainty that he is himself and not his body."

78. While Hubbard generally dated his policy letters and bulletins in the British way (date/month/year), he sometimes measured time as beginning with the publication of his book *Dianetics*. Thus he used A.D., After Dianetics, as the beginning of a new time, as *Anno Domini* or Common Era establishes a new era beginning with the birth of Christ.

79. *Tech Dictionary*. 3) HCOB 3 July 1959.

80. Beckett, Samuel. *Waiting for Godot*. Grove Press. New York, NY. 1954. Excerpts from *Waiting for Godot*, copyright © 1954 by Grove Press, Inc; copyright © renewed 1982 by Samuel Beckett. Used by permission of Grove/Atlantic, Inc. Any third-party use of this material, outside of this publication, is prohibited.

BECAUSE, YOU KNOW, YOU DID JUST TURN THIRTY-SIX

81. Rehabilitation Project Force (rpf): "The RPF is based upon one of the oldest and most fundamental concepts in religion—a religious retreat in the form of a cloister focusing on intensive spiritual introspection and study and balanced by some form of physical labor." "What Is the Rehabilitation Project Force?" www.scientologynews.org/faq/what-is-the-rehabilitation-project-force.html (accessed July 31, 2017).

82. rundown. *Tech Dictionary*: "a series of steps which are auditing actions and processes designed to handle a specific aspect of a case and which have a known end phenomena." (LRH Def. Notes)

Scientology Glossary: "a series of related actions in Scientology which culminate in a specific end result."

83. karma. *American Heritage*: The total effect of one's actions and conduct during the successive phases of one's existence, regarded as determining one's destiny. From the Sanskrit for "deed, action that has consequences."

84. Quad Flows. *Tech Dictionary*: "F-1 is flow one, something happening to self. F-2 is flow two, doing something to another. F-3 is flow three, others doing something to others. F-0 is flow zero, self doing something to self." (HCOB 4 Apr 1971-1R)

85. HCOB 23 Jan 1974RB revised 25 Apr 1991, "The Introspection Rundown."

BINDING BACK

86. Childs, Joe, and Thomas C. Tobin. "Two Detectives Describe Their Two-Decade Pursuit of an Exiled Scientology Leader." September

29, 2012. www.tampabay.com/news/scientology/two-detectives-describe-their-two-decade-pursuit-of-an-exiled-scientology/1254129 (accessed July 31, 2017).

87. Ortega, Tony. "Death of a Scientologist." January 30, 2012. www.village voice.com/2012/01/30/death-of-a-scientologist-why-annie-broeker-famous-in-the-church-had-to-die-in-secret (accessed July 31, 2017).

THAT SPIRITUAL STUFF DOES MATTER

88. See Note 69.

89. BLOWDOWN. *Tech Dictionary*: "a period of relief and cognition to a pc while it is occurring and for a moment after it stops. When the auditor has to move the tone arm from right to left to keep the needle on the dial . . . then a blowdown is occurring." (HCOB 3 Aug 1965)

SPIT HAPPENS

90. The definition of PROFOUND is "penetrating beyond what is superficial or obvious," from Lat. *profundus*: *pro*, "before" + *fundus*, "bottom." I find this derivation intriguing—"before the bottom"—as it seems to echo the sense of the underworld I was occupying at the time; the idea, perhaps, that it is darkest before the dawn, that one has such insights and epiphanies on the way to being able to rise again—to return. The idea of "we," of "us," replacing, or, rather, replenishing "I" is definitely one of the boons I found down there in the darkness.

THE LOSS OF NAMELESS THINGS

91. The title of Bill Rose's documentary is a line in Oakley's play *Grinder's Stand*. Meriwether Lewis is speaking with the recently widowed Mrs. Grinder. The play is written in blank verse.

LEWIS: I'll toast, ma'am. But I do not drink strong liquor.
It affects me strangely, and quite fast.
MRS. G: You are no gentleman if you condemn
a lady to drink whiskey by herself.
LEWIS: In that case, ma'am, I'll risk embarrassment.
But if I start to weep, please understand:
I am in mourning, too.
MRS. G: Have you lost someone?

LEWIS: Some thing, although I'm not sure what it was.
I had it, on the trail to Oregon,
but sometime after that, it disappeared.
MRS. G: I'll drink to that: the loss of nameless things.

PILGRIMAGE SEASON

92. That David Miscavige catapulted to the top of the Church so immediately and unexpectedly after Hubbard "dropped his body" was part of what led me to follow link after link regarding that death. Most of the following is based on Robert Vaughn Young's description of what happened during the days surrounding Hubbard's death, which is available on the website Operation Clambake, a site set up in 1996 by Andreas Heldal-Lund to debunk Scientology. Also on this site is the link to the coroner's report from which I quote below, as well as information about the drug Vistaril, an antipsychotic given to Hubbard in the days before he died. Heldal-Lund, Andreas. (n.d.) www.xenu.net/archive/hubbardcoroner (accessed July 31, 2017).

Lawrence Wright substantiates these and gives further sad details in *Going Clear.*

Some of the details surrounding Hubbard's death seem suspicious, many pathetic. It almost made me weep, that this supposed Operating Thetan of all Operating Thetans, with his vaunted power over Matter, Energy, Space, and Time, who created a religion designed to let its practitioners live "at cause" for all eternity, spent his last years hiding out in a motorhome. The Blue Bird was tucked behind the stables at Star Ranch, 160 acres near San Luis Obispo. Loyal Pat and Annie Broeker attended to housekeeping tasks. They served Hubbard well, but he lived in that trailer all alone.

The week before he died, Hubbard appears to have suffered a stroke. Perhaps because of this, his personal physician, Dr. Gene Denk, injected him with Vistaril. Used to relieve nausea and insomnia, Vistaril is also known to calm the "acutely disturbed or hysterical patient." Some ex-Scientologists find it the highest of ironies that at the end of his life Hubbard would rely on a "psychiatric" drug. Others argue that the drug was used merely to help him sleep.

Whatever the case, the night Hubbard died, less than a week after that stroke, Dr. Denk was nowhere near his patient. He was in Lake

Tahoe, having been taken there for a weekend of fun and gambling by David Miscavige. The timing of this vacation is, at the very least, interesting. The coroner's report can be found at the abovementioned link and is a public document, available from the San Luis Obispo Sheriff's Office. Coroner's file #8936.

The report states that L. Ron Hubbard was seventy-four when he died, on January 24, 1986.

> . . . The body shows abundant reddish-white facial hair and eyebrows of reddish-white color. Scalp hair is long, thinning, receding at the forehead and of greyish-white color. Reddish-white body hair is present on the surface. Fingernails are long, unkempt. Nail beds are of bluish-red discoloration. Toenails are long, unkempt, and there is a bluish-red cyanosis present. The back is covered by livores. There is a bandaide [*sic*] affixed to the right gluteal area where 10 recent needle marks are recognized of 5–8 cm. There are no abnormalities upon inspection of the back. The body is without bruises or injuries or palpable masses.

The toenails—"long, unkempt"—particularly sadden me. Not long before Dad died, Brett realized that when rolling over in the night, he sometimes scratched open his own parchment-thin skin with the jagged edges of his toenails. On the porch of their house, she arranged a chair and a bowl of warm water in which to soak his feet, and she sawed away at those thick nails as he stared out over the lawn and sipped a glass of wine. It was a most loving act. I was struck that no matter the care Hubbard might have been provided, or the money he could have lavished on that care, that act of intimate affection was simply not available to him.

Because Scientologists view the body as a kind of "shell," of no use without the spirit/thetan activating it, the next sentence in the coroner's report strikes me as peculiar:

> Post mortem examination was refused because of religious reasons.

Details such as this one, and quite a number of others found in the coroner's report and other legal documents describing the circumstances surrounding Hubbard's death, make it hard for me not to imagine foul play—if not connected to the death itself, then in what was done regarding his body.

And especially in regards to his will, which was altered twenty-four hours before his death.

Also, although he died at 8:00 P.M., it was not until the following morning that an attorney, Mr. Cooley, reported it. It's easy to imagine the scurrying that may have taken place during those hours: Cooley zipping down to Star Ranch from Los Angeles, Dr. Denk and Miscavige hustling back from Tahoe.

The author of the coroner's report certainly appears to feel something is amiss. He refers to himself as Writer—as in, "Writer asked Mr. Cooley if the decedent had executed a Last Will and Testament."

> Mr. Cooley stated that he had the decedent's will in his possession. That a Mr. Norman F. Starke . . . was named as executor.

Writer telephones the sheriff's department and gets a deputy (Deputy Gasset, whose own report makes for interesting reading) to head out to Star Ranch; he asks another deputy to telephone Starke and "obtain his permission to release custody of the ranch to Mr. Cooley."

> Upon completion of the assignment Deputy telephoned writer to report his observations. Deputy Gassett reported that there was nothing suspicious about the scene but that the copy of the Last Will and Testament revealed that the Will was dated January 23, 1986, one day prior to decedent's death.

Curiouser and curiouser. At this point,

> Writer decided to reconsider the matter and instead of permitting the doctor to certify the cause of death, writer ordered an autopsy performed. The decision was not based on whether or not Dr. Denk has properly diagnosed the immediate cause of death, but to avoid possible questions pertaining to the cause of death and whether or not the decedent was of sound mind when he signed his Last Will and Testament, should this be challenged in a civil court.

One thinks Writer is thinking clearly, and is grateful to him.

In addition to the reason Writer decides to "reconsider the matter"—that is, the recently dated will—one could also have misgivings about the motivation behind that other document, signed and witnessed January 20, just four days before Hubbard's death, attesting to his spiritual beliefs regarding autopsy.

The attorneys—there are two of them by the time Hubbard's body arrives at the mortuary—present that document, but agree to a toxicology test. This test, completed, indicates that while trace amounts of Vistriol can be noted, there is nothing to indicate suicide or foul play.

Nevertheless, a whole lot of things certainly changed quickly and without explanation. After years of being named as executor in Hubbard's will, Norman Starke doesn't wind up in that position. Pat Broeker and his wife, Annie—Loyal Officers #1 and #2—are mysteriously whisked out of sight. Pat leaves the Church altogether. Annie finds herself in the RPF, where she is sighted looking hollow-eyed and "broken," and is never again seen outside of Scientology's desert compound near Hemet, California. (For more on what happened to Annie Broeker, see Note 93.)

A dozen more troubling, suspicious matters unfold on the way to young Miscavige being named, just a week later, leader of the Church of Scientology.

However, far more knowledgeable people than I have sifted through these and many other documents and have been unable to substantiate foul play.

The last paragraph of the coroner's report reads:

> Writer, accompanied by Dr. Denk, took the specimen to the Sierra Vista Hospital where the toxicology studies were performed. The results of the toxicology studies revealed no presence of any substance that would be contributory to the decedent's death. Dr. Denk accompanied writer back to the mortuary where writer thanked the attorneys for their understanding and cooperation. The body was released to their custody.

One can imagine the scene: Writer—who signs this fascinating document Jon Hines, Chief Deputy Coroner—intent on making absolutely sure nothing untoward has gone on; the attorneys and Dr. Denk hoping to God nothing has (or, if it has, that they waited long enough before reporting the death to have it disappear). Disappointment and relief in equal measure at the benign toxicology reports. Shaking of hands, tense and male. Writer wondering if perhaps he imagined something, maybe worried about what he may have missed; attorney and doctor scurrying back to the mortuary to see to the immediate cremation of Hubbard's body.

93. See Tony Ortega's excellent piece of investigative journalism in *The Village Voice*: www.villagevoice.com/2012/01/30/death-of-a-scientologist-why-annie-broeker-famous-in-the-church-had-to-die-in-secret (accessed July 31, 2017).

94. Many have described disturbing incidents that characterize Miscavige's abusive nature: Lawrence Wright's well-documented and clear-eyed *Going Clear: Scientology, Hollywood, and the Prison of Belief*, as well as Tony Ortega in his blog, *The Underground Bunker*; Mark Headley, in his memoir, *Blown for Good: Behind the Iron Curtain of Scientology*; Marty Rathbun, in his blog, *Moving On Up a Little Higher*, as well as in several of his books; Mike Rinder in his blog, *Something Can Be Done About It*. The Church denies all these allegations.

WHO NEVER LEFT HER BROTHER FOR DEAD

95. Campbell, Joseph. *The Hero with a Thousand Faces*. New World Library. Novato, CA. 2008.

In this seminal volume, first published in 1949, Campbell describes the basic pattern of the "hero's journey": "A hero ventures forth from the world of common day into a region of supernatural wonder: fabulous forces are there encountered and a decisive victory is won: the hero comes back from this mysterious adventure with the power to bestow boons on his fellow man."

96. Campbell, Joseph. "The Self as Hero." *Pathways to Bliss*. New World Library. Novato, CA. 2004.

TREASURE

97. See notes 54 and 61.

98. See notes 56, 57, and 58.

99. There are numerous reports of the tactics Church management employed to accomplish this, including ones found in Lawrence Wright's *Going Clear: Scientology, Hollywood, and the Prison of Belief*, and in the documentary based on Wright's book, *Going Clear*, directed by Alex Gibney.

100. SQUANDER. As the meaning seemed quite clear from context, it took a long time before I looked it up: "To spend or use money or time extrava-

gantly or wastefully; to use up needlessly or foolishly, to lose. Thought to be an obsolete form of *scatter*." Also, Tony Ortega's terrific piece of journalistic investigation, *The Unbreakable Miss Lovely: How the Church of Scientology Tried to Destroy Paulette Cooper*. In the process of revealing the lengths to which the Church is willing to go to harass and terrify its critics, Ortega also lays out the timeline of Scientology's infiltration of the IRS. A chilling and compelling read.

AFTERWORD: DISCONNECTION

101. In 2016, Leah Remini launched a television show on A&E called *Scientology and the Aftermath*, in which, as its website states, "along with high-level former Scientology executives and members, [she] relates shocking stories of abuse and harassment alleged by ex-practitioners who claim their lives have been affected even well after they left the organization." In September 2017, *Scientology and the Aftermath*'s first season won an Emmy for Outstanding Informational Series.

102. Mark "Marty" Rathbun's memoir is called *Memoirs of a Scientology Warrior*. A former senior executive in the Church, he left Scientology in 2004 and for years was an Independent Scientologist. His blog, *Moving On Up a Little Higher*, which for more than a decade was committed to attacking the Church, now addresses broader issues of communication and information. Tony Ortega writes about what may be, in fact, Rathbun's intriguing about-face: Ortega, Tony. "Memories of a Scientology Warrior: Marty Rathbun's Curious Career as a Church Rebel." March 14, 2017. www.tonyortega.org/2017/03/14/memories-of-a-scientology-warrior-marty-rathbuns-curious-career-as-church-rebel/ (accessed November 21, 2017).

103. Mike Rinder, in his blog, *Something Can Be Done About It*, offers a thorough discussion of the Church's contradictory policies regarding disconnection: Rinder, Mark. February 28, 2017. www.mikerindersblog.org/scientology-disconnection-policy-exposed (accessed July 31, 2017).

104. The Greek word for spirit, *psyche*, descends, ultimately, from the idea of breath, as does its word for soul, *pneuma*.

105. LIBERAL: www.etymonline.com/index.php?term=liberal (accessed September 14, 2017).

© Graham Hayes

ABOUT THE AUTHOR

SANDS HALL is the author of the novel *Catching Heaven*, a WILLA Award Finalist for Best Contemporary Fiction, and a Random House Reader's Circle selection; and of a book of craft essays and writing exercises, *Tools of the Writer's Craft*. She teaches at the Iowa Summer Writing Festival and at the Community of Writers at Squaw Valley, and is an associate teaching professor at Franklin & Marshall College in Lancaster, Pennsylvania. Sands lives in Nevada City.